Practical Python

MAGNUS LIE HETLAND

Apress™

Practical Python
Copyright ©2002 by Magnus Lie Hetland

ISBN (pbk): 1-59059-006-6

Printed and bound in the United States of America 12345678910
Trademarked names may appear in this book. Rather than use a trademark symbol with every occurrence of a trademarked name, we use the names only in an editorial fashion and to the benefit of the trademark owner, with no intention of infringement of the trademark.

Editorial Directors: Dan Appleman, Gary Cornell, Jason Gilmore, Karen Watterson
Marketing Manager: Stephanie Rodriguez
Technical Reviewers: Jason Gilmore and Alex Martelli
Project Managers: Erin Mulligan and Tory McLearn
Copy Editor: Nancy Rapoport
Production Editor: Tory McLearn
Compositor: Impressions Book and Journal Services, Inc.
Indexer: Carol Burbo
Cover Designer: Kurt Krames

Distributed to the book trade in the United States by Springer-Verlag New York, Inc., 175 Fifth Avenue, New York, NY, 10010
and outside the United States by Springer-Verlag GmbH & Co. KG, Tiergartenstr. 17, 69112 Heidelberg, Germany
In the United States, phone 1-800-SPRINGER, email orders@springer-ny.com, or visit http://www.springer-ny.com.
Outside the United States, fax +49 6221 345229, email orders@springer.de, or visit http://www.springer.de.

For information on translations, please contact Apress directly at 2560 Ninth Street, Suite 219, Berkeley, CA 94710. Phone 510-549-5930, fax: 510-549-5939, email info@apress.com, or visit http://www.apress.com.

The source code for this book is available to readers at http://www.apress.com in the Downloads section. You will need to answer questions pertaining to this book in order to successfully download the code.

For Anne, my favorite little sister.

Contents at a Glance

Contents

Chapter 14 Project 1: Instant Markup 365

Chapter 15 Project 2: Painting a Pretty Picture 387

Chapter 16 Project 3: XML for All Occasions 401

Chapter 17 Project 4: In the News 421

Chapter 18 Project 5: A Virtual Tea Party 439

Chapter 19 Project 6: Remote Editing with CGI 461

Chapter 20 Project 7: Your Own Bulletin Board 481

Chapter 21 Project 8: File Sharing with XML-RPC 501

Chapter 22 Project 9: File Sharing II—Now with GUI!

Chapter 23 Project 10: Do-It-Yourself Arcade Game

Appendix A The Short Version

Appendix B Python Reference

Appendix C Online Resources

About the Author

MAGNUS LIE HETLAND is currently a Ph.D. student at the Norwegian University of Science and Technology where he works with algorithms for knowledge discovery in temporal sequences. Even though he loves learning new programming languages—even quite obscure ones—Magnus has been a devoted Python fan and an active member of the Python community for several years. He is the author of the popular online tutorials "Instant Python" and "Instant Hacking," and is the founder and lead programmer of the Anygui project (http://www.anygui.org). When he isn't busy staring at a computer screen, he may be found reading (even while bicycling), acting (in a local theater group), or gaming (mostly roleplaying games).

About the Technical Reviewers

W. JASON GILMORE is an aficionado of all sorts of scripting languages, and spends an inordinate amount of time playing with them both at work and in his free time. Jason is a regular contributor to numerous IT publications, and is the author of *A Programmer's Introduction to PHP 4.0* (Apress, 2001). During his rare moments spent away from the computer, Jason can be found rummaging through bookstores, searching for the perfect meal, and wondering why he's not in front of his computer.

Alex Martelli is an active member of the Python community, having contributed numerous articles on the subject to various IT publications, participated in the technical editing and review of many Python books, and shared an editorial role in the *Python Cookbook* (O'Reilly, 2002). He is also the author of the upcoming *Python in a Nutshell* (O'Reilly, 2002). Alex is also a C++ MVP for Brainbench, a member of the Python Software Foundation, and a Board Member of the Python Business Forum.

After a decade with IBM Research, followed by a ten-year stint as Senior Software Consultant for think3, inc, Alex now telecommutes (from his home in Bologna, Italy) for AB Strakt (a Python-centered Swedish firm that develops innovative technologies for application frameworks), and moonlights as a Python author, teacher, consultant and mentor.

Acknowledgments

WITHOUT THE PERSISTENT HELP and encouragement from several people, this book would never have been written. My heartfelt thanks go out to all of them. In particular, I would like to thank the team that has worked directly with me in the process of writing the book: Jason Gilmore and Alex Martelli for their excellent technical editing (Jason on the entire book, and Alex on the first half) and for going above and beyond the call of duty in dispensing advice and suggestions; Erin Mulligan and Tory McLearn for holding my hand through the process and for nudging me along when that was needed; Nancy Rapoport for her help polishing my prose; and Grace Wong for providing answers when no one else could. I would also like to thank all the other people at Apress and elsewhere who have worked to transform what started as rough drafts on my computer into words on paper. Even though I might not know who all of you are, I'm sure you do. I owe great thanks to the Anygui team for their effort in making the Anygui project a reality. Without them, Chapters 12 and 22 would not have been possible. Pete Shinners gave me several helpful suggestions on the game in Chapter 23, for which I am very grateful. Finally, I would like to thank my family and friends who put up with me while I was writing this book. Perhaps now I will have more time to spend with all of you—at least until the next book.

Introduction

"A C program is like a fast dance on a newly waxed dance floor by people carrying razors."

—Waldi Ravens

"C++: Hard to learn and built to stay that way."

—Anonymous

"Java is, in many ways, C++−−."

—Michael Feldman

"And now for something completely different. . . ."

—Monty Python's Flying Circus

I'VE STARTED THIS INTRODUCTION with a few quotes to set the tone for the book—which is rather informal. In the hope of making it an easy read, I've tried to approach the topic of Python programming with a healthy dose of humor, and true to the traditions of the Python community, much of this humor is related to Monty Python sketches. As a consequence, some of my examples may seem a bit silly; I hope you will bear with me. (And, yes, the name Python is derived from Monty Python, not from snakes belonging to the family *Pythonidae*.)

In this introduction I give you a quick look at what Python is, why you should use it, who uses it, who this book's intended audience is, and how the book is organized. Finally, I'll address some technical issues.

So, what is Python, and why should you use it? To quote an official blurb (available from `http://www.python.org/doc/essays/blurb.html`), it is "an interpreted, object-oriented, high-level programming language with dynamic semantics." Many of these terms will become clear as you read this book, but the gist of it is that Python is a programming language that knows how to stay out of your way when you write your programs. It enables you to implement the functionality you want without any hassle, and lets you write programs that are clear and readable (much more so than programs in most other currently popular programming languages).

Even though Python might not be as fast as compiled languages such as C or C++, what you save in programming time will probably be worth using it; in most programs the speed difference won't be noticeable anyway. If you are a C programmer you can easily implement the critical parts of your program in C at a later date, and have them interoperate with the Python parts. If you haven't done any programming before (and perhaps are a bit confused by my references to C and C++), Python's combination of simplicity and power make it an ideal choice as a place to start.

So, who uses Python? Since Guido van Rossum created the language in the early 1990s, its following has grown steadily, and interest has increased markedly in the last couple of years. Python is used extensively for system administration tasks (it is, for instance, a vital component of several Linux distributions), but it is also used to teach programming to complete beginners. NASA uses Python for several of its software systems, and has adopted it as the standard scripting language for its Integrated Planning System; Industrial Light & Magic uses Python in its production of special effects for large budget feature films; Yahoo! uses it (among other things) to manage its discussion groups; and Google has used it to implement many components of its Web crawler and search engine. Python is being used in such diverse areas as computer games and bioinformatics. Soon one might as well ask, who *isn't* using it?

This book is for those of you who want to learn how to program in Python. It is intended to suit a wide audience, from neophyte programmer to advanced computer wiz. If you have never programmed before, you should start by reading Chapter 1 and continue until you find that things get too advanced for you (if, indeed, they do). Then you should start practicing, and write some programs of your own. When the time is right, you can return to the book and proceed with the more intricate stuff.

If you already know how to program, then some of the introductory material might not be new to you. You could skim through the early chapters to get an idea of how Python works, or perhaps read through Appendix A, "The Short Version," which is based on my online Python tutorial "Instant Python." It will get you up to speed on the most important Python concepts. After getting the big picture, you could jump straight to Chapter 10 (which describes the Python standard libraries).

The second half of the book consists of ten programming projects, which show off various capabilities of the Python language. These projects should be of interest to beginner and expert alike. Although some of the material in the later projects may be a bit difficult for an inexperienced programmer, following the projects in order (after reading the material in the first part of the book) should be possible.

The projects touch upon a wide range of topics, most of which will be very useful to you when writing programs of your own. You will learn how to do things that may seem completely out of reach to you at this point, such as creating a chat server, a peer-to-peer file sharing system, or a full-fledged graphical computer game. Although much of the material may seem hard at first glance, I think you will be surprised by how easy most of it really is.

Before I conclude the introduction, there are some technical issues to address. First, the source code for all the examples and projects in this book is available online. You can download it from `http://www.apress.com`. Second, several parts of the Python language are described in this book by *syntax summaries* such as this:

```
pow(x, y[, z])
```

The text set in code font (`like this`) is to be taken literally. In the preceding line of code, the word "pow," the commas, and the parentheses are actually parts of the language and should be typed exactly as shown. The italicized text (in this case *x*, *y*, and *z*) should be replaced with something else. In this example, you could, for instance, replace them with numbers, as in

```
pow(2, 3, 4)
```

The brackets indicate optional pieces of code. In this example, you could omit the *z*, as in

```
pow(2, 3)
```

There is one last issue I'd like to mention (although it is rather minor). As this book neared completion, a change was introduced into the Python language: the words `True` and `False` were added. This does not in any way invalidate the material in this book, but when you run the examples (as explained in Chapter 1), you may sometimes see `True` where my examples show 1, and `False` where my examples show 0. This is nothing to worry about (`True` is essentially the same as 1, and `False` is essentially the same as 0) but is nice to know, so you don't have to fret about why you don't get the same results as I do.

Well, that's it. I always find long introductions boring myself, so I'll let you continue with your Pythoneering, either in Chapter 1 or in Appendix A. Good luck, and happy hacking.

CHAPTER 1

Instant Hacking: The Basics

IT'S TIME TO START HACKING.[1] In this chapter, you learn how to take control of your computer by speaking a language it understands: Python. Nothing here is particularly difficult, so if you know the basics of how your computer works, you should be able to follow the examples and try them out yourself. I'll go through the basics, starting with the excruciatingly simple, but because Python is such a powerful language, you'll soon be able to do pretty advanced things.

First, you take a quick look at how you can get the software you need. Then I tell you a bit about algorithms and their main components, expressions, and statements. Throughout these sections, there are numerous small examples (most of them using only simple arithmetic) that you can try out in the Python interactive interpreter (see the section "The Interactive Interpreter," later in this chapter). You learn about variables, functions, and modules, and after handling these topics, I show you how to write and run larger programs. Finally, I deal with strings, an important aspect of almost any Python program.

Installing Python

Before you can start programming, you need some new software. What follows is a short description of how to download and install Python.

Windows

To install Python on a Windows machine, follow these steps:

1. Open a Web browser and go to `http://www.python.org`.

2. Click the "Download" link.

---

1. "Hacking" is not the same as "cracking," which is a term describing computer crime. The two are often confused. "Hacking" basically means having fun while programming.

3. You should see several links here, with names such as Python 1.6.1, Python 2.2, and so on. Click the one with the highest version number. It will probably be the topmost link.

4. Follow the instructions for Windows users. You will download a file called `Python-2.2.exe` (or something similar), where 2.2 should be the version number of the newest release.

5. Store the file somewhere on your computer, for instance `C:\download\Python-2.2.exe`. (Just create a directory where you can find it later.)

6. Run the downloaded file by double-clicking it. This brings up the Python install wizard, which is really easy to use. Just accept the default settings, wait until the install is finished, and you're ready to roll!

Assuming that the installation went well, you now have a new program in your Windows Start menu. Run the Python Integrated Development Environment (IDLE) by selecting Start ➤ Programs ➤ Python[2] ➤ IDLE (Python GUI).

You should now see a window that looks like the one shown in Figure 1-1. If you feel a bit lost, simply press F1 (or select Help ➤ "Help…" from the menu), and you get a simple description of the various menu items. For more documentation on IDLE, check out `http://www.python.org/idle`. (Here you will also find more information on running IDLE on platforms other than Windows.)

---

2. This menu option will probably include your version number: for example, Python 2.2.

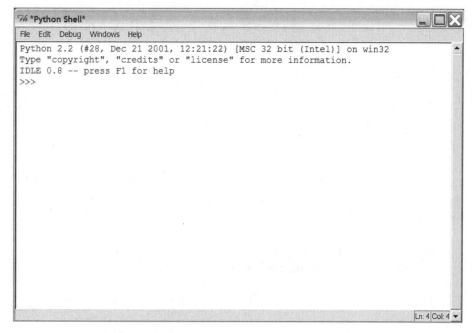

Figure 1-1. The IDLE interactive Python shell

Linux and UNIX

In many Linux and UNIX installations, Python is already present. You can check
by running python at the prompt, as follows:

```
$ python
```

which should output something like this:

```
Python 2.2 (#4, Dec 30 2001, 10:23:57)
[GCC 3.0.1] on sunos5
Type "help", "copyright", "credits" or "license" for more information.
>>>
```

If that doesn't work, you have to install it yourself.

NOTE *To exit the interactive interpreter, use Ctrl-D (press the Ctrl key and while keeping that depressed, press D).*

Linux with RPM

If you are running Red Hat Linux, or some other Linux distribution with the Red Hat Package Manager (RPM) installed, follow these steps to install the Python RPM packages:

1. Go to the download page (refer to Steps 1 through 3 in the instructions for installing Python on a Windows system).

2. Follow the instructions for Red Hat Linux: follow the link "Linux RPMs."

3. Download all the binary RPMs. Store them in a temporary location (such as ~/rpms/python).

4. Make sure you are logged in as root and are currently in the directory where you stored the RPMs. Make sure there are no other RPMs in this directory.

5. Install the packages by executing the command rpm --install *.rpm. If you already have an older version of Python installed, you should instead use rpm --upgrade *.rpm.

CAUTION *The preceding command installs all the RPM files in the current directory. Make sure that you are in the correct directory and that it only contains the packages you want to install. If you want to be more careful, you can specify the name of each package separately. For more information about RPMs, check out the man page.*

You should now be able to run Python. On occasion, you may run into some unresolved dependencies—you may lack other RPM packages needed to install Python. To locate these packages, visit a search facility such as http://www.rpmfind.net.

Sometimes a binary RPM package designed for one Linux distribution (for example, Red Hat Linux) may not work smoothly with another (for example, Mandrake Linux). If you find that the binary package is giving you grief, try downloading a source RPM instead (with a name like <packagename>.src.rpm). You can then build a set of binary packages tailored for your system with the command

```
rpm --rebuild <packagename>.src.rpm
```

where <packagename>.src.rpm is the real file name of the package you're rebuilding. After you have done this, you should have a brand new set of RPM files that you can install as described previously.

 NOTE *To use the RPM installation, you must be logged in as* root *(the administrator account). If you don't have root access, you should compile Python yourself, as described in the section "Compiling from Sources," which follows.*

Compiling from Sources

If you don't have RPM, or would rather not use it, you can compile Python yourself. This may be the method of choice if you are on a UNIX box but you don't have root access (installation privileges). This method is very flexible, and enables you to install Python wherever you want, including in your own home directory. To compile and install Python, follow these steps:

1. Go to the download page (refer to Steps 1 through 3 in the instructions for installing Python on a Windows system).

2. Follow the instructions for downloading the sources. You may choose between using HTTP and FTP. HTTP usually works just fine.

3. Download the file with the extension .tgz. Store it in a temporary location. Assuming that you want to install Python in your home directory, you may want to put it in a directory such as ~/python.

4. Unpack the archive with the command `tar -xzvf Python-2.2.tgz`
   (where 2.2 is the version number of the downloaded source code). If your
   version of `tar` doesn't support the `z` option, you may want to uncompress
   the archive with `gunzip` first, and then use `tar -xvf` afterward. If there is
   something wrong with the archive, try downloading it again. Sometimes
   errors occur during download.

5. Enter the unpacked directory:

```
$ cd Python-2.2
```

Now you should be able to execute the following commands:

```
./configure --prefix=.
make
make install
```

You should end up with an executable file called `python` in the current
directory. (If this doesn't work, please consult the README file included
in the distribution.) Put the current directory in your PATH environment
variable, and you're ready to rock.

To find out about the other configuration directives, execute

```
./configure --help
```

CAUTION *Using the current directory (". ") as a prefix may give
you problems later. A safer solution would be to explicitly provide the full path to the current directory, as in this example:*

```
./configure --prefix=/home/mlh/python/Python-2.2
```

Macintosh

If you're using a Macintosh, follow these steps:

1. Go to the standard download page (Step 1 from the UNIX/Linux instructions earlier in this chapter).

2. Follow the link for "Mac users." There you'll find information about MacPython, and detailed instructions on how to download and install it.

Other Distributions

You now have the standard Python distribution installed. There are others, and the most well-known ones are perhaps ActivePython, The PythonWare Python Distribution, and Jython.

ActivePython is a Python distribution from ActiveState (http://www.activestate.com). At its core, it's the same as the standard Python distribution for Windows. The main difference is that it includes lots of extra goodies (modules) that are available separately. Definitely worth a look if you are running Windows.

The PythonWare distribution also contains some extra goodies—but not the same ones as ActivePython. PythonWare's specialty is allowing non-administrator installation, and coexisting with other Python versions, in Windows. For more information about this distribution, see http://www.pythonware.com/downloads.

Jython is different—it's a version of Python implemented in Java (another programming language). It enables you to use Python and Java together, in the same program. More information (and the software) is available from http://www.jython.org.

The Interactive Interpreter

When you start up Python, you get a prompt similar to the following:

```
Python 2.2 (#4, Dec 30 2001, 10:23:57)
[GCC 3.0.1] on sunos5
Type "help", "copyright", "credits" or "license" for more information.
>>>
```

NOTE *The exact appearance of the interpreter and its error messages will depend on which version you are using.*

This might not seem very interesting, but believe me—it is. This is your gateway to hackerdom—your first step in taking control over your computer. In more pragmatic terms, it's an interactive Python interpreter. Just to see if it's working, try the following:

```
>>> print "Hello, world!"
```

When you press the Return/Enter key, the following output appears:

```
Hello, world!
>>>
```

NOTE *If you are familiar with other computer languages, you may be used to terminating every line with a semicolon. There is no need to do so in Python. A line is a line, more or less. You* may *add a semicolon if you like, but it won't have any effect (unless more code follows on to the same line), and it is not a common thing to do.*

What happened here? The >>>-thingy is the *prompt*. You can write something in this space, like print "Hello, world!". If you press Enter, the Python interpreter prints out the string Hello, world! and you get a new prompt below that.

NOTE *The term "printing" in this context refers to writing text to the screen, not producing hardcopies with a printer.*

What if you write something completely different? Try it out. For instance:

```
>>> The Spanish Inquisition
SyntaxError: invalid syntax
>>>
```

Obviously, the interpreter didn't understand that. (If you are running an interpreter other than IDLE, such as the command-line version for Linux, the error message will be slightly different.) The interpreter also indicates what's wrong: it will emphasize the word "Spanish" by giving it a red background (or, in the command-line version, by using a caret, "^").

If you feel like it, play around with the interpreter some more. (For some guidance, try entering the command help at the prompt and press Enter. As mentioned, you can press F1 for help about IDLE.) Otherwise, let's press on. After all, the interpreter isn't much fun when you don't know what to tell it, is it?

Algo...What?

Before you start programming in earnest, let's get an idea of what computer programming *is*. So, what is it? It's telling a computer what to do. Computers can do lots of things, but they aren't very good at thinking for themselves. They really need to be spoon-fed the details. You have to feed the computer an *algorithm*, in some language it understands. "Algorithm" is just a fancy word for a procedure or recipe—a detailed description of how to do something. Consider the following:

```
SPAM with SPAM, SPAM, Eggs, and SPAM:
First, take some SPAM.
Then add some SPAM, SPAM, and eggs.
If a particularly spicy SPAM is desired, add some SPAM.
Cook until done - Check every 10 minutes.
```

This recipe may not be very interesting, but how it's constructed is. It consists of a series of instructions to be followed in order. Some of the instructions may be done directly ("take some SPAM"), while some require some deliberation ("If a particularly spicy SPAM is desired") and others must be repeated several times ("Check every 10 minutes.")

Recipes and algorithms consist of *ingredients* (objects, things), and *instructions* (statements). In this example, SPAM and eggs were the ingredients, while the instructions consisted of adding SPAM, cooking for a given length of time, and so on. Let's start with some reasonably simple Python ingredients and see what you can do with them.

Numbers and Expressions

The interactive Python interpreter can be used as a powerful calculator. Try the following:

```
>>> 2 + 2
```

This ought to give you the answer 4. That wasn't too hard. Well, what about this:

```
>>> 53672 + 235253
288925
```

Still not impressed? Admittedly, this is pretty standard stuff. (I assume that you've used a calculator enough to know the difference between 1+2*3 and (1+2)*3.) All the usual arithmetic operators work as expected—almost. There is one potential trap here, and that is integer division (in Python versions up to and including 2.2):

```
>>> 1/2
0
```

What happened here? I divided one integer (a non-fractional number) by another, and the result was rounded down to give an integer result. This behavior can be useful at times, but often, you need ordinary division. What do you do to get that? You use real numbers (numbers with decimal points) rather than integers. These real numbers are called *floats* (or floating-point numbers) in Python:

```
>>> 1.0 / 2.0
0.5
```

Ah. There it was. In fact, only one of the two numbers has to be a float:

```
>>> 1/2.0
0.5
>>> 1.0/2
0.5
```

You don't even have to spell out the fractional part:

```
>>> 1/2.
0.5
```

NOTE   *If you are using Python 2.2 or a more recent version, you have another division operator available, which rounds down even if you are using floats:*

```
>>> 1.0 // 2.0
0.0
```

The main motivation for this new operator is that the old division operator is going to change in a later Python version. It will then be a true division operator, returning the exact answer even when dividing integers. To test this behavior, you can use the following statement:

```
>>> from __future__ import division
```

After executing this, the division behavior will have changed:

```
>>> 1 / 2
0.5
```

While this may seem like the natural behavior (I certainly think so), using floats to ensure correct division ensures that your program works in older versions of Python as well. (You get an explanation of the __future__ stuff in the section about modules, which follows.)

Now you've seen the basic arithmetic operators (addition, subtraction, multiplication, and division) but one more operator is quite useful at times:

```
>>> 1%2
1
```

This is the *remainder* (modulus) operator—x%y gives the remainder of x divided by y. For example:

```
>>> 10/3
3
>>> 10%3
1
>>> 9/3
3
```

```
>>> 9%3
0
>>> 2.75 % 0.5
0.25
```

Here 10/3 is 3 because the result is rounded down. But 3×3 is 9, so you get a remainder of 1. When you divide 9 by 3, the result is exactly 3, with no rounding. Therefore, the remainder is zero. This may be useful if you want to check something "every 10 minutes" as in the recipe earlier in the chapter. You can simply check whether `minute % 10` is zero. (For a description on how to do this, see the sidebar "Sneak Peek: The `if` Statement," later in the chapter.) As you can see from the final example, the remainder operator works just fine with floats as well.

The last operator is the *exponentiation* (or *power*) operator:

```
>>> 2 ** 3
8
>>> -3 ** 2
-9
>>> (-3) ** 2
9
```

Note that the exponentiation operator binds tighter than the negation (unary minus), so -3**2 is in fact the same as -(3**2). If you want to calculate (-3)**2, you must say so explicitly.

Large Integers

Python can handle really large integers:

```
>>> 1000000000000000000
1000000000000000000L
```

What happened here? The number suddenly got an "L" tucked onto the end.

NOTE *If you're using a version of Python older than 2.2, you get the following behavior:*

```
>>> 1000000000000000000
OverflowError: integer literal too large
```

In general, the newer versions of Python are more flexible when dealing with big numbers.

Ordinary integers can't be larger than 2147483647 (or smaller than –2147483648); if you want really big numbers, you have to use *longs*. A long (or long integer) is written just like an ordinary integer but with an "L" at the end. (You can, in theory, use a lowercase "l" as well, but that looks all too much like the digit 1, so I'd advise against it.)

In the previous attempt, Python converted the integer to a long, but you can do that yourself, too. Let's try that big number again:

```
>>> 1000000000000000000L
1000000000000000000L
```

Of course, this is only useful in old versions of Python that aren't capable of figuring out this stuff.

Well, can you do math with these monster numbers, too? Sure thing. Consider the following:

```
>>> 1987163987163981639186L * 1987639981726391826L + 23
3949766264320055676130001437847916936591L
```

As you can see, you can mix long integers and plain integers as you like.

Hexadecimals and Octals

To conclude this section, I should mention that hexadecimal numbers are written like this:

```
>>> 0xAF
175
```

and octal numbers like this:

```
>>> 010
8
```

The first digit in both of these is zero. (If you don't know what this is all about, just close your eyes and skip to the next section—you're not missing anything important)

 NOTE *For a summary of Python's numeric types and operators, see Appendix B.*

Variables

Another concept that might be familiar to you is *variables*. If math makes you queasy, don't worry: Variables in Python are easy to understand. A variable is basically a name that represents some value. For instance, you might want the name x to represent 3. To make it so, simply execute the following:

```
>>> x = 3
```

This is called an *assignment*. We *assign* the value 3 to the variable x. After a variable has had a value assigned to it, you can use the variable in expressions:

```
>>> x * 2
6
```

Note that you have to assign a value to a variable before you use it. After all, it doesn't make any sense to use a variable if it doesn't represent a value, does it?

 NOTE *Variable names can consist of letters, numbers, and underscore characters ("_"). A variable can't begin with a number, so* Plan9 *is a valid variable name, whereas* 9Plan *is not.*

Statements

Until now we've been working (almost) exclusively with expressions, the *ingredients* of the recipe. But what about statements—the instructions?

In fact, I've cheated. I've introduced two types of statements already: the `print` statement, and assignments. So, what's the difference between a statement and an expression? Well, an expression *is* something, while a statement *does* something. For instance, 2*2 *is* 4, whereas print 2*2 *prints* 4. What's the difference, you may ask. After all, they behave very similarly. Consider the following:

```
>>> 2*2
4
>>> print 2*2
4
```

As long as you execute this in the interactive interpreter the results are similar, but that is only because the interpreter always prints out the values of all expressions (using the same representation as `repr`—see the section on string representations later in this chapter). That is *not* true of Python in general. Later in this chapter, you see how to make programs that run without this interactive prompt, and simply putting an expression such as 2*2 in your program won't do anything interesting. Putting print 2*2 in there, on the other hand, will in fact print out 4.

The difference between statements and expressions may be more obvious when dealing with assignments. Because they are not expressions, they have no values that can be printed out by the interactive interpreter:

```
>>> x = 3
>>>
```

As you can see, you get a new prompt immediately. Something has changed, however; x now has the value 3.

This is a defining quality of statements in general: They *change* things. For instance, assignments change variables, and print statements change how your screen looks.

Assignments are, perhaps, the most important type of statement in any programming language. It may be difficult to grasp their importance right now. Variables may just seem like temporary storage (like the pots and pans of a cooking recipe), but the real power of variables is that you needn't know what values they hold to manipulate them. For instance, you know that x*y evaluates to the product of x and y even though you may have no knowledge of what x and y *are*. So, you may write programs that use variables in various ways without knowing the values they will eventually hold when the program is run.

Getting input from the User

You've seen that you can write programs with variables without knowing their values. Of course, the interpreter must know the values eventually. So how can it be that *we* don't? The interpreter knows only what we tell it, right?

Not necessarily. You may have written a program, and somebody else may use it. You cannot predict what values they will supply to the program. Let's take a look at the useful function input. (I'll have more to say about functions in a minute.)

```
>>> input("The meaning of life: ")
The meaning of life: 42
42
```

What happens here is that the first line (input(...)) is executed in the interactive interpreter. It prints out the string "The meaning of life: " as a new prompt. I type 42 and press Enter. The resulting value of input is that very number, which is automatically printed out in the last line. Not very useful. But look at the following:

```
>>> x = input("x: ")
x: 34
>>> y = input("y: ")
y: 42
>>> print x * y
1428
```

Here, the statements at the Python prompts (">>>") could be part of a finished program, and the values entered (34 and 42) would be supplied by some user. Your program would then print out the value 1428, which is the product of the two. And you didn't have to know these values when you wrote the program, right?

NOTE *This is much more useful when you save your programs in a separate file so other users can execute it. You learn to do that later in this chapter, in the section "Saving and Executing Your Programs."*

Sneak Peek: The `if` Statement

To make things a bit more fun, I'll give you a sneak peek of something you aren't really supposed to learn about until Chapter 5: the `if` statement. The `if` statement lets you perform an action (another statement) if a given condition is true. One type of condition is an equality test, using the equality operator `==`. (Yes, it's a *double* equality sign. I used the single one for assignments, remember?)

You simply put this condition after the word `if` and then separate it from the following statement with a colon:

```
>>> if 1 == 2: print 'One equals two'
...
>>> if 1 == 1: print 'One equals one'
...
One equals one
>>>
```

As you can see, nothing happens when the condition is false. When it is true, however, the following statement (in this case, a `print` statement) is executed. Note also that when using `if` statements in the interactive interpreter, you have to press Enter twice before it is executed. (The reason for this will become clear in Chapter 5—don't worry about it for now.)

So, if you have the current time in minutes stored in the variable `time`, you could check whether you're "on the hour" with the following statement:

```
if time % 60 == 0: print 'On the hour!'
```

Functions

In the section on numbers and expressions I used the exponentiation operator (`**`) to calculate powers. The fact is that you can use a *function* instead, called pow:

```
>>> 2**3
8
>>> pow(2,3)
8
```

A function is like a little program that you can use to perform a specific action. Python has lots of functions that can do many wonderful things. In fact, you can make your own functions, too (more about that later); therefore we often refer to standard functions such as pow as *built-in* functions.

When you use a function as I did in the preceding example, we say that we *call* the function. We supply it with *parameters* (in this case, 2 and 3) and it *returns* a value to us. Because it returns a value, a function call is simply another type of *expression*, like the arithmetic expressions discussed earlier in this chapter.[3] In fact, you can combine function calls and operators to create more complicated expressions:

```
>>> 10 + pow(2, 3*5)/3.0
10932.666666666666
```

 NOTE   *The exact number of decimals may vary depending on which version of Python you are using.*

There are several built-in functions that can be used in numeric expressions like this. For instance, abs gives the absolute value of a number, and round rounds floating numbers to the nearest integer:

```
>>> abs(-10)
10
>>> 1/ 2
0
>>> round(1.0/2.0)
1.0
```

Notice the difference between the two last expressions. Integer division always rounds down, whereas round rounds to the nearest integer. But what if you want to round a given number down? For instance, you might know that a person is 32.9 years old—but you would like to round that down to 32 because she isn't really 33 yet. Python has a function for this (called floor)—it just isn't available directly. As is the case with many useful functions, it is put away in a *module*.

---

3.   Function calls can also be statements if you simply ignore the return value.

Modules

You may think of modules as extensions that can be imported into Python to extend its capabilities. You import modules with a special command called (naturally enough) import. The function we needed in the previous section (floor) is in a module called math:

```
>>> import math
>>> math.floor(32.9)
32.0
```

Notice how this works: We import a module with import, and then use the functions from that module by writing module.function.

If you want the age to be an integer (32) and not a float (32.0), you can use the function int:[4]

```
>>> int(math.floor(32.9))
32
```

 NOTE *Similar functions exist to convert to other types (for example,* long *and* float*). The opposite of* floor *is* ceil *(short for "ceiling"), which finds the smallest integral value larger than or equal to the given number.*

If you are sure that you won't import more than one function with a given name (from different modules) you might not want to write the module name each time you call the function. Then you can use a variant of the import command:

```
>>> from math import sqrt
>>> sqrt(9)
3.0
```

After using from *module* import *function*, you can use the function without its module prefix.

---

4.   The int function will actually round down while converting to an integer, so when converting to an integer, using math.floor is superfluous.

Functions and Variables

You may, in fact, use variables to refer to functions (and most other things in Python). For instance, by performing the assignment foo = math.sqrt you can start using foo to calculate square roots; for example, foo(4) yields 2.

---

cmath *and Complex Numbers*

The sqrt function is used to calculate the square root of a number. Let's see what happens if we supply it with a negative number:

```
>>> from math import sqrt
>>> sqrt(-1)
Traceback (most recent call last):
  File "<pyshell#23>", line 1, in ?
    sqrt(-1)
ValueError: math domain error
```

Well, that's reasonable. You can't take the square root of a negative number. Or can you? Of course you can. The square root of a negative number is an *imaginary* number. (This is a standard mathematical concept—if you find it a bit too mind-bending, you are free to skip ahead.) So why couldn't sqrt deal with it? Because it only deals with floats, and imaginary numbers (and *complex* numbers, the sum of real and imaginary numbers) are something completely different— which is why they are covered by a different module, cmath (for *complex math*):

```
>>> import cmath
>>> cmath.sqrt(-1)
1j
```

Notice that I didn't use from...import... here. If I had, I would have lost my ordinary sqrt. Name clashes like these can be sneaky, so unless you *really* want to use the from version, you should probably stick with a plain import.

The 1j is an imaginary number. These are written with a trailing "j" (or "J"), just like longs used "L". Without delving into the theory of complex numbers, let me just show a final example of how you can use them:

```
>>> (1+3j) * (9+4j)
(-3+31j)
```

As you can see, the support for complex numbers is built into the language.

NOTE *There is no separate type for imaginary numbers in Python. They are treated as complex numbers whose real component is zero.*

Back to the __future__

It has been rumored that Guido (Python's creator) has a time machine because often when people request features in the language, the features have already been implemented. Of course, we aren't all allowed into this time machine, but Guido has been kind enough to build a part of it into Python, in the form of the magic module __future__. From it we can import features that will be standard in Python in the future but that aren't part of the language yet. You saw this in the section about numbers and expressions, and you'll be bumping into it from time to time throughout this book.

Saving and Executing Your Programs

The interactive interpreter is one of Python's great strengths. It makes it possible to test solutions and to experiment with the language in real time. If you want to know how something works, just try it! However, everything you write in the interactive interpreter is lost when you quit. What you really want to do is write *programs* that both you and other people can run. In this section, I tell you how to do just that.

First of all, you need a text editor, preferably one intended for programming. (If you use something like Microsoft Word, be sure to save your code as plain text.) If you are already using IDLE, you're in luck: Simply create a new editor window with File ➤ New Window. Another window appears—without an interactive prompt. Whew!

Start by entering the following:

```
print "Hello, world!"
```

Now select File ➤ Save to save your program (which is, in fact, a plain text file). Be sure to put it somewhere where you can find it later on. You might want to create a directory where you put all your Python projects, such as C:\python in Windows. (In a UNIX environment, you might use a directory like ~/python.) Give your file a logical name, such as hello.py. The ".py" ending is important.

NOTE *If you followed the installation instructions earlier in this chapter, you may have put your Python installation in* ~/python *already, but since that has a subdirectory of its own (such as* ~/python/Python-2.2/*), this shouldn't cause any problems. If you would rather put your own programs somewhere else, feel free to use a directory such as* ~/my_python_programs.

Got that? Don't close the window with your program in it. If you did, just open it again (File ➤ Open…). Now you can run it with Edit ➤ Run script, or by pressing Ctrl+F5. (If you aren't using IDLE, see the next section about running your programs from the command prompt.)

What happens? "Hello, world!" is printed in the interpreter windows, which is exactly what we wanted. The interpreter prompt is gone, but you can get it back by pressing Enter (in the interpreter window).

Let's extend our script to the following:

```
name = raw_input("What is your name? ")
print "Hello, " + name + "!"
```

NOTE *Don't worry about the difference between* input *and* raw_input—*I'll get to that.*

If you run this (remember to save it first), you should see the following prompt in the interpreter window:

```
What is your name?
```

Enter your name, (for example, "Gumby") and press Enter. You should get something like this:

```
Hello, Gumby!
```

Fun, isn't it?

Running Your Python Scripts from a Command Prompt

Actually, there are several ways to run your programs. First, let's assume that you have a DOS-window or a UNIX shell prompt before you and that the Python executable (called `python.exe` in Windows, and `python` in UNIX) has been put in your PATH environment variable.[5] Also, let's assume that your script from the previous section (`hello.py`) is in the current directory. Then you can execute your script with the following command in Windows:

```
C:\>python hello.py
```

or UNIX:

```
$ python hello.py
```

As you can see, the command is the same. Only the system prompt changes.

 NOTE *If you don't want to mess with environment variables, you can simply specify the full path of the Python interpreter. In Windows, you might do something like this:*

```
C:\>C:\Python22\python hello.py
```

Making Your Scripts Behave Like Normal Programs

Sometimes you want to execute a Python program (also called a *script*) the same way you execute other programs (such as your Web browser, or your text editor). In UNIX, there is a standard way of doing this: have the first line of your script begin with the character sequence #! (called "pound bang" or "shebang") followed by the absolute path to the program that interprets the script (in our case Python). Even if you didn't quite understand that, just put the following in the first line of your script if you want it to run easily on UNIX:

```
#!/usr/bin/env python
```

This should run the script, regardless of where the Python binary is located.

---

5.   If you don't understand this sentence, you should perhaps skip the section. You don't really need it.

NOTE   *In some systems (such as Red Hat Linux 7.2) if you install a recent version of Python (e.g., 2.2) you will still have an old one lying around (e.g., 1.5.2), which is needed by some system programs (so you can't uninstall it). In such cases, the* /usr/bin/env *trick is not a good idea, as you will probably end up with your programs being executed by the old Python. Instead, you should find the exact location of your new Python executable (probably called* python *or* python2*) and use the full path in the pound bang line, like this:*

```
#/usr/bin/python2
```

The exact path may vary from system to system.

Before you can actually run your script, you must make it executable:

```
$ chmod a+x hello.py
```

Now it can be run like this (assuming that you have the current directory in your path):

```
$ hello.py
```

NOTE   *If this doesn't work, try using* ./hello.py *instead, which will work even if the current directory (".") is not part of your execution path.*

If you like, you can rename your file and remove the "py" suffix to make it look more like a normal program.

What About Double-Clicking?

In Windows, the suffix (.py) is the key to making your script behave like a program. Try double-clicking on the file hello.py you saved in the previous section. If Python was installed correctly, a DOS window appears with the prompt "What is your name?" Cool, huh? (We'll make our programs look better, with buttons, menus, and so on later.)

There is one problem with running your program like this, however. Once you've entered your name, the program window closes before we can read the result. The window closes when the program is finished. Try changing the script by adding the following line at the end:

```
raw_input("Press <enter>")
```

Now, after running the program and entering your name, you should have a DOS window with the following contents:

```
What is your name? Gumby
Hello, Gumby!
Press <enter>
```

Once you press the Enter key, the window closes (because the program is finished). Just as a teaser, rename your file hello.pyw. (This is Windows-specific.) Double-click it as before. What happens? Nothing! How can that be? I will tell you later in the book—I promise.

Comments

The hash sign ("#") is a bit special in Python. When you put it in your code, everything to the right of it is ignored (which is why the Python interpreter didn't choke on the /usr/bin/env stuff we used earlier). For instance:

```
# Print the circumference of the circle:
print 2 * pi * radius
```

The first line here is called a *comment*, which can be useful in making programs easier to understand—both for other people and for yourself when you come back to old code. It has been said that the first commandment of programmers is "Thou Shalt Comment" (although some swear by the motto "If it was hard to write, it should be hard to read"). Make sure your comments say significant things and don't simply restate what is already obvious from the code. Useless, redundant comments may be worse than none. For instance, in the following example, a comment isn't really called for:

```
# Get the user's name:
user_name = raw_input("What is your name?")
```

Strings

Now what was all that `raw_input` and `"Hello, " + name + "!"` stuff about? Let's tackle the "Hello" part first and leave `raw_input` for later.

The first program in this chapter was simply

```
print "Hello, world!"
```

It is customary to begin with a program like this in programming tutorials—the problem is that I haven't really explained how it works yet. Well, you know the basics of the `print` statement (I'll have more to say about that later), but what is `"Hello, world!"`? It's called a *string* (as in "a string of characters"). Strings are found in almost every real Python program and have many uses, the main one being to represent a bit of text, such as the exclamation "Hello, world!"

Single-Quoted Strings and Escaping Quotes

Stringa are values, just like numbers are:

```
>>> "Hello, world!"
'Hello, world!'
```

But, let's consider this. When Python printed out our string it used *single* quotes, whereas we used *double* quotes. What's the difference? Actually, there is no difference:

```
>>> 'Hello, world!'
'Hello, world!'
```

Here, too, we use single quotes, and the result is the same. So why allow both? Because in some cases it may be useful:

```
>>> "Let's go!"
"Let's go!"
>>> '"Hello, world!" she said'
'"Hello, world!" she said'
```

In the preceding code, the first string contains a single quote (or apostrophe, as we should perhaps call it in this context), and therefore we can't use single quotes to enclose the string. If we did, the interpreter would complain (and rightly so):

```
>>> 'Let's go!'
SyntaxError: invalid syntax
```

Here, the string is `'Let'`, and Python doesn't quite know what to do with the following "s" (or the rest of the line, for that matter).

In the second string, we use double quotes as part of our sentence. Therefore, we have to use single quotes to enclose our string, for the same reasons as stated previously. Or, actually we don't *have* to. It's just convenient. An alternative is to use the backslash character ("\") to *escape* the quotes in the string, like this:

```
>>> 'Let\'s go!'
"Let's go!"
```

Python understands that the middle single quote is a character and not the end of the string. (Even so, Python chooses to use double quotes when printing out the string.) The same works with double quotes, of course:

```
>>> "\"Hello, world!\" she said"
'"Hello, world!" she said'
```

Escaping quotes like this can be useful, and sometimes necessary. For instance, what would you do without the backslash if your string contained both a single quote and a double quote, as in the string `'Let\'s say "Hello, world!"'`?

 NOTE *Tired of backslashes? As you will see in this chapter, you can avoid most of them by using* long strings *and* raw strings *(which can be combined).*

Concatenating Strings

Just to keep whipping this slightly tortured example, let me show you another way of writing the same string:

```
>>> "Let's say " '"Hello, world!"'
'Let\'s say "Hello, world!"'
```

I've simply written two strings, one after the other, and Python automatically concatenates them (makes them into one string). This is not a very well-known mechanism, but it can be useful at times. However, it only works when you actually write both strings at the same time, directly following one another:

```
>>> x = "Hello, "
>>> y = "world!"
>>> x y
SyntaxError: invalid syntax
```

In other words, this is just a special way of writing strings, not a general method of concatenating them. How, then, do you concatenate strings? Just like you add numbers:

```
>>> "Hello, " + "world!"
'Hello, world!'
>>> x = "Hello, "
>>> y = "world!"
>>> x + y
'Hello, world!'
```

String Representations, str and repr

Throughout these examples, you have probably noticed that all the strings printed out by Python are still quoted. That's because it prints out the value as it might be written in Python, not how you would like it to look for the user. If you use print, however, the result is different:

```
>>> "Hello, world!"
'Hello, world!'
>>> 10000L
10000L
>>> print "Hello, world!"
Hello, world!
>>> print 10000L
10000
```

As you can see, the long integer 10000L is simply the number 10,000 and should be written that way when presented to the user. But when you want to know what value a variable contains, you may be interested in whether it's a normal integer or a long, for instance.

What is actually going on here is that values are converted to strings through two different mechanisms. You can use both mechanisms yourself, through the functions str, which simply converts a value into a string in some reasonable fashion that will probably be understood by a user, for instance, and repr, which creates a string, which is a *representation* of the value as a legal Python expression:

```
>>> print repr("Hello, world!")
'Hello, world!'
>>> print repr(10000L)
10000L
>>> print str("Hello, world!")
Hello, world!
>>> print str(10000L)
10000
```

A synonym for repr(x) is `x` (here you use *backticks*, not single quotes). This can be useful when you want to print out a sentence containing a number, for instance:

```
>>> temp = 42
>>> print "The temperature is " + temp
Traceback (most recent call last):
  File "<pyshell#61>", line 1, in ?
    print "The temperature is " + temp
TypeError: cannot add type "int" to string
>>> print "The temperature is " + `temp`
The temperature is 42
```

The first print statement doesn't work because you can't add a string to a number. The second one, however, works because I have converted temp to the string 42 with the backticks. (I might, of course, just as well have used repr, which means the same thing. Actually, in this case, I could also have used str. Don't worry too much about this right now.)

In short: str, repr, and backticks are three ways of converting a Python value to a string. The function str makes it look good, while repr (and the backticks) tries to make the resulting string a legal Python expression.

input *vs.* raw_input

Now you've found out what "Hello, " + name + "!" means. But what about raw_input? Isn't input good enough? Let's try it. Enter the following in a separate script file:

```
name = input("What is your name? ")
print "Hello, " + name + "!"
```

This is a perfectly valid program, but as you will soon see, it's a bit unpractical. Let's try to run it:

```
What is your name? Gumby
Traceback (most recent call last):
  File "C:/python/test.py", line 2, in ?
    name = input("What is your name? ")
  File "<string>", line 0, in ?
NameError: name 'Gumby' is not defined
```

The problem is that input assumes that what you enter is a valid Python expression (it's more or less the inverse of repr). If you write your name as a string, that's no problem:

```
What is your name? "Gumby"
Hello, Gumby!
```

It's just a bit too much to ask that the user write his or her name in quotes like this; therefore we use raw_input, which treats all input as raw data, and puts it into a string:

```
>>> input("Enter a number: ")
Enter a number: 3
3
>>> raw_input("Enter a number: ")
Enter a number: 3
'3'
```

Unless you have a special need for input, you should probably use raw_input.

Long Strings, Raw Strings, and Unicode

Before ending this chapter, I want to first tell you about yet another couple of ways of writing strings. (I'm sure you're starting to understand that strings are pretty important.)

Long Strings

If you want to write a really long string, one that spans several lines, you can use triple quotes instead of ordinary quotes:

```
print '''This is a very long string.
It continues here.
And it's not over yet.
"Hello, world!"
Still here.'''
```

You can also use triple double quotes, `"""like this"""`. Note that because of the distinctive enclosing quotes, both single and double quotes are allowed inside, without being backslash-escaped.

 TIP *Ordinary strings can also span several lines. If the last character on a line is a backslash, the line break itself is "escaped," and is ignored. For instance,*

```
print "Hello, \
world!"
```

would print out `Hello, world!`. *The same goes for expressions and statements in general:*

```
>>> 1 + 2 + \
        4 + 5
12
>>> print \
        'Hello, world'
Hello, world
```

Raw Strings

Raw strings aren't too picky about backslashes, which can be very useful some-times.[6] In ordinary strings, the backslash has a special role: It *escapes* things, letting us put things into our string that we couldn't normally write directly. For instance, a new line is written \n, and can be put into a string like this:

```
>>> print 'Hello,\nworld!'
Hello,
world!
```

This is normally just dandy, but in some cases it's not what you want. What if you wanted the string to include a backslash followed by an "n"? You might want to put the DOS pathname C:\nowhere into a string, for instance:

```
>>> path = 'C:\nowhere'
>>> path
'C:\nowhere'
```

This looks correct, until you print it and discover the flaw:

```
>>> print path
C:
owhere
```

Not exactly what we were after, is it? So what do we do? We can escape the backslash itself:

```
>>> print 'C:\\nowhere'
C:\nowhere
```

This is just fine. But for long paths, you wind up with a *lot* of backslashes:

```
path = 'C:\\Program Files\\fnord\\foo\\bar\\baz\\frozz\\bozz'
```

Raw strings are useful in such cases. They don't treat the backslash as a special character at all. Every letter you put into a raw string stays the way you wrote it:

---

[6] Especially when writing regular expressions. More about those in Chapter 10.

```
>>> print r'C:\nowhere'
C:\nowhere
>>> print r'C:\Program Files\fnord\foo\bar\baz\frozz\bozz'
C:\Program Files\fnord\foo\bar\baz\frozz\bozz
```

As you can see, raw strings are written with an "r" in front. It would seem that you can put almost anything inside a raw string, and that is *almost* true. Of course, quotes have to be escaped as usual, although that means that you get a backslash in your final string, too:

```
>>> print r'Let\'s go!'
Let\'s go!
```

The one thing you *can't* have in a raw string is a final backslash. In other words, the last character in a raw string cannot be a backslash. Given the previous example, that ought to be obvious. If the last character (before the final quote) is a backslash, Python won't know whether to end the string or not:

```
>>> print r"This is illegal\"
SyntaxError: invalid token
```

Okay, so it's reasonable, but what if you *want* the last character in your raw string to be a backslash? (Perhaps it's the end of a DOS path, for instance.) Well, I've given you a whole bag of tricks in this section that should help you solve that problem, but basically you need to put the backslash in a separate string. A simple way of doing that is the following:

```
>>> print r'C:\Program Files\foo\bar' '\\'
C:\Program Files\foo\bar\
```

Note that you can use both single and double quotes with raw strings. Even triple-quoted strings can be raw.

Unicode Strings

The final type of string constant is the *Unicode string*. If you don't know what Unicode is, you probably don't need to know about this. (If you want to find out more about it, you can go to the Unicode Web site, www.unicode.org.) Normal strings in Python are stored internally as 8-bit ASCII, while Unicode strings are stored as 16-bit Unicode. This allows for a more varied set of characters, including special characters from most languages in the world. I'll restrict my treatment of Unicode strings to the following:

```
>>> u'Hello, world!'
u'Hello, world!'
```

As you can see, Unicode strings use the prefix u, just as raw strings use the prefix r.

A Quick Summary

I've covered quite a lot in this chapter. Let's take a look at what you've learned before moving on.

Algorithms. An algorithm is a recipe telling you exactly how to perform a task. When you program a computer, you are essentially describing an algorithm in a language the computer can understand, such as Python. Such a machine-friendly description is called a program, and it mainly consists of *expressions* and *statements*.

Expressions. An expression is a part of a computer program that represents a value. For instance, 2+2 is an expression, representing the value 4. Simple expressions are built from *literal values* (such as 2 or "Hello") by using *operators* (such as + or %) and *functions* (such as pow). More complicated expressions can be created by combining simpler expressions (e.g., (2+2)*(3-1)). Expressions may also contain *variables*.

Variables. A variable is a name that represents a value. New values may be assigned to variables through *assignments* such as x = 2. An assignment is a kind of *statement*.

Statements. A statement is an instruction that tells the computer to *do* something. That may involve changing variables (through assignments), printing things to the screen (such as print "Hello, world!"), importing modules, or a host of other stuff.

Functions. Functions in Python work just like functions in mathematics: They may take some arguments, and they return a result. (They may actually do lots of interesting stuff before returning, as you will find out when you learn to write your own functions in Chapter 6.)

Modules. Modules are extensions that can be imported into Python to extend its capabilities. For instance, several useful mathematical functions are available in the math module.

Programs. You have looked at the practicalities of writing, saving, and running Python programs.

Strings. Strings are really simple—they are just pieces of text. And yet there is a lot to know about them. In this chapter, you've seen many ways to write them, and in the next you learn many ways of using them.

New Functions in This Chapter

FUNCTION	DESCRIPTION
abs(*number*)	Returns the absolute value of a number
cmath.sqrt(*number*)	Square root, also for negative numbers
float(*object*)	Converts a string or number to a floating-point number
help()	Offers interactive help (new in Python 2.2)
input(*prompt*)	Gets input from the user
int(*object*)	Converts a string or number to an integer
long(*object*)	Converts a string or number to a long integer
math.ceil(*number*)	Returns the ceiling of a number as a float
math.floor(*number*)	Returns the floor of a number as a float
math.sqrt(*number*)	Square root, not for negative numbers
pow(*x*, *y*[, *z*])	*x* to the power of *y* (modulo *z*)
raw_input(*prompt*)	Gets input from the user, as a string
repr(*object*)	Returns a string-representation of a value
round(*number*[, *ndigits*])	Rounds a number to a given precision
str(*object*)	Converts a value to a string

What Now?

Now that you know the basics of expressions, let's move on to something a bit more advanced: data structures. Instead of dealing with simple values (such as numbers), you'll see how to bunch them together in more complex structures, such as *lists* and *dictionaries*. In addition, you'll take another close look at strings. In Chapter 5, you learn more about statements, and after that you'll be ready to write some really nifty programs.

CHAPTER 2

Lists and Tuples

IN THIS CHAPTER, you begin looking at *data structures*. A data structure is a collection of data elements (such as numbers or characters—or even other data structures) that is structured in some way, for instance by numbering the elements. The most basic data structure in Python is the *sequence*. Each element of a sequence is assigned a number, or *index*. The first index is zero, the second index is one, and so forth.

 NOTE *This numbering scheme may seem odd (you may wonder why the first element isn't number 1), but it is actually quite natural. As you see later in the chapter, the* last item *of a sequence is numbered –1, the next-to-last –2 and so forth. That means that you can count forward or backward from the first element, which lies at the beginning, or zero. Trust me: you get used to it.*

Python has six built-in types of sequences, but let's concentrate on two of the most common ones—lists and tuples. The main difference between these is that you can change a list but you can't change a tuple.

 NOTE *The other built-in sequence types are strings (which I revisit in the next chapter), Unicode strings,* buffer *objects, and* xrange *objects.*

Sequences are useful when you want to work with a collection of values. You might have a sequence representing a person in a database, with the first element being their name, and the second their age. Written as a list (the items of a list are separated by commas and enclosed in square brackets) that would look like this:

```
>>> edward = ['Edward Gumby', 42]
```

But sequences can contain other sequences, too, so you could make a list of such persons, which would be your database:

```
>>> edward = ['Edward Gumby', 42]
>>> john = ['John Smith', 50]
>>> database = [edward, john]
>>> database
[['Edward Gumby', 42], ['John Smith', 50]]
```

This chapter begins with some operations that are common to all sequences, including lists and tuples. These operations will also work with strings, which will be used in some of the examples, although for a full treatment of string operations, you have to wait until the next chapter.

After dealing with these basics, we start working with lists and see what's special about them. After lists, we come to tuples, which are very similar to lists, except that you can't change them.

> **NOTE** *Python has two basic types of data structures,* sequences *and* mappings. *While the elements of a sequence are numbered, each element in a mapping has a name (also called a* key*). You learn more about mappings in Chapter 4.*

Common Sequence Operations

There are certain things you can do with all sequence types. These operations include *indexing, slicing, adding, multiplying,* and checking for *membership.* In addition, Python has built-in functions for finding the length of a sequence, and for finding its largest and smallest elements.

> **NOTE** *One important operation not covered here is* iteration. *To iterate over a sequence means to perform certain actions repeatedly, once per element in the sequence. To learn more about this, see the section "Loops" in Chapter 5.*

Indexing

All elements in a sequence are numbered—from zero and upwards. You can access them individually with a number, like this:

```
>>> greeting = 'Hello'
>>> greeting[0]
'H'
```

> **NOTE**   *A string is just a sequence of characters. The index 0 refers to the first element, in this case the letter H.*

This is called *indexing*—you use an index to fetch an element. All sequences can be indexed in this way. When you use a negative index, Python counts *from the right*, e.g., from the last element. The last element is at position –1 (not –0, as that would be the same as the first element):

```
>>> greeting[-1]
'o'
```

String literals (and other sequence literals, for that matter) may be indexed directly, without putting them into a variable first. The effect is exactly the same:

```
>>> 'Hello'[1]
'e'
```

If a function returns a sequence, you can index it directly. For instance, if you are simply interested in the fourth digit in a year entered by the user, you could do something like this:

```
>>> fourth = raw_input('Year: ')[3]
Year: 2002
>>> fourth
'2'
```

Listing 2-1 contains an example program that asks you for a year, a month (as a number from 1 to 12), and a day (1 to 31), and then prints out the date with the proper month name and so on. An example session with this program might be as follows:

```
Year: 1974
Month (1-12): 8
Day (1-31): 16
August 16th, 1974
```

The last line is the output from the program.

Listing 2-1. Indexing Example

```
# Print out a date, given year, month, and day as numbers

months = [
    'January',
    'February',
    'March',
    'April',
    'May',
    'June',
    'July',
    'August',
    'September',
    'October',
    'November',
    'December'
]

# A list with one ending for each number from 1 to 31
endings = ['st', 'nd', 'rd'] + 17 * ['th'] \
        + ['st', 'nd', 'rd'] +  7 * ['th'] \
        + ['st']

year    = raw_input('Year: ')
month   = raw_input('Month (1-12): ')
day     = raw_input('Day (1-31): ')
```

```
# Remember to subtract 1 from month and day to get a correct index
month_name = months[int(month)-1]
ordinal = day + endings[int(day)-1]

print month_name + ' ' + ordinal + ', ' + year
```

Slicing

Just as you use indexing to access individual elements, you can use slicing to access *ranges* of elements. You do this by using *two* indices, separated by a colon:

```
>>> tag = '<a href="http://www.python.org">Python web site</a>'
>>> tag[9:30]
'http://www.python.org'
>>> tag[32:-4]
'Python web site'
```

As you can see, slicing is very useful for extracting parts of a sequence. The numbering here is very important. The *first* index is the number of the first element you want to include. However, the *last* index is the number of the first element *after* your slice. Consider the following:

```
>>> numbers = [1, 2, 3, 4, 5, 6, 7, 8, 9, 10]
>>> numbers[3:6]
[4, 5, 6]
>>> numbers[0:1]
[1]
```

In short, you supply two indices as limits for your slice, where the first is *inclusive*, and the second is *exclusive*.

A Nifty Shortcut

Let's say you want to access the last three elements of numbers (from the previous example). You could do it explicitly, of course:

```
>>> numbers[7:10]
[8, 9, 10]
```

Now, the index 10 refers to element eleven—which does not exist, but is one step after the last element you want. Got it?

Now, this is fine, but what if you want to count from the end?

```
>>> numbers[-3:-1]
[8, 9]
```

It seems you cannot access the last element this way. But, luckily you can use a shortcut: If the slice continues to the end of the sequence, you may simply leave out the last index:

```
>>> numbers[-3:]
[8, 9, 10]
```

The same thing works from the beginning:

```
>>> numbers[:3]
[1, 2, 3]
```

In fact, if you want to copy the entire sequence, you may leave out *both* indices:

```
>>> numbers[:]
[1, 2, 3, 4, 5, 6, 7, 8, 9, 10]
```

EXAMPLE

Listing 2-2 contains a small program that prompts you for a URL, and (assuming it is of the form http://www.somedomainname.com) extracts the domain name. Here is a sample run of the program:

```
Please enter the URL: http://www.python.org
Domain name: python
```

Listing 2-2. Slicing Example

```
# Split up a URL of the form http://www.something.com

url = raw_input('Please enter the URL: ')
domain = url[11:-4]

print "Domain name: " + domain
```

Adding Sequences

Sequences can be concatenated with the addition ("plus") operator:

```
>>> [1, 2, 3] + [4, 5, 6]
[1, 2, 3, 4, 5, 6]
>>> 'Hello, ' + 'world!'
'Hello, world!'
>>> [1, 2, 3] + 'world!'
Traceback (innermost last):
  File "<pyshell#2>", line 1, in ?
    [1, 2, 3] + 'world!'
TypeError: can only concatenate list (not "string") to list
```

As you can see from the error message, you can't concatenate a list and a string, although both are sequences. In general, you can only concatenate two sequences of the same type.

Multiplication

Multiplying a sequence by a number *x* creates a new sequence where the original sequence is repeated *x* times:

```
>>> 'python' * 5
'pythonpythonpythonpythonpython'
>>> [42] * 10
[42, 42, 42, 42, 42, 42, 42, 42, 42, 42]
```

None, Empty Lists, and Initialization

An empty list is simply written as two brackets ([ ])—there's nothing in it. But what if you want to have a list with room for ten elements but with nothing useful in it? You could use [42]*10, as before, or perhaps more realistically [0]*10. You now have a list with ten zeros in it. Sometimes, however, you would like a value that somehow means "nothing," as in "we haven't put anything here yet." That's when you use None. None is a Python value and means exactly that—"nothing here." So if you want to initialize a list of length 10, you could do the following:

```
>>> sequence = [None] * 10
>>> sequence
[None, None, None, None, None, None, None, None, None, None]
```

Listing 2-3 contains a program that prints (to the screen) a "box" made up of characters, which is centered on the screen and adapted to the size of a sentence supplied by the user. The following is a sample run:

```
Sentence: He's a very naughty boy!
```

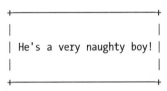

The code may look complicated, but it's basically just arithmetic—figuring out how many spaces, dashes, and so on you need to place things correctly.

Listing 2-3. Sequence (String) Multiplication Example

```python
# Prints a sentence in a centered "box" of correct width

# Note that the integer division operator (//) only works in Python
# 2.2 and newer. In earlier versions, simply use plain division (/)

sentence = raw_input("Sentence: ")

screen_width = 80
text_width   = len(sentence)
box_width    = text_width + 6
left_margin  = (screen_width - box_width) // 2

print
print ' ' * left_margin + '+'   + '-' * (box_width-2)  +   '+'
print ' ' * left_margin + '| '  + ' ' * text_width     + ' |'
print ' ' * left_margin + '| '  +        sentence       + ' |'
print ' ' * left_margin + '| '  + ' ' * text_width     + ' |'
print ' ' * left_margin + '+'   + '-' * (box_width-2)  +   '+'
print
```

Membership

To check whether a value can be found in a sequence, you use the in operator. This operator is a bit different from the ones discussed so far (such as multiplication or addition). It checks whether something is true, and returns a value accordingly: 1 means true, 0 means false. Such operators are called *Boolean operators*, and the truth values are called *Boolean values*. You learn more about Boolean expressions in the section on conditional statements in Chapter 5.

Here are some examples that use the in operator:

```
>>> permissions = 'rw'
>>> 'w' in permissions
1
>>> 'x' in permissions
0
>>> users = ['mlh', 'foo', 'bar']
>>> raw_input('Enter your user name: ') in users
Enter your user name: mlh
1
>>> subject = '$$$ Get rich now!!! $$$'
>>> '$$$' in subject
Traceback (innermost last):
  File "<pyshell#44>", line 1, in ?
    '$$$' in subject
TypeError: 'in <string>' requires character as left operand
```

The first two examples use the membership test to check whether 'w' and 'x' respectively are found in the string permissions. This could be a script on a UNIX machine checking for writing and execution permissions on a file. The next example checks whether a supplied user name (mlh) is found in a list of users. This could be useful if your program enforces some security policy. (In that case, you would probably want to use passwords as well.)

The last example doesn't work as well as the first ones. Had it worked, it could have become part of a spam filter, removing unsolicited commercial e-mail from your mailbox, for instance. The intention is to check whether a given string (subject) contains another string, '$$$'. So why doesn't it work? Because in only checks for single elements. In the case of a string, it only works with single characters (as the error message points out). To check whether a string is found within another string (whether the first is a *substring* of the second), you have to use a *string method*. You learn how to do that in Chapter 3, "Working with Strings."

Listing 2-4 shows a program that reads in a user name and checks the entered PIN code against a database (a list, actually) that contains pairs (more lists) of names and PIN codes. If the name/PIN pair is found in the database, the string 'Access granted' is printed. (The if statement was mentioned in Chapter 1 and will be fully explained in Chapter 5.)

Listing 2-4. Sequence Membership Example

```
# Check a user name and PIN code

database = [
    ['albert',  '1234'],
    ['dilbert', '4242'],
    ['smith',   '7524'],
    ['jones',   '9843']
]

username = raw_input('User name: ')
pin = raw_input('PIN code: ')

if [username, pin] in database: print 'Access granted'
```

Length, Minimum, and Maximum

The built-in functions len, min, and max can be quite useful. The function len returns the number of elements a sequence contains, while min and max return the smallest and largest element of the sequence respectively. (You learn more about comparing objects in Chapter 5, in the section "Comparison Operators.")

```
>>> numbers = [100, 34, 678]
>>> len(numbers)
3
>>> max(numbers)
678
>>> min(numbers)
34
>>> max(2, 3)
3
>>> min(9, 3, 2, 5)
2
```

How this works should be clear from the previous explanation, except possibly the last two expressions. Here max and min are not called with a sequence argument; the numbers are supplied directly as arguments.

Lists: Python's Workhorse

In the previous examples, I've used lists quite a bit. You've seen how useful they are, but in this section let's see what makes them different from tuples and strings: Lists are *mutable*—that is, you can change their contents.

The list *Function*

Because strings can't be modified in the same way as lists, often it can be useful to create a list from a string. You can do this with the list function:

```
>>> list('Hello')
['H', 'e', 'l', 'l', 'o']
```

Note that list works with all kinds of sequences, not just strings.

TIP *To convert a list of characters such as the preceding code back to a string, you have to use the following expression:*

```
''.join(somelist)
```

where somelist *is your list. For an explanation of what this really means, see the section about* join *in Chapter 3, "Working with Strings."*

Basic List Operations

You can perform all the standard sequence operations on lists, such as indexing, slicing, concatenating, and multiplying; but the interesting thing about lists is that they can be modified. In this section, you see some of the ways you can change a list: item assignments, item deletion, slice assignments, and list methods. (Note that not all list methods actually change their list.)

Changing Lists: Item Assignments

Changing a list is easy. You just use ordinary assignment as explained in the first chapter. However, instead of writing something like x = 2 you use the indexing notation to assign to a specific, existing position, such as x[1] = 2.

```
>>> x = [1, 1, 1]
>>> x[1] = 2
>>> x
[1, 2, 1]
```

NOTE   *You cannot assign to a position that doesn't exist; if your list is of length 2, you cannot assign a value to index 100. To do that, you would have to make a list of length 101 (or more). See the section "None, Empty Lists, and Initialization," earlier in this chapter.*

Deleting Elements

Deleting elements from a list is easy too. Actually, there are two ways of doing this, depending on what result you want.

Using None

If you just want to remove the value and leave the position "empty," you need a placeholder—something to occupy the position instead of the old value. For instance, let's say you have a list of the names of five persons working in a group:

```
>>> names = ['Alice', 'Beth', 'Cecil', 'Dee-Dee', 'Earl']
```

Let's say that this group has five positions allotted, so that if one person leaves, his or her place is kept open until another person joins the team. How can you do that? As you may remember, Python's value for representing "nothing" is None—so to remove a name, you simply assign None to that position in the list. For instance, if Cecil has left the group, you can simply do this:

```
>>> names[2] = None
>>> names
['Alice', 'Beth', None, 'Dee-Dee', 'Earl']
```

Now there is no name at position two in the list.

NOTE None *doesn't have any special meaning to Python; it doesn't mean that "this element has been deleted" or anything like that. It's just a value, like any other. We might just as well have used zero, or the string* 'No Name' *(although that would have the Boolean value* true, *while* None, *like 0 or an empty string, is* false*). We just choose to use* None *because it is convenient—because it is a value that is different from all other values, and that is often used for this sort of thing. (Boolean values are discussed in Chapter 5.)*

Using del

If you really want to *delete* one of the elements, removing it completely and not leaving anything in its place, use the del statement:

```
>>> names = ['Alice', 'Beth', 'Cecil', 'Dee-Dee', 'Earl']
>>> del names[2]
>>> names
['Alice', 'Beth', 'Dee-Dee', 'Earl']
```

Notice how Cecil is completely gone, and the length of the list has shrunk from five to four.

The del statement may be used to delete things other than list elements. It can be used with dictionaries (see Chapter 4) or even variables. For more information, see Chapter 5.

Assigning to Slices

Slicing is a very powerful feature, and it is made even more powerful by the fact that you can assign to slices:

```
>>> name = list('Perl')
>>> name
['P', 'e', 'r', 'l']
>>> name[2:] = list('ar')
>>> name
['P', 'e', 'a', 'r']
```

So you can assign to several positions at once. You may wonder what the big deal is. Couldn't you just have assigned to them one at a time? Sure, but when you use slice assignments, you may also replace the slice with a sequence whose length is different from that of the original:

```
>>> name = list('Perl')
>>> name[1:] = list('ython')
>>> name
['P', 'y', 't', 'h', 'o', 'n']
```

Slice assignments can even be used to *insert* elements without replacing any of the original ones:

```
>>> numbers = [1, 5]
>>> numbers[1:1] = [2, 3, 4]
>>> numbers
[1, 2, 3, 4, 5]
```

Here, I basically "replaced" an empty slice, thereby really inserting a sequence. You can do the reverse to delete a slice:

```
>>> numbers
[1, 2, 3, 4, 5]
>>> numbers[1:4] = []
>>> numbers
[1, 5]
```

As you may have guessed, this last example is equivalent to del numbers[1:4].

List Methods

You've encountered functions already, but now it's time to meet a close relative: *methods.*

NOTE *You get a much more detailed explanation of what methods really are in Chapter 7, "More Abstraction."*

A method is a function that is tightly coupled to some object, be it a list, a number, a string, or whatever. In general, a method is called like this:

```
object.method(arguments)
```

As you can see, a method call looks just like a function call, except that the object is put before the method name, with a dot separating them. Lists have several methods that allow you to examine or modify their contents.

append

The append method is used to append an object to the end of a list:

```
>>> lst = [1, 2, 3]
>>> lst.append(4)
>>> lst
[1, 2, 3, 4]
```

You might wonder why I have chosen such an ugly name as lst for my list. Why not call it list? I could do that, but as you might remember, list is a built-in function.[1] If I use the name for a list instead, I won't be able to call the function anymore. You can generally find better names for a given application. A name such as lst really doesn't tell you anything. So if your list is a list of prices, for instance, you probably ought to call it something like prices, prices_of_eggs, or pricesOfEggs.

It's also important to note that append, like several similar methods, changes the list *in place*. This means that it does *not* simply return a new, modified list—it modifies the old one directly. This is usually what you want, but it may sometimes cause trouble. I'll return to this discussion when I describe sort later in the chapter.

---

1. Actually, from version 2.2 of Python, list is a type, not a function. (This is the case with tuple and str as well.) For the full story on this, see the section "Subclassing list, dict, and str," in Chapter 9, "Magic Methods, Properties, and Iterators."

count

The `count` method counts the occurrences of an element in a list:

```
>>> ['to', 'be', 'or', 'not', 'to', 'be'].count('to')
2
>>> x = [[1, 2], 1, 1, [2, 1, [1, 2]]]
>>> x.count(1)
2
>>> x.count([1, 2])
1
```

extend

The extend method allows you to append several values at once by supplying a sequence of the values you want to append. In other words, your original list has been extended by the other one:

```
>>> a = [1, 2, 3]
>>> b = [4, 5, 6]
>>> a.extend(b)
>>> a
[1, 2, 3, 4, 5, 6]
```

This may seem similar to concatenation, but the important difference is that the extended sequence (in this case a) is modified. This is not the case in ordinary concatenation, in which a completely new sequence is returned:

```
>>> a = [1, 2, 3]
>>> b = [4, 5, 6]
>>> a + b
[1, 2, 3, 4, 5, 6]
>>> a
[1, 2, 3]
```

As you can see, the concatenated list looks exactly the same as the extended one in the previous example, yet a hasn't changed this time. Because ordinary concatenation has to make a new list that contains copies of a and b, it isn't quite as efficient as using extend if what you want is something like this:

```
>>> a = a + b
```

The effect of extend can be achieved by assigning to slices, as follows:

```
>>> a = [1, 2, 3]
>>> b = [4, 5, 6]
>>> a[len(a):] = b
>>> a
[1, 2, 3, 4, 5, 6]
```

While this works, it isn't quite as readable.

index

The index method is used for searching lists to find the index of the first occurrence of a value:

```
>>> knights = ['We', 'are', 'the', 'knights', 'who', 'say', 'ni']
>>> knights.index('who')
4
>>> knights.index('herring')
Traceback (innermost last):
  File "<pyshell#76>", line 1, in ?
    knights.index('herring')
ValueError: list.index(x): x not in list
```

When you search for the word "who," you find that it's located at index 4:

```
>>> knights[4]
'who'
```

However, when you search for "herring," you get an exception because the word is not found at all.

insert

The insert method is used to insert an object into a list:

```
>>> numbers = [1, 2, 3, 5, 6, 7]
>>> numbers.insert(3, 'four')
>>> numbers
[1, 2, 3, 'four', 5, 6, 7]
```

As with extend, you can implement insert with slice assignments:

```
>>> numbers = [1, 2, 3, 5, 6, 7]
>>> numbers[3:3] = ['four']
>>> numbers
[1, 2, 3, 'four', 5, 6, 7]
```

This may be fancy, but it is hardly as readable as using insert.

pop

The pop method removes an element (by default the last one) from the list and returns it:

```
>>> x = [1, 2, 3]
>>> x.pop()
3
>>> x
[1, 2]
>>> x.pop(0)
1
>>> x
[2]
```

 NOTE *The* pop *method is the only list method that both modifies the list and returns a value (other than* None*).*

Using pop, you can implement a common data structure called a *stack*. A stack like this works just like a stack of plates. You can put plates on top, and you can remove plates from the top. The last one you put into the stack is the first one to be removed. (This principle is called *Last-In-First-Out*, or LIFO.)

The generally accepted names for the two stack operations (putting things in and taking them out) are push and pop. Python doesn't have push, but you can use append instead. The pop and append methods reverse each other's results, so if you push (or append) the value you just popped, you end up with the same stack:

```
>>> x = [1, 2, 3]
>>> x.append(x.pop())
>>> x
[1, 2, 3]
```

 TIP   *If you want a* First-In-First-Out *(FIFO) queue, you can use* insert(0,...) *instead of* append. *Alternatively, you could keep using* append *but substitute* pop(0) *for* pop().

remove

The remove method is used to remove the first occurrence of a value:

```
>>> x = ['to', 'be', 'or', 'not', 'to', 'be']
>>> x.remove('be')
>>> x
['to', 'or', 'not', 'to', 'be']
>>> x.remove('bee')
Traceback (innermost last):
  File "<pyshell#3>", line 1, in ?
    x.remove('bee')
ValueError: list.remove(x): x not in list
```

As you can see, only the first occurrence is removed, and you cannot remove something (in this case, the string 'bee') if it isn't in the list to begin with.

It's important to note that this is one of the "non-returning in-place changing" methods. It modifies the list, but returns nothing (as opposed to pop).

reverse

The reverse method reverses the elements in the list. (Not very surprising, I guess.)

```
>>> x = [1, 2, 3]
>>> x.reverse()
>>> x
[3, 2, 1]
```

Note that `reverse` changes the list and does not return anything (just like `remove` and `sort`, for instance).

sort

The `sort` method is used to sort lists in place. Sorting "in place" means changing the original list so its elements are in sorted order, rather than simply returning a sorted copy of the list:

```
>>> x = [4, 6, 2, 1, 7, 9]
>>> x.sort()
>>> x
[1, 2, 4, 6, 7, 9]
```

You've encountered several methods already that modify the list without returning anything, and in most cases that behavior is quite natural (as with append, for instance). But I want to emphasize this behavior in the case of `sort` because so many people seem to be confused by it. The confusion usually occurs when users want a sorted copy of a list while leaving the original alone. An intuitive (but *wrong*) way of doing this is as follows:

```
>>> x = [4, 6, 2, 1, 7, 9]
>>> y = x.sort() # Don't do this!
>>> print y
None
```

Because `sort` modifies x but returns nothing, you end up with a sorted x and a y containing None. The *right* way to do this would be to *first* put a copy of x into y, and then sort y, as follows:

```
>>> x = [4, 6, 2, 1, 7, 9]
>>> y = x[:]
>>> y.sort()
>>> x
[4, 6, 2, 1, 7, 9]
>>> y
[1, 2, 4, 6, 7, 9]
```

Recall that x[:] is a slice containing all the elements of x, effectively a copy of the entire list. Simply assigning x to y wouldn't work because both x and y would contain the same list:

```
>>> y = x
>>> y.sort()
>>> x
[1, 2, 4, 6, 7, 9]
>>> y
[1, 2, 4, 6, 7, 9]
```

If you want to sort the elements in reverse order, simply use sort, followed by reverse:

```
>>> names = ['Gumby', 'Smith', 'Jones']
>>> names.sort()
>>> names.reverse()
>>> names
['Smith', 'Jones', 'Gumby']
```

Advanced Sorting

If you want to have your elements sorted in a specific manner (other than sort's default behavior, which is to sort elements in ascending order) you can define your own *comparison function*, of the form compare(x,y), which returns a negative number when x < y, a positive number when x > y, and zero when x == y (according to your definition). You can then supply this as a parameter to sort. The built-in function cmp provides the default behavior:

```
>>> cmp(42, 32)
1
>>> cmp(99, 100)
-1
>>> cmp(10, 10)
0
>>> numbers = [5, 2, 9, 7]
>>> numbers.sort(cmp)
>>> numbers
[2, 5, 7, 9]
```

You learn how to define your own functions in Chapter 6, "Abstraction."

TIP *If you would like to read more about sorting, you may want to check out Andrew Dalke's "Sorting Mini-HOWTO" at* http://py-howto.sourceforge.net/sorting/sorting.html.

Tuples: Immutable Sequences

Tuples are sequences, just like lists. The only difference is that tuples *can't be changed.*[2] (As you may have noticed, this is also true of strings.) The tuple syntax is simple—if you separate some values with commas you automatically have a tuple:

```
>>> 1, 2, 3
(1, 2, 3)
```

As you can see, tuples may also be (and often are) enclosed in parentheses:

```
>>> (1, 2, 3)
(1, 2, 3)
```

The empty tuple is written as two parentheses containing nothing:

```
>>> ()
()
```

So, you may wonder how to write a tuple containing a single value. This is a bit peculiar—you have to include a comma, even though there is only one value:

```
>>> 42
42
>>> 42,
(42,)
>>> (42,)
(42,)
```

---

2. There are some technical differences in the way tuples and lists work behind the scenes, but you probably won't notice it in any practical way. And tuples don't have methods. Don't ask me why.

The last two examples produce tuples of length one, while the first is not a tuple at all. The comma is crucial. Simply adding parentheses won't help: (42) is exactly the same as 42. One lonely comma, however, can change the value of an expression completely:

```
>>> 3*(40+2)
126
>>> 3*(40+2,)
(42, 42, 42)
```

The tuple Function

The tuple function works in pretty much the same way as list: It takes one sequence argument and converts it to a tuple. If the argument is already a tuple, it is returned unchanged:

```
>>> tuple([1, 2, 3])
(1, 2, 3)
>>> tuple('abc')
('a', 'b', 'c')
>>> tuple((1, 2, 3))
(1, 2, 3)
```

Basic Tuple Operations

As you may have gathered, tuples aren't very complicated—and there isn't really much you can do with them except make them and access their elements, and you do this the same as with other sequences:

```
>>> x = 1, 2, 3
>>> x[1]
2
>>> x[0:2]
(1, 2)
```

As you can see, slices of a tuple are also tuples, just as list slices are themselves lists.

So What's the Point?

By now you are probably wondering why anyone would ever want such a thing as an immutable (unchangeable) sequence. Can't you just stick to lists and leave them alone when you don't want them to change? Basically: Yes. However, there are two important reasons why you need to know about tuples:

- They can be used as keys in mappings—lists can't be. (You may remember that mappings were mentioned in the introduction to this chapter. You learn more about them in Chapter 4.)

- They are returned by some built-in functions and methods, which means that you have to deal with them. As long as you don't try to change them, "dealing" with them most often means treating them just like lists (unless you need methods such as index and count, which tuples don't have).

In general, lists will probably be adequate for all your sequencing needs.

A Quick Summary

Let's review some of the most important concepts covered in this chapter:

Sequences. A sequence is a data structure in which the elements are numbered (starting with zero). Examples of sequence types are lists, strings, and tuples. Of these, lists are mutable (you can change them) whereas tuples and strings are immutable (once they're created, they're fixed). Parts of a sequence can be accessed through slicing, supplying two indices, indicating the starting and ending position of the slice. To change a list, you assign new values to its positions, or use assignment to overwrite entire slices.

Membership. Whether a value can be found in a sequence is decided with the operator in.

Methods. Some of the built-in types (such as lists and strings, but not tuples) have many useful methods attached to them. These are a bit like functions, except that they are tied closely to a specific value. Methods are an important aspect of object-oriented programming, which we look at later, in Chapter 7, "More Abstraction."

New Functions in This Chapter

FUNCTION	DESCRIPTION
cmp(*x*, *y*)	Compares two values
len(*seq*)	Returns the length of a sequence
list(*seq*)	Converts a sequence to a list
max(*args*)	Returns the maximum of a sequence or set of arguments
min(*args*)	Returns the minimum of a sequence or set of arguments
tuple(*seq*)	Converts a sequence to a tuple

What Now?

Now that you're acquainted with sequences, let's move on to character sequences, also known as strings.

Working with Strings

You've seen strings before, and know how to make them. You've also looked at how to access their individual characters by indexing and slicing. In this chapter, you see how to use them to format other values (for printing, for example), and take a quick look at the useful things you can do with string methods, such as splitting, joining, searching, and more.

Basic String Operations

All the standard sequence operations (indexing, slicing, multiplication, membership, length, minimum, and maximum) work with strings, as you saw in the previous chapter. Remember, however, that strings are immutable, so all kinds of item or slice assignments are illegal:

```
>>> website = 'http://www.python.org'
>>> website[-3:] = 'com'
Traceback (most recent call last):
  File "<pyshell#19>", line 1, in ?
    website[-3:] = 'com'
TypeError: object doesn't support slice assignment
```

String Formatting: The Short Version

If you are new to programming, chances are you won't need all the options that are available in Python string formatting so I'll give you the short version here. If you are interested in the details, take a look at the section "String Formatting: The Long Version," which follows. Otherwise, just read this and skip down to the section "String Methods."

String formatting is done with the string formatting operator, "%" (percent).

 NOTE   *As you may remember, % is also used as a modulus operator.*

To the left of it you place a string (the format string), and to the right of it you place the value (or values) you want to format:

```
>>> format = "Hello, %s. %s enough for ya?"
>>> values = ('world', 'Hot')
>>> print format % value
Hello, world. Hot enough for ya?
```

The %s parts of the format string are called *conversion specifiers*. They mark the places where the values are to be inserted. The s means that the values should be formatted as if they were strings—if they aren't, they'll be converted with str. This works with most values; for a list of other types, see Table 3-1 later in the chapter.

NOTE *To actually include a percent sign in the format string, you must write %% so Python doesn't mistake it for the beginning of a conversion specifier.*

If you are formatting real numbers (floats), you can use the f type and supply the *precision* as a "." (dot) followed by the number of decimals you want to keep. The format specifier always ends with a type character, so you must put the precision before that:

```
>>> format = "Pi with three decimals: %.3f"
>>> from math import pi
>>> print format % pi
Pi with three decimals: 3.142
```

String Formatting: The Long Version

The right operand of the formatting operator may be anything; if it is either a tuple or a mapping (like a dictionary), it is given special treatment. We haven't looked at mappings (dictionaries) yet, so let's focus on tuples here. We'll use mappings in formatting in Chapter 4, where they're discussed in greater detail. If the right operand is a tuple, each of its elements is formatted separately, and you need a conversion specifier for each of the values.

NOTE *If you write the tuple to be converted as part of the conversion expression, you must enclose it in parentheses to avoid confusing Python:*

```
>>> '%s plus %s equals %s' % (1, 1, 2)
'1 plus 1 equals 2'
>>> '%s plus %s equals %s' % 1, 1, 2 # Lacks parentheses!
Traceback (most recent call last):
  File "<stdin>", line 1, in ?
TypeError: not enough arguments for format string
```

In the material that follows, I walk you through the various parts of the conversion specifier. For a summary, see the sidebar "Conversion Specifier Anatomy."

Conversion Specifier Anatomy

A basic conversion specifier (as opposed to a full conversion specifier, which may contain a mapping key as well; see Chapter 4 for more information) consists of the items that follow. Note here that the order is crucial.

- The "%" character. This marks the beginning of the conversion specifier.

- *Conversion flags* (optional). These may be either "-", indicating left alignment, "+", indicating that a sign should precede the converted value, " " (a space character), indicating that a space should precede positive numbers, or "0", indicating that the conversion should be zero-padded.

- The *minimum field width* (optional). The converted string will be at least this wide. If this is an "*" (asterisk), the width will be read from the value tuple.

- A "." (dot) followed by the *precision* (optional). If a real number is converted, this many decimals should be shown. If a string is converted, this number is that *maximum field width*. If this is an "*" (asterisk), the precision will be read from the value tuple.

- The *conversion type* (see Table 3-1).

Simple Conversion

The simple conversion, with only a conversion type, is really easy to use:

```
>>> 'Price of eggs: $%d' % 42
'Price of eggs: $42'
>>> 'Hexadecimal price of eggs: %x' % 42
'Hexadecimal price of eggs: 2a'
>>> from math import pi
>>> 'Pi: %f...' % pi
'Pi: 3.141593...'
>>> 'Very inexact estimate of pi: %i' % pi
'Very inexact estimate of pi: 3'
>>> 'Using str: %s' % 42L
'Using str: 42'
>>> 'Using repr: %r' % 42L
'Using repr: 42L'
```

For a list of all conversion types, see Table 3-1.

Table 3-1. String Formatting Conversion Types

CONVERSION TYPE	MEANING
d, i	Signed integer decimal
o	Unsigned octal
u	Unsigned decimal
x	Unsigned hexadecimal (lowercase)
X	Unsigned hexadecimal (uppercase)
e	Floating point exponential format (lowercase)
E	Floating point exponential format (uppercase)
f, F	Floating point decimal format
g	Same as "e" if exponent is greater than –4 or less than precision, "f" otherwise
G	Same as "E" if exponent is greater than –4 or less than precision, "F" otherwise
c	Single character (accepts integer or single character string)
r	String (converts any Python object using repr)
s	String (converts any Python object using str)

Width and Precision

A conversion specifier may include a field width and a precision. The width is the minimum number of characters reserved for a formatted value, while the precision is (for a numeric conversion) the number of decimals that will be included in the result, or (for a string conversion) the maximum number of characters the formatted value may have.

These two parameters are supplied as two integer numbers (width first, then precision), separated by a "." (dot). Both are optional, but if you want to supply only the precision, you must also include the dot:

```
>>> '%10f' % pi        # Field width 10
'  3.141593'
>>> '%10.2f' % pi      # Field width 10, precision 2
'      3.14'
>>> '%.2f' % pi        # Precision 2
'3.14'
>>> '%.5s' % 'Guido van Rossum'
'Guido'
```

You can use an asterisk ("*") as the width or precision (or both), in which case the number will be read from the tuple argument:

```
>>> '%.*s' % (5, 'Guido van Rossum')
'Guido'
```

Signs, Alignment, and Zero-Padding

Before the width and precision numbers, you may put a "flag," which may be either zero, plus, minus, or blank. A zero means that the number will be zero-padded:

```
>>> '%010.2f' % pi
'0000003.14'
```

It's important to note here that the leading zero in 010 in the preceding code does *not* mean that the width specifier is an octal number, as it would in a normal Python number. When you use 010 as the width specifier, it means that the width should be 10 and that the number should be zero-padded, not that the width should be 8:

```
>>> 010
8
```

A minus sign ("-") left-aligns the value:

```
>>> '%-10.2f' % pi
'3.14      '
```

As you can see, any extra space is put on the right-hand side of the number.

A blank (" ") means that a blank should be put in front of positive numbers. This may be useful for aligning positive and negative numbers:

```
>>> print ('% 5d' % 10) + '\n' + ('% 5d' % -10)
   10
  -10
```

Finally, a plus ("+") means that a sign (either plus or minus) should precede both positive and negative numbers (again, useful for aligning):

```
>>> print ('%+5d' % 10) + '\n' + ('%+5d' % -10)
  +10
  -10
```

EXAMPLE

In the following example, I use the asterisk width specifier to format a table of fruit prices, where the user enters the total width of the table. Because this information is supplied by the user, I can't hard-code the field widths in my conversion specifiers; by using the asterisk, I can have the field width read from the converted tuple. The source code is given in Listing 3-1.

Listing 3-1. String Formatting Example

```
# Print a formatted price list with a given width

width = input('Please enter width: ')

price_width = 10
item_width  = width - price_width

header_format = '%-*s%*s'
format        = '%-*s%*.2f'

print '=' * width
```

```
print header_format % (item_width, 'Item', price_width, 'Price')

print '-' * width

print format % (item_width, 'Apples', price_width, 0.4)
print format % (item_width, 'Pears', price_width, 0.5)
print format % (item_width, 'Cantaloupes', price_width, 1.92)
print format % (item_width, 'Dried Apricots (16 oz.)', price_width, 8)
print format % (item_width, 'Prunes (4 lbs.)', price_width, 12)

print '=' * width
```

The following is a sample run of the program:

```
Please enter width: 35
===================================
Item                      Price
-----------------------------------
Apples                     0.40
Pears                      0.50
Cantaloupes                1.92
Dried Apricots (16 oz.)    8.00
Prunes (4 lbs.)           12.00
===================================
```

String Methods

You have already encountered methods in lists. Strings have a much richer set of methods, in part because strings have "inherited" many of their methods from the string module where they resided as functions in earlier versions of Python (and where you may still find them, if you feel the need).

But string Isn't Dead

Even though string methods have completely upstaged the string module, the module still includes a few constants and functions that *aren't* available as string methods. The maketrans function is one example and will be discussed together with the translate method in the material that follows. Table 3-2 shows some useful constants available from string. For a more thorough description of the module, check out section 4.1 of the Python Library Reference (http://www.python.org/doc/lib/module-string.html).

Table 3-2. Useful Values from the string *Module*

CONSTANT	DESCRIPTION
string.digits	A string containing the digits 0–9
string.letters	A string containing all letters (upper and lowercase)
string.lowercase	A string containing all lowercase letters
string.printable	A string containing all printable characters
string.punctuation	A string containing all punctuation characters
string.uppercase	A string containing all uppercase letters
string.whitespace	A string containing all whitespace characters

Because there are so many string methods, only some of the most useful ones are described here. For a full reference, see Appendix B. In the description of the string methods you will find references to other, related string methods in this chapter (marked "See also") or in the appendix (marked "In the appendix").

find

The find method finds a substring within a larger string. It returns the leftmost index where the substring is found. If it is *not* found, –1 is returned:

```
>>> 'With a moo-moo here, and a moo-moo there'.find('moo')
7
>>> title = "Monty Python's Flying Circus"
>>> title.find('Monty')
0
>>> title.find('Python')
6
>>> title.find('Flying')
15
>>> title.find('Zirquss')
-1
```

In our first encounter with membership in Chapter 2, we tried to create a spam filter by using the expression '$$$' in subject, which didn't work. Our attempt was as follows:

```
>>> subject = '$$$ Get rich now!!! $$$'
>>> '$$$' in subject
Traceback (most recent call last):
```

```
  File "<stdin>", line 1, in ?
TypeError: 'in <string>' requires character as left operand
```

Now you have the tool to fix that:

```
>>> subject = '$$$ Get rich now!!! $$$'
>>> subject.find('$$$')
0
```

 NOTE *The string method* find *does* not *return a Boolean value. If* find *returns 0, as it did here, it means that it* has *found the substring, at index zero.*

You may also supply a starting point for your search and, optionally, also an ending-point:

```
>>> subject = '$$$ Get rich now!!! $$$'
>>> subject.find('$$$')
0
>>> subject.find('$$$', 1) # Only supplying the start
20
>>> subject.find('!!!')
16
>>> subject.find('!!!', 0, 16) # Supplying start and end
-1
```

Note that the range specified by the start and stop values (second and third parameter) includes the first index but not the second. This is common practice in Python.

In the appendix: rfind, index, rindex, count, startswith, endswith.

join

A very important string method, join is the inverse of split, and is used to join the elements of a sequence:

```
>>> seq = [1, 2, 3, 4, 5]
>>> sep = '+'
```

```
>>> sep.join(seq) # Trying to join a list of numbers
Traceback (most recent call last):
  File "<stdin>", line 1, in ?
TypeError: sequence item 0: expected string, int found
>>> seq = ['1', '2', '3', '4', '5']
>>> sep.join(seq) # Joining a list of strings
'1+2+3+4+5'
>>> dirs = '', 'usr', 'bin', 'env'
>>> '/'.join(dirs)
'/usr/bin/env'
>>> print 'C:' + '\\'.join(dirs)
C:\usr\bin\env
```

As you can see, the sequence elements that are to be joined must all be strings. Note how in the last two examples I make use of a list of directories and format them according to the conventions of UNIX and DOS/Windows simply by using a different separator (and adding a drive name in the DOS version).

See also: split.

lower

The lower method returns a lowercase version of the string:

```
>>> 'Trondheim Hammer Dance'.lower()
'trondheim hammer dance'
```

This can be useful if you want to write code that is "case-insensitive"—that is, code that ignores the difference between uppercase and lowercase letters. For instance, you want to check whether a user name is found in a list. If your list contains the string 'gumby' and the user enters his name as 'Gumby', you won't find it:

```
>>> if 'Gumby' in ['gumby', 'smith', 'jones']: print 'Found it!'
...
>>>
```

The same will of course happen if you have stored 'Gumby' and the user writes 'gumby', or even 'GUMBY'. A solution to this is to convert all names to lowercase both when storing and searching. The code would look something like this:

```
>>> name = 'Gumby'
>>> names = ['gumby', 'smith', 'jones']
```

```
>>> if name.lower() in names: print 'Found it!'
...
Found it!
>>>
```

> **See also:** translate.
> **In the appendix:** islower, capitalize, swapcase, title, istitle, upper, isupper.

replace

The replace method returns a string where all the occurrences of one string have been replaced by another:

```
>>> 'This is a test'.replace('is', 'eez')
'Theez eez a test'
```

If you have ever used the "search and replace" feature of a word processing program, you will no doubt see the usefulness of this method.
>   **See also:** translate.
>   **In the appendix:** expandtabs.

split

A very important string method, split is the inverse of join, and is used to split a string into a sequence:

```
>>> '1+2+3+4+5'.split('+')
['1', '2', '3', '4', '5']
>>> '/usr/bin/env'.split('/')
['', 'usr', 'bin', 'env']
>>> 'Using    the    default'.split()
['Using', 'the', 'default']
```

Note that if no separator is supplied, the default is to split on all occurrences of whitespace (spaces, tabs, newlines, and so on).
>   **See also:** join.
>   **In the appendix:** splitlines.

strip

The strip method returns a string where whitespace on the left and right (but not internally) has been stripped (removed):

```
>>> '    internal whitespace is kept    '.strip()
'internal whitespace is kept'
```

As with lower, strip can be useful when comparing input to stored values. Let's return to the user name example from the section on lower, and let's say that the user inadvertently types a space after his name:

```
>>> names = ['gumby', 'smith', 'jones']
>>> name = 'gumby '
>>> if name in names: print 'Found it!'
...
>>> if name.strip() in names: print 'Found it!'
...
Found it!
>>>
```

In the appendix: lstrip, rstrip.

translate

Similar to replace, translate replaces parts of a string, but unlike replace, translate only works with single characters. Its strength lies in that it can perform several replacements simultaneously, and can do so more efficiently than replace.

There are quite a few rather technical uses for this method (such as translating newline characters or other platform-dependent special characters) but let's consider a simpler (although slightly more silly) example. Let's say you want to translate a plain English text into one with a German accent. To do this, you must replace the character "c" with "k," and "s" with "z."

Before you can use translate, however, you must make a *translation table*. This translation table is a full listing of which characters should be replaced by which. Because this table (which is actually just a string) has 256 entries, you won't write it out yourself: You'll use the function maketrans from the string module.

The `maketrans` function takes two arguments: two strings of equal length, indicating that each character in the first string should be replaced by the character in the same position in the second string. Got that? In the case of our simple example, the code would look like the following:

```
>>> from string import maketrans
>>> table = maketrans('cs', 'kz')
```

....

What's in a Translation Table?

A translation table is a string containing one replacement letter for each of the 256 characters in the ASCII character set:

```
>>> table = maketrans('cs', 'kz')
>>> len(table)
256
>>> table[97:123]
'abkdefghijklmnopqrztuvwxyz'
>>> maketrans('', '')[97:123]
'abcdefghijklmnopqrstuvwxyz'
```

As you can see, I've sliced out the part of the table that corresponds to the lowercase letters. Take a look at the alphabet in the table and that in the empty translation (which doesn't change anything). The empty translation has a normal alphabet, while in the preceding code, the letter "c" has been replaced by "k," and "s" has been replaced by "z."

....

Once you have this table, you can use it as an argument to the `translate` method, thereby translating your string:

```
>>> 'this is an incredible test'.translate(table)
'thiz iz an inkredible tezt'
```

An optional second argument can be supplied to `translate`, specifying letters that should be deleted. If you wanted to emulate a really fast-talking German, for instance, you could delete all the spaces:

```
>>> 'this is an incredible test'.translate(table, ' ')
'thizizaninkredibletezt'
```

TIP *Sometimes string methods such as* lower *won't work quite the way you want them to—for instance, if you happen to use a non-English alphabet. Let's say you want to convert the uppercase Norwegian word "BØLLEFRØ" to its lowercase equivalent:*

```
>>> print 'BØLLEFRØ'.lower()
bØllefrØ
```

As you can see, this didn't really work because Python doesn't consider "Ø" a real letter. In this case, you can use translate *to do the translation:*

```
>>> table = maketrans('ÆØÅ', 'æøå')
>>> word = 'KÅPESØM'
>>> print word.lower()
kÅpesØm
>>> print word.translate(table)
KåPESøM
>>> print word.translate(table).lower()
kåpesøm
```

See also: replace, lower.

A Quick Summary

In this chapter, you have seen two important ways of working with strings:

> **String formatting.** The modulo operator (%) can be used to splice values into a string that contains conversion flags, such as %s. You can use this to format values in many ways, including right or left justification, setting a specific field width and precision, adding a sign (plus or minus), or left-padding with zeros.

> **String methods.** Strings have a plethora of methods. Some of them are extremely useful (such as split and join), while others are used less often (such as istitle or capitalize).

New Functions in This Chapter

FUNCTION	DESCRIPTION
string.maketrans(*from*, *to*)	Makes a translation table for translate

What Now?

Lists, strings, and dictionaries are three of the most important data types in Python. You've seen lists and strings, so guess what's next? In the next chapter, you see how dictionaries not only support indices, but other kinds of keys (such as strings or tuples) as well. Dictionaries also support a few methods, although not as many as strings.

CHAPTER 4

Dictionaries:
When Indices Won't Do

You've seen that lists are useful when you want to group values into a structure and refer to each value by number. In this chapter, you learn about a data structure in which you can refer to each value by name. This type of structure is called a mapping, and the only built-in mapping type in Python is the *dictionary*. The values in a dictionary don't have any particular order but are stored under a *key*, which may be either a number, a string, or even a tuple.

But What Are They For?

There are many situations where a dictionary is more appropriate than a list. The name "dictionary" should give you a clue: an ordinary book is made for reading from start to finish. If you like, you can quickly open it to any given page. This is a bit like a Python list. Dictionaries, however (both real ones and their Python equivalent) are constructed so that you can look up a specific word (key) easily, to find its definition (value). Some arbitrary uses of Python dictionaries are as follows:

- Representing the state of a gaming board, with each key being a tuple of coordinates

- Storing file modification times, with file names as keys

- A digital telephone/address book

Let's say you have a list of people:

```
>>> names = ['Alice', 'Beth', 'Cecil', 'Dee-Dee', 'Earl']
```

What if you wanted to make yourself a little database where you could store the telephone numbers of these people—how would you do that? One way would be to make another list. Let's say you're only storing their four-digit extensions. Then you would get something like this:

```
>>> numbers = ['2341', '9102', '3158', '0142', '5551']
```

NOTE *You might wonder why I have used strings to represent the telephone numbers—why not integers? Consider what would happen to Dee-Dee's number then:*

```
>>> 0142
98
```

Not exactly what we wanted, is it? As mentioned briefly in Chapter 1, octal numbers are written with an initial zero. It is impossible to write decimal numbers like that.

```
>>> 0912
  File "<stdin>", line 1
    0912
       ^
SyntaxError: invalid syntax
```

The lesson is: Telephone numbers (and other numbers that may contain leading zeros) should always be represented as strings of digits—not integers.

Once you've created these lists, you can look up Cecil's telephone number as follows:

```
>>> numbers[names.index('Cecil')]
3158
```

It works, but it's a bit impractical. What you *really* would want to do is something like the following:

```
>>> phonebook['Cecil']
3158
```

Guess what? If phonebook is a dictionary, you can do just that.

Dictionary Syntax

Dictionaries are written like this:

```
phonebook = {'Alice': '2341', 'Beth': '9102', 'Cecil': '3258'}
```

Dictionaries consist of pairs (called *items*) of *keys* and their corresponding *values*. In the preceding example, the names are the keys and the telephone numbers are the values. Each key is separated from its value by a colon (":"), the items are separated by commas, and the whole thing is enclosed in curly braces. An empty dictionary (without any items) is written with just two curly braces, like this: {}.

The dict *Function*

You can use the dict function to construct dictionaries from sequences of (*key, value*) pairs:

```
>>> items = [('name', 'Gumby'), ('age', 42)]
>>> d = dict(items)
>>> d
{'age': 42, 'name': 'Gumby'}
>>> d['name']
'Gumby'
```

Although this is probably the most useful application of dict, you can also use it with a mapping argument to create a dictionary with the same items. (If used without any arguments, it returns a new empty dictionary, just like other similar functions such as list, tuple, or str.)

 NOTE *The* dict *function was not available in Python versions prior to 2.2. It is actually the constructor for the dictionary type, just as* list *is for the list type.*

Basic Dictionary Operations

The basic behavior of a dictionary in many ways mirrors that of a sequence: len(d) returns the number of items (key-value pairs) in d, d[k] returns the value associated with the key k, d[k] = v associates the value v with the key k, del d[k] deletes the item with key k, and k in d checks whether there is an item in d that has the key k. Although they share several common characteristics, there are some important distinctions:

- Dictionary keys don't have to be integers (though they may be). They may be any immutable type, such as floating-point (real) numbers, strings, or tuples.

- You can assign a value to a key even if that key isn't in the dictionary to begin with; a new item will be created. You cannot assign a value to an index outside the list's range (without using append or something like that).

- The expression k in d (where d is a dictionary) looks for a *key*, not a *value*. The expression v in l, on the other hand (where l is a list) looks for a *value*, not an *index*. This may seem a bit inconsistent, but it is actually quite natural when you get used to it.

 TIP *Checking for key membership in a dictionary is much more efficient than checking for membership in a list—and the difference is greater the larger the data structures are.*

The first point—that the keys may be of any immutable type—is the main strength of dictionaries, while the second point is important, too. Just look at the difference here:

```
>>> x = []
>>> x[42] = 'Foobar'
Traceback (most recent call last):
  File "<stdin>", line 1, in ?
IndexError: list assignment index out of range
>>> x = {}
>>> x[42] = 'Foobar'
>>> x
{42: 'Foobar'}
```

First, I try to assign the string 'Foobar' to position 42 in an empty list—clearly impossible because that position does not exist. To make this possible, I would have to initialize x with [None]*43 or something, rather than simply [ ]. The next attempt, however, works perfectly. Here I assign 'Foobar' to the key 42 of an empty dictionary; no problem! A new item is simply added to the dictionary and I'm in business.

EXAMPLE

Listing 4-1 shows the code for the telephone book example. Here is a sample run of the program:

```
Name: Beth
Phone number (p) or address (a)? p
Beth's phone number is 9102.
```

Listing 4-1. Dictionary Example

```python
# A simple database

# A dictionary with person names as keys.  Each person is represented as
# another dictionary with the keys 'phone' and 'addr' referring to their phone
# number and address, respectively.
people = {

    'Alice': {
        'phone': '2341',
        'addr': 'Foo drive 23'
    },

    'Beth': {
        'phone': '9102',
        'addr': 'Bar street 42'
    },

    'Cecil': {
        'phone': '3158',
        'addr': 'Baz avenue 90'
    }

}
```

```
# Descriptive labels for the phone number and address. These will be used
# when printing the output.
labels = {
    'phone': 'phone number',
    'addr': 'address'
}

name = raw_input('Name: ')

# Are we looking for a phone number or an address?
request = raw_input('Phone number (p) or address (a)? ')

# Use the correct key:
if request == 'p': key = 'phone'
if request == 'a': key = 'addr'

# Only try to print the information if the name is a valid key in our dictionary:
if name in people: print "%s's %s is %s." % (name, labels[key], people[name][key])
```

String Formatting with Dictionaries

In Chapter 3, you saw how you could use string formatting to format all the values in a tuple. If you use a dictionary (with only strings as keys) instead of a tuple, you can make the string formatting even snazzier. After the % character in each conversion specifier, you add a key (enclosed in parentheses), which is followed by the other specifier elements:

```
>>> phonebook
{'Beth': '9102', 'Alice': '2341', 'Cecil': '3258'}
>>> "Cecil's phone number is %(Cecil)s." % phonebook
"Cecil's phone number is 3258."
```

Except for the added string key, the conversion specifiers work as before. When using dictionaries like this, you may have any number of conversion specifiers, as long as all the given keys are found in the dictionary. This sort of string formatting can be very useful in template systems (in this case using HTML):

```
>>> template = '''<html>
    <head><title>%(title)s</title></head>
    <body>
    <h1>%(title)s</h1>
    <p>%(text)s</p>
    </body>'''
```

```
>>> data = {'title': 'My Home Page', 'text': 'Welcome to my home page!'}
>>> print template % data
<html>
<head><title>My Home Page</title></head>
<body>
<h1>My Home Page</h1>
<p>Welcome to my home page!</p>
</body>
```

Dictionary Methods

Just like the other built-in types, dictionaries have methods. While these methods can be very useful at times, you probably will not need them as often as the list and string methods. You might want to skim this section first to get a picture of which methods are available, and then come back later if you need to find out exactly how a given method works.

clear

The clear method removes all items from the dictionary. This is an in-place operation (like list.sort), so it returns nothing (or, rather, None):

```
>>> d = {}
>>> d['name'] = 'Gumby'
>>> d['age'] = 42
>>> d
{'age': 42, 'name': 'Gumby'}
>>> returned_value = d.clear()
>>> d
{}
>>> print returned_value
None
```

Why is this useful? Consider the following scenarios, and notice the difference in behavior.

Scenario 1:

```
>>> x = {}
>>> y = x
>>> x['key'] = 'value'
```

```
>>> y
{'key': 'value'}
>>> x = {}
>>> y
{'key': 'value'}
```

Scenario 2:

```
>>> x = {}
>>> y = x
>>> x['key'] = 'value'
>>> y
{'key': 'value'}
>>> x.clear()
>>> y
{}
```

In both scenarios, x and y originally refer to the same dictionary. In the first scenario, I "blank out" x by assigning a new, empty dictionary to it. That doesn't affect y at all, which still refers to the original dictionary. This may be the behavior you want, but if you really want to remove all the elements of the *original* dictionary, you must use clear. As you can see in the second scenario, y is then also empty afterward.

copy

The copy method returns a new dictionary with the same key-value pairs (a "shallow copy," since the values themselves are the *same*, not copies):

```
>>> x = {'username': 'admin', 'machines': ['foo', 'bar', 'baz']}
>>> y = x.copy()
>>> y['username'] = 'mlh'
>>> y['machines'].remove('bar')
>>> y
{'username': 'mlh', 'machines': ['foo', 'baz']}
>>> x
{'username': 'admin', 'machines': ['foo', 'baz']}
```

As you can see, when you replace a value in the copy, the original is unaffected. *However*, if you *modify* a value (in place, without replacing it), the original is changed as well because the same value is stored there (like the "machines" list in this example).

TIP   *One way to avoid that problem is to make a "deep copy," copying the values, any values they contain, and so forth as well. You accomplish this using the function* deepcopy *from the* copy *module:*

```
>>> from copy import deepcopy
>>> d = {}
>>> d['names'] = ['Alfred', 'Bertrand']
>>> c = d.copy()
>>> dc = deepcopy(d)
>>> d['names'].append('Clive')
>>> c
{'names': ['Alfred', 'Bertrand', 'Clive']}
>>> dc
{'names': ['Alfred', 'Bertrand']}
```

get

The get method is a forgiving way of accessing dictionary items. Ordinarily, when you try to access an item that is not present in the dictionary, things go very wrong:

```
>>> d = {}
>>> print d['name']
Traceback (most recent call last):
  File "<stdin>", line 1, in ?
KeyError: name
```

Not so with get:

```
>>> print d.get('name')
None
```

As you can see, when you use get to access a nonexistent key, there is no exception. Instead, you get the value None. You may supply your own "default" value, which is then used instead of None:

```
>>> d.get('name', 'N/A')
'N/A'
```

If the key *is* there, get works like ordinary dictionary lookup:

```
>>> d['name'] = 'Eric'
>>> d.get('name')
'Eric'
```

has_key

The has_key method checks whether a dictionary has a given key. The expression d.has_key(k) is equivalent to k in d. The choice of which to use is largely a matter of taste. (The membership operator didn't work on dictionaries before Python 2.2.)

Here is an example of how you might use has_key:

```
>>> d = {}
>>> d.has_key('name')
0
>>> d['name'] = 'Eric'
>>> d.has_key('name')
1
```

items *and* iteritems

The items method returns all the items of the dictionary as a list of items in which each item is of the form (key, value). The items are not returned in any specific order:

```
>>> d = {'title': 'Python Web Site', 'url': 'http://www.python.org', 'spam': 0}
>>> d.items()
[('url', 'http://www.python.org'), ('spam', 0), ('title', 'Python Web Site')]
```

The iteritems method works in much the same way, but returns an *iterator* instead of a list.

```
>>> it = d.iteritems()
>>> it
<dictionary-iterator object at 169050>
>>> list(it) # Convert the iterator to a list
[('url', 'http://www.python.org'), ('spam', 0), ('title', 'Python Web Site')]
```

Using iteritems may be more efficient in many cases (especially if you want to *iterate* over the result). For more information on iterators, see Chapter 9.

NOTE *The method* iteritems *is not available in Python versions prior to 2.2.*

keys *and* iterkeys

The keys method returns a list of the keys in the dictionary, while iterkeys returns an iterator over the keys.

 NOTE *The* iterkeys *method is not available in Python versions prior to 2.2.*

popitem

The popitem method is similar to list.pop. Unlike list.pop, however, popitem pops off a random item because dictionaries don't have a "last element" or any order whatsoever. This may be very useful if you want to remove and process the items one by one in an efficient way (without retrieving a list of the keys first):

```
>>> d
{'url': 'http://www.python.org', 'spam': 0, 'title': 'Python Web Site'}
>>> d.popitem()
('url', 'http://www.python.org')
>>> d
{'spam': 0, 'title': 'Python Web Site'}
```

Although popitem is similar to the list method pop, there is no dictionary equivalent of append. Because dictionaries have no order, such a method wouldn't make any sense.

setdefault

The setdefault method is somewhat similar to get, except that in addition to the get functionality, setdefault *sets* the value corresponding to the given key if it is not already in the dictionary:

```
>>> d = {}
>>> d.setdefault('name', 'N/A')
'N/A'
>>> d
{'name': 'N/A'}
>>> d['name'] = 'Gumby'
>>> d.setdefault('name', 'N/A')
'Gumby'
>>> d
{'name': 'Gumby'}
```

As you can see, when the key is missing, setdefault returns the default and updates the dictionary accordingly. If the key is present, its value is returned and the dictionary is left unchanged. The default is optional, as with get; if it is left out, None is used:

```
>>> d = {}
>>> print d.setdefault('name')
None
>>> d
{'name': None}
```

update

The update method updates one dictionary with the items of another:

```
>>> d = {
        'title': 'Python Web Site',
        'url': 'http://www.python.org',
        'changed': '3. august 2001 21:08:05 GMT'
    }
>>> x = {'title': 'Python Language Website'}
>>> d.update(x)
>>> d
{'url': 'http://www.python.org', 'changed': '3. august 2001 21:08:05 GMT', 'title': 'Python Language Website'}
```

The items in the supplied dictionary are added to the old one, overwriting any items there with the same keys.

values *and* itervalues

The values method returns a list of the values in the dictionary (and itervalues returns an iterator of the values). Unlike keys, the list returned by values may contain duplicates:

```
>>> d = {}
>>> d[1] = 1
>>> d[2] = 2
>>> d[3] = 3
>>> d[4] = 1
>>> d.values()
[1, 2, 3, 1]
```

NOTE   *The* itervalues *method is not available in Python versions prior to 2.2.*

OUR EXAMPLE REVISITED

Listing 4-2 shows a modified version of the program from Listing 4-1, which uses the get method to access the "database" entries. An example run of this program follows. Notice how the added flexibility of get allows the program to give a useful response even though the user enters values we weren't prepared for:

```
Name: Gumby
Phone number (p) or address (a)? batting average
Gumby's batting average is not available.
```

Listing 4-2. Dictionary Method Example

```
# A simple database using get()

# Insert database ("people") from Listing 4-1 here.
```

```
labels = {
    'phone': 'phone number',
    'addr': 'address'
}

name = raw_input('Name: ')

# Are we looking for a phone number or an address?
request = raw_input('Phone number (p) or address (a)? ')

# Use the correct key:
key = request # In case the request is neither 'p' nor 'a'
if request == 'p': key = 'phone'
if request == 'a': key = 'addr'

# Use get to provide default values:
person = people.get(name, {})
label = labels.get(key, key)
result = person.get(key, 'not available')

print "%s's %s is %s." % (name, label, result)
```

A Quick Summary

In this chapter, you learned about the following:

Mappings. A mapping enables you to label its elements with any immutable object, the most usual types being strings and tuples. The only built-in mapping type in Python is the dictionary.

String formatting with dictionaries. You can apply the string formatting operation to dictionaries by including names (keys) in the formatting specifiers. When using tuples in string formatting, you need to have one formatting specifier for each element in the tuple. When using dictionaries, you can have fewer specifiers than you have items in the dictionary.

Dictionary methods. Dictionaries have quite a few methods, which are called in the same way as list and string methods.

New Functions in This Chapter

FUNCTION	DESCRIPTION
dict(*seq*)	Creates dictionary from (*key, value*) pairs

What Now?

You now know a lot about Python's basic data types and how to use them to form expressions. As you may remember from Chapter 1, computer programs have another important ingredient—statements. They're covered in detail in the next chapter.

CHAPTER 5

Conditionals, Loops, and Some Other Statements

By now, I'm sure you are getting a bit impatient. All right—all these data types are just dandy, but you can't really *do* much with them, can you?

Let's crank up the pace a bit. You've already encountered a couple of statement types (print statements, import statements, assignments). Let's first take a look at some more ways to use these before diving into the world of *conditionals* and *loops*. Then, you'll see how *list comprehensions* work almost like conditionals and loops, even though they are expressions, and finally you take a look at pass, del, and exec.

More About print and import

As you learn more about Python, you may notice that some aspects of Python that you thought you knew have hidden features just waiting to pleasantly surprise you. Let's take a look at a couple of such nice features in print and import.

Printing with Commas

You've seen how print can be used to print an expression, which is either a string or is automatically converted to one. But you can actually print more than one expression, as long as you separate them with commas:

```
>>> print 'Age:', 42
Age: 42
```

As you can see, a space character is inserted between each argument.

NOTE   *The arguments of* print *do not form a tuple, as one might expect:*

```
>>> 1, 2, 3
(1, 2, 3)
>>> print 1, 2, 3
1 2 3
>>> print (1, 2, 3)
(1, 2, 3)
```

This behavior can be very useful if you want to combine text and variable values without using the full power of string formatting:

```
>>> name = 'Gumby'
>>> salutation = 'Mr.'
>>> greeting = 'Hello,'
>>> print greeting, salutation, name
Hello, Mr. Gumby
```

NOTE   *If the* greeting *string had no comma, how would you get the comma in the result? You couldn't just use*

```
print greeting, ',', salutation, name
```

because that would introduce a space before the comma. One solution would be the following:

```
print greeting + ',', salutation, name
```

Here the comma is simply added to the greeting.

If you add a comma at the end, your next print statement will continue printing on the same line. For instance, the statements

```
print 'Hello,',
print 'world!'
```

print out Hello, world!

Importing Something as Something Else

Usually when you import something from a module you either use

```
import somemodule
```

or

```
from somemodule import somefunction
```

or

```
from somemodule import *
```

The latter should only be used when you are certain that you want to import *everything* from the given module. But what if you have two modules each containing a function called open, for instance—what do you do then? You could simply import the modules using the first form, and then use the functions as follows:

```
module1.open(...)
module2.open(...)
```

But there is another option: You can add an as clause to the end and supply the name you want to use, either for the entire module:

```
>>> import math as foobar
>>> foobar.sqrt(4)
2.0
```

or for the given function:

```
>>> from math import sqrt as foobar
>>> foobar(4)
2.0
```

For the open functions you might use the following:

```
from module1 import open as open1
from module2 import open as open2
```

Assignment Magic

The humble assignment statement also has a few tricks up its sleeve.

Sequence Unpacking

You've seen quite a few examples of assignments, both for variables and for parts of data structures (such as positions and slices in a list, or slots in a dictionary), but there is more. You can perform several different assignments *simultaneously*:

```
>>> x, y, z = 1, 2, 3
>>> print x, y, z
1 2 3
```

Doesn't sound useful? Well, you can use it to switch the contents of two variables:

```
>>> x, y = y, x
>>> print x, y, z
2 1 3
```

Actually, what I'm doing here is called "sequence unpacking"—I have a sequence of values, and I unpack it into a sequence of variables. Let me be more explicit:

```
>>> values = 1, 2, 3
>>> values
(1, 2, 3)
>>> x, y, z = values
>>> x
1
```

This is particularly useful when a function or method returns a tuple; let's say that you want to retrieve (and remove) a random key-value pair from a dictionary. You can then use the popitem method, which does just that, returning the pair as a tuple. Then you can unpack the returned tuple directly into two variables:

```
>>> scoundrel = {'name': 'Robin', 'girlfriend': 'Marion'}
>>> key, value = scoundrel.popitem()
>>> key
```

```
'girlfriend'
>>> value
'Marion'
```

This allows functions to return more than one value, packed as a tuple, easily accessible through a single assignment. The sequence you unpack must have exactly as many items as the targets you list on the left of the = sign; otherwise Python raises an exception when the assignment is performed.

Chained Assignments

Chained assignments are used as a shortcut when you want to bind several variables to the same value. This may seem a bit like the simultaneous assignments in the previous section, except that here you are only dealing with one value:

```
x = y = somefunction()
```

is the same as

```
y = somefunction()
x = y
```

Note that the statements above may *not* be the same as

```
x = somefunction()
y = somefunction()
```

For more information, see the section about the identity operator (is), later in this chapter.

Augmented Assignments

Instead of writing x = x + 1 you can just put the expression operator (in this case +) before the assignment operator (=) and write x += 1.This is called an augmented assignment, and it works with all the standard operators, such as *, /, %, and so on:

```
>>> x = 2
>>> x += 1
>>> x *= 2
>>> x
6
```

It also works with other data types:

```
>>> fnord = 'foo'
>>> fnord += 'bar'
>>> fnord
'foobar'
```

Augmented assignments can make your code more compact and concise, yet some argue that it can also make it harder to read.

TIP   *In general, you should not use* += *with strings, especially if you are building a large string piece by piece in a loop (see the section "Loops" later in this chapter for more information about loops). Each addition and assignment needs to create a new string, and that takes time, making your program slower. A much better approach is to append the small strings to a list, and use the string method* join *to create the big string when your list is finished.*

Blocks: The Joy of Indentation

This isn't really a type of statement but something you're going to need when you tackle the next two sections.

A block is a *group* of statements that can be executed if a condition is true (conditional statements), or executed several times (loops), and so on. A block is created by *indenting* a part of your code; that is, putting spaces in front of it.

NOTE   *You can use tab characters to indent your blocks as well. Python interprets a tab as moving to the next tab stop, with one tab stop every eight spaces, but the standard and preferable style is to use spaces only, no tabs, and specifically four spaces per each level of indentation.*

Each line in a block must be indented by the *same amount*. The following is pseudocode (not real Python code) but shows how the indenting works:

```
this is a line
this is another line:
    this is another block
    continuing the same block
```

```
the last line of this block
phew, there we escaped the inner block
```

In many languages a special word or character (for example, "begin" or "{") is used to start a block, and another (such as "end" or "}") is used to end it. In Python, a colon (":") is used to indicate that a block is about to begin, and then every line in that block is indented (by the same amount). When you go back to the same amount of indentation as some enclosing block, you know that the current block has ended.

Now I'm sure you are curious to know how to use these blocks. So, without further ado, let's have a look.

Conditions and Conditional Statements

Until now you've only written programs in which each statement is executed, one after the other. It's time to move beyond that and let your program choose whether or not to execute a block of statements.

So That's What Those Boolean Values Are For

Now you are finally going to need those *truth values* we've been bumping into repeatedly.

NOTE *If you've been paying close attention, you noticed the sidebar in Chapter 1, "Sneak Peek: The* if *Statement," which describes the* if *statement. I haven't really introduced it formally until now, and as you'll see, there is a bit more to it than what I've told you so far.*

The following values are considered by the interpreter to mean *false*:

```
None     0     ""     ()     []     {}
```

That is, the standard value None, numeric zero of all types (including float, long, and so on), all empty sequences (such as empty strings, tuples, and lists), and empty dictionaries. *Everything else* is interpreted as *true*. Laura Creighton describes this as discerning between *something* and *nothing*, rather than *true* and *false*.

Got it? This means that every value in Python can be interpreted as a truth value, which can be a bit confusing at first, but it can also be extremely useful. And even though you have all these truth values to choose from, the "standard" truth values are 0 (for *false*) and 1 (for *true*).

 NOTE   *In Python 2.3 a separate Boolean type is introduced, with the values* True *and* False, *which are basically equivalent to* 1 *and* 0, *but will eventually replace them as "standard" truth values.*

Conditional Execution and the if Statement

Truth values can be combined (which you'll see in a while), but let's first see what you can use them for. Try running the following script:

```
name = raw_input('What is your name? ')
if name.endswith('Gumby'):
    print 'Hello, Mr. Gumby'
```

This is the if statement, which lets you do *conditional execution*. That means that if the *condition* (the expression after if but before the colon) evaluates to *true* (as defined previously), the following block (in this case, a single print statement) is executed. If the condition is *false*, then the block is *not* executed (but you guessed that, didn't you?).

 NOTE   *In the sidebar "Sneak Peek: The* if *Statement" in Chapter 1, the statement was written on a single line. That is equivalent to using a single-line block, as in the preceding example.*

else Clauses

In the example from the previous section, if you enter a name that ends with "Gumby," the method name.endswith returns 1, making the if statement enter the block, and the greeting is printed. If you want, you can add an alternative, with the else clause (called a "clause" because it isn't really a separate statement, just a part of the if statement):

```
name = raw_input('What is your name? ')
if name.endswith('Gumby'):
    print 'Hello, Mr. Gumby'
else:
    print 'Hello, stranger'
```

Here, if the first block isn't executed (because the condition evaluated to false), you enter the second block instead. This really makes you see how easy it is to read Python code, doesn't it? Just read the code aloud (from if) and it sound just like a normal (or perhaps not *quite* normal) sentence.

elif *Clauses*

If you want to check for several conditions, you can use elif, which is short for "else if." It is a combination of an if clause and an else clause—an else clause with a condition:

```
num = input('Enter a number: ')
if num > 0:
    print 'The number is positive'
elif num < 0:
    print 'The number is negative'
else:
    print 'The number is zero'
```

Nesting Blocks

Let's throw in a few bells and whistles. You can have if statements inside other if statement blocks, as follows:

```
name = raw_input('What is your name? ')
if name.endswith('Gumby'):
    if name.startswith('Mr.'):
        print 'Hello, Mr. Gumby'
    elif name.startswith('Mrs.'):
        print 'Hello, Mrs. Gumby'
    else:
        print 'Hello, Gumby'
else:
    print 'Hello, stranger'
```

Here, if the name ends with "Gumby," you check the start of the name as well—in a separate if statement inside the first block. Note the use of elif here. The last alternative (the else clause) has no condition—if no other alternative is chosen, you use the last one. If you want to, you can leave out either of the else clauses. If you leave out the inner else clause, names that don't start with either "Mr." or "Mrs." are ignored (assuming the name was "Gumby"). If you drop the outer else clause, strangers are ignored.

More Complex Conditions

That's really all there is to know about if statements. Now let's return to the conditions themselves because they are the really interesting part of conditional execution.

Comparison Operators

Perhaps the most basic operators used in conditions are the *comparison operators*. They are used (surprise, surprise) to compare things. The comparison operators are summed up in Table 5-1.

Table 5-1. The Python Comparison Operators

EXPRESSION	DESCRIPTION
x == y	x equals y
x < y	x is less than y
x > y	x is greater than y
x >= y	x is greater than or equal to y
x <= y	x is less than or equal to y
x != y	x is not equal to y
x is y	x and y are the same object
x is not y	x and y are different objects
x in y	x is a member of the container (e.g., sequence) y
x not in y	x is not a member of the container (e.g., sequence) y

Comparisons can be *chained* in Python, just like assignments—you can put several comparison operators in a chain, like this: 0 < age < 100.

TIP   *When comparing things, you can also use the built-in function* cmp *as described in Chapter 2.*

Some of these operators deserve some special attention and will be described in the following sections.

The Equality Operator

If you want to know if two things are equal, you use the equality operator, written as a double equality sign, ==:

```
>>> "foo" == "foo"
1
>>> "foo" == "bar"
0
```

Double? Why can't you just use a *single* equality sign, like they do in mathematics? I'm sure you're clever enough to figure this out for yourself, but let's try it:

```
>>> "foo" = "foo"
SyntaxError: can't assign to literal
```

The single equality sign is the assignment operator, which is used to *change* things, which is *not* what you want to do when you compare things.

is: *The Identity Operator*

The is operator is interesting. It seems to work just like ==, but it doesn't:

```
>>> x - y - [1, 2, 3]
>>> z = [1, 2, 3]
>>> x == y
1
>>> x == z
1
>>> x is y
1
>>> x is z
0
```

Until the last example, this looks fine, but then you get that strange result, that x is not z even though they are equal. Why? Because is tests for *identity*, rather than *equality*. The variables x and y have been bound to the *same list*, while z is simply bound to another list that happens to contain the same values in the same order. They may be equal, but they aren't the *same object*.

Does that seem unreasonable? Consider this example:

```
>>> x = [1, 2, 3]
>>> y = [2, 4]
>>> x is not y
1
>>> del x[2]
>>> y[1] = 1
>>> y.reverse()
```

In this example, I start with two different lists, x and y. As you can see, x is not y (just the inverse of x is y), which you already know. I change the lists around a bit, and though they are now equal, they are still two separate lists:

```
>>> x == y
1
>>> x is y
0
```

Here it is obvious that the two lists are equal but not identical.

To summarize: Use == to see if two objects are *equal*, and use is to see if they are *identical* (the same object).

CAUTION   *Avoid the use of is with basic, immutable values such as numbers and strings. The result is unpredictable because of the way Python handles these internally.*

in: *The Membership Operator*

I have already introduced the in operator (in Chapter 2, in the section "Membership"). It can be used in conditions, just like all the other comparison operators:

```
name = raw_input('What is your name? ')
if 's' in name:
```

```
    print 'Your name contains the letter "s".'
else:
    print 'Your name does not contain the letter "s".'
```

Comparing Strings and Sequences

Strings are compared according to their order when sorted alphabetically:

```
>>> "alpha" < "beta"
1
```

If you throw in capital letters, things get a bit messy. (Actually, characters are sorted by their ordinal values. The ordinal value of a letter can be found with the ord function, whose inverse is chr.) To avoid this, use the string methods upper or lower:

```
>>> 'FnOrD'.lower() == 'Fnord'.lower()
1
```

Other sequences are compared in the same manner, except that instead of letters you have other types of elements:

```
>>> [1, 2] < [2, 1]
1
```

If the sequences contain lists as elements, the same rule applies to these sublists:

```
>>> [2, [1, 4]] < [2, [1, 5]]
1
```

Boolean Operators

Now, you've got plenty of things that return truth values. (Given the fact that all values can be interpreted as truth values, *all* expressions return them.) But you may want to check for more than one condition. For instance, let's say you want to write a program that reads a number and checks whether it's between 1 and 10 (inclusive). You *can* do it like this:

```
number = input('Enter a number between 1 and 10: ')
if number <= 10:
```

```
    if number >= 1:
        print 'Great!'
    else:
        print 'Wrong!'
else:
    print 'Wrong!'
```

This will work, but it's clumsy. The fact that you have to write `print 'Wrong!'` in two places should alert you to this clumsiness. Duplication of effort is not a good thing. So what do you do? It's so simple:

```
if number <= 10 and number >= 1:
    print 'Great!'
else:
    print 'Wrong!'
```

 NOTE *In this example, you could (and quite probably should) have made this even simpler by using the following chained comparison:*

```
    1 <= number <= 10
```

The and operator is a so-called Boolean operator (named after George Boole, who did a lot of smart stuff on truth values, also called *logical* or *Boolean* values). It takes two truth values, and returns true if both are true, and false otherwise. You have two more of these operators, or and not. With just these three, you can combine truth values in any way you like:

```
if ((cash > price) or customer_has_good_credit) and not out_of_stock:
    give_goods()
```

Short-Circuit Logic

The Boolean operators have one interesting property: They only evaluate what they need to. For instance, the expression x and y requires both x and y to be true; so if x is false, the expression returns false immediately, without worrying about y. Actually, if x is false, it returns x—otherwise it returns y. (Can you see how this gives the expected meaning?) This behavior is called *short-circuit logic:* the Boolean operators are often called logical operators, and as you can see, the second value is sometimes "short-circuited." This works with or, too. In the expression x or y, if x is true, it is returned, otherwise y is returned. (Can you see how this makes sense?)

So, how is this useful? Let's say a user is supposed to enter his or her name, but may opt to enter nothing, in which case you want to use the default value '<unknown>'. You could use an if statement, but you could also state things very succinctly:

```
name = raw_input('Please enter your name: ') or '<unknown>'
```

In other words, if the return value from raw_input is true (not an empty string) it is assigned to name (nothing changes); otherwise, the default '<unknown>' is assigned to name.

This sort of short-circuit logic can be used to implement the so-called "ternary operator" (or conditional operator), found in languages such as C and Java. For a thorough explanation, see Alex Martelli's recipe on the subject in the Python Cookbook (http://aspn.activestate.com/ASPN/Cookbook/Python/Recipe/52310).

Assertions

There is a useful relative of the if statement, which works more or less like this (pseudocode):

```
if not condition:
    crash program
```

Now, why on earth would you want something like that? Simply because it's better that your program crashes when an error condition emerges than at a much later time. Basically, you can require that certain things be true. The keyword used in the statement is assert:

```
>>> age = 10
>>> assert 0 < age < 100
>>> age = -1
```

```
>>> assert 0 < age < 100
Traceback (most recent call last):
  File "<stdin>", line 1, in ?
AssertionError
```

It can be useful to put the `assert` statement in your program as a checkpoint, if you know something *has* to be true for your program to work correctly.

A string may be added after the condition, to explain the assertion:

```
>>> age = -1
>>> assert 0 < age < 100, 'The age must be realistic'
Traceback (most recent call last):
  File "<stdin>", line 1, in ?
AssertionError: The age must be realistic
```

Loops

Now you know how to do something if a condition is true (or false), but how do you do something several times? For instance, you might want to create a program that reminds you to pay the rent every month, but with the tools we have looked at until now, you'd have to write the program like this (pseudocode):

```
send mail
wait one month
send mail
wait one month
send mail
wait one month
(...and so on)
```

But what if you wanted it to continue doing this until you stopped it? Basically, you want something like this (again, pseudocode):

```
while we aren't stopped:
    send mail
    wait one month
```

Or, let's take a simpler example. Let's say that you want to print out all the numbers from 1 to 100. Again, you could do it the stupid way:

```
print 1
print 2
print 3
```

…and so on. But you didn't start using Python because you wanted to do stupid things, right?

while *Loops*

In order to avoid the cumbersome code of the preceding example, it would be useful to be able to do something like this:

```
x = 1
while x <= 100:
    print x
    x += 1
```

Now, how do you do that in Python? You guessed it—you do it just like that. Not that complicated is it? You could also use a loop to ensure that the user enters a name, as follows:

```
name = ''
while not name:
    name = raw_input('Please enter your name: ')
print 'Hello, %s!' % name
```

Try running this, and then just pressing the Enter key when asked to enter your name: the question appears again because name is still an empty string, which evaluates to *false*.

> **TIP** *What would happen if you entered just a space charac-*
> *ter as your name? Try it. It is accepted because a string with*
> *one space character is not empty, and therefore not* false. *This*
> *is definitely a flaw in our little program, but easily corrected:*
> *just change* while not name *to* while name.isspace().

for *Loops*

The while statement is very flexible. It can be used to repeat a block of code while *any condition* is true. While this may be very nice in general, sometimes you may want something tailored to your specific needs. One such need is to perform a block of code *for each* element of a set (or, actually, sequence) of values. You can do this with the for statement:

```
words = ['this', 'is', 'an', 'ex', 'parrot']
for word in words:
    print word
```

Or...

```
range = [0, 1, 2, 3, 4, 5, 6, 7, 8, 9]
for number in range:
    print number
```

Because iterating (another word for "looping") over a range of numbers is a common thing to do, there is a built-in function to make ranges for you:

```
>>> range(0, 10)
[0, 1, 2, 3, 4, 5, 6, 7, 8, 9]
```

Ranges work like slices. They include the first limit (in this case 0), but not the last (in this case 10). Quite often, you want the ranges to start at 0, and this is actually assumed if you only supply one limit (which will then be the last):

```
>>> range(10)
[0, 1, 2, 3, 4, 5, 6, 7, 8, 9]
```

 TIP *There is also another function called* range *that works just like* range *in loops, but where* range *creates the whole sequence at once,* xrange *creates only one number at a time. This can be useful when iterating over* huge *sequences more efficiently, but in general you needn't worry about it.*

The following program writes out the numbers from 1 to 100:

```
for number in range(1,101):
    print number
```

Notice that this is much more compact than the while loop I used earlier.

TIP *If you can use a* for *loop rather than a* while *loop, you should probably do so.*

Iterating over Dictionaries

To loop over the keys of a dictionary, you can use a plain for statement, just as you can with sequences:

```
d = {'x': 1, 'y': 2, 'z': 3}
for key in d:
    print key, 'corresponds to', d[key]
```

In Python versions before 2.2, you would have used a dictionary method such as keys to retrieve the keys (since direct iteration over dictionaries wasn't allowed). If only the values were of interest, you could have used d.values instead of d.keys. You may remember that d.items returns key-value pairs as tuples. One great thing about for loops is that you can use sequence unpacking in them:

```
for key, value in d.items():
    print key, 'corresponds to', value
```

To make your iteration more efficient, you can use the methods iterkeys (equivalent to the plain for loop), itervalues, or iteritems. (These don't return lists, but iterators. Iterators are explained in Chapter 9, "Magic Methods and Iterators.")

NOTE *As always, the order of dictionary elements is undefined. In other words, when iterating over either the keys or the values of a dictionary, you can be sure that you'll process all of them, but you can't know in which order. If the order is important, you can store the keys or values in a separate list and sort it before iterating over it.*

Parallel Iteration

Sometimes you want to iterate over two sequences at the same time. Let's say that you have the following two lists:

```
names = ['anne', 'beth', 'george', 'damon']
ages = [12, 45, 32, 102]
```

If you want to print out names with corresponding ages, you *could* do the following:

```
for i in range(len(names)):
    print names[i], 'is', ages[i], 'years old'
```

Here I use i as a standard variable name for loop indices (as these things are called).

A useful tool for parallel iteration is the built-in function zip, which "zips" together the sequences, returning a list of tuples:

```
>>> zip(names, ages)
[('anne', 12), ('beth', 45), ('george', 32), ('damon', 102)]
```

Now I can unpack the tuples in my loop:

```
for name, age in zip(names, ages):
    print name, 'is', age, 'years old'
```

The zip function works with as many sequences as you want. It's important to note what zip does when the sequences are of different lengths: it stops when the shortest sequence is "used up":

```
>>> zip(range(5), xrange(100000000))
[(0, 0), (1, 1), (2, 2), (3, 3), (4, 4)]
```

I wouldn't recommend using range instead of xrange in the preceding example—although only the first five numbers are needed, range calculates all the numbers, and that may take a lot of time. With xrange, this isn't a problem because it calculates only those numbers needed.

Breaking Out of Loops

Usually, a loop simply executes a block until its condition becomes false, or until it has used up all sequence elements—but sometimes you may want to interrupt the loop, to start a new iteration (one "round" of executing the block), or to simply end the loop.

break

To end (break out of) a loop, you use break. Let's say you wanted to find the largest square (an integer that is the square of another integer) below 100. Then you start at 100 and iterate downwards to 0. When you've found a square, there's no need to continue, so you simply break out of the loop:

```
from math import sqrt
for n in range(99, 0, -1):
    root = sqrt(n)
    if root == int(root):
        print n
        break
```

If you run this program, it will print out 81, and stop. Notice that I've added a third argument to range—that's the *step*, the difference between every pair of adjacent numbers in the sequence. It can be used to iterate downwards as I did here, with a negative step value, and it can be used to skip numbers:

```
>>> range(0, 10, 2)
[0, 2, 4, 6, 8]
```

continue

The continue statement is used less often than break. It causes the current iteration to end, and to "jump" to the beginning of the next. It basically means "skip the rest of the loop body, but don't end the loop." This can be useful if you have a large and complicated loop body and several possible reasons for skipping it—in that case you can use continue as follows:

```
for x in seq:
    if condition1: continue
    if condition2: continue
    if condition3: continue
```

```
do_something()
do_something_else()
do_another_thing()
etc()
```

In many cases, however, simply using an if statement is just as good:

```
for x in seq:
    if not (condition1 or condition2 or condition3):
        do_something()
        do_something_else()
        do_another_thing()
        etc()
```

Even though continue can be a useful tool, it is not essential. The break statement, however, is something you should get used to because it is used quite often in concert with while 1, as explained in the next section.

The while 1/break *Idiom*

The while and for loops in Python are quite flexible, but every once in a while you may encounter a problem that makes you wish you had more functionality. For instance, let's say you want to do something while a user enters words at a prompt, and you want to end the loop when no word is provided. One way of doing that would be

```
word = 'dummy'
while word:
    word = raw_input('Please enter a word: ')
    # do something with the word:
    print 'The word was ' + word
```

Here is an example session:

```
Please enter a word: first
The word was first
Please enter a word: second
The word was second
Please enter a word:
```

This works just like you want it to. (Presumably you'd do something more useful with the word than print it out, though.) However, as you can see, this code is a bit ugly. To enter the loop in the first place, you have to assign a dummy (unused) value to word. Dummy values like this are usually a sign that you aren't doing things quite right. Let's try to get rid of it:

```
word = raw_input('Please enter a word: ')
while word:
    # do something with the word:
    print 'The word was ' + word
    word = raw_input('Please enter a word: ')
```

Here the dummy is gone, but I have repeated code (which is also a bad thing): I have to use the same assignment and call to raw_input in two places. How can I avoid that? I can use the while 1/break idiom:

```
while 1:
    word = raw_input('Please enter a word: ')
    if not word: break
    # do something with the word:
    print 'The word was ' + word
```

NOTE *An idiom is a common way of doing things that people who know the language are assumed to know.*

The while 1 part gives you a loop that will never terminate by itself. Instead you put the condition in an if statement inside the loop, which calls break when the condition is fulfilled. Thus you can terminate the loop anywhere inside the loop instead of only at the beginning (as with a normal while loop). The if/break line splits the loop naturally in two parts: The first takes care of setting things up (the part that would be duplicated with a normal while loop), and the other part makes use of the initialization from the first part, provided that the loop condition is true.

Although you should be wary of using break too often (because it can make your loops harder to read), this specific technique is so common that most Python programmers (including yourself) will probably be able to follow your intentions.

Chapter 5

else *Clauses in Loops*

When you use break statements in loops, it is often because you have "found" something, or because something has "happened." It's easy to do something when you break out (like print n), but sometimes you may want to do something if you *didn't* break out. But how do you find out? You could use a Boolean variable, set it to 0 before the loop, and set it to 1 when you break out. Then you can use an if statement afterwards to check whether you did break out or not:

```
broke_out = 0
for x in seq:
    do_something(x)
    if condition(x):
        broke_out = 1
        break
    do_something_else(x)
if not broke_out:
    print "I didn't break out!"
```

A simpler way is to add an else clause to your loop—it is only executed if you didn't call break. Let's reuse the example from the preceding section on break:

```
from math import sqrt
for n in range(99, 81, -1):
    root = sqrt(n)
    if root == int(root):
        print n
        break
else:
    print "Didn't find it!"
```

Notice that I changed the lower (exclusive) limit to 81 to test the else clause. If you run the program, it prints out "Didn't find it!" because (as you saw in the section on break) the largest square below 100 is 81. You can use continue, break, and else clauses both with for loops and while loops.

List Comprehension–Slightly Loopy

List comprehension is a way of making lists from other lists (similar to *set comprehension*, if you know that term from mathematics). It works in a way similar to for loops, and is actually quite simple:

118

```
>>> [x*x for x in range(10)]
[0, 1, 4, 9, 16, 25, 36, 49, 64, 81]
```

The list is composed of x*x for each x in range(10). Pretty straightforward? What if you only want to print out those squares that are divisible by 3? Then you can use the modulo operator—y % 3 returns zero when y is divisible by 3. (Note that x*x is divisible by 3 only if x is divisible by 3.) You put this into your list comprehension by adding an if part to it:

```
>>> [x*x for x in range(10) if x % 3 == 0]
[0, 9, 36, 81]
```

You can also add more for parts:

```
>>> [(x, y) for x in range(3) for y in range(3)]
[(0, 0), (0, 1), (0, 2), (1, 0), (1, 1), (1, 2), (2, 0), (2, 1), (2, 2)]
```

This can be combined with an if clause, just like before:

```
>>> girls = ['alice', 'bernice', 'clarice']
>>> boys = ['chris', 'arnold', 'bob']
>>> [b+'+'+g for b in boys for g in girls if b[0] == g[0]]
['chris+clarice', 'arnold+alice', 'bob+bernice']
```

This gives the pairs of boys and girls who have the same initial letter in their first name.

....

A Better Solution

The boy/girl pairing example isn't particularly efficient because it checks every possible pairing. There are many ways of solving this problem in Python. The following was suggested by Alex Martelli:

```
girls = ['alice', 'bernice', 'clarice']
boys = ['chris', 'arnold', 'bob']
letterGirls = {}
for girl in girls:
    letterGirls.setdefault(girl[0], []).append(girl)
print [b+'+'+g for b in boys for g in letterGirls[b[0]]]
```

This program constructs a dictionary called letterGirl where each entry has a single letter as its key and a list of girls' names as its value. (The setdefault dictionary method is described in the previous chapter.) After this dictionary has been constructed, the list comprehension loops over all the boys and looks up all the girls whose name begins with the same letter as the current boy. This way the list comprehension doesn't have to try out every possible combination of boy and girl and check whether the first letters match.

And Three for the Road

To end the chapter, let's take a quick look at three more statements: pass, del, and exec.

Nothing Happened!

Sometimes you need to do nothing. This may not be very often, but when it happens, it's good to know that you have the pass statement:

```
>>> pass
>>>
```

Not much going on here.

Now, why on earth would you want a statement that does nothing? It can be useful as a placeholder while you are writing code. For instance, you may have written an if statement and you want to try it, but you lack the code for one of your blocks. Consider the following:

```
if name == 'Ralph Auldus Melish':
    print 'Welcome!'
elif name == 'Enid':
    # Not finished yet...
elif name == 'Bill Gates':
    print 'Access Denied'
```

This code won't run because an empty block is illegal in Python. To fix this, simply add a pass statement to the middle block:

```
if name == 'Ralph Auldus Melish':
    print 'Welcome!'
elif name == 'Enid':
    # Not finished yet...
    pass
```

```
elif name == 'Bill Gates':
    print 'Access Denied'
```

 NOTE *An alternative to the combination of a comment and a* pass *statement is to simply insert a string. This is especially useful for unfinished functions (see Chapter 6) and classes (see Chapter 7) because they will then act as "docstrings" (explained in Chapter 6).*

Deleting with del

In general, Python deletes objects that you don't use anymore:

```
>>> scoundrel = {'age': 42, 'first name': 'Robin', 'last name': 'of Locksley'}
>>> robin = scoundrel
>>> scoundrel
{'age': 42, 'first name': 'Robin', 'last name': 'of Locksley'}
>>> robin
{'age': 42, 'first name': 'Robin', 'last name': 'of Locksley'}
>>> scoundrel = None
>>> robin
{'age': 42, 'first name': 'Robin', 'last name': 'of Locksley'}
>>> robin = None
```

At first, robin and scoundrel both contain (or "point to") the same dictionary. So when I assign None to scoundrel, the dictionary is still available through robin. But when I assign None to robin as well, the dictionary suddenly floats around in the memory of the computer with no name attached to it. There is no way I can retrieve it or use it, so the Python interpreter (in its infinite wisdom) simply deletes it. (This is called "garbage collection.") Note that I could have used any value other than None as well. The dictionary would be just as gone.

Another way of doing this is to use the del statement (which we used to delete sequence and dictionary elements in Chapters 2 and 4, remember?). This not only removes a reference to an object, it also removes the name itself:

```
>>> x = 1
>>> del x
>>> x
Traceback (most recent call last):
```

```
    File "<pyshell#255>", line 1, in ?
      x
NameError: name 'x' is not defined
```

This may seem easy, but it can actually be a bit tricky to understand at times. For instance, in the following example, x and y refer to the same list:

```
>>> x = ["Hello", "world"]
>>> y = x
>>> y[1] = "Python"
>>> x
['Hello', 'Python']
```

You might assume that by deleting x, you would also delete y, but that is *not* the case:

```
>>> del x
>>> y
['Hello', 'Python']
```

Why is this? x and y referred to the *same* list, but deleting x didn't affect y at all. The reason for this is that you only delete the *name*, not the list itself (the value). In fact, there is no way to delete values in Python (and you don't really need to because the Python interpreter does it by itself whenever you don't use the value anymore).

Executing and Evaluating Strings with exec and eval

Sometimes you may want to create Python code "on the fly" and execute it as a statement or evaluate it as an expression. This may border on dark magic at times—consider yourself warned.

 CAUTION *In this section, you learn to execute Python code stored in a string. This is a potential security hole of great dimensions. If you execute a string where parts of the contents have been supplied by a user, you have little or no control over what code you are executing. This is especially dangerous in network applications, such as CGI scripts, which you will learn about in Chapter 19.*

exec

The statement for executing a string is exec:

```
>>> exec "print 'Hello, world!'"
Hello, world!
```

However, using this simple form of the exec statement is rarely a good thing; in most cases you want to supply it with a *namespace*, a place where it can put its variables. You want to do this so that the code doesn't corrupt *your* namespace (that is, change your variables). For instance, let's say that the code uses the name sqrt:

```
>>> from math import sqrt
>>> exec "sqrt = 1"
>>> sqrt(4)
Traceback (most recent call last):
  File "<pyshell#18>", line 1, in ?
    sqrt(4)
TypeError: object is not callable: 1
```

Well, why would you do something like that in the first place, you ask? The exec statement is mainly useful when you build the code string on the fly. And if the string is built from parts that you get from other places, and possibly from the user, you can rarely be certain of exactly what it will contain. So to be safe, you give it a dictionary, which will work as a namespace for it.

NOTE *The concept of namespaces, or* scopes, *is a very important one. You will look at it in depth in the next chapter, but for now you can think of a namespace as a place where you keep your variables, much like an invisible dictionary. So when you execute an assignment like* x = 1, *you store the key* x *with the value* 1 *in the* current namespace, *which will often be the global namespace (which we have been using, for the most part, up until now), but doesn't have to be.*

You do this by adding in scope, where scope is some dictionary that will function as the namespace for your code string:

```
>>> from math import sqrt
>>> scope = {}
>>> exec 'sqrt = 1' in scope
>>> sqrt(4)
2.0
>>> scope['sqrt']
1
```

Now you have full control over the variables that are changed by the code because they are all kept inside scope. If you try to print out scope, you see that it contains a *lot* of stuff because the dictionary called __builtins__ is automatically added and contains all built-in functions and values:

```
>>> len(scope)
2
>>> scope.keys()
['sqrt', '__builtins__']
```

eval

A built-in function that is similar to exec is eval (for "evaluate"). Just as exec executes a series of Python *statements*, eval evaluates a Python *expression* (written in a string) and returns the value. (exec doesn't return anything because it is a statement itself.) For instance, you can use the following to make a Python calculator:

```
>>> eval(raw_input("Enter an arithmetic expression: "))
Enter an arithmetic expression: 6 + 18 * 2
42
```

 NOTE *The expression* eval(raw_input(...)) *is, in fact, equivalent to* input(...).

You can supply a namespace with eval, just as with exec, although expressions rarely rebind variables in the way statements usually do.

 CAUTION *Even though expressions don't rebind variables as a rule, they certainly can (for instance by calling functions that rebind global variables). Therefore, using* eval *with an untrusted piece of code is no safer than using* exec. *For a more secure alternative, see the standard library modules* rexec *and* Bastion, *mentioned in Chapter 10.*

Priming the Scope

When supplying a namespace for exec or eval, you can also put some values in before actually using the namespace:

```
>>> scope = {}
>>> scope['x'] = 2
>>> scope['y'] = 3
>>> eval('x * y', scope)
6
```

In the same way, a scope from one exec or eval call can be used again in another one:

```
>>> scope = {}
>>> exec 'x = 2' in scope
>>> eval('x*x', scope)
4
```

Actually, exec and eval are not used all that often, but they can be nice tools to keep in your back pocket (figuratively, of course).

A Quick Summary

In this chapter you've seen several kinds of statements:

Printing. You can use the print statement to print several values by separating them with commas. If you end the statement with a comma, later print statements will continue printing on the same line.

Importing. Sometimes you don't like the name of a function you want to import—perhaps you've already used the name for something else. You can use the `import...as...` statement, to locally rename a function.

Assignments. You've seen that through the wonder of sequence unpacking and chained assignments, you can assign values to several variables at once, and that with augmented assignments you can change a variable in place.

Blocks. Blocks are used as a means of grouping statements through indentation. They are used in conditionals and loops, and as you see later in the book, in function and class definitions, among other things.

Conditionals. A conditional statement either executes a block or not, depending on a condition (Boolean expression). Several conditionals can be strung together with `if`/`elif`/`else`.

Assertions. An assertion simply asserts that something (a Boolean expression) is true, optionally with a string explaining why it has to be so. If the expression happens to be false, the assertion brings your program to a halt (or actually raises an exception—more on that in Chapter 8). It's better to find an error early than to let it sneak around your program until you don't know where it originated.

Loops. You either can execute a block for each element in a sequence (such as a range of numbers) or continue executing it while a condition is true. To skip the rest of the block and continue with the next iteration, use the `continue` statement; to break out of the loop, use the `break` statement. Optionally, you may add an `else` clause at the end of the loop, which will be executed if you didn't execute any `break` statements inside the loop.

List comprehension. These aren't really statements—they are expressions that look a lot like loops, which is why I grouped them with the looping statements. Through list comprehension you can build new lists from old ones, applying functions to the elements, filtering out those you don't want, and so on. The technique is quite powerful, but in many cases using plain loops and conditionals (which will always get the job done) may be more readable.

pass, del, exec, and eval. The `pass` statement does nothing, which can be useful as a placeholder, for instance. The `del` statement is used to delete variables or parts of a datastructure, but cannot be used to delete values. The `exec` statement is used to execute a string as if it were a Python program. The built-in function `eval` evaluates an expression written in a string and returns the result.

New Functions in This Chapter

FUNCTION	DESCRIPTION
chr(n)	Returns a one-character string with ordinal n ($0 \leq n \leq 256$)
eval(*source*[, *globals*[, *locals*]])	Evaluates a string as an expression and returns the value
ord(c)	Returns the integer ordinal value of a one-character string
range([*start*,] *stop*[, *step*])	Creates a list of integers
xrange([*start*,] *stop*[, *step*])	Creates an xrange object, used for iteration
zip(*seq1*, *seq2*,...)	Creates a new sequence suitable for parallel iteration

What Now?

Now you've cleared the basics. You can implement any algorithm you can dream up; you can read in parameters and print out the results. In the next couple of chapters, you learn about something that will help you write larger programs without losing the big picture. That something is called *abstraction.*

CHAPTER 6

Abstraction

IN THIS CHAPTER, you learn how to group statements into functions, which enables you to tell the computer how to do something, and to tell it only once. You won't have to give it the same detailed instructions over and over. The chapter provides a thorough introduction to parameters and scoping; you learn what recursion is and what it can do for your programs, and you see how functions can be used as parameters, just like numbers, strings, and other objects.

Laziness Is a Virtue

The programs we've written so far have been pretty small, but if you want to make something bigger, you'll soon run into trouble. Consider what happens if you have written some code in one place and need to use in another place as well. For instance, let's say you wrote a snippet of code that computed some *Fibonacci numbers* (a series of numbers in which each number is the sum of the two previous ones):

```
fibs = [0, 1]
for i in range(8):
    fibs.append(fibs[-2] + fibs[-1])
```

After running this, fibs contains the first ten Fibonacci numbers:

```
>>> fibs
[0, 1, 1, 2, 3, 5, 8, 13, 21, 34]
```

This is all right if what you want is to calculate the first ten Fibonacci numbers once. You could even change the for loop to work with a dynamic range, with the length of the resulting sequence supplied by the user:

```
fibs = [0, 1]
num = input('How many Fibonacci numbers do you want? ')
for i in range(num-2):
    fibs.append(fibs[-2] + fibs[-1])
print fibs
```

NOTE *Remember that you can use* raw_input *if you want to read in a plain string. In this case, you would then have had to convert it to an integer by using the* int *function.*

But what if you also want to use the numbers for something else? You could certainly just write the same loop again when needed, but what if you had written a more complicated piece of code, for instance one that downloaded a set of Web pages and computed the frequencies of all the words used. Would you still want to write all the code several times, once for each time you needed it? No, real programmers don't do that. Real programmers are lazy. Not lazy in a bad way, but in the sense that they don't do unnecessary work.

So what do real programmers do? They make their programs more *abstract*. You could make the previous program more abstract as follows:

```
num = input('How many numbers do you want? ')
print fibs(num)
```

Here, only what is specific to *this program* is written concretely (reading in the number, and printing out the result). Actually computing the Fibonacci numbers is done in an abstract manner: you simply tell the computer to do it. You don't say specifically how it should be done. You have made a function called fibs, and use it when you need the functionality of the little Fibonacci program. It saves you a lot of effort if you need it in several places.

Abstraction and Structure

Abstraction can be useful as a labor-saver, but it is actually more important than that. It is the key to making computer programs understandable to humans (which is essential, whether you're writing them or reading them). The computers themselves are perfectly happy with very concrete and specific instructions, but humans generally aren't. If you ask me for directions to the cinema, for instance, you wouldn't want to answer, "Walk ten steps forward, turn ninety degrees to your left, walk another five steps, turn forty-five degrees to your right, walk 123 steps." You would soon lose track, wouldn't you?

Now, if I instead told you to "Walk down this street until you get to a bridge, cross the bridge, and the cinema is to your left" then you'd certainly understand me. The point is that you already know how to walk down the street, and how to cross a bridge. You don't need explicit instructions on how to do either.

You structure computer programs in a similar fashion. Your programs should be quite abstract, as in "download page, compute frequencies, print the frequency of each word." This is easily understandable. In fact, let's translate this high-level description to a Python program right now:

```
page = download_page()
freqs = compute_frequencies(page)
for word, freq in freqs:
    print word, freq
```

From reading this, you can understand what the program does. However, you haven't explicitly said anything about *how* it should do it. You just tell the computer to download the page and compute the frequencies. The specifics of these operations will have to be written somewhere else—in separate *function definitions*.

Creating Your Own Functions

A function is something you can call (possibly with some parameters, the things you put in the parentheses), which performs an action and returns a value. In general, you can tell whether something is callable or not with the built-in function `callable`:

```
>>> import math
>>> x = 1
>>> y = math.sqrt
>>> callable(x)
0
>>> callable(y)
1
```

As you know from the previous section, making functions is central to structured programming. So how do you define a function? With the `def` (or "function definition") statement:

```
def hello(name):
    return 'Hello, ' + name + '!'
```

After running this, you have a new function available, called `hello`, which returns a string with a greeting for the name given as the only parameter. You can use this function just like you used the built-in ones:

```
>>> print hello('world')
Hello, world!
>>> print hello('Gumby')
Hello, Gumby!
```

Pretty neat, huh? Consider how you would write a function that returned a list of Fibonacci numbers. Easy! You just use the code from before, and instead of reading in a number from the user, you receive it as a parameter:

```
def fibs(num):
    result = [0, 1]
    for i in range(num-2):
        result.append(result[-2] + result[-1])
    return result
```

After running this statement, you've basically told the interpreter how to calculate Fibonacci numbers—so now you don't have to worry about the details anymore. You simply use the function fibs:

```
>>> fibs(10)
[0, 1, 1, 2, 3, 5, 8, 13, 21, 34]
>>> fibs(15)
[0, 1, 1, 2, 3, 5, 8, 13, 21, 34, 55, 89, 144, 233, 377]
```

The names num and result are quite arbitrary in this example, but return is important. The return statement is used to return something from the function (which is also how we used it in the preceding hello function).

 TIP *Your functions can return more than one value—simply collect them in a tuple and return that.*

Documenting Functions

If you want to document your functions so that you're certain that others will understand them later on, you can add comments (beginning with the hash sign, "#"). Another way of writing comments is simply to write strings by themselves. Such strings can be particularly useful in some places, such as right after a def statement (and at the beginning of a module or a class—you learn more about those later in the book). If you put a string at the beginning of a function, it is stored as part of the function and is called a *docstring*. The following code demonstrates how to add a docstring to a function:

```
def square(x):
    'Calculates the square of the number x.'
    return x*x
```

The docstring may be accessed like this:

```
>>> square.__doc__
'Calculates the square of the number x.'
```

NOTE   __doc__ *is a* function attribute. *You'll learn a lot more about attributes in Chapter 7. The double underscores in the attribute name mean that this is a special attribute. Special or "magic" attributes like this are discussed in Chapter 9.*

Newer versions of Python have a function called help, which can be quite useful. If you use it in the interactive interpreter, you can get information about a function, including its docstring:

```
>>> help(square)
Help on function square in module __main__:

square(x)
    Calculates the square of the number x.
```

You meet the help function again in Chapter 10.

Functions That Aren't Really Functions

Functions, in the mathematical sense, always return something that is calculated from their parameters. In Python, some functions don't return anything. In other languages (such as Pascal) such functions may be called other things (such as "procedures"), but in Python a function is a function, even if it technically isn't. Functions that don't return anything simply don't have a return statement. Or, if they *do* have return statements, there is no value after the word return:

```
def test():
    print 'This is printed'
    return
    print 'This is not'
```

Here, the `return` statement is used simply to end the function:

```
>>> x = test()
This is printed
```

As you can see, the second `print` statement is skipped. (This is a bit like using break in loops, except that you break out of the function.) But if `test` doesn't return anything, what's in x? Let's see:

```
>>> x
>>>
```

Nothing there. Let's look a bit closer:

```
>>> print x
None
```

That's a familiar value: None. So all functions *do* return something: it's just that they return None when you don't tell them what to return. I guess I was a bit unfair when I said that some functions aren't really functions.

The Magic of Parameters

Using functions is pretty straightforward, and creating them isn't all that complicated either. The way parameters work may, however, seem a bit like magic at times. First, let's do the basics.

Where Do the Values Come From?

Sometimes, when defining a function, you may wonder where parameters get their values from. In general, you shouldn't worry about that. Writing a function is a matter of providing a service to whatever part of your program (and possibly even other programs) that might need it. Your task is to make sure the function does its job if it is supplied with acceptable parameters, and preferably fails in an obvious manner if the parameters are wrong. (You do this with `assert` or exceptions in general. More about exceptions in Chapter 8, "Exceptions.")

NOTE *The variables you write after your function name in a* def *statements are often called the* formal *parameters of the function, while the values you supply when you* call *the function are called the* actual *parameters. In general, I won't be too picky about the distinction. If it is important, I will call the actual parameters "values" to distinguish them from the formal parameters.*

Can I Change a Parameter?

So, your function gets a set of values in through its parameters. Can you change them? And what happens if you do? Well, the parameters are just variables like all others, so this works as you would expect. Assigning a new value to a parameter inside a function won't change the outside world at all:

```
>>> def try_to_change(n):
        n = 'Mr. Gumby'

>>> name = 'Mrs. Entity'
>>> try_to_change(name)
>>> name
'Mrs. Entity'
```

Inside try_to_change, the parameter n gets a new value, but as you can see, that doesn't affect the variable name. After all, it's a completely different variable. It's just as if you did something like this:

```
>>> name = 'Mrs. Entity'
>>> n = name # This is almost what happens when passing a parameter
>>> n = 'Mr. Gumby' # This is done inside the function
>>> name
'Mrs. Entity'
```

Here, the result is obvious. While the variable n is changed, the variable name is not. Similarly, when you rebind (assign to) a parameter inside a function, variables outside the function will not be affected.

NOTE *Parameters are stored in what is called a* local scope. *Scoping is discussed later in this chapter.*

Strings (and numbers and tuples) are *immutable:* you can't modify them. Therefore there isn't much to say about them as parameters. But consider what happens if you use a mutable data structure such as a list:

```
>>> def change(n):
        n[0] = 'Mr. Gumby'

>>> names = ['Mrs. Entity', 'Mrs. Thing']
>>> change(names)
>>> names
['Mr. Gumby', 'Mrs. Thing']
```

In this example, the parameter is changed. There is one crucial difference between this example and the previous one. In the previous one, we simply gave the local variable a new value, but in this one we actually *modify* the list that the variable names is bound to. Sound strange? It's not really that strange; let's do it again without the function call:

```
>>> names = ['Mrs. Entity', 'Mrs. Thing']
>>> n = names # Again pretending to pass names as a parameter
>>> n[0] = 'Mr. Gumby' # Change the list
>>> names
['Mr. Gumby', 'Mrs. Thing']
```

You've seen this sort of thing before. When two variables refer to the same list, they...refer to the same list. It's really as simple as that. If you want to avoid this, you have to make a *copy* of the list. When you do slicing on a sequence, the returned slice is always a copy. Thus, if you make a slice of the *entire list* you get a copy:

```
>>> names = ['Mrs. Entity', 'Mrs. Thing']
>>> n = names[:]
```

Now n and names contain two *separate* (nonidentical) lists that are *equal*:

```
>>> n is names
0
>>> n == names
1
```

If you change n now (as you did inside the function change) it won't affect names:

```
>>> n[0] = 'Mr. Gumby'
>>> n
['Mr. Gumby', 'Mrs. Thing']
>>> names
['Mrs. Entity', 'Mrs. Thing']
```

Let's try this trick with change:

```
>>> change(names[:])
>>> names
['Mrs. Entity', 'Mrs. Thing']
```

Now, the parameter n contains a copy, and your original list is safe.

Why Would I Want to Modify My Parameters?

Using a function to change a data structure (such as a list or a dictionary) can be a good way of introducing abstraction into your program. Let's say you want to write a program that stores names and that allows you to look up people either by their first, middle, or last names. You might use a data structure like this:

```
storage = {}
storage['first'] = {}
storage['middle'] = {}
storage['last'] = {}
```

The data structure storage is a dictionary with three keys: 'first', 'middle', and 'last'. Under each of these keys, you store another dictionary. In these sub-dictionaries, you'll use names (first, middle, or last) as keys, and insert lists of people as values. For instance, to add me to this structure, you could do the following:

```
>>> me = 'Magnus Lie Hetland'
>>> storage['first']['Magnus'] = [me]
>>> storage['middle']['Lie'] = [me]
>>> storage['last']['Hetland'] = [me]
```

Under each key, you store a list of people. In this case, the lists contain only me.

Now, if you want a list of all the people registered who have the middle name Lie, you could do the following:

```
>>> storage['middle']['Lie']
['Magnus Lie Hetland']
```

As you can see, adding people to this structure is a bit tedious, especially when you get more people with the same first, middle, or last names, because then you have to extend the list that is already stored under that name. Let's add my sister, for instance, and let's assume you don't know what is already stored in the database:

```
>>> my_sister = 'Anne Lie Hetland'
>>> storage['first'].setdefault('Anne', []).append(my_sister)
>>> storage['middle'].setdefault('Lie', []).append(my_sister)
>>> storage['last'].setdefault('Hetland', []).append(my_sister)
>>> storage['first']['Anne']
['Anne Lie Hetland']
>>> storage['middle']['Lie']
['Magnus Lie Hetland', 'Anne Lie Hetland']
```

Imagine writing a large program filled with updates like this—it would quickly become quite unwieldy.

The point of abstraction is to hide all the gory details of the updates, and you can do that with functions. Let's first make a function to initialize a data structure:

```
def init(data):
    data['first'] = {}
    data['middle'] = {}
    data['last'] = {}
```

In the preceding code, I've simply moved the initialization statements inside a function. You can use it like this:

```
>>> storage = {}
>>> init(storage)
>>> storage
{'middle': {}, 'last': {}, 'first': {}}
```

As you can see, the function has taken care of the initialization, making the code much more readable.

 NOTE *The keys of a dictionary don't have a specific order, so when a dictionary is printed out the order may vary. If the order is different in your interpreter, don't worry about it.*

Before writing a function for storing names, let's write one for getting them.

```
def lookup(data, label, name):
    return data[label].get(name)
```

With lookup you can take a label (such as 'middle') and a name (such as 'Lie') and get a list of full names returned. In other words, assuming my name was stored, you could do this:

```
>>> lookup(storage, 'middle', 'Lie')
['Magnus Lie Hetland']
```

It's important to notice that the list that is returned is the same list that is stored in the data structure. So if you change the list, the change also affects the data structure. (This is not the case if no people are found: then you simply return None.)

Now it's time to write the function that stores a name in your structure:

```
def store(data, full_name):
    names = full_name.split()
    if len(names) == 2: names.insert(1, '')
    labels = 'first', 'middle', 'last'
    for label, name in zip(labels, names):
```

```
        people = lookup(data, label, name)
        if people:
            people.append(full_name)
        else:
            data[label][name] = [full_name]
```

The store function performs the following steps:

1. You enter the function with the parameters data and full_name set to some values that you receive from the outside world.

2. You make yourself a list called names by splitting full_name.

3. If the length of names is 2 (you only have a first and a last name) you insert an empty string as a middle name.

4. You store the strings 'first', 'middle', and 'last' as a tuple in labels. (You could certainly use a list here: it's just convenient to drop the brackets.)

5. You use the zip function to combine the labels and names so they line up properly, and for each pair (label, name), you do the following: (1) Fetch the list belonging to the given label and name; (2) Append full_name to that list, or insert a new list if needed.

Let's try it out:

```
>>> MyNames = {}
>>> init(MyNames)
>>> store(MyNames, 'Magnus Lie Hetland')
>>> lookup(MyNames, 'middle', 'Lie')
['Magnus Lie Hetland']
```

It seems to work. Let's try some more:

```
>>> store(MyNames, 'Robin Hood')
>>> store(MyNames, 'Robin Locksley')
>>> lookup(MyNames, 'first', 'Robin')
['Robin Hood', 'Robin Locksley']
>>> store(MyNames, 'Mr. Gumby')
>>> lookup(MyNames, 'middle', '')
['Robin Hood', 'Robin Locksley', 'Mr. Gumby']
```

As you can see, if more people share the same first, middle, or last name, you can retrieve them all together.

 NOTE *This sort of application is well-suited to object-oriented programming, which is explained in the next chapter.*

What If My Parameter Is Immutable?

In some languages (such as C++, Pascal, or Ada), rebinding parameters and having these changes affect variables outside the function is an everyday thing. In Python, it's not directly possible: you can only modify the parameter objects themselves. But what if you have an immutable parameter, such as a number?

Sorry but it can't be done. What you should do is return all the values you need from your function (as a tuple, if there is more than one). For instance, a function that increments the numeric value of a variable by one could be written like this:

```
>>> def inc(x): return x + 1

>>> foo = 10
>>> foo = inc(foo)
>>> foo
11
```

What If I Really Want To?

If you really want to modify your parameter, you can use a little trick— wrap your value in a list:

```
>>> def inc(x): x[0] = x[0] + 1

>>> foo = [10]
>>> inc(foo)
>>> foo
[11]
```

Simply returning the new value is generally considered a cleaner solution.

Keyword Parameters and Defaults

The parameters we've been using until now are called *positional parameters* because their positions are important—more important than their names, in fact. Consider the following two functions:

```
def hello_1(greeting, name):
    print '%s, %s!' % (greeting, name)

def hello_2(name, greeting):
    print '%s, %s!' % (name, greeting)
```

They both do *exactly* the same thing, only with their parameter names reversed:

```
>>> hello_1('Hello', 'world')
Hello, world!
>>> hello_2('Hello', 'world')
Hello, world!
```

Sometimes (especially if you have many parameters) the order may be hard to remember. To make things easier, you can supply the *name* of our parameter:

```
>>> hello_1(greeting='Hello', name='world')
Hello, world!
```

The order here doesn't matter at all:

```
>>> hello_1(name='world', greeting='Hello')
Hello, world!
```

The names *do*, however (as you may have gathered):

```
>>> hello_2(greeting='Hello', name='world')
world, Hello!
```

The parameters that are supplied with a name like this are called *keyword parameters*. On their own, the key strength of keyword parameters is that they can help clarify the role of each parameter. Instead of having to use some odd and mysterious call like

```
>>> store('Mr. Brainsample', 10, 20, 13, 5)
```

you could use

```
>>> store(patient='Mr. Brainsample', hour=10, minute=20, day=13, month=5)
```

Even though it takes a bit more typing, it is absolutely clear what each parameter does. Also, if you get the order mixed up, it doesn't matter.

What really makes keyword arguments rock, however, is that you can give the parameters in the function default values:

```
def hello_3(greeting='Hello', name='world'):
    print '%s, %s!' % (greeting, name)
```

When a parameter has a default value like this, you don't have to supply it when you call the function! You can supply none, some, or all, as the situation might dictate:

```
>>> hello_3()
Hello, world!
>>> hello_3('Greetings')
Greetings, world!
>>> hello_3('Greetings', 'universe')
Greetings, universe!
```

As you can see, this works well with positional parameters, except that you have to supply the greeting if you want to supply the name. What if you want to supply *only* the name, leaving the default value for the greeting? I'm sure you've guessed it by now:

```
>>> hello_3(name='Gumby')
Hello, Gumby!
```

Pretty nifty, huh? And that's not all. You can combine positional and keyword parameters. The only requirement is that all the positional parameters come first. If they don't, the interpreter won't know which ones they are (that is, which position they are supposed to have).

NOTE *Unless you know what you're doing, you might want to avoid such mixing. It is generally used when you have a small number of mandatory parameters and many modifying parameters with default values. (For some real-world examples, see the* add *method from Anygui in Chapter 12 or the ReportLab package in Chapter 15.)*

For instance, our `hello` function might require a name, but allow us to (optionally) specify the greeting and the punctuation:

```
def hello_4(name, greeting='Hello', punctuation='!'):
    print '%s, %s%s' % (greeting, name, punctuation)
```

This function can be called in many ways. Here are some of them:

```
>>> hello_4('Mars')
Hello, Mars!
>>> hello_4('Mars', 'Howdy')
Howdy, Mars!
>>> hello_4('Mars', 'Howdy', '...')
Howdy, Mars...
>>> hello_4('Mars', punctuation='.')
Hello, Mars.
>>> hello_4('Mars', greeting='Top of the morning to ya')
Top of the morning to ya, Mars!
>>> hello_4()
Traceback (most recent call last):
  File "<pyshell#64>", line 1, in ?
    hello_4()
TypeError: hello_4() takes at least 1 argument (0 given)
```

 NOTE *If I had given* name *a default value as well, the last example wouldn't have raised an exception.*

That's pretty flexible, isn't it? And we didn't really have to do much to achieve it either. In the next section we get even *more* flexible.

Collecting Parameters

Sometimes it can be useful to allow the user to supply any number of parameters. For instance, in the name-storing program (described earlier in this chapter) you can store only one name at a time. It would be nice to be able to store more names, like this:

```
>>> store(data, name1, name2, name3)
```

For this to be useful, you should be allowed to supply as many names as you wanted. Actually, that's quite possible.

Try the following function definition:

```
def print_params(*params):
    print params
```

Here, I seemingly specify only one parameter, but it has an odd little star (or asterisk) in front of it. What does that mean? Let's call the function with a single parameter and see what happens:

```
>>> print_params('Testing')
('Testing',)
```

You can see that what is printed out is a tuple because it has a comma in it. (Those tuples of length one are a bit odd, aren't they?) So using a star in front of a parameter puts it in a tuple? The plural in params ought to give a clue about what's going on:

```
>>> print_params(1, 2, 3)
(1, 2, 3)
```

The star in front of the parameter puts all the values into the same tuple. It gathers them up, so to speak. I wonder if we can combine this with ordinary parameters. Let's write another function and see:

```
def print_params_2(title, *params):
    print title
    print params
```

Let's try it:

```
>>> print_params_2('Params:', 1, 2, 3)
Params:
(1, 2, 3)
```

It works! So the star means "gather up the rest of the positional parameters." I bet if I don't give any parameters to gather, params will be an empty tuple:

```
>>> print_params_2('Nothing:')
Nothing:
()
```

Indeed. How useful. Does it handle keyword arguments (the same as parameters), too?

```
>>> print_params_2('Hmm...', something=42)
Traceback (most recent call last):
  File "<pyshell#60>", line 1, in ?
    print_params_2('Hmm...', something=42)
TypeError: print_params_2() got an unexpected keyword argument 'something'
```

Doesn't look like it. So we probably need another "gathering" operator for keyword arguments. What do you think that might be? Perhaps **?

```
def print_params_3(**params):
    print params
```

At least the interpreter doesn't complain about the function. Let's try to call it:

```
>>> print_params_3(x=1, y=2, z=3)
{'z': 3, 'x': 1, 'y': 2}
```

Yep. We get a dictionary rather than a tuple. Let's put them all together:

```
def print_params_4(x, y, z=3, *pospar, **keypar):
    print x, y, z
    print pospar
    print keypar
```

This works just like expected:

```
>>> print_params_4(1, 2, 3, 5, 6, 7, foo=1, bar=2)
1 2 3
(5, 6, 7)
{'foo': 1, 'bar': 2}
>>> print_params_4(1, 2)
1 2 3
()
{}
```

By combining all these techniques, you can do quite a lot. If you wonder how some combination might work (or whether it's allowed), just try it! (In the next section you see how * and ** can be used at the point of call as well, regardless of whether it was used in the function definition.)

Now, back to the original problem. How you can use this in the name-storing example. The solution is shown below:

```
def store(data, *full_names):
    for full_name in full_names:
        names = full_name.split()
        if len(names) == 2: names.insert(1, '')
        labels = 'first', 'middle', 'last'
        for label, name in zip(labels, names):
            people = lookup(data, label, name)
            if people:
                people.append(full_name)
            else:
                data[label][name] = [full_name]
```

Using this function is just as easy as using the previous version, which only accepted one name:

```
>>> d = {}
>>> init(d)
>>> store(d, 'Han Solo')
```

But now you can also do this:

```
>>> store(d, 'Luke Skywalker', 'Anakin Skywalker')
>>> lookup(d, 'last', 'Skywalker')
['Luke Skywalker', 'Anakin Skywalker']
```

Reversing the Process

Now you've learned about gathering up parameters in tuples and dictionaries, but it is in fact possible to do the "opposite" as well, with the same two operators, * and **. What might the opposite of parameter-gathering be? Let's say we have the following function available:

```
def add(x, y): return x + y
```

NOTE *You can find a more efficient version of this function in the* operator *module.*

Also, let's say you also have a tuple with two numbers that you want to add:

```
params = (1, 2)
```

This is more or less the opposite of what we did previously. Instead of gathering the parameters, we want to *distribute* them. That is simply done by using the asterisk operator in the "other end," that is, when calling the function rather than when defining it:

```
>>> add(*params)
3
```

This works with parts of a parameter list, too, as long as the expanded part is last. You can use the same technique with dictionaries, using the double asterisk operator. Assuming that you have defined hello_3 as before, you can do the following:

```
>>> params = {'name': 'Sir Robin', 'greeting': 'Well met'}
>>> hello_3(**params)
Well met, Sir Robin!
```

Using the asterisk (or double asterisk) both when you define and call the function will simply pass the tuple or dictionary right through, so you might as well not have bothered:

```
>>> def with_stars(**kwds):
        print kwds['name'], 'is', kwds['age'], 'years old'

>>> def without_stars(kwds):
        print kwds['name'], 'is', kwds['age'], 'years old'

>>> args = {'name': 'Mr. Gumby', 'age': 42}
>>> with_stars(**args)
Mr. Gumby is 42 years old
>>> without_stars(args)
Mr. Gumby is 42 years old
```

As you can see, in `with_stars`, I use stars both when defining and calling the function. In `without_stars`, I don't use the stars in either place but achieve exactly the same effect. So the stars are only really useful if you use them *either* when defining a function (to allow a varying number of arguments) *or* when calling a function (to "splice in" a dictionary or a sequence).

With so many ways of supplying and receiving parameters, it's easy to get confused. So let me tie it all together with an example. First, let me define some functions:

```python
def story(**kwds):
    return 'Once upon a time, there was a ' \
           '%(job)s called %(name)s.' % kwds

def power(x, y, *others):
    if others:
        print 'Received redundant parameters:', others
    return pow(x, y)

def interval(start, stop=None, step=1):
    'Imitates range() for step > 0'
    if stop is None:            # If the stop is not supplied...
        start, stop = 0, start  # shuffle the parameters
    result = []
    i = start                   # We start counting at the start index
    while i < stop:             # Until the index reaches the stop index...
        result.append(i)        # ...append the index to out result...
        i += step               # ...and increment the index with the step (> 0)
    return result
```

Now let's try them out:

```python
>>> print story(job='king', name='Gumby')
Once upon a time, there was a king called Gumby.
>>> print story(name='Sir Robin', job='brave knight')
Once upon a time, there was a brave knight called Sir Robin.
>>> params = {'job': 'language', 'name': 'Python'}
>>> print story(**params)
Once upon a time, there was a language called Python.
>>> del params['job']
```

```
>>> print story(job='stroke of genius', **params)
Once upon a time, there was a stroke of genius called Python.
>>> power(2,3)
8
>>> power(3,2)
9
>>> power(y=3,x=2)
8
>>> params = (5,) * 2
>>> power(*params)
3125
>>> power(3, 3, 'Hello, world')
Received redundant parameters: ('Hello, world',)
27
>>> interval(10)
[0, 1, 2, 3, 4, 5, 6, 7, 8, 9]
>>> interval(1,5)
[1, 2, 3, 4]
>>> interval(3,12,4)
[3, 7, 11]
>>> power(*interval(3,7))
Received redundant parameters: (5, 6)
81
```

Feel free to experiment with these functions and functions of your own until you are confident that you understand how this stuff works.

Scoping

What *are* variables, really? You can think of them as names referring to values. So, after the assignment x = 1, the name x refers to the value 1. It's almost like using dictionaries, where keys refer to values, except that you're using an "invisible" dictionary. Actually, this isn't far from the truth. There is a built-in function called vars, which returns this dictionary:

```
>>> x = 1
>>> scope = vars()
>>> scope['x']
1
>>> scope['x'] += 1
>>> x
2
```

CAUTION   *You should not modify the dictionary returned by* vars *because, according to the official Python documentation, the result is undefined. In other words, you might not get the result you're after.*

This sort of "invisible dictionary" is called a *namespace* or *scope.* So, how many namespaces are there? In addition to the global scope, each function call creates a new one:

```
>>> def foo(): x = 42

>>> x = 1
>>> foo()
>>> x
1
```

Here foo changes (rebinds) the variable x, but when you look at it in the end, it hasn't changed after all. That's because when you call foo a *new* namespace is created, which is used for the block *inside* foo. The assignment x = 42 is performed in this inner scope (the *local* namespace), and therefore it doesn't affect the x in the outer (*global*) scope. Variables that are used inside functions like this are called *local variables* (as opposed to global variables). The parameters work just like local variables, so there is no problem in having a parameter with the same name as a global variable:

```
>>> def output(x): print x

>>> x = 1
>>> y = 2
>>> output(y)
2
```

So far, so good. But what if you want to access the global variables inside a function? As long as you only want to *read* the value of the variable (i.e., you don't want to rebind it), there is generally no problem:

```
>>> def combine(parameter): print parameter + external

>>> external = 'berry'
>>> combine('Shrub')
Shrubberry
```

The Problem of "Shadowing"

Reading the value of global variables is not a problem in general, but one thing may make it problematic. If a local variable or parameter exists with the same name as the global variable you want to access, you can't do it directly. The global variable is "shadowed" by the local one.

If needed, you can still gain access to the global variable by using the function globals, a close relative of vars, which returns a dictionary with the global variables. (locals returns a dictionary with the local variables.)

For instance, if you had a global variable called parameter in the previous example, you couldn't access it from within combine because you have a parameter with the same name. In a pinch, however, you could have referred to it as globals()['parameter']:

```
>>> def combine(parameter):
        print parameter + globals()['parameter']

>>> parameter = 'berry'
>>> combine('Shrub')
Shrubberry
```

Rebinding Global Variables

Rebinding global variables (making them refer to some new value) is another matter. If you assign a value to a variable inside a function it automatically becomes local unless you tell Python otherwise. And how do you think you can tell it to make a variable global?

```
>>> x = 1
>>> def change_global():
        global x
        x = x + 1

>>> change_global()
>>> x
2
```

Piece of cake!

NOTE *Use global variables only when you have to. They tend to make your code less readable and less robust. Local variables make your program more abstract because they are "hidden" inside functions.*

Nested Scopes

Beginning with version 2.2, Python supports *nested scopes*. They give you (among other things) the capability to write functions like the following:

```python
def multiplier(factor):
    def multiplyByFactor (number):
        return number*factor
    return multiplyByFactor
```

One function is inside another, and the outer function returns the inner one. Each time the outer function is called, the inner one gets redefined, and each time, the variable factor may have a new value. With nested scopes, this variable from the outer local scope (of multiplier) is accessible in the inner function later on, as follows:

```python
>>> double = multiplier(2)
>>> double(5)
10
>>> triple = multiplier(3)
>>> triple(3)
9
>>> multiplier(5)(4)
20
```

A function such as multiplyByFactor which stores its enclosing scopes is called a *closure*.

If you're using Python 2.1, you have to add the following line at the beginning of your program:

```python
from __future__ import nested_scopes
```

In older versions of Python, variables from surrounding nested scopes are not available. You get an error message like this:

```
>>> double = multiplier(2)
>>> double(2)
Traceback (innermost last):
  File "<stdin>", line 1, in ?
  File "<stdin>", line 3, in multiplyByFactor
NameError: factor
```

Because old versions of Python only have local and global scopes, and `factor` is not a local variable in `multiplyByFactor`, Python assumes that it must be a global variable. But it isn't, so you get an exception. To store a variable from an enclosing scope, you can use a trick—storing it as a default value:

```
def multiplier(factor):
    def multiplyByFactor(number, factor=factor):
        return number*factor
    return multiplyByFactor
```

This works because default values are "frozen" when a function is defined.

Recursion

You've learned a lot about making functions and calling them. You also know that functions can call other functions. What *might* come as a surprise is that functions can call *themselves*.

If you haven't encountered this sort of thing before, you may wonder what this word "recursion" is. It simply means referring to (or, in our case, "calling") yourself. A humorous definition goes like this:

re·cur·sion \ri-'k&r-zh&n\ *n: see* recursion.

Recursive definitions (including recursive function definitions) include references to the term they are defining. Depending on the amount of experience you have with it, recursion can be either mind-boggling or quite straightforward. For a deeper understanding of it, you should probably buy yourself a good textbook on computer science, but playing around with the Python interpreter can certainly help.

In general, you don't want recursive definitions like the humorous one of the word "recursion" because you won't get anywhere. You look up recursion, which again tells you to look up recursion, and so on. A similar function definition would be:

```
def recursion():
    return recursion()
```

It is obvious that this doesn't *do* anything—it's just as silly as the mock dictionary definition. But what happens if you run it? You're welcome to try: The program simply crashes (raises an exception) after a while. Theoretically, it should simply run forever. However, each time a function is called, it uses up a little bit of memory, and after enough function calls have been made, there is no more room, and the program ends with the error message `maximum recursion depth exceeded`.

The sort of recursion you have in this function is called *infinite recursion* (just as a loop beginning with `while 1` and containing no `break` or `return` statements is an *infinite loop*) because it never ends (in theory). What you want is a recursive function that does something useful. A useful recursive function usually consists of the following parts:

- A "base case" (for the *smallest possible problem*) when the function returns a value directly.

- A "recursive case," which contains one or more recursive calls on *smaller parts of the problem.*

The point here is that by breaking the problem up into smaller pieces, the recursion can't go on forever because you always end up with the smallest possible problem, which is covered by the base case.

So you have a function calling itself. But how is that even possible? It's really not as strange as it might seem. As I said before, each time a function is called, a new namespace is created for that specific call; that means that when a function calls "itself," you are actually talking about two different functions (or, rather, the same function with two different namespaces). You might think of it as one creature of a certain species talking to another one of the same species.

Two Classics: Factorial and Power

In this section, we examine two classic recursive functions. First, let's say you want to compute the *factorial* of a number n. The factorial of n is defined as $n \times (n-1) \times (n-2) \times ... \times 1$. It's used in many mathematical applications (for instance, in calculating how many different ways there are there of putting *n* people in a line). How do you calculate it? You could always use a loop:

```
def factorial(n):
    result = n
    for i in range(1,n):
        result *= i
    return result
```

This works and is a straightforward implementation. Basically, what it does is this: first, it sets the result to *n*; then, the result is multiplied by each number from 1 to n–1 in turn; finally, it returns the result. But you can do this differently if you like. The key is the mathematical definition of the factorial, which can be stated as follows:

- The factorial of 1 is 1.

- The factorial of a number *n* greater than 1 is the product of *n* and the factorial of *n*–1.

As you can see, this definition is exactly equivalent to the one given at the beginning of this section.

Now, consider how you implement this definition as a function. It is actually pretty straightforward, once you understand the definition itself:

```
def factorial(n):
    if n == 1:
        return 1
    else:
        return n * factorial(n-1)
```

This is a direct implementation of the definition. Just remember that the function call `factorial(n)` is a different entity from the call `factorial(n-1)`.

Let's consider another example. Assume you want to calculate powers, just like the built-in function pow, or the operator **. You can define the (integer) power of a number in several different ways, but let's start with a simple one: power(x,n) (x to the power of n) is the number x multiplied by itself n-1 times (so that x is used as a factor n times). So power(2,3) is 2 multiplied with itself twice, or $2 \times 2 \times 2 = 8$.

This is easy to implement:

```
def power(x, n):
    result = 1
```

```
    for i in range(n):
        result *= x
    return result
```

This is a sweet and simple little function, but again you can change the definition to a recursive one:

- power(x, 0) is 1 for all numbers x.

- power(x, n) for n > 0 is the product of x and power(x, n-1).

Again, as you can see, this gives exactly the same result as in the simpler, iterative definition.

Understanding the definition is the hardest part—implementing it is easy:

```
def power(x, n):
    if n == 0:
        return 1
    else:
        return x * power(x, n-1)
```

Again, I have simply translated my definition from a slightly formal textual description into a programming language (Python).

 TIP   *If a function or an algorithm is complex and difficult to understand, clearly defining it in your own words before actually implementing it can be very helpful. Programs in this sort of "almost-programming-language" are often referred to as "pseudocode."*

So what is the point of recursion? Can't you just use loops instead? The truth is—yes, you can. But in many cases, recursion can be more readable (although it is usually less efficient), especially if one understands the recursive definition of a function. And even though you could conceivably avoid ever writing a recursive function, as a programmer you will most likely have to understand recursive algorithms and functions created by others.

Another Classic: Binary Search

As a final example of recursion in practice, let's have a look at the algorithm called *binary search*.

You probably know of the game where you are supposed to guess what someone is thinking about by asking twenty yes-or-no questions. To make the most of your questions, you try to cut the number of possibilities in (more or less) half. For instance, if you know the subject is a person, you might ask "Are you thinking of a woman?" You don't start by asking "Are you thinking of John Cleese?" unless you have a very strong hunch. A version of this game for those more numerically inclined is to guess a number. For example, your partner is thinking of a number between 1 and 100, and you have to guess which one it is. Of course, you could do it in a hundred guesses, but how many do you really need?

As it turns out, you only need seven questions. The first one is something like "Is the number greater than 50?" If it is, then you ask "Is it greater than 75?" You keep halving the interval until you find the number. You can do this without much thought.

The same tactic can be used in many different contexts. One common problem is to find out whether a number is to be found in a (sorted) sequence, and even to find out where it is. Again, you follow the same procedure: "Is the number to the right of the middle of the sequence?" If it isn't, "Is it in the second quarter (to the right of the middle of the left half)?" and so on. You keep an upper and a lower limit to where the number *may* be, and keep splitting that interval in two with every question.

The point is that this algorithm lends itself naturally to a recursive definition and implementation. Let's review the definition first, to make sure we know what we're doing:

- If the upper and lower limits are the same, they both refer to the correct position of the number, so return it.

- Otherwise, find the middle of the interval (the average of the upper and lower bound), and find out if the number is in the right or left half. Keep searching in the proper half.

The key to the recursive case is that the numbers are sorted, so when you have found the middle element you can just compare it to the number you're looking for. If your number is larger, then it must be to the right, and if it is smaller, it must be to the left. The recursive part is "Keep searching in the proper half," because the search will be performed in exactly the manner described in the definition. (Note that the search algorithm returns the position where the number *should* be—if it's not present in the sequence, this position will naturally be occupied by another number.)

You're now ready to implement binary search:

```
def search(sequence, number, lower, upper):
    if lower == upper:
        return upper
    else:
        middle = (lower + upper) // 2
        if number > sequence[middle]:
            return search(sequence, number, middle+1, upper)
        else:
            return search(sequence, number, lower, middle)
```

This does exactly what the definition said it should: If lower == upper, then return upper, which is the upper limit. Note that you assume (assert) that the number you are looking for (number) has actually been found (number == sequence[upper]). If you haven't reached your base case yet, you find the middle, check whether your number is to the left or right, and call search recursively with new limits. You could even make this easier to use by making the limit specifications optional. You simply add the following conditional to the beginning of the function definition:

```
def search(sequence, number, lower=0, upper=None):
    if upper is None: upper = len(sequence)-1
    ...
```

Now, if you don't supply the limits, they are set to the first and last positions of the sequence. Let's see if this works:

```
>>> seq = [34, 67, 8, 123, 4, 100, 95]
>>> seq.sort()
>>> seq
[4, 8, 34, 67, 95, 100, 123]
>>> search(seq, 34)
2
>>> search(seq, 100)
5
```

But why go to all this trouble, you ask? For one thing, you could simply use the list method index, and if you wanted to implement this yourself, you could just make a loop starting at the beginning and iterating along until you found the number.

Sure. Using index is just fine. But using a simple loop may be a bit inefficient. Remember I said you needed seven questions to find one number (or position) among 100? And the loop obviously needs 100 questions in the worst case scenario. Big deal, you say. But if the list has 100,000,000,000,000,000,000,000,000,000,000 elements (and the same number of questions with a loop), this sort of thing starts to matter. Binary search would then need only 117 questions. Pretty efficient, huh?

 TIP *There is a standard library module called* bisect, *which implements binary search.*

Throwing Functions Around

By now, you are probably used to using functions just like other objects (strings, number, sequences, and so on) by putting them into variables, passing them as parameters, and returning them from other functions. Some programming languages (such as Scheme or LISP) use functions in this way to accomplish almost everything. Even though you usually don't rely that heavily on functions in Python (you usually make your own kinds of objects—more about that in the next chapter), you *can*. This section describes a few functions that are useful for this sort of "functional programming." These functions are map, filter, reduce, and apply.

Lambda Expressions

In the material that follows, I sometimes use something called *lambda expressions*. These are small, unnamed functions that can only contain an expression, and that return its value. A lambda expression is written like this:

```
lambda x, y, z: x + y + z
```

The first word, lambda, is a reserved word (keyword).[1] It is followed by the parameters, a colon (":"), and finally the body (an expression).

Although lambdas can be useful at times, you are usually better off writing a full-fledged function, especially since the function name will then say something about what your function does.

---

1. The name "lambda" comes from the Greek letter λ, which is used in mathematics to indicate an anonymous function.

map

The map function "maps" one sequence into another (of the same length) by applying a function to each of the elements. For instance, you may have a list of numbers, and you want to create another list in which all the numbers are doubled:

```
>>> numbers = [72, 101, 108, 108, 111, 44, 32, 119, 111, 114, 108, 100, 33]
>>> map(lambda n: 2*n, numbers)
[144, 202, 216, 216, 222, 88, 64, 238, 222, 228, 216, 200, 66]
```

You don't have to use lambda expressions—it works just fine with named functions as well:

```
>>> map(chr, numbers)
['H', 'e', 'l', 'l', 'o', ',', ' ', 'w', 'o', 'r', 'l', 'd', '!']
```

The built-in function chr takes a number as its only parameter and returns the character corresponding to that number (the so-called "ordinal number," which is really its ASCII code). The reverse of chr is ord:

```
>>> map(ord, 'Hello, world!')
[72, 101, 108, 108, 111, 44, 32, 119, 111, 114, 108, 100, 33]
```

Because strings are just sequences of characters, you can use map directly. Note that the result is a list, not another string.

filter

The filter function returns a new sequence in which the elements that you don't want have been filtered out. Or, to put it another way, it returns exactly those you *do* want. You supply filter with a function that returns a Boolean (truth) value for a given sequence element. If the function returns *true*, the element is part of the returned sequence; if it returns *false*, the element is not included in the returned sequence. (The original sequence is not modified.) For instance, you might want to retain only the even numbers from the list numbers:

```
>>> numbers = [72, 101, 108, 108, 111, 44, 32, 119, 111, 114, 108, 100, 33]
>>> filter(lambda n: n % 2 == 0, numbers)
[72, 108, 108, 44, 32, 114, 108, 100]
```

The lambda expression simply checks whether the remainder of a given number when divided by 2 is zero (which is another way of saying that the number is even).

Now, map and filter can be very useful, but they were added to the language before list comprehension came along. If you think about it, all that map and filter can accomplish can also be done with list comprehensions:

```
>>> [chr(n) for n in numbers] # characters corresponding to numbers
['H', 'e', 'l', 'l', 'o', ',', ' ', 'w', 'o', 'r', 'l', 'd', '!']
>>> [ord(c) for c in 'Hello, world!'] # numbers corresponding to characters
[72, 101, 108, 108, 111, 44, 32, 119, 111, 114, 108, 100, 33]
>>> [n for n in numbers if n % 2 == 0] # filters out the odd numbers
[72, 108, 108, 44, 32, 114, 108, 100]
```

In my opinion, list comprehensions are, in many cases, more readable than using map and filter. I won't go so far as to say that you *always* should use list comprehensions: it's largely a matter of taste, and the demands of each specific programming task.

> **NOTE**   *If it is speed you are after, you may want to go with* map *and* filter *after all. When used with built-in functions, they are much faster than list comprehensions.*

reduce

But what about the third function, reduce? This is a tricky one, and I confess that I rarely use it. But people used to functional programming may find it useful. It combines the first two elements of a sequence with a given function, and combines the result with the third element, and so on until the entire sequence has been processed and a single result remains. For instance, if you wanted to sum all the numbers of a sequence, you could use reduce with lambda x, y: x+y (still using the same numbers):[2]

```
>>> numbers = [72, 101, 108, 108, 111, 44, 32, 119, 111, 114, 108, 100, 33]
>>> reduce(lambda x, y: x+y, numbers)
1161
```

---

2.   Actually, instead of this lambda function, you could import the function add from the operator module, which has a function for each of the built-in operators. Using functions from the operator module is always more efficient than using your own functions.

In this example, all the numbers of numbers are summed by successively adding the current sum and the next number in the sequence. What actually happens is very close to this: ·

```
sum = 0
for number in numbers:
    sum = sum + number
```

In the original example, reduce takes care of the sum and the looping, while the lambda represents the expression sum + number. Let's take a peek at what's happening. The following defines a function for adding numbers that also prints out its arguments:

```
def peek_sum(x, y):
    print 'Adding', x, 'and', y
    return x + y
```

Let's use this with reduce:

```
>>> reduce(peek_sum, [1, 2, 3, 4, 5])
Adding 1 and 2
Adding 3 and 3
Adding 6 and 4
Adding 10 and 5
15
```

What happens is that reduce first adds 1 and 2, then adds the result with 3, and so on until all the elements have been added. Finally, after printing out all the operations it goes through, the sum (15) is returned.

As another example, let's imagine that you could only use max with two arguments (in fact, it works with entire sequences) and you wanted to use it on a sequence. Then you could use reduce:

```
>>> reduce(max, numbers)
119
```

The max function is used here to return the maximum of two numbers, and instead of keeping track of a sum, reduce keeps track of the maximum so far. Let's take another peek under the hood:

```
def peek_max(x, y):
    print 'Finding max of', x, 'and', y
    return max(x, y)
```

Just like peek_sum, peek_max prints out its arguments when it is executed. Let's use it with reduce:

```
>>> reduce(peek_max, [3, 5, 2, 6, 9, 2])
Finding max of 3 and 5
Finding max of 5 and 2
Finding max of 5 and 6
Finding max of 6 and 9
Finding max of 9 and 2
9
```

As you can see, the left argument is always the largest number found so far, while the right argument is the next number in the sequence.

> **NOTE** *You have seen that* reduce *can be replaced by a* for *loop, but it cannot be reduced (pun intended) to a list comprehension because it doesn't return a list.*

apply

Before leaving the subject of functional programming, I'll touch upon the built-in function apply. It takes a function as an argument and calls it. You may also optionally supply a tuple of positional parameters and a dictionary of keyword arguments. You use this if you have a tuple (or dictionary) of arguments and want to apply a function to it:

```
>>> def rectangleArea(width, height):
        return width * height

>>> rectangle = 20, 30
>>> apply(rectangleArea, rectangle)
600
```

However, this function is a bit outdated now that you can simply use the nifty little stars to unpack the arguments (as discussed earlier in this chapter, in the section "Collecting Parameters"):

```
>>> rectangleArea(*rectangle)
600
```

Even though you'll probably rarely use `apply`, it has been used extensively in older programs, and you never know when you'll have to read someone else's code.

A Quick Summary

In this chapter you've learned several things about abstraction in general, and functions in particular:

Abstraction. Abstraction is the art of hiding unnecessary details. You can make your program more abstract by defining functions that handle the details.

Function definition. Functions are defined with the `def` statement. They are blocks of statements that receive values (parameters) from the "outside world" and may return one or more values as the result of their computation.

Parameters. Functions receive what they need to know in the form of parameters—variables that are set when the function is called. There are two types of parameters in Python, positional parameters and keyword parameters. Parameters can be made optional by giving them default values.

Scopes. Variables are stored in scopes (also called namespaces). There are two main scopes in Python—the global scope and the local scope. Scopes may be nested.

Recursion. A function can call itself—and if it does, it's called recursion. Everything you can do with recursion can also be done by loops, but sometimes a recursive function is more readable.

Functional programming. Python has some facilities for programming in a functional style. Among these are lambda expressions and the `map`, `filter`, and `reduce` functions.

New Functions in This Chapter

FUNCTION	DESCRIPTION
map(*func, seq* [, *seq*, …])	Applies the function to all the elements in the sequences
filter(*func, seq*)	Returns a list of those elements for which the function is true
reduce(*func, seq* [, *initial*])	Equivalent to *func*(*func*(*func*(*seq*[0], *seq*[1]), *seq*[2]), …)
apply(*func*[, *args*[, *kwargs*]])	Calls the function, optionally supplying arguments

What Now?

The next chapter takes abstractions to another level, through *object-oriented programming*. You learn how to make your own types (or *classes*) of objects to use alongside those provided by Python (such as strings, lists, and dictionaries) and you learn how this enables you to write better programs. Once you've worked your way through the next chapter, you'll be able to write some really *big* programs without getting lost in the source code.

CHAPTER 7

More Abstraction

In the previous chapters, you looked at Python's main built-in object types (numbers, strings, lists, tuples, and dictionaries); you peeked at the wealth of built-in functions and standard libraries; you even created your own functions. Now, only one thing seems to be missing—making your own objects. And that's what you do in this chapter.

You may wonder how useful this is. It might be cool to make your own kinds of objects, but what would you use them for? With all the dictionaries and sequences and numbers and strings available, can't you just use them and make the functions do the job? Certainly. But making your own objects (and especially types or *classes* of objects) is a central concept in Python—so central, in fact, that Python is called an *object-oriented* language (along with SmallTalk, C++, Java, and many others). In this chapter, you learn how to make objects, and you learn about polymorphism and encapsulation, methods and attributes, superclasses and inheritance—you learn a lot. So let's get started.

 NOTE *If you're already familiar with the concepts of object-oriented programming, you probably know about* constructors. *Constructors will not be dealt with in this chapter; for a full discussion, see Chapter 9, "Magic Methods, Properties, and Iterators."*

The Magic of Objects

In object-oriented programming, the term *object* loosely means a collection of data (attributes) with a set of methods for accessing and manipulating those data. There are several reasons for using objects instead of sticking with global variables and functions. Some of the most important benefits of objects include the following:

- Polymorphism

- Encapsulation

- Inheritance

Roughly, these terms mean that you can use the same operations on objects of different classes, and they will work as if "by magic" (polymorphism), you hide unimportant details of how objects work from the outside world (encapsulation), and you can create specialized classes of objects from general ones (inheritance).

In many presentations of object-oriented programming the order of these concepts is different. Encapsulation and inheritance are presented first, and then they are used to model real-world objects. That's all fine and dandy, but in my opinion, the most interesting feature of object-oriented programming is polymorphism. It is also the feature most people (in my experience) get confused by. Therefore I'll start with polymorphism, and show that this concept alone should be enough to make you like object-oriented programming.

Polymorphism

The term polymorphism is derived from a Greek word meaning "having multiple forms." Basically, that means that even if you don't know what kind of object a variable refers to, you may still be able to perform operations on it that will work differently depending on the type (or class) of the object. For example, assume that you are creating an online payment system for a commercial Web site that sells food. Your program receives a "shopping cart" of goods from another part of the system (or other similar systems that may be designed in the future)—all you need to worry about is summing up the total and billing some credit card.

Your first thought may be to specify exactly how the goods must be represented when your program receives them. For instance, you may want to receive them as tuples, like this:

```
('SPAM', 2.50)
```

If all you need is a descriptive tag and a price, this is fine. But it's not very flexible. Let's say that some clever person starts an auctioning service as part of the Web site—where the price of an item is gradually reduced until somebody buys it. It would be nice if the user could put the object in his or her shopping cart and proceed to the checkout (your part of the system) and just wait until the price was right before pressing the "Pay" button.

But that wouldn't work. For that to work, the object would have to check its current price (through some network magic) each time your code asked for it—it couldn't be frozen like in a tuple. You can solve that; just make a function:

```
# Don't do it like this...
def getPrice(object):
    if isinstance(object, type(())):
        return object[1]
    else:
        return magic_network_method(object)
```

NOTE *The type/class checking and use of* isinstance *here is meant to illustrate a point—namely that type checking isn't generally a satisfactory solution. Avoid type checking if you possibly can. The function* isinstance *is described in the section "Investigating Inheritance," later in this chapter.*

In the preceding code, I use the functions type and isinstance to find out whether the object is a tuple (or, equivalently, whether it has the same type as the empty tuple). If it is, its second element is returned; otherwise, some "magic" network method is called.

TIP *In Python 2.2 and later, you can use* tuple *instead of* type(()). *Similarly, in the next example you can use* dict *instead of* type({}).

Assuming that the network stuff already exists, you've solved the problem—for now. But this still isn't very flexible. What if some clever programmer decides that she'll represent the price as a string with a hex value, stored in a dictionary under the key "price"? No problem: you just update your function:

```
# Don't do it like this...
def getPrice(object):
    if isinstance(object, type(())):
        return object[1]
    elif isinstance(object, type({})):
        return int(object['price'])
    else:
        return magic_network_method(object)
```

Now, surely you must have covered every possibility? But let's say someone decides to add a new type of dictionary with the price stored as under a different key. What do you do now? You could certainly update getPrice again, but for how long could you continue doing that? Every time someone wanted to implement some priced object differently, you would have to reimplement your module. But what if you already sold your module and moved on to other, cooler projects—what would the client do then? Clearly this is an inflexible and impractical way of coding the different behaviors.

So what do you do instead? You let the objects handle the operation themselves. It sounds really obvious, but think about how much easier things will get.

Every new object type can retrieve or calculate its own price and return it to you—all you have to do is ask for it.

And this is where polymorphism enters the scene. You receive an object and have no idea of how it is implemented—it may have any one of many "shapes." All you know is that you can ask for its price, and that's enough for you. The way you do that should be familiar:

```
>>> object.getPrice()
2.5
```

Functions that are bound to objects like this are called *methods*. You've already encountered them in the form of string, list, and dictionary methods. There, too, you saw some polymorphism:

```
>>> 'abc'.count('a')
1
>>> [1, 2, 'a'].count('a')
1
```

If you had a variable x, you wouldn't have to know whether it was a string or a list to call the count method—it would work regardless (as long as you supplied a single character as the argument).

Let's do an experiment. The standard library random contains a function called choice that selects a random element from a sequence. Let's use that to give your variable a value:

```
>>> from random import choice
>>> x = choice(['Hello, world!', [1, 2, 'e', 'e', 4]])
```

After performing this, x can either contain the string 'Hello, world!', *or* the list [1, 2, 'e', 'e', 4]—you don't know, and you don't have to worry about it. All you care about is how many times you find "e" in x, and you can find that out regardless of whether x is a list or a string. By calling the count method as before, you find out just that:

```
>>> x.count('e')
2
```

In this case, it seems that the list won out. But the point is that you didn't have to check: Your only requirement was that x had a method called count that took a single character as an argument and returned an integer. If someone else had made their own class of objects that had this method, it wouldn't matter to you—you could use their objects just as well as the strings and lists.

Polymorphism Comes in Many Forms

Polymorphism is at work every time you can "do something" to an object without having to know exactly what kind of object it is. This doesn't only apply to methods—we've already used polymorphism a lot in the form of built-in operators and functions. Consider the following:

```
>>> 1+2
3
>>> 'Fish'+'license'
'Fishlicense'
```

Here the *plus* operator works fine for both numbers (integers in this case) and strings (as well as other types of sequences). To illustrate the point, let's say you wanted to make a function called add that added two things together. You could simply define it like this (equivalent to, but less efficient than, the add function from the operator module):

```
def add(x, y):
    return x+y
```

This would also work with many kinds of arguments:

```
>>> add(1, 2)
3
>>> add('Fish', 'license')
'Fishlicense'
```

This might seem silly, but the point is that the arguments can be *anything that supports addition.*[1] If you want to write a function that prints a message about the length of an object, all that's required is that it *have* a length (that the len function work on it):

```
def length_message(x):
    print "The length of", repr(x), "is", len(x)
```

---

1. Note that these objects have to support addition with each other. So calling add(1, 'license') would not work.

NOTE *As described in Chapter 1,* repr *gives a string represen-*
tation of a Python value.

As you can see, the function also uses repr, but repr is one of the grand mas-
ters of polymorphism—it works with anything. Let's see how this works:

```
>>> length_message('Fnord')
The length of 'Fnord' is 5
>>> length_message([1, 2, 3])
The length of [1, 2, 3] is 3
```

Many functions and operators are polymorphic—probably most of yours will
be, too, even if you don't intend them to be. Just by using polymorphic functions
and operators, the polymorphism "rubs off." In fact, virtually the only thing you
can do to destroy this polymorphism is to do explicit type checking with
functions such as type, isinstance, and issubclass.

Encapsulation

Encapsulation is the principle of hiding unnecessary details from the rest of the
world. This may sound like polymorphism—there, too, you use an object without
knowing its inner details. The two concepts are similar because they are both
principles of abstraction—they both help you deal with the components of your
program without caring about unnecessary detail, just like functions do.

But encapsulation isn't the same as polymorphism. Polymorphism enables
you to call the methods of an object without knowing its class (type of object).
Encapsulation enables you to use the object without worrying about how it's constructed. Does it still sound similar? Let's construct an example *with*
polymorphism, but *without* encapsulation. Assume that you have a class called
OpenObject (you learn how to create classes later in this chapter):

```
>>> o = OpenObject() # This is how we create objects...
>>> o.setName('Sir Lancelot')
>>> o.getName()
'Sir Lancelot'
```

You create an object (by calling the class as if it were a function) and bind the variable o to it. You can then use the methods setName and getName (assuming that they are methods that are supported by the class OpenObject). Everything seems to be working perfectly. However, let's assume that o stores its name in the global variable globalName:

```
>>> globalName
'Sir Lancelot'
```

This means that you have to worry about the contents of globalName when you use instances (objects) of the class OpenObject. In fact, you have to make sure that nobody changes it:

```
>>> globalName = 'Sir Gumby'
>>> o.getName()
'Sir Gumby'
```

Things get even more problematic if you try to create more than one OpenObject because they will all be messing with the same variable:

```
>>> o1 = OpenObject()
>>> o2 = OpenObject()
>>> o1.setName('Robin Hood')
>>> o2.getName()
'Robin Hood'
```

As you can see, setting the name of one automatically sets the name of the other. Not exactly what you want.

Basically, you want to treat objects as abstract. When you call a method you don't want to worry about anything else, such as not disturbing global variables. So how can you "encapsulate" the name within the object? No problem. You make it an *attribute*. Attributes are variables that are a part of the object, just like methods; actually methods are almost like attributes bound to functions. (You'll see an important difference between methods and functions in the section "Attributes, Functions, and Methods," later in this chapter.)

If you rewrite the class to use an attribute instead of a global variable, and you rename it ClosedObject, it works like this:

```
>>> c = ClosedObject()
>>> c.setName('Sir Lancelot')
>>> c.getName()
'Sir Lancelot'
```

So far, so good. But for all you know, this could still be stored in a global variable. Let's make another object:

```
>>> r = ClosedObject()
>>> r.setName('Sir Robin')
r.getName()
'Sir Robin'
```

Here we can see that the new object has its name set properly. Well, we expected that. But what has happened to the first object now?

```
>>> c.getName()
'Sir Lancelot'
```

The name is still there! What I have done is give the object its own *state*. The state of an object is described by its attributes (like its name, for instance). The methods of an object may change these attributes. So it's like lumping together a bunch of functions (the methods) and giving them access to some variables (the attributes) where they can keep values stored between function calls.

In Private

But that's not all. In fact, you can access the attributes of an object from the "outside," too:

```
>>> c.name
'Sir Lancelot'
>>> c.name = 'Sir Gumby'
>>> c.getName()
'Sir Gumby'
```

Some programmers are okay with this, but some (like the creators of SmallTalk, a language where attributes of an object are only accessible to the methods of the same object) feel that it breaks with the principle of encapsulation. They believe that the state of the object should be *completely hidden* (inaccessible) to the outside world. You might wonder why they take such an extreme stand. Isn't it enough that each object manages its own attributes? Why should you hide them from the world? After all, if you just used the name attribute directly in ClosedObject you wouldn't have to make the setName and getName methods.

The point is that other programmers may not know (and perhaps shouldn't know) what's going on inside your object. For instance, ClosedObject may send an e-mail to some administrator every time an object changes its name. This could be part of the setName method. But what happens when you set c.name directly? Nothing. No e-mail is sent. To avoid this sort of thing, you have "private" attributes, attributes that are not accessible outside the object but only through "accessor" methods such as getName and setName.

 NOTE *In Chapter 9, you learn about* properties, *a powerful alternative to accessors.*

Python doesn't support privacy directly, but relies on the programmer to know when it is safe to modify an attribute from the outside. After all, you ought to know how to use an object before using it. It *is*, however, possible to achieve something like private attributes with a little trickery.

To make a method or attribute private (inaccessible from the outside), simply start its name with two underscores:

```
class Secretive:
    def __inaccessible(self):
        print "Bet you can't see me..."
    def accessible(self):
        print "The secret message is:"
        self.__inaccessible()
```

Now __inaccessible is inaccessible to the outside world, while it can still be used inside the class (for example, from accessible):

```
>>> s = Secretive()
>>> s.__inaccessible()
Traceback (most recent call last):
  File "<pyshell#112>", line 1, in ?
    s.__inaccessible()
AttributeError: Secretive instance has no attribute '__inaccessible'
>>> s.accessible()
The secret message is:
Bet you can't see me...
```

Although the double underscores are a bit strange, this seems like a standard private method, as found in other languages. What's not so standard is what actually happens. Inside a class definition, all names beginning with a double underscore are "translated" by adding a single underscore and the class name to the beginning:

```
>>> Secretive._Secretive__inaccessible
<unbound method Secretive.__inaccessible>
```

If you know how this works behind the scenes, it is still possible to access private methods outside the class, even though you're not supposed to:

```
>>> s._Secretive__inaccessible()
Bet you can't see me...
```

So, in short, you can't be sure that others won't access the methods and attributes of your objects, but this sort of name-mangling is a pretty strong signal that they *shouldn't*.

 NOTE *Some languages support several degrees of privacy for its member variables (attributes). Java, for instance, has four different levels. Python has no equivalent privacy support.*

Inheritance

Inheritance is another way of dealing with laziness (in the positive sense). Programmers want to avoid typing the same code more than once. We avoided that earlier by making functions, but now I will address a more subtle problem. What if you have a class already, and you want to make one that is very similar? Perhaps one that adds only a few methods? When making this new class, you don't want to have to copy all the code from the old one over to the new one. You may already have a class called Shape, which knows how to draw itself on the screen.

Now you want to make a class called Rectangle, which *also* knows how to draw itself on the screen, but which can, in addition, calculate its own area. You wouldn't want to do all the work of making a new draw method when Shape has one that works just fine. So what do you do? You let Rectangle *inherit* the methods from Shape. You can do this in such a way that when draw is called on a Rectangle object, the method from the Shape class is called automatically. I go into the details of this a bit later in this chapter.

Classes and Types

By now, you're getting a feeling for what classes are—or you *may* be getting impatient for me to tell you how to make the darn things. Before jumping into the technicalities, let's have a look at what a class is, and how it is different from (or similar to) a type.

What Is a Class, Exactly?

I've been throwing around the word *class* a lot, using it more or less synonymously with words such as "kind" or "type." In many ways that's exactly what a class is—a kind of object. All objects *belong* to one class and are said to be *instances* of that class.

So, for example, if you look outside your window and see a bird, that bird is an instance of the class "birds." This is a very general (abstract) class that has several subclasses: your bird might belong to the subclass "larches." You can think of the class "birds" as the set of all birds, while the class "larches" is just a subset of that. When the objects belonging to one class form a subset of the objects belonging to another class, the first is called a *subclass* of the second. Thus, "larches" is a subclass of "birds." Conversely, "birds" is a *superclass* of "larches."

> **NOTE** *In everyday speech, we denote classes of objects with plural nouns such as "birds" or "larches." In Python, it is customary to use singular, capitalized nouns such as* Bird *and* Larch.

When stated like this, subclasses and superclasses are easy to understand. But in object-oriented programming, the subclass relation has important implications because a class is defined by what methods it supports. All the instances of a class have these methods, so all the instances of all *subclasses* must *also* have them. Defining subclasses is then only a matter of defining *more* methods.

For instance, Bird might supply the method fly while Penguin (a subclass of Bird) might add the method eatFish. When making a penguin class you would probably also want to *override* a method of the superclass, namely the fly method. In a Penguin instance, this method should either do nothing, or possibly raise an exception (see Chapter 8), given that penguins can't fly.

Types and Classes in Python 2.2

Both classes and types represent sets of objects. In some languages (such as SmallTalk) there is no difference between classes and types; in Python, however, there is.

Simply put, you can make classes, but you can't make types. Types are built-in and very basic. In recent versions of Python (2.2) things are starting to change. The division between basic types and classes is blurring. You can now make subclasses (or subtypes) of the built-in types, and the types are behaving more like classes. Chances are you won't notice this change much until you become more familiar with the language.

Making Your Own Classes

Finally! You get to make your own classes! Okay, enough enthusiasm. Let's get down to it—here is a simple class:

```
class Person:
    def setName(self, name):
        self.name = name
    def getName(self):
        return self.name
    def greet(self):
        print "Hello, world! I'm %s." % self.name
```

This example contains three method definitions, which are like function definitions except that they are written inside a class statement. Person is, of course, the name of the class. The class statement creates its own namespace where the functions are defined. (See the section "The Class Namespace" later in this chapter.) All this seems fine, but you may wonder what this self parameter is. It refers to the object itself. And what object is that? Let's make a couple of instances and see:

```
>>> foo = Person()
>>> bar = Person()
>>> foo.setName('Luke Skywalker')
>>> bar.setName('Anakin Skywalker')
>>> foo.greet()
Hello, world! I'm Luke Skywalker.
>>> bar.greet()
Hello, world! I'm Anakin Skywalker.
```

Okay, so this example may be a bit obvious, but perhaps it clarifies what `self` is. When I call `setName` and `greet` on `foo`, `foo` itself is automatically passed as the first parameter in each case—the parameter that I have so fittingly called `self`. You may, in fact, call it whatever you like, but because it is always the object itself, it is almost always called `self`, by convention.

It should be obvious why `self` is useful, and even necessary here. Without it, none of the methods would have access to the object itself, the object whose attributes they are supposed to manipulate.

As before, the attributes are also accessible from the outside:

```
>>> foo.name
'Luke Skywalker'
>>> bar.name = 'Yoda'
>>> bar.greet()
Hello, world! I'm Yoda.
```

Attributes, Functions, and Methods

The `self` parameter (mentioned in the previous section) is, in fact, what distinguishes methods from functions. Methods (or, more technically, *bound* methods) have their first parameter bound to the instance they belong to: you don't have to supply it. So while you can certainly bind an attribute to a plain function, it won't have that special `self` parameter:

```
>>> class Class:
        def method(self):
            print 'I have a self!'

>>> def function():
        print "I don't..."

>>> instance = Class()
>>> instance.method()
I have a self!
>>> instance.method = function
>>> instance.method()
I don't...
```

Note that the `self` parameter is not dependent on calling the method the way I've done until now, as `instance.method`. You're free to use another variable that refers to the same method:

```
>>> class Bird:
        song = 'Squaawk!'
        def sing(self):
            print self.song

>>> bird = Bird()
>>> bird.sing()
Squaawk!
>>> birdsong = bird.sing
>>> birdsong()
Squaawk!
```

Even though the last method call looks exactly like a function call, the variable `birdsong` refers to the bound method `bird.sing`, which means that it still has access to the `self` parameter.

> **NOTE**   *In Chapter 9, you see how classes can call methods in their superclasses (more specifically, the* constructors *of their superclasses). Those methods are called directly on the* class; *they haven't bound their* self *parameter to anything and are therefore called* unbound *methods.*

Throwing Methods Around

In the previous section, I showed how you could use a bound method just like a function without losing the `self` parameter. That means that you can use methods in many of the fancy ways that I've used functions previously, with handy tools such as `map`, `filter`, and `reduce` (see the section "Throwing Functions Around" in Chapter 6). In this section, I provide some examples of these capabilities. They should all be fairly self-explanatory.

Let's start by creating a class:

```
class FoodExpert:
    def init(self):
        self.goodFood = []

    def addGoodFood(self, food):
        self.goodFood.append(food)
```

```
    def likes(self, x):
        return x in self.goodFood

    def prefers(self, x, y):
        x_rating = self.goodFood.index(x)
        y_rating = self.goodFood.index(y)
        if x_rating > y_rating:
            return y
        else:
            return x
```

This class has more code than earlier examples, but it is still pretty simple. It is meant to represent some sort of food expert (as the name implies) who likes only some types of food, and likes some more than others.

The init method simply initializes the objects by giving them an attribute called goodFood containing an empty list. The addGoodFood method adds a type of food to the list, where the first food type added is the expert's favorite, the next one is the second choice, and so on. The likes method simply checks whether the expert likes a certain type of food (whether it has been added to goodFood), and finally the prefers method is given two food types (both of which must be liked) and returns the preferred one (based on their position in goodFood).

Now, let's play. In the following example, a FoodExpert is created and its taste buds initialized:

```
>>> f = FoodExpert()
>>> f.init()
>>> map(f.addGoodFood, ['SPAM', 'Eggs', 'Bacon', 'Rat', 'Spring Surprise'])
[None, None, None, None, None]
```

The first two lines instantiate FoodExpert and initialize the instance, which is stored in f. The map call simply uses the method addGoodFood with its self parameter bound to f. Because this method doesn't return anything, the result is a list filled with None. However, a side effect is that f has been updated:

```
>>> f.goodFood
['SPAM', 'Eggs', 'Bacon', 'Rat', 'Spring Surprise']
```

Let's use this expert to give us a list of recommendations:

```
>>> menu = ['Filet Mignon', 'Pasta', 'Pizza', 'Eggs', 'Bacon', 'Tomato', 'SPAM']
>>> rec = filter(f.likes, menu)
>>> rec
['Eggs', 'Bacon', 'SPAM']
```

What I did here was simply apply f.likes as a filter to a menu; the dishes the expert didn't like were simply discarded. But what if you want to find out which of these dishes the expert would prefer? I once again turn to the trusty (if rarely used) reduce:

```
>>> reduce(f.prefers, rec)
'SPAM'
```

This basically works just like the example using reduce with max in Chapter 6 (in the section "reduce").

If I had used a different expert, initialized with different preferences, of course, I'd get completely different results, even though the method definitions would be exactly the same. This is the primary difference between standard functional programming and this quasi-functional programming using bound methods; the methods have access to a state that can be used to "customize" them.

The Class Namespace

The following two statements are (more or less) equivalent:

```
def foo(x): return x*x
foo = lambda x: x*x
```

Both create a function that returns the square of its argument, and both bind the variable foo to that function. The name foo may be defined in the global (module) scope, or it may be local to some function or method. The same thing happens when you define a class; all the code in the class statement is executed in a special namespace—the *class namespace*. This namespace is accessible later by all members of the class. Not all Python programmers know that class definitions are simply code sections that are executed, but it can be useful information. For instance, you aren't restricted to def statements:

```
>>> class C:
        print 'Class C being defined...'

Class C being defined...
>>>
```

Okay, that was a bit silly. But consider the following:

```
class MemberCounter:
    members = 0
    def init(self):
        MemberCounter.members += 1

>>> m1 = MemberCounter()
>>> m1.init()
>>> MemberCounter.members
1
>>> m2 = MemberCounter()
>>> m2.init()
>>> MemberCounter.members
2
```

In the preceding code, a variable is defined in the class scope, which can be accessed by all the members (instances), in this case to count the number of class members. Note the use of init to initialize all the instances: I'll automate that in Chapter 9.

This class scope variable is accessible from every instance as well, just as methods are:

```
>>> m1.members
2
>>> m2.members
2
```

What happens when you rebind the members attribute in an instance?

```
>>> m1.members = 'Two'
>>> m1.members
'Two'
>>> m2.members
2
```

The new members value has been written into an attribute in m1, shadowing the classwide variable. This mirrors the behavior of local and global variables.

Specifying a Superclass

As I discussed earlier in the chapter, subclasses expand on the definitions in their superclasses. You indicate the superclass in a class statement by writing it in parentheses after the class name:

```
class Filter:
    def init(self):
        self.blocked = []
    def filter(self, sequence):
        return filter(lambda x: x not in self.blocked,
                        sequence)

class SPAMFilter(Filter): # SPAMFilter is a subclass of Filter
    def init(self): # Overrides init method from Filter superclass
        self.blocked = ['SPAM']
```

NOTE *This code relies on nested scopes. If you are using Python 2.1, remember to include*

```
from __future__ import nested_scopes
```

at the beginning.

Filter is a general class for filtering sequences. Actually it doesn't filter out anything:

```
>>> f = Filter()
>>> f.init()
>>> f.filter([1, 2, 3])
[1, 2, 3]
```

The usefulness of the Filter class is that it can be used as a base class (superclass) for other classes, such as SPAMFilter, which filters out 'SPAM' from sequences:

```
>>> s = SPAMFilter()
>>> s.init()
>>> s.filter(['SPAM', 'SPAM', 'SPAM', 'SPAM', 'eggs', 'bacon', 'SPAM'])
['eggs', 'bacon']
```

Note two important points in the definition of SPAMFilter:

- I *override* the definition of init from Filter by simply providing a new definition.

- The definition of the filter method carries over (is inherited) from Filter, so you don't have to write the definition again.

The second point demonstrates why inheritance is useful: I can now make a number of different filter classes, all subclassing Filter, and for each one I can simply use the filter method I have already implemented. Talk about useful laziness...

Investigating Inheritance

If you want to find out whether a class is a subclass of another, you can use the built-in method issubclass:

```
>>> issubclass(SPAMFilter, Filter)
1
>>> issubclass(Filter, SPAMFilter)
0
```

If you have a class and want to know its base classes, you can access its special attribute __bases__:

```
>>> SPAMFilter.__bases__
(<class __main__.Filter at 0x171e40>,)
>>> Filter.__bases__
()
```

In a similar manner, you can check whether an object is an instance of a class by using isinstance:

```
>>> s = SPAMFilter()
>>> isinstance(s, SPAMFilter)
1
```

```
>>> isinstance(s, Filter)
1
>>> isinstance(s, type(''))
0
```

 TIP *In Python 2.2 and later you can use* str *instead of* type('').

As you can see, s is a (direct) member of the class SPAMFilter, but it is also an indirect member of Filter because SPAMFilter is a subclass of Filter. Another way of putting it is that all SPAMFilters are Filters. As you can see in the last example, isinstance also works with types, such as the string type returned by type('').

If you just want to find out which class an object belongs to, you can use the __class__ attribute:

```
>>> s.__class__
<class __main__.SPAMFilter at 0x1707c0>
```

Multiple Superclasses

I'm sure you noticed a small detail in the previous section that may have seemed odd: the plural form in __bases__. I said you could use it to find the base classes of a class, which implies that it may have more than one. This is, in fact, the case. To show how it works, let's create a few classes:

```
class Calculator:
    def calculate(self, expression):
        self.value = eval(expression)

class Talker:
    def talk(self):
        print 'Hi, my value is', self.value

class TalkingCalculator(Calculator, Talker):
    pass
```

The subclass (TalkingCalculator) does nothing by itself; it inherits all its behavior from its superclasses. The point is that it inherits both calculate from Calculator and talk from Talker, making it a talking calculator:

```
>>> tc = TalkingCalculator()
>>> tc.calculate('1+2*3')
>>> tc.talk()
Hi, my value is 7
```

This is called *multiple inheritance*, and is a very powerful tool.

 NOTE *When using multiple inheritance, there is one thing you should look out for. If a method is implemented differently by two or more of the superclasses, you must be careful about the order of these superclasses (in the class statement): The methods in the earlier classes* override *the methods in the later ones. So if the* Calculator *class in the preceding example had a method called* talk, *it would override (and make inaccessible) the* talk *method of the* Talker. *Reversing their order, like this*

```
class TalkingCalculator(Talker, Calculator): pass
```

would have made the talk *method of the* Talker *accessible. The normal way of handling multiple inheritance is to have one "substantial" base class, and to add so-called* mix-in *classes that implement a few methods, "modifying" the inheritance. If the mix-ins are to override something in the base class, they must be put first.*

Interfaces and Introspection

The "interface" concept is related to polymorphism. When you handle a polymorphic object, you only care about its interface—the methods and attributes known to the world. In Python, you don't explicitly specify which methods an object needs to have to be acceptable as a parameter. For instance, you don't write interfaces explicitly (as you do in Java); you just assume that an object can do what you ask it to. If it can't, the program will fail.

NOTE *There is some talk of adding explicit interface functionality to Python. For more information, take a look at Python Enhancement Proposal number 245* (http://www.python.org/peps/pep-0245.html).

Usually, you simply require that objects conform to a certain interface (in other words, implement certain methods), but if you want to, you can be quite flexible in your demands. Instead of just calling the methods and hoping for the best, you can check whether the required methods are present—and if not, perhaps do something else:

```
>>> hasattr(tc, 'talk')
1
>>> hasattr(tc, 'fnord')
0
```

In the preceding code, you find that that tc (a TalkingCalculator, as described earlier in this chapter) has the attribute talk (which contains a method), but not the attribute fnord. If you wanted to, you could even check whether the talk attribute was callable:

```
>>> callable(getattr(tc, 'talk', None))
1
>>> callable(getattr(tc, 'fnord', None))
0
```

Note that instead of using hasattr in an if statement and accessing the attribute directly, I'm using getattr, which allows me to supply a default value (in this case None) that will be used if the attribute is not present. I then use callable on the returned object.

NOTE *The inverse of* getattr *is* setattr, *which can be used to set the attributes of an object:*

```
>>> setattr(tc, 'name', 'Mr. Gumby')
>>> tc.name
'Mr. Gumby'
```

If you want to see all the values stored in an object, you can examine its __dict__ attribute. And if you *really* want to find out what an object is made of, you should take a look at the inspect module. It is meant for fairly advanced users who want to make object browsers (programs that enable you to browse Python objects in a graphical manner) and other similar programs that require such functionality. For more information on exploring objects and modules, see the section "Exploring Modules" in Chapter 10.

Some Thoughts on Object-Oriented Design

Many books have been written about object-oriented program design, and although that's not the focus of this book, I'll give you some pointers:

- Gather what belongs together. If a function manipulates a global variable, the two of them might be better off in a class, as an attribute and a method.

- Don't let objects become too intimate. Methods should mainly be concerned with the attributes of their own instance. Let other instances manage their own state.

- Keep it simple. Keep your methods small. As a rule of thumb, it should be possible to read (and understand) each of your methods in 30 seconds.

When determining which classes you need and what methods they should have, you may try something like this:

1. Write down a description of your problem (what should the program do?). Underline all the nouns, verbs, and adjectives.

2. Go through the nouns, looking for potential classes.

3. Go through the verbs, looking for potential methods.

4. Go through the adjectives, looking for potential attributes.

5. Allocate methods and attributes to your classes.

Now you have a first sketch of an *object-oriented model*. You may also want to think about what relationships (such as inheritance) the classes and objects will have. To refine your model, you can do the following:

6. Write down (or dream up) a set of *use cases*—scenarios of how your program may be used. Try to cover all the functionality.

7. Think through every use case step by step, making sure that everything you need is covered by your model. If something is missing, add it. If something isn't quite right, change it. Continue until you are satisfied.

When you have a model you think will work, you can start hacking away. Chances are you'll have to revise your model—or revise parts of your program. Luckily, that's easy in Python, so don't worry about it. Just dive in.

A Quick Summary

This chapter has given you more than just information about the Python language; it has introduced you to several concepts that may have been completely foreign to you. Let me try to summarize them for you:

Objects. An object consists of attributes and methods. An attribute is merely a variable that is part of an object, and a method is more or less a function that is stored in an attribute. One difference between (bound) methods and other functions is that methods always receive the object they are part of as their first argument, usually called `self`.

Classes. A class represents a set (or kind) of objects, and every object (instance) has a class. The class's main task is to define the methods its instances will have.

Polymorphism. Polymorphism is the characteristic of being able to treat objects of different types and classes alike—you don't have to know which class an object belongs to in order to call one of its methods.

Encapsulation. Objects may hide (or encapsulate) their internal state. In some languages this means that their state (their attributes) is only available through their methods. In Python, all attributes are publicly available, but programmers should still be careful about accessing an object's state directly, since they might unwittingly make the state inconsistent in some way.

Inheritance. One class may be the subclass of one or more other classes. The subclass then inherits all the methods of the superclasses.

Interfaces and introspection. In general, you don't want to prod an object too deeply. You rely on polymorphism, and call the methods you need. However, if you want to find out what methods or attributes an object has, there are functions that will do the job for you.

Object-oriented design. There are many opinions about how (or whether!) to do object-oriented design. No matter where you stand on the issue, it's important to understand your problem thoroughly, and to create a design that is easy to understand.

New Functions in This Chapter

FUNCTION	DESCRIPTION
callable(*object*)	Determines if the object is callable (such as a function or a method)
getattr(*object, name[, default]*)	Gets the value of an attribute, optionally providing a default
hasattr(*object, name*)	Determines if the object has the given attribute
isinstance(*object, class*)	Determines if the object is an instance of the class
issubclass(*A, B*)	Determines if *A* is a subclass of *B*
random.choice(*sequence*)	Choose a random element from a non-empty sequence
setattr(*object, name, value*)	Sets the given attribute of the object to *value*
type(*object*)	Returns the type of the object

What Now?

You've learned a lot about creating your own objects and how useful that can be. Before diving headlong into the magic of Python's special methods (Chapter 9, "Magic Methods, Properties, and Iterators"), let's take a breather with a little chapter about exception handling.

Exceptions

WHEN WRITING COMPUTER PROGRAMS it is usually possible to discern between a normal course of events and something that's exceptional (out of the ordinary). Such exceptional events might be errors (such as trying to divide a number by zero), or simply something you might not expect to happen very often. To handle such exceptional events you might use conditionals everywhere the events might occur (for instance, have your program check whether the denominator is zero for every division). However, this would not only be inefficient and inflexible, but would also make the programs illegible. You might be tempted to ignore these exceptions and just hope they won't occur, but Python offers a powerful alternative.

What Is an Exception?

To represent exceptional conditions, Python uses *exception objects*. If such an exception object is not handled in any way, the program terminates with a so-called *traceback* (an error message):

```
>>> 1/0
Traceback (most recent call last):
  File "<stdin>", line 1, in ?
ZeroDivisionError: integer division or modulo by zero
```

If such error messages were all you could use exceptions for, exceptions wouldn't be very interesting. The fact is, however, that each exception is an instance of some class (in this case ZeroDivisionError), and these instances may be raised and caught in various ways, allowing you to trap the error and do something about it instead of allowing the entire program to fail.

In the next section, you learn how to create and raise your own exceptions. In the following sections, you learn about handling exceptions in various ways.

....

Warnings

Exceptions may be used to represent exceptional or illegal states in your program (such as trying to divide a number by zero, or reading from a nonexistent file), and will, unless caught by you, terminate the program. Warnings, on the other hand, are mild error messages; they notify you that something isn't quite right, but your program keeps running. For instance, try to import the regex module:

```
>>> import regex
__main__:1: DeprecationWarning: the regex module is deprecated; please
use the re module
>>> regex
<module 'regex' (built-in)>
```

It's obvious that the interpreter didn't like this; the regex module is old, and you should use the re module instead. (You learn more about the re module in Chapter 10). However, because a lot of code already uses the regex module, it would be unreasonable to *demand* that re be used; that would simply break all the older code. So instead, a warning is issued.

If, for some reason, you are stuck with the regex module, you can happily ignore the warning (although you probably *should* rewrite your code). You can even filter it out (with the function filterwarnings), so it isn't printed:

```
>>> from warnings import filterwarnings
>>> filterwarnings('ignore')
>>> import regex
```

If you want to learn more about warnings, you can check out the warnings module in the standard library documentation at http://www.python.org/doc/lib.

....

Making Things Go Wrong...Your Way

As you've seen, exceptions are raised automatically when something is wrong. Before looking at how to deal with those exceptions, let's take a look at how you can raise exceptions yourself—and even create your own kinds of exceptions.

The raise *Statement*

To raise an exception, you use the raise statement with an argument that is either a class or an instance. When using a class, an instance is created automatically; you can optionally provide a string argument after the class, separated by a comma. Here are some simple examples, using the built-in exception class Exception:

```
>>> raise Exception
Traceback (most recent call last):
  File "<stdin>", line 1, in ?
Exception
>>> raise Exception, 'hyperdrive overload'
Traceback (most recent call last):
  File "<stdin>", line 1, in ?
Exception: hyperdrive overload
>>> raise Exception('hyperdrive overload')
Traceback (most recent call last):
  File "<stdin>", line 1, in ?
Exception: hyperdrive overload
```

 NOTE   *There are actually two other ways to use* raise. *The argument may be a string, or you can call* raise *without any arguments. Using a string argument is considered obsolete; calling* raise *without arguments is covered in the section "Look, Ma, No Arguments!" later in this chapter.*

The first example (raise Exception) raises a generic exception with no information of what went wrong. In the last two examples, I added the error message hyperdrive overload. As you can see, the two forms raise *class, message* and raise *class*(*message*) are equivalent; both raise an exception with the given error message.

There are many built-in classes available. You can find a description of all of them in the Python Library Reference, in the section "Built-in Exceptions." You can also explore them yourself with the interactive interpreter; they are all found in the module exceptions, for your convenience (as well as in the built-in namespace). To list the contents of a module, you can use the dir function, which is described in Chapter 10:

```
>>> import exceptions
>>> dir(exceptions)
['ArithmeticError', 'AssertionError', 'AttributeError', ...]
```

In your interpreter, this list will be quite a lot longer. I've deleted most of the names in the interest of legibility. All of these exceptions can be used in your raise statements:

```
>>> raise ArithmeticError
Traceback (most recent call last):
  File "<stdin>", line 1, in ?
ArithmeticError
```

Table 8-1 describes some of the most important built-in exceptions.

Table 8-1. Some Built-in Exceptions

CLASS NAME	DESCRIPTION
Exception	The root class for all exceptions
AttributeError	Raised when attribute reference or assignment fails
IOError	Raised when trying to open a nonexistent file (among other things)
IndexError	Raised when using a nonexistent index on a sequence
KeyError	Raised when using a nonexistent key on a mapping
NameError	Raised when a name (variable) is not found
SyntaxError	Raised when the code is ill-formed
TypeError	Raised when a built-in operation or function is applied to an object of the wrong type
ValueError	Raised when a built-in operation or function is applied to an object with correct type, but with an inappropriate value
ZeroDivisionError	Raised when the second argument of a division or modulo operation is zero

Custom Exception Classes

Although the built-in exceptions cover a lot of ground and are sufficient for many purposes, there are times when you might want to create your own. For instance, in the "hyperdrive overload" example, wouldn't it be more natural to have a specific HyperDriveError class representing error conditions in the hyperdrive? It might seem that the error message is sufficient, but as you will see in the next section ("Catching Exceptions"), you can selectively handle certain types of exceptions based on their class. Thus, if you want to handle hyperdrive errors with special error-handling code, you would need a separate class for the exceptions.

So, how do you create exception classes? Just like any other class—but be sure to subclass Exception (either directly or indirectly, which means that subclassing any other built-in exception is okay). Thus, writing a custom exception basically amounts to something like this:

```
class SomeCustomException(Exception): pass
```

Really not much work, is it?

Catching Exceptions

As mentioned earlier, the interesting thing about exceptions is that you can handle them (often called "trapping" or "catching" the exceptions). You do this with the try/except statement. Let's say you have created a program that lets the user enter two numbers and then divides one by the other, like this:

```
x = input('Enter the first number: ')
y = input('Enter the second number: ')
print x/y
```

This would work nicely until the user entered zero as the second number:

```
Enter the first number: 10
Enter the second number: 0
Traceback (most recent call last):
  File "exceptions.py", line 3, in ?
    print x/y
ZeroDivisionError: integer division or modulo by zero
```

To catch the exception and perform some error handling (in this case simply printing a more user-friendly error message) you could rewrite the program like this:

```
try:
    x = input('Enter the first number: ')
    y = input('Enter the second number: ')
```

```
    print x/y
except ZeroDivisionError:
    print "The second number can't be zero!"
```

It might seem that a simple if statement checking the value of y would be easier to use, and in this case it might indeed be a better solution. But if you added more divisions to your program, you would need one if statement per division; by using try/except you need only one error handler.

Look, Ma, No Arguments!

If you have caught an exception but you want to raise it again (pass it on, so to speak) you can call raise without any arguments. (You can also supply the exception explicitly if you catch it, as explained in the section "Catching the Object," later in this chapter.)

As an example of how this might be useful, consider a calculator class that has the capability to "muffle" ZeroDivisionErrors. If this behavior is turned on, the calculator prints out an error message instead of letting the exception propagate. This is useful if the calculator is used in an interactive session with a user, but if it is used internally in a program, raising an exception would be better. Therefore the muffling can be turned off. Here is the code for such a class:

```
class MuffledCalculator:
    muffled = 0
    def calc(self, expr):
        try:
            return eval(expr)
        except ZeroDivisionError:
            if self.muffled:
                print 'Division by zero is illegal'
            else:
                raise
```

 NOTE *If division by zero occurs and muffling is turned on, the* calc *method will (implicitly) return* None. *In other words, if you turn on muffling, you should not rely on the return value.*

The following is an example of how this class may be used, both with and without muffling:

```
>>> calculator = MuffledCalculator()
>>> calculator.calc('10/2')
5
>>> calculator.calc('10/0') # No muffling
Traceback (most recent call last):
  File "<stdin>", line 1, in ?
  File "MuffledCalculator.py", line 6, in calc
    return eval(expr)
  File "<string>", line 0, in ?
ZeroDivisionError: integer division or modulo by zero
>>> calculator.muffled = 1
>>> calculator.calc('10/0')
Division by zero is illegal
```

As you can see, when the calculator is not muffled, the ZeroDivisionError is caught but passed on.

More Than One except Clause

If you run the program from the previous section again, and enter a non-numeric value at the prompt, another exception occurs:

```
Enter the first number: 10
Enter the second number: "Hello, world!"
Traceback (most recent call last):
  File "exceptions.py", line 4, in ?
    print x/y
TypeError: unsupported operand type(s) for /: 'int' and 'str'
```

Because the except clause only looked for ZeroDivisionError exceptions, this one slipped through and halted the program. To catch this as well, you can simply add another except clause to the same try/except statement:

```
try:
    x = input('Enter the first number: ')
    y = input('Enter the second number: ')
    print x/y
```

```
except ZeroDivisionError:
    print "The second number can't be zero!"
except TypeError:
    print "That wasn't a number, was it?"
```

This time using an `if` statement would be more difficult. How do you check whether a value can be used in division? There are a number of ways, but by far the best way is, in fact, to simply divide the numbers to see if it works.

Also notice how the exception handling doesn't clutter the original code; adding lots of `if` statements to check for possible error conditions could easily have made the code quite unreadable.

Catching Two Exceptions with One Block

If you want to catch more than one exception type with one block, you can specify them all in a tuple, as follows:

```
try:
    x = input('Enter the first number: ')
    y = input('Enter the second number: ')
    print x/y
except (ZeroDivisionError, TypeError):
    print 'Your numbers were bogus...'
```

In the preceding code, if the user either enters a string or something other than a number, or if the second number is zero, the same error message is printed. Simply printing an error message isn't very helpful, of course. An alternative could be to keep asking for numbers until the division works. I show you how to do that in the section "When All Is Well," later in this chapter.

Note that the parentheses around the exceptions in the except clause are important; a common error is to omit them, in which case you may end up with something other than what you want. For an explanation, see the next section, "Catching the Object."

Catching the Object

If you want access to the exception itself in an except clause, you can use two arguments instead of one. (Note that even when you are catching multiple exceptions, you are only supplying except with one argument—a tuple). This can be useful (for instance) if you want your program to keep running, but you want to log the error somehow (perhaps just printing it out to the user). The following is an example program that prints out the exception (if it occurs), but keeps running:

```
try:
    x = input('Enter the first number: ')
    y = input('Enter the second number: ')
    print x/y
except (ZeroDivisionError, TypeError), e:
    print e
```

The except clause in this little program again catches two types of exceptions, but because you also explicitly catch the object itself, you can print it out so the user can see what happened. (You see a more useful application of this later in this chapter, in the section "When All Is Well.")

A Real Catchall

Even if the program handles several types of exceptions, some may still slip through. For instance, using the same division program, simply try to press Enter at the prompt, without writing anything. You should get a stack trace somewhat like this:

```
Traceback (most recent call last):
  File 'exceptions.py', line 3, in ?
    x = input('Enter the first number: ')
File '<string>', line 0

    ^
SyntaxError: unexpected EOF while parsing
```

This exception got through the try/except statement—and rightly so. You hadn't foreseen that this could happen, and weren't prepared for it. In these cases it is better that the program crash immediately (so you can see what's wrong) than that it simply hide the exception with a try/except statement that isn't meant to catch it.

However, if you *do* want to catch *all* exceptions in a piece of code, you can simply omit the exception class from the except clause:

```
try:
    x = input('Enter the first number: ')
    y = input('Enter the second number: ')
```

```
    print x/y
except:
    print 'Something wrong happened...'
```

Now you can do practically whatever you want:

```
Enter the first number: "This" is *completely* illegal 123
Something wrong happened...
```

CAUTION   *Catching all exceptions like this is risky business because it will hide errors you haven't thought of as well as those you're prepared for. It will also trap attempts by the user to terminate execution by Ctrl-C, attempts by functions you call to terminate by* sys.exit, *and so on.*

When All Is Well

In some cases it can be useful to have a block of code that is executed *unless* something bad happens; as with conditionals and loops, you can add an else clause:

```
try:
    print 'A simple task'
except:
    print 'What? Something went wrong?'
else:
    print 'Ah...It went as planned.'
```

If you run this, you get the following output:

```
A simple task
Ah...It went as planned.
```

With this else clause, you can implement the loop hinted at in the section "Catching Two Exceptions with One Block," earlier in this chapter:

```
while 1:
    try:
        x = input('Enter the first number: ')
        y = input('Enter the second number: ')
        value = x/y
        print 'x/y is', value
    except:
        print 'Invalid input. Please try again.'
    else:
        break
```

Here the loop is only broken when no exception is raised (by the break statement in the else clause). In other words, as long as something wrong happens, the program keeps asking for new input. The following is an example run:

```
Enter the first number: 1
Enter the second number: 0
Invalid input. Please try again.
Enter the first number: 'foo'
Enter the second number: 'bar'
Invalid input. Please try again.
Enter the first number: baz
Invalid input. Please try again.
Enter the first number: 10
Enter the second number: 2
x/y is 5
```

An alternative to using an empty except clause is to catch all exceptions of the Exception class (which will catch all exceptions of any subclass as well). You cannot be 100 percent certain that you'll catch everything then because the code in your try/except statement may be naughty and use the old-fashioned string exceptions, or perhaps create a custom exception that doesn't subclass Exception. However, if you go with the except Exception version, you can use the technique from the section "Catching the Object" earlier in this chapter to print out a more instructive error message in your little division program:

```
while 1:
    try:
        x = input('Enter the first number: ')
        y = input('Enter the second number: ')
        value = x/y
```

```
        print 'x/y is', value
    except Exception, e:
        print 'Invalid input:', e
        print 'Please try again'
    else:
        break
```

The following is a sample run:

```
Enter the first number: 1
Enter the second number: 0
Invalid input: integer division or modulo by zero
Please try again
Enter the first number: 'x'
Enter the second number: 'y'
Invalid input: unsupported operand type(s) for /: 'str' and 'str'
Please try again
Enter the first number: foo
Invalid input: name 'foo' is not defined
Please try again
Enter the first number: 10
Enter the second number: 2
x/y is 5
```

And Finally...

Finally, there is the finally clause. You use it to do housekeeping after a possible exception. It is combined with a try clause (but not an except clause):

```
x = None
try:
    x = 1/0
finally:
    print 'Cleaning up...'
    del x
```

In the preceding, you are *guaranteed* that the finally clause will get executed, no matter what exceptions occur in the try clause. (The reason for initializing x before the try clause is that otherwise it would never get assigned a value because of the ZeroDivisionError. This would lead to an exception when using del on it within the finally clause, which you *wouldn't* catch.)

If you run this, the cleanup comes *before* the program crashes and burns:

```
Cleaning up...
Traceback (most recent call last):
  File "C:\python\div.py", line 4, in ?
    x = 1/0
ZeroDivisionError: integer division or modulo by zero
```

Exceptions and Functions

Exceptions and functions work together quite naturally. If an exception is raised inside a function, and isn't handled there, it propagates ("bubbles up") to the place where the function was called. If it isn't handled there either, it continues propagating until it reaches the main program (the global scope), and if there is no exception handler there, the program halts with an error message and some information about what went wrong (a "stack trace"). Let's take a look at an example:

```
>>> def faulty():
        raise Exception('Something is wrong')
>>> def ignore_exception():
        faulty()
>>> def handle_exception():
        try:
            faulty()
        except:
            print 'Exception handled'
>>> ignore_exception()
Traceback (most recent call last):
  File '<stdin>', line 1, in ?
  File '<stdin>', line 2, in ignore_exception
  File '<stdin>', line 2, in faulty
Exception: Something is wrong
>>> handle_exception()
Exception handled
```

As you can see, the exception raised in faulty propagates through faulty and ignore_exception, and finally causes a stack trace. Similarly, it propagates through to handle_exception, but there it is handled with a try/except statement.

The Zen of Exceptions

Exception handling isn't very complicated. If you know that some part of your code may cause a certain kind of exception, and you don't want your program to terminate with a stack trace if and when that happens, then you add the necessary try/except or try/finally statements to deal with it, as needed.

Sometimes, you can accomplish the same thing with conditional statements as you can with exception handling, but the conditional statements will probably end up being less natural and less readable. On the other hand, some things that might seem like natural applications of if/else may in fact be implemented much better with try/except. Let's take a look at a couple of examples.

Let's say you have a dictionary and you want to print the value stored under a specific key—if it is there. If it isn't there, you don't want to do anything. The code might be something like this:

```
def describePerson(person):
    print 'Description of', person['name']
    print 'Age:', person['age']
    if 'occupation' in person:
        print 'Occupation:', person['occupation']
```

If you supply this function with a dictionary containing the name Throatwobbler Mangrove and the age 42 (but no occupation), you get the following output:

```
Description of Throatwobbler Mangrove
Age: 42
```

If you add the occupation "camper," you get the following output:

```
Description of Throatwobbler Mangrove
Age: 42
Occupation: camper
```

The code is intuitive, but a bit inefficient. It has to look up the key 'occupation' twice—once to see whether the key exists (in the condition) and once to get the value (to print it out). An alternative definition is

```
def describePerson(person):
    print 'Description of', person['name']
    print 'Age:', person['age']
    try: print 'Occupation:', person['occupation']
    except KeyError: pass
```

Here the function simply assumes that the key `'occupation'` is present. If you assume that it normally is, this saves some effort: The value will be fetched and printed—no extra fetch to check whether it is indeed there. If the key doesn't exist, a `KeyError` exception is raised, which is trapped by the except clause.

You may also find `try/except` useful when checking whether an object has a specific attribute or not. Let's say you want to check whether an object has a `write` attribute, for instance. Then you could use code like this:

```
try: obj.write
except AttributeError:
    print 'The object is not writeable'
else:
    print 'The object is writeable'
```

Here the `try` clause simply accesses the attribute without doing anything useful with it. If an `AttributeError` is raised, the object doesn't have the attribute; otherwise, it has the attribute. This is a natural alternative to the `getattr` solution introduced in Chapter 7 (in the section "Interfaces and Introspection"). Which one you prefer is largely a matter of taste. Indeed, `getattr` is internally implemented exactly this way: It tries to access the attribute and catches the `AttributeError` that this attempt may raise.

Note that the gain in efficiency here isn't great. In general (unless your program is having performance problems), you shouldn't worry about that sort of optimization too much. The point is that using a `try/except` statement is in many cases much more natural (more "Pythonic") than `if/else`, and you should get into the habit of using it where you can.

 NOTE *The preference for* try/except *in Python is often explained by the slogan "It's Easier to Ask Forgiveness than Permission."*

A Quick Summary

The main topics covered in this chapter are as follows:

Exception objects. Exceptional situations (such as when an error has occurred) are represented by exception objects. These can be manipulated in several ways, but if ignored they terminate your program.

Warnings. Warnings are similar to exceptions, but will (in general) just print out an error message.

Raising exceptions. You can raise exceptions with the `raise` statement. It accepts either an exception class or an exception instance as its argument. You can also supply two arguments (an exception and an error message). If you call `raise` with no arguments in an `except` clause, it "re-raises" the exception caught by that clause.

Custom exception classes. You can create your own kinds of exceptions by subclassing `Exception`.

Catching exceptions. You catch exceptions with the `except` clause of a `try` statement. If you don't specify a class in the `except` clause, all exceptions are caught. You can specify more than one class by putting them in a tuple. If you give two arguments to `except`, the second is bound to the exception object. You can have several `except` clauses in the same `try`/`except` statement, to react differently to different exceptions.

`else` clauses. You can use an `else` clause in addition to `except`. The `else` clause is executed if no exceptions are raised in the main `try` block.

`finally`. You can use `try`/`finally` if you need to make sure that some code (for example, cleanup code) is executed regardless of whether an exception is raised or not. This code is then put in the `finally` clause. Note that you cannot have both `except` clauses and a `finally` clause in the same `try` statement—but you can put one inside the other.

Exceptions and functions. When you raise an exception inside a function, it propagates to the place where the function was called. (The same goes for methods.)

New Functions in This Chapter

FUNCTION	DESCRIPTION
`warnings.filterwarnings(`*action*`, ...)`	Used to filter out warnings

What Now?

While you might think that the material in this chapter was exceptional (pardon the pun), the next chapter is truly magical. Well, *almost* magical.

#### CHAPTER 9

Magic Methods, Properties, and Iterators

IN PYTHON, some names are spelled in a peculiar manner, with two leading and two trailing underscores. You have already encountered some of these (such as __future__ for instance). This spelling signals that the name has a special significance—you should never invent such names for your own programs. One set of such names that is very prominent in the language is the set of "magic" (or special) method names. If one of your objects implements one of these methods, that method will be called under specific circumstances (exactly which will depend on the name) by Python. There is rarely any need to call these methods directly. This chapter deals with a few important magic methods (most notably the __init__ method and some methods dealing with item access, allowing you to create sequences or mappings of your own). It also tackles two related topics: properties (previously dealt with through magic methods, now handled by the property function), and iterators (which use the magic method __iter__ to enable them to be used in for loops). You'll find a meaty example at the end of the chapter, which uses some of the things you have learned so far to solve a fairly difficult problem.

Before We Begin...

In Python 2.2 a change is taking place in the way Python objects work. I mentioned this briefly in a sidebar in Chapter 7, and I discuss it again later in this chapter (in the section "Subclassing list, dict, and str"). This change has several consequences, most of which won't be important to you as a beginning Python programmer.[1] One thing is worth noting, though: even if you're using Python 2.2, some features (such as properties and the super function) won't work on "old-style" classes. To make your classes "new-style" you should (directly or indirectly) subclass the built-in class (or, actually, type) object. Consider the following two classes:

---

1. For a thorough description of the differences between old-style and new-style classes, see Chapter 8 in Alex Martelli's *Python in a Nutshell* (scheduled for publication in late 2002 by O'Reilly & Associates).

```
class NewStyle(object):
    more_code_here
class OldStyle:
    more_code_here
```

Of these two, NewStyle is a new-style class, while OldStyle is an old-style class.

In this book, I have taken the conservative approach of subclassing object only where it is needed (because object did not exist before version 2.2) but if you do not specifically have to make your programs compatible with old versions of Python, I would advise you to make all your classes new-style, and consistently use features such as the super function (described in the section "Using the super Function," later in this chapter).

Constructors

The first magic method we'll take a look at is the constructor. In case you have never heard the word "constructor" before, it's basically a fancy name for the kind of initializing method I have already used in some of the examples, under the name init. What separates constructors from ordinary methods, however, is that the constructors are called automatically right after an object has been created. Thus, instead of doing what I've been doing up until now,

```
>>> f = FooBar()
>>> f.init()
```

constructors make it possible to simply do this:

```
>>> f = FooBar()
```

Creating constructors in Python is really easy; simply change the init method's name from the plain old init to the magic version, __init__:

```
class FooBar:
    def __init__(self):
        self.somevar = 42

>>> f = FooBar()
>>> f.somevar
42
```

Now, that's pretty nice. But you may wonder what happens if you give the constructor some parameters to work with. Consider the following:

```
class FooBar:
    def __init__(self, value=42):
        self.somevar = value
```

How do you think you could use this? Because the parameter is optional, you certainly could go on like nothing had happened. But what if you wanted to use it (or you hadn't made it optional)? I'm sure you've guessed it, but let me show you anyway:

```
>>> f = FooBar('This is a constructor argument')
>>> f.somevar
'This is a constructor argument'
```

Of all the magic methods in Python, __init__ is quite certainly the one you'll be using the most.

 NOTE *Python has a magic method called __del__, also known as the "destructor." It is called just before the object is destroyed, but because you cannot really know when this happens, I would advise you to stay away from __del__ if at all possible.*

Overriding the Constructor

In Chapter 7, "More Abstraction" you learned about inheritance. Each class may have one or more superclasses, from which they inherit behavior. If a method is called on (or an attribute is accessed) an instance of class B and it is not found, its superclass A would be searched. Consider the following two classes:

```
class A:
    def hello(self):
        print "Hello, I'm A."

class B(A):
    pass
```

The class A defines a method called `hello`, which is inherited by B. Here is an example of how these classes work:

```
>>> a = A()
>>> b = B()
>>> a.hello()
Hello, I'm A.
>>> b.hello()
Hello, I'm A.
```

Because B does not define a `hello` method of its own, the original message is printed when `b.hello` is called. It is possible for B to override this method. Consider, for instance, this modified definition of B:

```
class B(A):
    def hello(self):
        print "Hello, I'm B."
```

Using this definition, `b.hello()` will give a different result:

```
>>> b = B()
>>> b.hello()
Hello, I'm B.
```

Overriding is an important aspect of the inheritance mechanism in general, but you will most likely encounter one particular problem more often when dealing with constructors than when overriding ordinary methods. If you override the constructor of a class, you need to call the constructor of the superclass (the class you inherit from) or risk having an object that isn't properly initialized.

Consider the following class, `Bird`:

```
class Bird:
    def __init__(self):
        self.hungry = 1
    def eat(self):
        if self.hungry:
            print 'Aaaah...'
            self.hungry = 0
        else:
            print 'No, thanks!'
```

This class defines one of the most basic capabilities of all birds: eating. Here is an example of how you might use it:

```
>>> b = Bird()
>>> b.eat()
Aaaah...
>>> b.eat()
No, thanks!
```

As you can see from this example, once the bird has eaten it is no longer hungry. Now consider the subclass SongBird, which adds singing to the repertoire of behaviors:

```
class SongBird(Bird):
    def __init__(self):
        self.sound = 'Squawk!'
    def sing(self):
        print self.sound
```

The SongBird class is just as easy to use as Bird:

```
>>> sb = SongBird()
>>> sb.sing()
Squawk!
```

Because SongBird is a subclass of Bird, it inherits the eat method, but if you try to call it, you'll discover a problem:

```
>>> sb.eat()
Traceback (most recent call last):
  File "<stdin>", line 1, in ?
  File "birds.py", line 6, in eat
    if self.hungry:
AttributeError: SongBird instance has no attribute 'hungry'
```

The exception is quite clear about what's wrong: the SongBird has no attribute called 'hungry'. Why should it? In SongBird the constructor is overridden, and the new constructor doesn't contain any initialization code dealing with the hungry attribute. To rectify the situation, the SongBird constructor must call the constructor of its superclass, Bird, to make sure that the basic initialization takes place. There are basically two ways of doing this: calling the unbound version of the superclass's constructor, and using the new (in Python 2.2) super function. In the next two sections I explain both.

NOTE *Although this discussion centers around overriding constructors, the techniques apply to all methods.*

Calling the Unbound Superclass Constructor

If you find the title of this section a bit intimidating, relax. Calling the constructor of a superclass is, in fact, very easy (and useful). I'll start by giving you the solution to the problem posed at the end of the previous section:

```
class SongBird(Bird):
    def __init__(self):
        Bird.__init__(self)
        self.sound = 'Squawk!'
    def sing(self):
        print self.sound
```

Only one line has been added to the SongBird class, containing the code Bird.__init__(self). Before I explain what this really means, let me just show you that this really works:

```
>>> sb = SongBird()
>>> sb.sing()
Squawk!
>>> sb.eat()
Aaaah...
>>> sb.eat()
No, thanks!
```

But why does this work? When you retrieve a method from an instance, the self argument of the method is automatically *bound* to the instance (a so-called "bound method"). You've seen several examples of that. However, if you retrieve the method directly from the class (such as in Bird.__init__), there is no instance to bind to. Therefore, you are free to supply any self you want to. Such a method is called "unbound," which explains the title of this section.

By supplying the current instance as the self argument to the unbound method, the songbird gets the full treatment from its superclass's constructor (which means that it has its hungry attribute set).

This technique works well in most situations, and knowing how to use unbound methods like this is important. However, if you are using new-style classes, you should use the other alternative: the super function.

Using the super Function

The super function is new in Python 2.2 and only works in new-style classes. It is called with the current class and instance as its arguments, and any method you call on the returned object will be fetched from the superclass rather than the current class. So, instead of using Bird in the SongBird constructor, you can use super(SongBird, self). Also, the __init__ method can be called in a normal (bound) fashion.

The following is an updated version of the bird example. Note that Bird now subclasses object to make the classes new-style:

```
class Bird(object):
    def __init__(self):
        self.hungry = 1
    def eat(self):
        if self.hungry:
            print 'Aaaah...'
            self.hungry = 0
        else:
            print 'No, thanks!'

class SongBird(Bird):
    def __init__(self):
        super(SongBird, self).__init__()
        self.sound = 'Squawk!'
    def sing(self):
        print self.sound
```

This new-style version works just like the old-style one:

```
>>> sb = SongBird()
>>> sb.sing()
Squawk!
>>> sb.eat()
Aaaah...
>>> sb.eat()
No, thanks!
```

Item Access

Although __init__ is by far the most important special method you'll encounter, there are many others that enable you to achieve quite a lot of cool things. One useful set of magic methods described in this section enables you to create objects that behave like sequences or mappings.

The basic sequence and mapping protocol is pretty simple. However, to implement all the functionality of sequences and mappings, there are many magic functions to implement. Luckily, there are some shortcuts, but I'll get to that.

 NOTE *The word* protocol *is often used in Python to describe the rules governing some form of behavior. This is somewhat similar to the notion of* interfaces *mentioned earlier. The protocol says something about which methods you should implement and what those methods should do. Because polymorphism in Python is only based on the object's behavior (and not on its "ancestry," e.g., its class or superclass and so forth) this is an important concept: Where other languages might require an object to belong to a certain class, or to implement a certain interface, Python often simply requires it to follow some given protocol. So, to be a sequence, all you have to do is follow the sequence protocol.*

The Basic Sequence and Mapping Protocol

Sequences and mappings are basically collections of *items*. To implement their basic behavior (protocol), you need two magic methods if your objects are immutable, four if they are mutable:

__len__(*self*): This method should return the number of items contained in the collection. For a sequence, this would simply be the number of elements; for a mapping, it would be the number of key-value pairs. If __len__ returns zero (and you don't implement __nonzero__, which overrides this behavior), the object is treated as *false* in a Boolean context (as with empty lists, tuples, strings, and dictionaries).

__getitem__(*self*, *key*): This should return the value corresponding to the given key. For a sequence, the key should be an integer from zero to *n*–1, where *n* is the length of the sequence; for a mapping, you could really have any kind of keys.

__setitem__(*self*, *key*, *value*): This should store *value* in a manner associated with *key*, so it can later be retrieved with __getitem__. Of course, you define this method only for mutable objects.

__delitem__(*self*, *key*): This is called when someone uses the del statement on a part of the object, and should delete the element associated with *key*. Again, only mutable objects (and not all of them—only those for which you want to let items be removed) should define this method.

Some extra requirements are imposed on these methods:

- For a sequence, if the key is a negative integer, it should be used to count from the end. In other words, treat x[-n] the same as x[len(x)-n].

- If the key is of an inappropriate type (such as a string key used on a sequence) a TypeError may be raised.

- If the index of a sequence is of the right type, but outside its range, an IndexError should be raised.

Let's have a go at it:

```
def checkIndex(key):
    """

    Is the given key an acceptable index?

    To be acceptable, the key should be a non-negative integer. If it
    is not an integer, a TypeError is raised; if it is negative, an
    IndexError is raised (since the sequence is of infinite length).
    """
    if not isinstance(key, (int, long)): raise TypeError
    if key<0: raise IndexError

class ArithmeticSequence:
    def __init__(self, start=0, step=1):
        """

        Initialize the arithmetic sequence.

        start   - the first value in the sequence
        step    - the difference between two adjacent values
        changed - a dictionary of values that have been modified by
                  the user
        """
        self.start = start                    # Store the start value
        self.step = step                      # Store the step value
        self.changed = {}                     # No items have been modified

    def __getitem__(self, key):
        """

        Get an item from the arithmetic sequence.
        """
        checkIndex(key)

        try: return self.changed[key]         # Modified?
        except KeyError:                      # otherwise...
            return self.start + key*self.step # ...calculate the value

    def __setitem__(self, key, value):
        """

        Change an item in the arithmetic sequence.
        """
        checkIndex(key)

        self.changed[key] = value             # Store the changed value
```

This implements an *arithmetic sequence*, a sequence of numbers in which each is greater than the previous one by a constant amount. The first value is given by the constructor parameter start (defaulting to zero), while the step between the values is given by step (defaulting to one). You allow the user to change some of the elements by storing the exceptions to the general rule in a dictionary called changed. If the element hasn't been changed, it is calculated as start+key*step.

Here is an example of how you can use this class:

```
>>> s = ArithmeticSequence(1, 2)
>>> s[4]
9
>>> s[4] = 2
>>> s[4]
2
>>> s[5]
11
```

Note that it is illegal to delete items, which is why I haven't implemented __del__:

```
>>> del s[4]
Traceback (most recent call last):
  File "<stdin>", line 1, in ?
AttributeError: ArithmeticSequence instance has no attribute '__delitem__'
```

Also, the class has no __len__ method because it is of infinite length.

If an illegal type of index is used, a TypeError is raised, and if the index is the correct type but out of range (negative in the last of the following two examples), an IndexError is raised:

```
>>> s["four"]
Traceback (most recent call last):
  File "<stdin>", line 1, in ?
  File "arithseq.py", line 31, in __getitem__
    checkIndex(key)
  File "arithseq.py", line 10, in checkIndex
    if not isinstance(key, int): raise TypeError
TypeError
>>> s[-42]
Traceback (most recent call last):
  File "<stdin>", line 1, in ?
  File "arithseq.py", line 31, in __getitem__
```

```
        checkIndex(key)
  File "arithseq.py", line 11, in checkIndex
    if key<0: raise IndexError
IndexError
```

The index checking is taken care of by a utility function I've written for the purpose, checkIndex.

....

But Isn't That Type Checking?

One thing that might surprise you about the checkIndex function is the use of isinstance (which you should rarely use because type or class checking goes against the grain of Python's polymorphism). I've used it because the language reference explicitly states that the index should be an integer (this includes long integers). And complying with standards is one of the (very few) valid reasons for using type checking.

If you're using Python 2.1 or older, you cannot use int and long in a call to isinstance like this. You have to use IntType and LongType, and you have to use two separate calls to isinstance:

```
from types import IntType, LongType
if not (isinstance(key, IntType) or isinstance(key, LongType)):
    raise TypeError
```
....

> **NOTE**   *You can simulate slicing, too, if you like. When slicing an instance that supports __getitem__, a slice object is supplied as the key. (Slice objects are described in the Python Library Reference (*http://python.org/doc/lib*) in Section 2.1, "Built-in Functions" under the* slice *function.)*

Subclassing list, dict, *and* str

While the four methods of the basic sequence/mapping protocol will get you far, the official language reference also recommends that several other magic and ordinary methods be implemented (see the section "Emulating Container Types" in the Python Reference Manual, http://www.python.org/doc/ref/sequence-types.html), including the __iter__ method, which I describe in the section "Iterators," later in this chapter. Implementing all these methods (to make your objects fully polymorphically equivalent to lists or dictionaries) is a lot of work and hard to get right. If you want custom behavior in only *one* of the operations, it makes no sense that you should have to reimplement all of the others. It's just programmer laziness (also called common sense).

So what should you do? The magic word is "inheritance." Why reimplement all of these things when you can inherit them? The standard library comes with three ready-to-use implementations of the sequence and mapping protocols (see the sidebar), and in Python 2.2, you can subclass the built-in types themselves. (Note that this is mainly useful if your class's behavior is close to the default. If you have to reimplement most of the methods, it might be just as easy to write a new class.)

UserList, UserString, and UserDict

The standard library contains three modules called UserList, UserString, and UserDict, each containing a class with the same name as the module. These classes satisfy all the requirements of the sequence and mapping protocols. UserList and UserString are custom sequences that behave just like ordinary lists and strings, while UserDict is a custom mapping that behaves just like ordinary dictionaries. Until Python 2.2 these were the best option as superclasses when creating your own mappings and sequences. In Python 2.2 the capability to subclass built-in types was added, making these less useful.

So, if you want to implement a sequence type that behaves similarly to the built-in lists, you can simply subclass list.

NOTE *When you subclass a built-in type such as* list, *you are indirectly subclassing* object. *Therefore your class is automatically new-style, which means that such features as the* super *function are available.*

Let's just do a quick example—a list with an access counter:

```
class CounterList(list):
    def __init__(self, *args):
        super(CounterList, self).__init__(*args)
        self.counter = 0
    def __getitem__(self, index):
        self.counter += 1
        return super(CounterList, self).__getitem__(index)
```

The CounterList class relies heavily on the behavior of its subclass (list). Any methods not overridden by CounterList (such as append, extend, index, and so on) may be used directly. In the two methods that *are* overridden, super is used to call the superclass version of the method, only adding the necessary behavior of initializing the counter attribute (in __init__) and updating the counter attribute (in __getitem__).

 NOTE *Overriding __getitem__ is not a bullet-proof way of trapping user access because there are other ways of accessing the list contents, such as through the* pop *method.*

Here is an example of how CounterList may be used:

```
>>> cl = CounterList(range(10))
>>> cl
[0, 1, 2, 3, 4, 5, 6, 7, 8, 9]
>>> cl.reverse()
>>> cl
[9, 8, 7, 6, 5, 4, 3, 2, 1, 0]
>>> del cl[3:6]
>>> cl
[9, 8, 7, 3, 2, 1, 0]
>>> cl.counter
0
>>> cl[4] + cl[2]
9
>>> cl.counter
2
```

As you can see, CounterList works just like list in most respects. However, it has a counter attribute (initially zero), which is incremented each time you access a list element. After performing the addition cl[4] + cl[2], the counter has been incremented twice, to the value 2.

More Magic

There are special (magic) names for many purposes—what I've shown you so far is just a small taste of what is possible. Most of the magic methods available are meant for fairly advanced use, so I won't go into detail here. However, if you are interested, it is possible to emulate numbers, make objects that can be called as if they were functions, influence how objects are compared, and much more.

For more information on which magic methods are available, see the section "Special Method Names" in the Python Reference Manual (http://www.python.org/doc/ref/specialnames.html).

Properties

In Chapter 7, "More Abstraction," I mentioned *accessor methods*. Accessors are simply methods with names such as getHeight and setHeight and are used to retrieve or rebind some attribute (which may be private to the class—see the section "In Private" in Chapter 7). Encapsulating state variables (attributes) like this can be important if certain actions must be taken when accessing the given attribute. For instance, consider the following Rectangle class:

```
class Rectangle:
    def __init__(self):
        self.width = 0
        self.height = 0
    def setSize(self, size):
        self.width, self.height = size
    def getSize(self):
        return self.width, self.height
```

Here is an example of how you can use the class:

```
>>> r = Rectangle()
>>> r.width = 10
>>> r.height = 5
>>> r.getSize()
(10, 5)
>>> r.setSize((150, 100))
>>> r.width
150
```

The getSize and setSize methods are accessors for a fictitious attribute called size—which is simply the tuple consisting of width and height. This code isn't directly wrong, but it is flawed. The programmer using this class shouldn't have to worry about how it is implemented (encapsulation). If you some day wanted to change the implementation so that size was a real attribute and width and height were calculated on the fly, you would have to wrap *them* in accessors, and any programs using the class would also have to be rewritten. The client code (the code using your code) should be able to treat all your attributes in the same manner.

So what is the solution? To wrap all your attributes in accessors? That is a possibility, of course. However, it would be impractical (and kind of silly) if you had lots of simple attributes; you would have to write many accessors that did nothing but retrieve or set these attributes, with no useful action taken. This smells of *copy-paste* programming, or *cookie-cutter code,* which is clearly a bad thing. Luckily, Python can hide your accessors for you, making all of your attributes look alike. Those attributes that are defined through their accessors are often called *properties.*

There are, in fact, two mechanisms for creating properties in Python. I will focus on the most recent one, the property function (introduced in Python 2.2), which only works on new-style classes. Then, I'll give you a short description of how to implement properties with magic methods.

The property Function

Using the property function is delightfully simple. If you have already written a class such as Rectangle from the previous section, you only have to add a single line of code (in addition to subclassing object):

```
class Rectangle(object):
    def __init__(self):
        self.width = 0
        self.height = 0
    def setSize(self, size):
        self.width, self.height = size
    def getSize(self):
        return self.width, self.height
    size = property(getSize, setSize)
```

In this new version of Rectangle, a property is created with the property function with the accessor functions as arguments (the "getter" first, then the "setter"), and this property is stored under the name size. After this, you no longer have to worry about how things are implemented, but can treat width, height, and size the same way:

```
>>> r = Rectangle()
>>> r.width = 10
>>> r.height = 5
>>> r.size
(10, 5)
>>> r.size = 150, 100
>>> r.width
150
```

As you can see, the size attribute is still subject to the calculations in getSize and setSize, but it looks just like a normal attribute.

 TIP *If your properties are behaving oddly, make sure your class subclasses* object *(either directly or indirectly). If it doesn't, the* getter *part of the property will still work, but the* setter *part won't. This can be a bit confusing.*

In fact, the property function may be called with zero, one, three, or four arguments as well. If called with no arguments, the resulting property is neither readable nor writeable. If called with only one argument (a getter method) the property is readable only. The third (optional) argument is a method used to *delete* the attribute (it takes no arguments). The fourth (optional) argument is a documentation string.

Although this section has been short (a testament to the simplicity of the property function) it is very important. The moral is: With new-style classes, you should use property rather than accessors.

__getattr__, __setattr__, *and* Friends

It is possible to implement properties with old-style classes, too, but you have to use magic methods rather than the property function. The following four methods provide all the functionality you need (in old-style classes you only use the last three):

__getattribute__(*self, name*): Automatically called when the attribute *name* is accessed. (Works correctly on new-style classes only.)

__getattr__(*self, name*): Automatically called when the attribute *name* is accessed and the object has no such attribute.

__setattr__(*self, name, value*): Automatically called when an attempt is made to bind the attribute *name* to *value*.

__delattr__(*self, name*): Automatically called when an attempt is made to delete the attribute *name*.

Although a bit trickier (and less efficient) to use than property, these magic methods are quite powerful because you can write code in one of these methods that deals with several properties. (If you have a choice, though, stick with property.)

Here is the `Rectangle` example again, this time with magic methods:

```
class Rectangle:
    def __init__(self):
        self.width = 0
        self.height = 0
    def __setattr__(self, name, value):
        if name == 'size':
            self.width, self.height = value
        else:
            self.__dict__[name] = value
    def __getattr__(self, name):
        if name == 'size':
            return self.width, self.height
        else:
            raise AttributeError
```

As you can see, this version of the class needs to take care of additional administrative details. When considering this code example, it's important to note the following:

- The __setattr__ method is called even if the attribute in question is not size. Therefore, the method must take both cases into consideration: If the attribute is size, the same operation is performed as before; otherwise, the magic attribute __dict__ is used. It contains a dictionary with all the instances attributes. It is used instead of ordinary attribute assignment to avoid having __setattr__ called again (which would cause the program to loop endlessly).

- The __getattr__ method is called only if a normal attribute is not found, which means that if the given name is not size, the attribute does not exist, and the method raises an AttributeError. This is important if you want the class to work correctly with built-in functions such as hasattr and getattr. If the name *is* size, the expression found in the previous implementation is used.

··

Another Trap

Just as there is an "endless loop" trap associated with __setattr__, there is a trap associated with __getattribute__ as well. Because it intercepts *all* attribute accesses (in new-style classes), it will intercept accesses to __dict__ as well! The only safe way to access attributes on self inside __getattribute__ is to use the __getattribute__ method of the superclass (using super).

....

Iterators

In this section I cover only one magic method, __iter__, which is the basis of the iterator protocol.

The Iterator Protocol

To *iterate* means to repeat something several times—what you do with loops. Until now I have only iterated over sequences and dictionaries in for loops, but the truth is that you can iterate over other objects, too: objects that implement the __iter__ method.

The __iter__ method returns an iterator, which is any object with a method called next, which is callable without any arguments. When you call the next method, the iterator should return its "next value." If the method is called, and the iterator has no more values to return, it should raise a StopIteration exception.

What's the point, you say? Why not just use a list? Because it may often be overkill. If you have an function that can compute values one by one, you may need them only one by one—not all at once, stored in a list. If the number of values is large, the list may take up too much memory. But there are other reasons: using iterators is more general, simpler, and more elegant. Let's take a look at an example you couldn't do with a list, simply because the list would have to be of infinite length!

Our "list" is the sequence of Fibonacci numbers. An iterator for these could be the following:

```
class Fibs:
    def __init__(self):
        self.a = 0
        self.b = 1
    def next(self):
        self.a, self.b = self.b, self.a+self.b
        return self.a
    def __iter__(self):
        return self
```

Note that the iterator implements the `__iter__` method, which will, in fact, return the iterator itself. In many cases, you'd put the `__iter__` method in *another* object, which you would use in the `for` loop. That would then return your iterator. It is recommended that iterators implement an `__iter__` method of their own in addition (returning `self`, just as I did here), so they themselves can be used directly in `for` loops.

NOTE *In formal terms, an object that implements the* `__iter__` *method is* iterable *while the object implementing* `next` *is the* iterator.

First, make a `Fibs` object:

```
>>> fibs = Fibs()
```

You can then use it in a `for` loop—for instance to find the smallest Fibonacci number that is greater than 1,000:

```
>>> for f in fibs:
        if f > 1000:
            print f
            break

1597
```

Here the loop stops because I issue a `break` inside it; if I didn't, the `for` loop would never end.

TIP *The built-in function* `iter` *can be used to extract the iterator from an object.*

Making Sequences from Iterators

In addition to iterating over the iterators (which is what you normally do), you can convert them to sequences. In most contexts in which you can use a sequence (except in operations such as indexing or slicing) you can use an iterator instead. One useful example of this is explicitly converting an iterator to a list using the list constructor:

```
>>> class TestIterator:
        value = 0
        def next(self):
            self.value += 1
            if self.value > 10: raise StopIteration
            return self.value
        def __iter__(self):
            return self

>>> ti = TestIterator()
>>> list(ti)
[1, 2, 3, 4, 5, 6, 7, 8, 9, 10]
```

Generators

Generators (also called "simple generators" for historical reasons) are relatively new to Python, and are (along with iterators) perhaps one of the most powerful features to come along for years. Generators are a kind of iterators that are defined with normal function syntax. Exactly how they work is best shown through example. Let's first have a look at how you make them and use them, and then take a peek under the hood afterward.

NOTE *If you are using Python version 2.2, you should remember to put the line*

```
from __future__ import generators
```

at the beginning of any script using generators.

Making a Generator

Making a generator is simple; it's just like making a function. I'm sure you are starting to tire of the good old Fibonacci sequence by now, so let me do something else. I'll make a function that flattens nested lists. The argument is a list that may look something like this:

```
nested = [[1, 2], [3, 4], [5]]
```

In other words, a list of lists. My function should then give me the numbers in order. Here's a solution:

```
def flatten(nested):
    for sublist in nested:
        for element in sublist:
            yield element
```

Most of this function is pretty simple. First it iterates over all the sublists of the supplied nested list; then it iterates over the elements of each sublist in order. If the last line had been print element, for instance, the function would have been easy to understand, right?

So what's new here is the yield statement. Any function that contains a yield statement is called a *generator*. And it's not just a matter of naming; it will behave quite differently from ordinary functions. The difference is that instead of returning *one* value, as you do with return, you can yield *several* values, one at a time. Each time a value is yielded (with yield) the function *freezes*, stops its execution at exactly that point, and waits to be reawakened. When it is, it resumes its execution at the point where it stopped.

I can make use of all the values by iterating over the generator:

```
>>> nested = [[1, 2], [3, 4], [5]]
>>> for num in flatten(nested):
        print num

1
2
3
4
5
```

...or...

```
>>> list(flatten(nested))
[1, 2, 3, 4, 5]
```

A Recursive Generator

The generator I designed in the previous section could only deal with lists nested two levels deep, and to do that it used two for loops. What if you have a set of lists nested arbitrarily deeply? Perhaps you use them to represent some tree structure, for instance. (You can also do that with specific tree classes, but the strategy is the same.) You need a for loop for each level of nesting, but because you don't know how many levels there are, you have to change your solution to be more flexible. It's time to turn to the magic of recursion:

```
def flatten(nested):
    try:
        for sublist in nested:
            for element in flatten(sublist):
                yield element
    except TypeError:
        yield nested
```

When flatten is called, you have two possibilities (as is always the case when dealing with recursion): the *base* case and the *recursive* case. In the base case, the function is told to flatten a single element (for example, a number), in which case the for loop raises a TypeError (because you're trying to iterate over a number), and the generator simply yields the element.

If you are told to flatten a list (or any iterable), however, you have to do some work. You go through all the sublists (some of which may not really be lists) and call flatten on them. Then you yield all the elements of the flattened sublists by using another for loop. It may seem slightly magical, but it works:

```
>>> list(flatten([[[1],2],3,4,[5,[6,7]],8]))
[1, 2, 3, 4, 5, 6, 7, 8]
```

Making It Safer

There is one problem with this, however. If nested is a string-like object (string, Unicode, UserString, and so on), it is a sequence and will not raise TypeError, yet you do *not* want to iterate over it.

NOTE   *There are two main reasons why you shouldn't iterate over string-like objects in the* flatten *function. First, you want to treat string-like objects as atomic values, not as sequences that should be flattened. Second, iterating over them would actually lead to infinite recursion because the first element of a string is another string of length one, and the first element of that string is the string itself(!).*

To deal with this, you must add a test at the beginning of the generator. Trying to concatenate the object with a string and seeing if a TypeError results is the simplest and fastest way to check whether an object is string-like.[2] Here is the generator with the added test:

```
def flatten(nested):
    try:
        # Don't iterate over string-like objects:
        try: nested + ''
        except TypeError: pass
        else: raise TypeError
        for sublist in nested:
            for element in flatten(sublist):
                yield element
    except TypeError:
        yield nested
```

As you can see, if the expression nested + '' raises a TypeError, it is ignored; however, if the expression does *not* raise a TypeError, the else clause of the inner try statement raises a TypeError of its own. This causes the string-like object to be yielded as is (in the outer except clause). Got it?

Here is an example to demonstrate that this version works with strings as well:

---

2.   Thanks to Alex Martelli for pointing out this idiom and the importance of using it here.

```
>>> list(flatten(['foo', ['bar', ['baz']]]))
['foo', 'bar', 'baz']
```

Note that there is no type checking going on here. I don't test whether nested *is* a string (which I could do by using isinstance), only whether it *behaves* like one (it can be concatenated with a string).

Generators in General

If you followed the examples so far, you know how to use generators, more or less. Let me just give you a general description: A generator is a function that contains the keyword yield. When it is called, the generator is "frozen," but can be used in a for loop or other similar contexts, such as the list or tuple functions, tuple unpacking, and so on. Each time a value is requested, the code in the generator is executed until a yield or a return is encountered. A yield means that a value should be yielded. A return means that the generator should stop executing (without yielding anything more; return can only be called without arguments when used inside a generator).

How Do They Work?

Actually, generators consist of two separate components: the *generator-function*, and the *generator-iterator*. The generator-function is what is defined by the def statement containing a yield; the generator-iterator is what this function returns. In less precise terms, these two entities are often treated as one, and collectively called "a generator."

```
>>> def simple_generator():
        yield 1

>>> simple_generator
<function simple_generator at 153b44>
>>> simple_generator()
<generator object at 1510b0>
```

The iterator returned by the generator-function can be used just like any other iterator.

Avoiding Generators

If you have to use a Python version prior to 2.2 generators aren't available. What follows is a simple recipe for simulating them with normal functions.

Starting with the code for the generator, begin by inserting the following line at the beginning of the function body:

```
result = []
```

If the code already uses the name `result` you should come up with another. (Using a more descriptive name may be a good idea anyway.) Then, substitute all lines of the form

```
yield some_expression
```

with

```
result.append(some_expression)
```

Finally, at the end of the function, add

```
return result
```

Although this may not work with all generators, it works with most. (For instance, it fails with infinite generators, which of course can't stuff their values into a list.)

Here is the `flatten` generator rewritten as a plain function:

```
def flatten(nested):
    result = []
    try:
        # Don't iterate over string-like objects:
        try: nested + ''
        except TypeError: pass
        else: raise TypeError
        for sublist in nested:
            for element in flatten(sublist):
                result.append(element)
    except TypeError:
        result.append(nested)
    return result
```

The Eight Queens

Now that you've learned about all this magic, it's time to put it to work. In this section, you see how to use generators to solve a classic programming problem.

Generators are ideal for complex recursive algorithms that gradually build a result. Without generators, these algorithms usually require you to pass a half-built solution around as an extra parameter so that the recursive calls can build on it. With generators, all the recursive calls have to do is `yield` their part. That is what I did with the preceding recursive version of `flatten`, and you can use the exact same strategy to traverse graphs and tree structures.

Graphs and Trees

If you have never heard of graphs and trees before, you ought to learn about them as soon as possible; they are very important concepts in programming and computer science. To find out more, you should probably get a book about computer science, discrete mathematics, data structures, or algorithms. For some concise definitions, you can check out the following Web pages:

```
http://mathworld.wolfram.com/Graph.html
```

```
http://mathworld.wolfram.com/Tree.html
```

```
http://www.nist.gov/dads/HTML/tree.html
```

```
http://www.nist.gov/dads/HTML/graph.html
```

A quick Web search ought to turn up a lot of material.

Backtracking

In some applications, however, you don't get the answer right away; you have to try several alternatives. And not only do you have to try several alternatives on *one* level, but on *every* level in your recursion. To draw a parallel from real life, imagine that you have an important meeting to go to. You're not sure where it is, but you have two doors in front of you, and the meeting room has to be behind one of them. You choose the left, and step through. There you face another two doors. You choose the left, but it turns out to be wrong. So you *backtrack*, and choose the right door, which also turns out to be wrong (excuse the pun). So, you backtrack again, to the point where you started, ready to try the right door.

This strategy of backtracking is useful for solving problems that require you try every combination until you find a solution. Such problems are solved like this:

```
# Pseudocode
for each possibility at level 1:
    for each possibility at level 2:
        ...
                for each possibility at level n:
                    is it viable?
```

To implement this directly with for loops, you have to know how many levels you'll encounter. If that is not possible, you use recursion.

The Problem

This is a much loved computer science puzzle: You have a chessboard, and eight queen pieces to place on it. The only requirement is that none of the queens can capture any of the others; that is, you must place them so that no two queens can capture each other. How do you do this? Where should the queens be placed?

This is a typical backtracking problem: you try one position for the first queen (in the first row), advance to the second, and so on. If you find that you are unable to place a queen, you backtrack to the previous one and try another position. Finally, you either exhaust all possibilities, or find a solution.

In the problem as stated, you are provided with information that there will be only eight queens, but let's assume that there can be any number of queens. (This is more similar to real-world backtracking problems.) How do you solve that? If you want to try to solve it yourself, you should stop reading now because I'm about to give you the solution.

State Representation

To represent a possible solution (or part of it), you simply use a tuple. Each element of the tuple indicates the position of the queen of the corresponding row. So if state[0] == 3, you know that the queen in row one is positioned in column four (we are counting from zero, remember?). When working at one level of recursion (one specific row) you know only what positions the queens above have, so you may have a state tuple whose length is less than eight (or whatever the number of queens is).

NOTE   *I could well have used a list instead of a tuple to represent the state. It's mostly a matter of taste in this case. In general, if the sequence is small and static, tuples are a good choice.*

Finding Conflicts

Let's start by doing some simple abstraction. To find a configuration in which there are no conflicts (where no queen may capture another), you first have to define what a conflict is. And why not define it as a function while you're at it?

The conflict function is given the positions of the queens *so far* (in the form of a state tuple) and determines if a position for the *next* queen generates any new conflicts:

```
def conflict(state, nextX):
    nextY = len(state)
    for i in range(nextY):
        if abs(state[i]-nextX) in (0, nextY-i):
            return 1
    return 0
```

The nextX parameter is the suggested horizontal position (*x* coordinate, or column) of the next queen, and nextY is the vertical position (*y* coordinate, or row) of the next queen. This function does a simple check for each of the previous queens. If the next queen has the same *x* coordinate, or is on the same diagonal as (nextX, nextY), a conflict has occurred, and *true* is returned. If no such conflicts arise, *false* is returned. The tricky part is the following expression:

```
abs(state[i]-nextX) in (0, nextY-i)
```

It simply returns *true* if the horizontal distance between the next queen and the previous one under consideration is either zero (same column) or equal to the vertical distance (on a diagonal)—and *false* otherwise.

The Base Case

The Eight Queens problem can be a bit tricky to implement, but with generators it isn't so bad. If you aren't used to recursion, I wouldn't expect you to come up with this solution by yourself, though. Note also that this solution isn't particularly efficient, so with a very large number of queens, it might be a bit slow.

Let's begin with the base case: the last queen. What would you want her to do? Let's say you want to find all possible solutions; in that case you would expect her to produce (generate) all the positions she could occupy (possibly none) given the positions of the others. You can sketch this out directly:

```
def queens(num, state):
    if len(state) == num-1:
        for pos in range(num):
            if not conflict(state, pos):
                yield pos
```

In human speak this means: If all but one queen have been placed, go through all possible positions for the last one, and return the ones that don't give rise to any conflicts. The num parameter is the number of queens in total, and the state parameter is the tuple of positions for the previous queens. For instance, let's say you have four queens, and that the first three have been given the positions 1, 3, and 0, respectively, as shown in Figure 9-1. (Pay no attention to the white queen at this point.)

Figure 9-1. Placing four queens on a 4×4 board

As you can see in the figure, each queen gets a (horizontal) row, and their positions are numbered across the top (beginning with zero, as is normal in Python):

```
>>> list(queens(4, (1,3,0)))
[2]
```

It works like a charm. Using `list` simply forces the generator to yield all of its values. In this case only one position qualifies. The white queen has been put in this position in Figure 9-1. (Note that color has no special significance and is not part of the program.)

The Recursive Case

Now, let's turn to the recursive part of the solution. When you have your base case covered, the recursive case may correctly assume (by induction) that all results from lower levels (the queens with higher numbers) are correct. So what you have to do is add an `else` clause to the `if` statement in the previous implementation of the `queens` function.

What results do you expect from the recursive call? You want the positions of all the lower queens, right? Let's say they are returned as a tuple. In that case you probably have to change your base case to return a tuple as well (of length one)—but I get to that later.

So, you're supplied with one tuple of positions from "above," and for each legal position of the current queen you are supplied with a tuple of positions from "below." All you have to do to keep things flowing is to yield the result from below with your own position added to the front:

```
    ...
    else:
        for pos in range(num):
            if not conflict(state, pos):
                for result in queens(num, state + (pos,)):
                    yield (pos,) + result
```

The for pos and if not conflict parts of this are identical to what you had before so you can rewrite this a bit to simplify the code. Let's add some default arguments as well:

```
def queens(num=8, state=()):
    for pos in range(num):
        if not conflict(state, pos):
            if len(state) == num-1:
                yield (pos,)
            else:
                for result in queens(num, state + (pos,)):
                    yield (pos,) + result
```

If you find the code hard to understand, you might find it helpful to formulate what it does in your own words. (And, you do remember that the comma in (pos,) is necessary to make it a tuple, and not simply a parenthesized value?)

The queens generator gives you all the solutions (that is, all the legal ways of placing the queens):

```
>>> list(queens(3))
[]
>>> list(queens(4))
[(1, 3, 0, 2), (2, 0, 3, 1)]
>>> for solution in queens(8):
        print solution

(0, 4, 7, 5, 2, 6, 1, 3)
(0, 5, 7, 2, 6, 3, 1, 4)
...
(7, 2, 0, 5, 1, 4, 6, 3)
(7, 3, 0, 2, 5, 1, 6, 4)
>>>
```

If you run queens with eight queens, you see a lot of solutions flashing by. Let's find out how many:

```
>>> len(list(queens(8)))
92
```

Wrapping It Up

Before leaving the queens, let's make the output a bit more understandable. Clear output is always a good thing because it makes it easier to spot bugs, among other things.

```
def prettyprint(solution):
    def line(pos, length=len(solution)):
        return '. ' * (pos) + 'X ' + '. ' * (length-pos-1)
    for pos in solution:
        print line(pos)
```

Note that I've made a little helper function inside `prettyprint`. I put it there because I assumed I wouldn't need it anywhere outside. In the following, I print out a random solution to satisfy myself that it is correct:

```
>>> import random
>>> prettyprint(random.choice(list(queens(8))))
.  .  .  .  .  X  .  .
.  X  .  .  .  .  .  .
.  .  .  .  .  .  X  .
X  .  .  .  .  .  .  .
.  .  .  X  .  .  .  .
.  .  .  .  .  .  .  X
.  .  .  .  X  .  .  .
.  .  X  .  .  .  .  .
```

This "drawing" corresponds to the diagram in Figure 9-2. Fun to play with Python, isn't it?

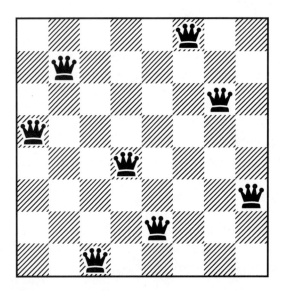

Figure 9-2. One of many possible solutions to the Eight Queens problem

A Quick Summary

A lot of magic here. Let's take stock:

> **New-style classes.** The way classes work in Python is changing. In Python 2.2 new-style classes were introduced, and they provide several new features (for example, they work with super and property while old-style classes do not). To create a new-style class you must subclass object, either directly or indirectly.

> **Magic methods.** Several special methods (with names beginning and ending with double underscores) exist in Python. These methods differ quite a bit in function, but most of them are called automatically by Python under certain circumstances. (For instance, __init__ is called after object creation.)

> **Constructors.** These are common to many object-oriented languages, and you'll probably implement one for almost every class you write. Constructors are named __init__ and are automatically called right after an object is created.

> **Overriding.** A class can override methods (or any other attributes) defined in its superclasses simply by implementing the methods. If the new method needs to call the overridden version it can either call the unbound

version from the superclass directly (old-style classes) or use the super function (new-style classes).

Sequences and mappings. Creating a sequence or mapping of your own requires implementing all the methods of the sequence and mapping protocols, including such magic methods as __getitem__ and __setitem__. By subclassing list (or User List) and dict (or User Dict) you can save a lot of work.

Iterators. An *iterator* is simply an object that has a next method. Iterators can be used to iterate over a set of values. When there are no more values, the next method should raise a StopIteration exception. *Iterable* objects have an __iter__ method, which returns an iterator, and can be used in for loops, just like sequences. Often, an iterator is also iterable, that is, it has an __iter__ method returning the iterator itself.

Generators. A *generator function* (or method) is a function (or method) that contains the keyword yield. When called, the generator function returns a *generator*, which is a special type of iterator.

Eight Queens. The Eight Queens problem is well-known in computer science and lends itself easily to implementation with generators. The goal is to position eight queens on a chess board so that none of the queens is in a position from which she can attack any of the others.

New Functions in This Chapter

FUNCTION	DESCRIPTION
iter(*obj*)	Extracts an iterator from an iterable object.
property(*fget, fset, fdel, doc*)	Returns a property. All arguments are optional.
super(*class, obj*)	Returns a bound instance of *class*'s superclass.

Note that iter and super may be called with other parameters than those described here. For more information see the standard Python documentation (http://python.org/doc).

What Now?

Now you know most of the Python language. So why are there still so many chapters left, you ask? Chapters 14 through 23 show you how to use Python in the real world, and walk you through the implementation of various useful (or at least interesting) projects; and Chapter 13 is an introduction to these projects. But what about the three chapters that follow this one? They are about wonderful resources that aren't part of the Python language itself, but which can be used in your programs. (Okay—not quite true. The files described in Chapter 11 are part of the core language.) In the next chapter, you learn about the invaluable standard modules that ship with Python and that make it easy to write really advanced programs by using code others have written for you. In Chapter 11, you learn how to make your programs communicate with the environment around it in more advanced ways than using the `print` statement, and in Chapter 12, you learn about some third-party packages for creating graphical user interfaces.

CHAPTER 10

Batteries Included

You now know most of the basic Python language. While the core language is powerful in itself, Python gives you more tools to play with. A standard installation includes a set of modules called the *standard library*. You have already seen some of them (math and cmath, containing mathematical functions for real and complex numbers, for instance), but there are many more. This chapter shows you a bit about how modules work, and how to explore them and learn what they have to offer. Then the chapter offers an overview of the standard library with a few selected useful modules.

Modules

You already know about making your own programs (or "scripts") and executing them. You have also seen how you can fetch functions into your programs from external modules using import:

```
>>> import math
>>> math.sin(0)
0.0
```

Let's take a look at how you can write your own modules.

Modules Are Programs

Any Python program can be imported as a module. Let's say you have written the program in Listing 10-1 and stored it in a file called hello.py (the name is important):

Listing 10-1. A Simple Module

```
# hello.py
print "Hello, world!"
```

Where you save it is also important; in the next section you learn more about that, but for now let's say you save it in the directory C:\python (Windows) or

~/python (UNIX). Then you can tell your interpreter where to look for the module by executing the following (using the Windows directory):

```
>>> import sys
>>> sys.path.append('c:/python')
```

NOTE *In the path of the preceding directory I used forward slashes, while on Windows, backslashes are the norm. Both are legal, but because backslashes are used to write certain special characters (such as newlines), the forward slashes are safer. If you use backslashes, you can use either a raw string (r'c:\python') or escape the backslash ('c:\\python').*

What I did here was simply to tell the interpreter that it should look for modules in the directory c:\python in addition to the places it would normally look. After having done this, your can import your module (which is stored in the file c:\python\hello.py, remember?):

```
>>> import hello
Hello, world!
```

NOTE *When you import a module, you may notice that a new file appears—in this case c:\python\hello.pyc. The file with the .pyc extension is a processed ("compiled") Python file that has been translated to a format that Python can handle more efficiently. If you import the same module later, Python will import the .pyc file rather than the .py file, unless the .py file has changed; in that case, a new .pyc file is generated. Deleting the .pyc file causes no harm (as long as there is an equivalent .py file available)—a new one is created when needed.*

As you can see, the code in the module is executed when you import it. However, if you try to import it again, nothing happens:

```
>>> import hello
>>>
```

Why doesn't it work this time? Because modules aren't really meant to *do* things (such as printing text) when they're imported. They are mostly meant to *define* things, such as variables, functions, classes, and so on. And because you only need to define things once, importing a module several times has the same effect as importing it once.

Why Only Once?

The import-only-once behavior is a substantial optimization in most cases, and it can be very important in one special case: if two modules import each other.

In many cases you may write two modules that need to access functions and classes from each other to function properly. For instance, you may have created two modules—clientdb and billing—containing code for a client database and a billing system, respectively. Your client database may contain calls to your billing system (for instance, automatically sending a bill to a client every month), while the billing system probably needs to access functionality from your client database to do the billing correctly.

If each module could be imported several times, you would end up with a problem here. The module clientdb would import billing, which again imports clientdb, which.... You get the picture. You get an endless loop of imports (endless recursion, remember?). However, because nothing happens the second time you import the module, the loop is broken.

If you *insist* on reloading your module, you can use the built-in function reload. It takes a single argument (the module you want to reload) and returns the reloaded module. This may be useful if you have made changes to your module and want those changes reflected in your program while it is running. To reload the simple hello module (containing only a print statement), you would use the following:

```
>>> hello = reload(hello)
Hello, world!
```

Here I assume that hello has already been imported (once). By assigning the result of reload to hello, I have replaced the previous version with the reloaded one. As you can see from the printed greeting, I am really importing the module here.

Modules Are Used to Define Things

So modules are executed the first time they are imported into your program. That seems sort of useful—but not very. What makes them worthwhile is that they (just like classes) keep their scope around afterward. That means that any class or function you define, and any variable you assign a value to, becomes an attribute of the module. This may seem complicated, but in practice it is very simple. Let's say you have written a module like the one in Listing 10-2 and stored it in a file called hello2.py. Also assume that you've put it in a place where the Python interpreter can find it, either using the sys.path trick from the previous section, or the more conventional methods from the section "Making Your Modules Available," which follows.

Listing 10-2. A Simple Module Containing a Function

```
# hello2.py
def hello():
    print "Hello, world!"
```

You can then import it like this:

```
>>> import hello2
```

The module is then executed, which means that the function hello is defined in the scope of the module, which means that you can access the function like this:

```
>>> hello2.hello()
Hello, world!
```

Any name defined in the global scope of the module will be available in the same manner.

....

Why Bother?

Why would you want to do this, you may wonder. Why not just define everything in your main program? The primary reason is *code reuse*. If you put your code in a module, you can use it in more than one of your programs, which means that if you write a good client database and put it in a module called clientdb, you can use it both when billing, when sending out spam (though I hope you won't), and in any program that needs access to your client data. If you hadn't put this in a separate module, you would have to rewrite the code in each one of these programs. So, remember: To make your code reusable, make it modular! (And, yes, this is definitely related to abstraction.)

....

if __name__ == "__main__"

Modules are used to define things such as functions and classes, but every once in a while (quite often, actually) it is useful to add some test code that checks whether things work as they should. For instance, if you wanted to make sure that the `hello` function worked, you might rewrite the module `hello2` into a new one, `hello3`, defined in Listing 10-3.

Listing 10-3. A Simple Module with Some Problematic Test Code

```
# hello3.py
def hello():
    print "Hello, world!"

# A test:
hello()
```

This seems reasonable—if you run this as a normal program, you will see that it works. However, if you import it as a module, to use the `hello` function in another program, the test code is executed, as in the first `hello` module in this chapter:

```
>>> import hello3
Hello, world!
>>> hello3.hello()
Hello, world!
```

This is not what you want. The key to avoiding it is "telling" the module whether it's being run as a program on its own, or being imported into another program. To do that, you need the variable __name__:

```
>>> __name__
'__main__'
>>> hello3.__name__
'hello3'
```

As you can see, in the "main program" (including the interactive prompt of the interpreter), the variable __name__ has the value '__main__', while in an imported module, it is set to the name of that module. Therefore, you can make your module's test code more well-behaved by putting in an if statement, as shown in Listing 10-4.

Listing 10-4. A Module with Conditional Test Code

```
# hello4.py

def hello():
    print "Hello, world!"

def test():
    hello()

if __name__ == '__main__': test()
```

If you run this as a program, the hello function is executed, whereas if you import it, it behaves like a normal module:

```
>>> import hello4
>>> hello4.hello()
Hello, world!
```

As you can see, I've wrapped up the test code in a function called test. I could have put the code directly into the if statement; however, by putting it in a separate test function, you can test the module even if you have imported it into another program:

```
>>> hello4.test()
Hello, world!
```

Making Your Modules Available

In the previous examples, I have altered sys.path, which contains a list of directories (as strings) in which the interpreter should look for modules. However, you don't want to do this in general. The ideal case would be for sys.path to contain the right directory (the one containing your module) to begin with. There are two ways of doing this:

Solution 1: Putting Your Module in the Right Place

Putting your module in the right place (or, rather *a* right place, because there may be several possibilities) is quite easy. It's just a matter of finding out where the Python interpreter looks for modules and then putting your file there.

NOTE *If the Python interpreter on the machine you're work-ing on has been installed by an administrator and you do not have administrator permissions, you may not be able to save your module in any of the directories used by Python. You will then have to skip ahead to solution number 2.*

As you may remember, the list of directories (the so-called "search path") can be found in the path variable in the sys module:

```
>>> import sys, pprint
>>> pprint.pprint(sys.path)
['C:\\Python22\\Tools\\idle',
 'C:\\Python22',
 'C:\\Python22\\DLLs',
 'C:\\Python22\\lib',
 'C:\\Python22\\lib\\lib-tk',
 'C:\\Python22\\lib\\site-packages']
```

TIP *If you have a data structure that is too big to fit on one line, you can use the* pprint *function from the* pprint *module instead of the normal* print *statement.* pprint *is a pretty-printing function, which makes a more intelligent printout.*

This is a relatively standard path for a Python 2.2 installation on Windows. You may not get the exact same result. The point is that each of these strings provides a place to put modules if you want your interpreter to find them. Even though all these will work, the site-packages directory is the best choice because it's meant for this sort of thing. Look through your sys.path and find your site-packages directory, and save the module from Listing 10-4 in it, but give it another name, such as another_hello.py. Then try the following:

```
>>> import another_hello
>>> another_hello.hello()
Hello, world!
```

As long as your module is located in a place like `site-packages`, all your programs will be able to import it.

Solution 2: Telling the Interpreter Where to Look

Solution 1 might not be the right for you for a number of reasons:

- You don't want to clutter the Python interpreter's directories with your own modules.

- You don't have permission to save files in the Python interpreter's directories.

- You would like to keep your modules somewhere else.

The bottom line is that if you place your modules somewhere else, you have to tell the interpreter where to look. As you saw earlier, one way of doing this is to edit `sys.path`, but that is *not* a common way to do it. The standard method is to include your module directory (or directories) in the environment variable `PYTHONPATH`.

Environment Variables

Environment variables are not part of the Python interpreter—they're part of your operating system. Basically, they are like Python variables, but they are set outside the Python interpreter. To find out how to set them you should consult your system documentation, but here are a few pointers:

In **UNIX**, you will probably set environment variables in some shell file that is executed every time you log in. If you use a shell such as `bash`, the file is `.bashrc`. Add the following to that file to add the directory `~/python` to your `PYTHONPATH`:

```
export PYTHONPATH=$PYTHONPATH:~/python
```

Note that multiple directories are separated by colons. Other shells may have a different syntax for this so you should consult the relevant documentation.

In **Windows**, you may be able to edit environment variables from your control panel (in reasonably advanced versions of Windows, such as

Windows XP, 2000, and NT; on older versions such as Windows 98, this does not work, and you would have to edit your autoexec.bat file instead, as covered in the next paragraph). From the Start menu, select Start ➢ Settings ➢ Control Panel. In the control panel, double-click the System icon. In the dialog box that opens, select the Advanced tab and press the Environment Variables button. That brings up another dialog box with two tables: one with your user variables and one with system variables. You are interested in the user variables. If you see PYTHONPATH there already, select it and press Edit, and edit it. Otherwise, press New and use PYTHONPATH as the name; enter your directory as the value. Note that multiple directories are separated by semicolons.

If the previous tactic doesn't work, you can edit the file autoexec.bat, which you can find (assuming that you have a relatively standard setup) in the top directory of the C drive. Open the file in Notepad (or the IDLE text editor, for that matter) and add a line setting the PYTHONPATH. If you want to add the directory C:\python you write the following:

```
set PYTHONPATH=%PYTHONPATH%;C:\python
```

For information on setting up Python in **Mac OS**, see the MacPython pages at http://www.cwi.nl/~jack/macpython.html.

Depending on which operating system you are using, the contents of PYTHONPATH varies (see the sidebar), but basically it's just like sys.path—a list of directories.

TIP *You don't have to change the* sys.path *by using* PYTHONPATH. Path configuration files *provide a useful shortcut to make Python do it for you. A path configuration file is a file with the file name extension* .pth *that contains directories that should be added to* sys.path; *empty lines and lines beginning with* # *are ignored. Files beginning with* import *are executed.*

For a path configuration file to be executed, it must be placed in a directory where it can be found. For Windows, use the directory named by sys.prefix *(probably something like* C:\Python22*) and in UNIX, use the* site-packages *directory. (For more information, look up the* site *module in the Python Library Reference. This module is automatically imported during initialization of the Python interpreter.)*

Naming Your Module

As you may have noticed, the file that contains the code of a module must be given the same name as the module—with an additional `.py` file name extension. In Windows you can use the file name extension `.pyw` instead. You learn more about what that file name extension means in Chapter 12, "Graphical User Interfaces."

Packages

To structure your modules, you can group them into *packages*. A package is basically just another type of module. The interesting thing about them is that they can contain other modules. While a module is stored in a file (with the file name extension `.py`), a package is a directory. To make Python treat it as a package, it must contain a file (module) named `__init__.py`. The contents of this file will be the contents of the package, if you import it as if it were a plain module. For instance, if you have a package named `constants`, and the file `constants/__init__.py` contains the statement `PI = 3.14`, you would be able to do the following:

```
import constants
print constants.PI
```

To put modules inside a package, simply put the module files inside the package directory.

For example, if you wanted a package called `drawing`, which contained one module called `shapes` and one called `colors`, you would need the files and directories (UNIX pathnames) shown in Table 10-1.

Table 10-1. A Simple Package Layout

FILE/DIRECTORY	DESCRIPTION
~/python/	Directory in PYTHONPATH
~/python/drawing/	Package directory (drawing package)
~/python/drawing/__init__.py	Package code ("drawing module")
~/python/drawing/colors.py	colors module
~/python/drawing/shapes.py	shapes module

In Table 10-1 it is assumed that you have placed the directory ~/python in your PYTHONPATH. In Windows, simply replace ~/python with c:\python and reverse the direction of the slashes (to backslashes).

With this setup, the following statements are all legal:

```
import drawing          # (1) Imports the drawing package
import drawing.colors   # (2) Imports the colors module
from drawing import shapes  # (3) Imports the shapes module
```

After the first statement (1), the contents of the __init__ module in drawing would be available; the drawing and colors modules, however, would not be. After the second statement (2), the colors module would be available, but only under its full name, drawing.colors. After the third statement (3), the shapes module would be available, under its short name (that is, simply shapes). Note that these statements are just examples. There is no need, for instance, to import the package itself before importing one of its modules as I have done here. The second statement could very well be executed on its own, as could the third.

Exploring Modules

Before I tackle some of the standard library modules, I'll show you how to explore modules on your own. This is a valuable skill because you will encounter lots of useful modules in your career as a Python programmer, and I couldn't possibly cover all of them here. The current standard library is large enough to warrant books all by itself (and such books have been written)—and it's growing. New modules are added with each release, and often some of the modules undergo slight changes and improvements. Also, you will most certainly find several useful modules on the Web, and being able to grok them quickly and easily will make your programming much more enjoyable.[1]

---

1. The term "grok" is hackerspeak, meaning "to understand fully," taken from Robert A. Heinlein's novel *Stranger in a Strange Land* (Ace Books, reissue 1995).

What's in a Module?

The most direct way of probing a module is to investigate it in the Python interpreter. The first thing you need to do is to import it, of course. Let's say you've
heard rumors about a standard module called copy:

```
>>> import copy
```

No exceptions are raised—so it exists. But what does it do? And what does it
contain?

Using dir

To find out what a module contains, you can use the dir function, which lists all
the attributes of an object (and therefore all functions, classes, variables, and so
on of a module). If you try to print out dir(copy) you get a long list of names. (Go
ahead, try it.) Several of these names begin with an underscore—a hint (by convention) that they aren't meant to be used outside the module. So let's filter them
out with a little list comprehension (check the section on list comprehension in
Chapter 5 if you don't remember how this works):

```
>>> [name for name in dir(copy) if name[0] != '_']
['Error', 'PyStringMap', 'copy', 'deepcopy', 'error']
```

The list comprehension is the list consisting of all the names from dir(copy)
that don't have an underscore as their first letter. This list is much less confusing
than the full listing.

The __all__ Variable

What I did with the little list comprehension in the previous section was to make
a guess about what I was *supposed* to see in the copy module. However, you can
get the correct answer directly from the module itself. In the full dir(copy) list,
you may have noticed the name __all__. This is a variable containing a list similar to the one I created with list comprehension—except that this list has been set
in the module itself. Let's see what it contains:

```
>>> copy.__all__
['Error', 'error', 'copy', 'deepcopy']
```

My guess wasn't so bad after all. I got only one extra name (PyStringMap) that wasn't intended for my use. But where did this __all__ list come from, and why is it really there? The first question is easy to answer. It was set in the copy module, like this (copied directly from copy.py):

```
__all__ = ["Error", "error", "copy", "deepcopy"]
```

So why is it there? It defines the *public interface* of the module. More specifically, it tells the interpreter what it means to import all the names from this module. So if you use

```
from copy import *
```

you get only the four functions listed in the __all__ variable. To import PyStringMap, for instance, you would have to be explicit, either importing copy and using copy.PyStringMap, or using

```
from copy import PyStringMap
```

Setting __all__ like this is actually a useful technique for you to use when writing modules too. Because you may have lots of variables, functions, and classes in your module that other programs might not need or want, it is only polite to filter them out. If you don't set __all__, the names exported in a *starred import* defaults to all global names in the module that don't begin with an underscore.

Getting Help with help

Until now, you've been using your ingenuity and knowledge of various Python functions and special attributes to explore the copy module. The interactive interpreter is a very powerful tool for this sort of exploration because your mastery of the language is the only limit to how deeply you can probe a module. However, there is one standard function (available from Python version 2.2) that gives you all the information you would normally need. That function is called help; let's try it on the copy function:

```
>>> help(copy.copy)
Help on function copy in module copy:

copy(x)
    Shallow copy operation on arbitrary Python objects.

    See the module's __doc__ string for more info.

>>>
```

This is interesting: it tells you that copy takes a single argument x, and that it is a "shallow copy operation." But it also mentions the module's __doc__ string. What's that? You may remember that I mentioned docstrings in Chapter 6, "Abstraction." A docstring is simply a string you write at the beginning of a function to document it. That string is then stored in the function attribute __doc__. As you may understand from the preceding help text, modules may also have docstrings (they are written at the beginning of the module), as may classes (they are written at the beginning of the class).

Actually, the preceding help text was extracted from the copy function's docstring:

```
>>> print copy.copy.__doc__
Shallow copy operation on arbitrary Python objects.

    See the module's __doc__ string for more info.
```

The advantage of using help over just examining the docstring directly like this is that you get more info, such as the function signature (that is, what arguments it takes). Try to call help(copy) (on the module itself) and see what you get. It prints out a lot of information, including a thorough discussion of the difference between copy and deepcopy (essentially that deepcopy(x) makes copies of the values stored in x as attributes and so on, while copy(x) just copies x, binding the attributes of the copy to the same values as those of x).

Documentation

A natural source for information about a module is, of course, its documentation. I've postponed the discussion of documentation because it's often much quicker to just examine the module a bit yourself first. For instance, you may wonder, "What were the arguments to range again?" Instead of searching through a Python book or the standard Python documentation for a description of range, you can just check it directly:

```
>>> print range.__doc__
range([start,] stop[, step]) -> list of integers

Return a list containing an arithmetic progression of integers.
range(i, j) returns [i, i+1, i+2,..., j-1]; start (!) defaults to 0.
When step is given, it specifies the increment (or decrement).
For example, range(4) returns [0, 1, 2, 3].  The end point is omitted!
These are exactly the valid indices for a list of 4 elements.
```

You now have a precise description of the range function, and because you probably had the Python interpreter running already (wondering about functions like this usually happens while you are programming), accessing this information took just a couple of seconds.

However, not every module and every function has a good docstring (although it should), and sometimes you may need a more thorough description of how things work. Most modules you download from the Web have some associated documentation. In my opinion, some of the most useful documentation for learning to program in Python is the Python Library Reference, which describes all of the modules in the standard library. If I want to look up some fact about Python, nine times out of ten, I find it there. The library reference is available for online browsing (at http://www.python.org/doc/lib) or for download, as are several other standard documents (such as the Python Tutorial, or the Python Language Reference). All of the documentation is available from the Python Web site, at http://www.python.org/doc.

Use the Source

The exploration techniques I've discussed so far will probably be enough for most cases. But those of you who wish to truly understand the Python language may want to know things about a module that can't be answered without actually reading the source code. Reading source code is in fact one of the best ways to learn Python—besides coding yourself.

Doing the actual reading shouldn't be much of a problem, but where is the source? Let's say you wanted to read the source code for the standard module copy. Where would you find it? One solution would be to examine sys.path again, and actually look for it yourself, just like the interpreter does. A faster way is to examine the module's __file__ property:

```
>>> print copy.__file__
C:\Python22\lib\copy.py
```

NOTE *If the file name ends with* .pyc, *just use the corresponding file whose name ends with* .py.

There it is! You can open the copy.py file in your code editor (for example, IDLE) and start examining how it works.

CAUTION *When opening a standard library file in a text editor like this you run the risk of accidentally modifying it. Doing so might break it, so when you close the file, make sure that you don't save any changes you might have made.*

Note that some modules don't have any Python source you can read. They may be built into the interpreter (such as the sys module) or they may be written in the C programming language. (The C source code is also available, but that's beyond the scope of this book.)

The Standard Library: A Few Favorites

Chances are that you're beginning to wonder what the title of this chapter means. The phrase was originally coined by Frank Stajano and refers to Python's copious standard library.[2] When you install Python you get lots of useful modules (the batteries) for "free." Because there are so many ways of getting more information about these modules (as explained in the first part of this chapter) I won't include a full reference here (which would take up far too much space anyway), but I'll describe a few of my favorite standard modules to whet your appetite for exploration. You encounter more standard modules in the project chapters (Chapters 14 through 23). The module descriptions are not complete but highlight some of the interesting features of each module.

---

2.   First use found in the article at http://www.uk.research.att.com/~fms/ipc7/tr-1998-9.html.

sys

This module gives you access to variables and functions that are closely linked to the Python interpreter. Some of these are shown in Table 10-2.

Table 10-2. Some Important Functions and Variables in the sys *Module*

FUNCTION/VARIABLE	DESCRIPTION
argv	The command-line arguments, including the script name
exit([*arg*])	Exits the current program, optionally with a given return value or error message
modules	A dictionary mapping module names to loaded modules
path	A list of directory names where modules can be found
platform	Contains a platform identifier such as sunos5 or win32
stdin	Standard input stream—a file-like object
stdout	Standard output stream—a file-like object
stderr	Standard error stream—a file-like object

The variable sys.argv contains the arguments passed to the Python interpreter, including the script name.

The function sys.exit exits the current program. (If called within a try/finally block, the finally clause is executed.) You can supply an integer to indicate whether the program succeeded or not—a UNIX convention. You'll probably be fine in most cases if you rely on the default (which is zero, indicating success). Alternatively, you can supply a string, which is used as an error message and can be very userful for a user trying to figure out why the program halted; then, the program exits with that error message and a code indicating failure.

The mapping sys.modules maps module names to actual modules. It only applies to currently imported modules.

The module variable sys.path was discussed earlier in this chapter. It's a list of strings, in which each string is the name of a directory where the interpreter will look for modules when an import statement is executed.

The module variable sys.platform (a string) is simply the name of the "platform" the interpreter is running on. This may be either a name indicating an operating system (such as sunos5 or win32) or it may indicate some other kind of platform, such as a Java virtual machine (for example, java1.4.0) if you're running Jython.

The module variables sys.stdin, sys.stdout, and sys.stderr are file-like *stream* objects. They represent the standard UNIX concepts of standard input, standard output, and standard error. To put it simply, sys.stdin is where Python gets its input (used in the functions input and raw_input for instance), and sys.stdout is where it prints to. You learn more about files (and these three streams) in Chapter 11, "Files and Stuff."

EXAMPLE

Printing the arguments in reverse order. When you call a Python script from the command line, you may add some arguments after it—the so-called *command-line arguments.* These will then be placed in the list sys.argv, with the name of the Python script as sys.argv[0]. Printing these out in reverse order is pretty simple, as you can see in Listing 10-5.

Listing 10-5. Reversing and Printing Command-Line Arguments

```
# reverseargs.py
import sys
args = sys.argv[1:]
args.reverse()
print ' '.join(args)
```

As you can see, I make a copy of sys.argv. You can modify the original, but in general it's safer not to because other parts of the program may also rely on sys.argv containing the original arguments. Notice also that I skip the first element of sys.argv—the name of the script. I reverse the list with args.reverse(), but I can't print the result of that operation. It is an in-place modification that returns None. Finally, to make the output prettier, I use the join string method. Let's try the result (assuming a UNIX shell here, but it will work equally well at an MS-DOS prompt, for instance):

```
$ python reverseargs.py this is a test
test a is this
```

os

The os module gives you access to several operating system services. The os module is extensive, and only a few of the most useful functions and variables are described in Table 10-3. In addition to these, os and its submodule os.path contain several functions to examine, construct, and remove directories and files. For more information about this functionality, see the standard library documentation.

Table 10-3. Some Important Functions and Variables in the os *Module*

FUNCTION/VARIABLE	DESCRIPTION
environ	Mapping with environment variables
system(*command*)	Executes an OS command in a subshell
sep	Separator used in paths
pathsep	Separator to separate paths
linesep	Line separator ('\n', '\r', or '\r\n')

The mapping os.environ contains environment variables described earlier in this chapter. For instance, to access the environment variable PYTHONPATH, you would use the expression os.environ['PYTHONPATH']. This mapping can also be used to change environment variables, although not all platforms support this.

The function os.system is used to run external programs. There are other functions for executing external programs, including execv, which exits the Python interpreter, yielding control to the executed program, and popen, which creates a file-like connection to the program. For more information about these functions, consult the standard library documentation.

The module variable os.sep is a separator used in pathnames. The standard separator in UNIX is '/', the standard in Windows is '\\' (the Python syntax for a single backslash), and in Mac OS, it is ':'. (On some platforms, os.altsep contains an alternate path separator, such as '/' in Windows.)

You use os.pathsep when grouping several paths, as in PYTHONPATH. The pathsep is used to separate the pathnames: ':' in UNIX, ';' in Windows, and '::' in Mac OS.

The module variable os.linesep is the line separator string used in text files. In UNIX this is a single newline character ('\n'), in Mac OS it's a single carriage return character ('\r'), and in Windows it's the combination of a carriage return and a newline ('\r\n').

EXAMPLE

Starting a Web browser. The `system` command can be used to execute any external program, which is very useful in environments such as UNIX where you can execute programs (or *commands*) from the command line to list the contents of a directory, send e-mail, and so on. But it can be useful for starting programs with graphical user interfaces, too—such as a Web browser. In UNIX, you can do the following (provided that you have a browser at `/local/bin/netscape`):

```
os.system('/local/bin/netscape')
```

A Windows version would be (again use the path of a browser you have installed):

```
os.system(r'c:\"Program Files"\Netscape\Communicator\Program\netscape.exe')
```

Note that I've been careful about enclosing `Program Files` in quotes; otherwise DOS (which handles the command) balks at the whitespace. Note also that you have to use backslashes here because DOS gets confused by forward slashes. If you run this, you will notice that the browser tries to open a Web site named `Files"\Netscape\...`—the part of the command after the whitespace. Also, if you try to run this from IDLE, a DOS window appears, but the browser doesn't start until you close that DOS window. All in all, not exactly ideal behavior.

Another function that suits the job better is the Windows-specific function `os.startfile`:

```
os.startfile(r'c:\Program Files\Netscape\Communicator\Program\netscape.exe')
```

As you can see, `os.startfile` accepts a plain path, even if it contains whitespace. (That is, don't enclose "Program Files" in quotes as in the `os.system` example.)

Note that in Windows, your Python program keeps on running after the external program has been started by `os.system` (or `os.startfile`) whereas in UNIX, your Python program waits for the `os.system` command to finish.

A Better Solution: `webbrowser`

The `os.system` function is useful for a lot of things, but for the specific task of launching a Web browser there's an even better solution: the `webbrowser` module. It contains a function called `open` that lets you automatically launch a Web browser to open the given URL. For instance, if you want your program to open the Python Web site in a Web browser (either starting a new browser or using one that is already running), you simply use

```
import webbrowser
webbrowser.open('http://www.python.org')
```

and the page should pop up. Pretty nifty, huh?

....

fileinput

You learn a lot about reading from and writing to files in Chapter 11, "Files and Stuff," but here is a sneak preview. The fileinput module enables you to easily iterate over all the lines in a series of text files. If you call your script like this (assuming a UNIX command-line)

```
$ python some_script.py file1.txt file2.txt file3.txt
```

you will be able to iterate over the lines of file1.txt through file3.txt in turn. You can also iterate over lines supplied to standard input (sys.stdin, remember?), for instance in a UNIX pipe (using the standard UNIX command cat):

```
$ cat file.txt | python some_script.py
```

If you use fileinput, this way of calling your script (with cat in a UNIX pipe) works just as well as the previous one (supplying the file names as command-line arguments to your script). The most important functions of the fileinput module are described in Table 10-4.

Table 10-4. Some Important Functions in the fileinput *Module*

FUNCTION	DESCRIPTION
input(*[files[, inplace[, backup]]]*)	Facilitates iteration over lines in multiple input streams
filename()	Returns name of current file
lineno()	Returns current (cumulative) line number
filelineno()	Returns line number within current file
isfirstline()	Checks whether current line is first in file
isstdin()	Checks whether last line was from sys.stdin
nextfile()	Closes current file and moves to the next
close()	Closes the sequence

The function `fileinput.input` is the most important of the functions. It returns an object that you can iterate over in a for loop. If you don't want the default behavior (in which `fileinput` finds out which files to iterate over) you can supply one or more file names to this function. You can also set the `inplace` parameter to a *true* value (`inplace=1`) to enable in-place processing. For each line you access, you'll have to print out a replacement, which will be put back into the current input file. The optional `backup` argument gives a file name extension to a backup file created from the original file when you do in-place processing.

The function `fileinput.filename` returns the file name of the file you are currently in (that is, the file that contains the line you are currently processing).

The function `fileinput.lineno` returns the number of the current line. This count is cumulative so that when you are finished with one file and begin processing the next, the line number is not reset but starts at one more than the last line number in the previous file.

The function `fileinput.filelineno` returns the number of the current line within the current file. Each time you are finished with one file and begin processing the next, the file line number is reset, and restarts at 1.

The function `fileinput.isfirstline` returns a *true* value if the current line is the first line of the current file—and a *false* value otherwise.

The function `fileinput.isstdin` returns a *true* value if the current file is `sys.stdin` and *false* otherwise.

The function `fileinput.nextfile` closes the current file and skips to the next one. The lines you skip do not count against the line count. This can be useful if you know that you are finished with the current file—for instance if each file contains words in sorted order, and you are looking for a specific word. If you have passed the word's position in the sorted order, you can safely skip to the next file.

The function `fileinput.close` closes the entire chain of files and finishes the iteration.

EXAMPLE

Numbering the lines of a Python script. Let's say you have written a Python script and you want to number the lines. Because you want the program to keep working after you've done this, you have to add the line numbers in comments to the right of each line. To line them up you can use string formatting. Let's allow each program line to get 40 characters maximum and add the comment after that. The program in Listing 10-6 shows a simple way of doing this with `fileinput` and the `inplace` parameter.

Listing 10-6. Adding Line Numbers to a Python Script

```
# numberlines.py

import fileinput

for line in fileinput.input(inplace=1):
    line = line.rstrip()
    num  = fileinput.lineno()
    print '%-40s # %2i' % (line, num)
```

If you run this program on itself, like this

```
$ python numberlines.py numberlines.py
```

you end up with the program in Listing 10-7. Note that the program itself has been modified, and that if you run it like this several times, you end up with multiple numbers on each line. Recall that rstrip is a string method that returns a copy of a string, where all the whitespace on the right has been removed (see the section "String Methods" in Chapter 3 and Table B-6 in Appendix B).

Listing 10-7. The Line Numbering Program with Line Numbers Added

```
# numberlines.py                          # 1
                                          # 2
import fileinput                          # 3
                                          # 4
for line in fileinput.input(inplace=1):   # 5
    line = line.rstrip()                  # 6
    num  = fileinput.lineno()             # 7
    print '%-40s # %2i' % (line, num)     # 8
```

 CAUTION   *Be careful about using the* inplace *parameter—it's an easy way to ruin a file. You should test your program carefully without setting* inplace *(this will simply print out the result), making sure the program works before you let it modify your files.*

For another example using `fileinput`, see the section about the `random` module, later in this chapter.

time

The `time` module contains functions for, among other things, getting the current time, manipulating times and dates, and reading dates from strings and formatting dates as strings. Dates can be represented as either a real number (the seconds since 0 hours, January 1 in the "epoch," a platform-dependent year; for UNIX it's 1970), or a tuple containing nine integers. These integers are explained in Table 10-5. For instance, the tuple

```
(2002, 1, 21, 12, 2, 56, 0, 21, 0)
```

represents January 21, 2002, at 12:02:56, which is a Monday, and the 21st day of the year. (No daylight savings.)

Table 10-5. The Fields of Python Date Tuples

INDEX	FIELD	VALUE
0	Year	e.g., 2000, 2001, and so on
1	Month	In the range 1–12
2	Day	In the range 1–31
3	Hour	In the range 0–23
4	Minute	In the range 0–59
5	Second	In the range 0–61
6	Weekday	In the range 0–6, where Monday is 0
7	Julian day	In the range 1–366
8	Daylight Savings	0, 1, or –1

Some of these values need some explaining: The range for seconds is 0–61 to account for leap seconds and double leap seconds. The Daylight Savings number is a Boolean value (*true* or *false*), but if you use –1, `mktime` (a function that converts such a tuple to a timestamp measured in seconds since the epoch) will probably get it right. Some of the most important functions in the `time` module are described in Table 10-6.

Table 10-6. Some Important Functions in the time *Module*

FUNCTION	DESCRIPTION
asctime([*tuple*])	Converts time tuple to a string
localtime([*secs*])	Converts seconds to a date tuple, local time
mktime(*tuple*)	Converts time tuple to local time
sleep(*secs*)	Sleeps (does nothing) for *secs* seconds
strptime(*string[, format]*)	Parses a string into a time tuple
time()	Current time (seconds since the epoch, UTC)

The function time.asctime formats the current time as a string, such as

```
>>> time.asctime()
'Fri Dec 21 05:41:27 2001'
```

You can also supply a date tuple (such as those created by localtime) if you don't want the current time. (For more elaborate formatting, see the strftime function, described in the standard documentation.)

The function time.localtime converts a real number (seconds since epoch) to a date tuple, local time. If you want universal time, use gmtime instead.

The function time.mktime converts a date tuple to the time since epoch in seconds; it is the inverse of localtime.

The function time.sleep makes the interpreter wait for a given number of seconds.

The function time.strptime converts a string of the format returned by asctime to a date tuple. (The optional format argument follows the same rules as those for strftime. See the standard documentation.) Note that strptime is not available in the Windows version of Python.

The function time.time returns the current (universal) time as seconds since the epoch. Even though the epoch may vary from platform to platform, you can reliably time something by storing the result of time before and after the event (such as a function call) and then computing the difference.

For an example of these functions, see the next section about the random module.

....

Other Time Functions

The functions shown in Table 10-6 are just a selection of those available from the time module. Most of the functions in that module perform tasks similar to or related to those described in this section. If you need something not covered by the functions described here, you should take a look at the section about the `time` module in the standard library reference (http://www.python.org/doc/lib/module-time.html); chances are you may find exactly what you are looking for.

random

The `random` module contains functions that return random numbers, which can be useful for simulations or any program that generates random output.

 NOTE *Actually, the numbers generated are* pseudo-random. *That means that while they appear completely random, there is a predictable system that underlies them. But because the module is so good at pretending to be random, you probably won't ever have to worry about this (unless you want to use these numbers for strong-cryptography purposes, in which case they may not be "strong" enough to withstand determined attack—but if you're into strong cryptography, you surely don't need me to explain such elementary issues).*

Some important functions in this module are shown in Table 10-7.

Table 10-7. Some Important Functions in the random *Module*

FUNCTION	DESCRIPTION
random()	Returns a random real number n such that $0 \leqslant n < 1$
uniform(*a, b*)	Returns a random real number n such that $a \leqslant n < b$
randrange(*[start], stop, [step]*)	Returns a random number from range(*start, stop, step*)
choice(*seq*)	Returns a random element from the sequence *seq*
shuffle(*seq[, random]*)	Shuffles the sequence *seq* in place

The function `random.random` is the base of the other functions; it simply returns a pseudo-random number n such that $0 \leqslant n < 1$. Unless this is exactly what you need, you should probably use one of the other functions, which offer extra functionality.

The function random.uniform, when supplied with two numerical parameters *a* and *b*, returns a random (uniformly distributed) real number *n* such that $a \leq n < b$. So, for instance, if you want a random angle, you could use uniform(0,360).

The function random.randrange is the standard function for generating a random integer in the range you would get by calling range with the same arguments. For instance, to get a random number in the range from 1 to 10 (inclusive), you would use randrange(1,11) (or, alternatively, randrange(10)+1), and if you want a random odd positive integer lower than 20, you would use randrange(1,20,2).

The function random.choice chooses (uniformly) a random element from a given sequence.

The function random.shuffle shuffles the elements of a (mutable) sequence randomly, such that every possible ordering is equally likely.

 NOTE *For the statistically inclined there are other functions like* uniform *that return random numbers sampled according to various other distributions, such as betavariate, exponential, Gaussian, and several others.*

EXAMPLES

Generating a random date in a given range. In the following examples, I use several of the functions from the time module described previously. First, let's get the real numbers representing the limits of the time interval (the year 2002). You do that by expressing the date as a time tuple (using -1 for day of the week, day of the year, and daylight savings, making Python calculate that for itself) and calling mktime on these tuples:

```
from random import *
from time import *
date1 = (2002, 1, 1, 0, 0, 0, -1, -1, -1)
time1 = mktime(date1)
date2 = (2003, 1, 1, 0, 0, 0, -1, -1, -1)
time2 = mktime(date2)
```

Then you generate a random number uniformly in this range (the upper limit excluded):

```
>>> random_time = uniform(time1, time2)
```

Then, you simply convert this number back to a legible date:

```
>>> print asctime(localtime(random_time))
Mon Jun 24 21:35:19 2002
```

Creating an electronic die-throwing machine. For this example, let's ask the user how many dice to throw, and how many sides each one should have. The die-throwing mechanism is implemented with randrange and a for loop:

```
from random import randrange
num   = input('How many dice? ')
sides = input('How many sides per die? ')
sum = 0
for i in range(num): sum += randrange(sides) + 1
print 'The result is', sum
```

If you put this in a script file and run it, you get an interaction something like the following:

```
How many dice? 3
How many sides per die? 6
The result is 10
```

Creating a fortune cookie program. Assume that you have made a text file in which each line of text contains a fortune. Then you can use the fileinput module described earlier to put the fortunes in a list, and then select one randomly:

```
# fortune.py
import fileinput, random
fortunes = []
for line in fileinput.input():
    fortunes.append(line)
print random.choice(fortunes)
```

In UNIX, you could test this on the standard dictionary file /usr/dict/words to get a random word:

```
$ python fortune.py /usr/dict/words
dodge
```

Creating an electronic deck of cards. You want your program to deal you cards, one at a time, each time you press Enter on your keyboard. Also, you want to make sure that you don't get the same card more than once. First, you make a "deck of cards"—a list of strings:

```
>>> values = range(1, 11) + 'Jack Queen King'.split()
>>> suits = 'diamonds clubs hearts spades'.split()
>>> deck = ['%s of %s' % (v, s) for v in values for s in suits]
```

The deck you just created isn't very suitable for a game of cards. Let's just peek at some of the cards:

```
>>> from pprint import pprint
>>> pprint(deck[:12])
['1 of diamonds',
 '1 of clubs',
 '1 of hearts',
 '1 of spades',
 '2 of diamonds',
 '2 of clubs',
 '2 of hearts',
 '2 of spades',
 '3 of diamonds',
 '3 of clubs',
 '3 of hearts',
 '3 of spades']
```

A bit too ordered, isn't it? That's easy to fix:

```
>>> from random import shuffle
>>> shuffle(deck)
>>> pprint(deck[:12])
['3 of spades',
 '2 of diamonds',
 '5 of diamonds',
 '6 of spades',
 '8 of diamonds',
 '1 of clubs',
 '5 of hearts',
 'Queen of diamonds',
 'Queen of hearts',
 'King of hearts',
 'Jack of diamonds',
 'Queen of clubs']
```

Note that I've just printed the 12 first cards here, to save some space. Feel free to take a look at the whole deck yourself.

Finally, to get Python to deal you a card each time you press Enter on your keyboard, until there are no more cards, you simply create a little while loop. Assuming that you put the code needed to create the deck into a program file, you could simply add the following at the end:

```
while deck: raw_input(deck.pop())
```

 NOTE *If you try the* while *loop shown here in the interactive interpreter, you'll notice that an empty string gets printed out every time you press Enter because* raw_input *returns what you write (which is nothing), and that will get printed. In a normal program, this return value from* raw_input *is simply ignored. To have it "ignored" interactively, too, just assign the result of* raw_input *to some variable you won't look at again and name it something like* ignore.

shelve

In the next chapter you learn how to store data in files, but if you want a really simple storage solution, the shelve module can do most of the work for you. All you have to do is supply it with a file name. The only function of interest in shelve is open. When called (with a file name) it returns a Shelf object, which you can use to store things. Just treat it as a normal dictionary (except that the keys must be strings), and when you're done (and want things saved to disk) you call its close method.

A Potential Trap

It is important to realize that the object returned by shelve.open is not an ordinary mapping, as the following example demonstrates:

```
>>> import shelve
>>> s = shelve.open('test.dat')
>>> s['x'] = ['a', 'b', 'c']
>>> s['x'].append('d')
>>> s['x']
['a', 'b', 'c']
```

Where did the 'd' go?

The explanation is simple: When you look up an element in a shelf object, the object is reconstructed from its stored version; and when you assign an element to a key, it is stored. What happened in the preceding example was the following:

1.   The list ['a', 'b', 'c'] was stored in s under the key 'x'.

2.   The stored representation was retrieved, a new list was constructed from it, and 'd' was appended to the copy. This modified version was *not* stored!

3.   Finally, the original is retrieved again—without the 'd'.

To correctly modify an object that is stored using the shelve module you must bind a temporary variable to the retrieved copy, and then store the copy again after it has been modified:

```
>>> temp = s['x']
>>> temp.append('d')
>>> s['x'] = temp
>>> s['x']
['a', 'b', 'c', 'd']
```

Thanks to Luther Blissett for pointing this out.

EXAMPLE

Listing 10-8 shows a simple database application that uses the shelve module.

Listing 10-8. A Simple Database Application

```
# database.py
import sys, shelve

def store_person(db):
    """
    Query user for data and store it in the shelf object
    """
    pid = raw_input('Enter unique ID number: ')
    person = {}
    person['name']  = raw_input('Enter name: ')
```

```python
        person['age']   = raw_input('Enter age: ')
        person['phone'] = raw_input('Enter phone number: ')

        db[pid] = person

def lookup_person(db):
    """
    Query user for ID and desired field, and fetch the corresponding data from
    the shelf object
    """
    pid = raw_input('Enter ID number: ')
    field = raw_input('What would you like to know? (name, age, phone)  ')
    field = field.strip().lower()
    print field.capitalize() + ':', \
            db[pid][field]

def print_help():
    print 'The available commands are:'
    print 'store: Stores information about a person'
    print 'lookup: Looks up a person from ID number'
    print 'quit: Save changes and exit'
    print '?: Prints this message'

def enter_command():
    cmd = raw_input('Enter command (? for help): ')
    cmd = cmd.strip().lower()
    return cmd

def main():
    database = shelve.open('c:\\database.dat')
    try:
        while 1:
            cmd = enter_command()
            if   cmd == 'store':
                store_person(database)
            elif cmd == 'lookup':
                lookup_person(database)
            elif cmd == '?':
                print_help()
            elif cmd == 'quit':
                return
```

```
finally:
    database.close()

if __name__ == '__main__': main()
```

 CAUTION *As you can see, the program specifies the file name* C:\database.dat. *If you, by any chance, have a database by that name that the* shelve *module can use, it will—and that database will be modified. So make sure that you use a file name for your database that isn't in use already. After running this program, the proper file appears.*

The program shown in Listing 10-8 has several interesting features:

- I have wrapped everything in functions to make the program more structured. (A possible improvement is to group those functions as the methods of a class.)

- I have put the main program in the main function, which is called only if __name__ == '__main__'. That means that you can import this as a module and then call the main function from another program.

- I open a database ("shelf") in the main function, and then pass it as a parameter to the other functions that need it. I could have used a global variable, too, because this program is so small, but it's better to avoid global variables in most cases, unless you have a reason to use them.

- After reading in some values, I make a modified version by calling strip and lower on them because if a supplied key is to match one stored in the database, the two must be *exactly* alike. If you always use strip and lower on what the user enters, you can allow him or her to be sloppy about using uppercase or lowercase letters and additional whitespace. Also, note that I've used capitalize when printing the field name.

- I have used try and finally to ensure that the database is closed properly. You never know when something might go wrong (and you get an exception), and if the program terminates without closing the database properly, you end up with a corrupt database file that is essentially useless. By using try and finally, you avoid that.

So, let's take this database out for a spin. Here is the interaction between the program and me:

```
Enter command (? for help): ?
The available commands are:
store  : Stores information about a person
lookup : Looks up a person from ID number
quit   : Save changes and exit
?      : Prints this message
Enter command (? for help): store
Enter unique ID number: 001
Enter name: Mr. Gumby
Enter age: 42
Enter phone number: 555-1234
Enter command (? for help): lookup
Enter ID number: 001
What would you like to know? (name, age, phone) phone
Phone: 555-1234
Enter command (? for help): quit
```

This interaction isn't terribly interesting. I could have done exactly the same thing with an ordinary dictionary instead of the shelf object. But now that I've quit the program, let's see what happens when I restart it—perhaps the following day?

```
Enter command (? for help): lookup
Enter ID number: 001
What would you like to know? (name, age, phone) name
Name: Mr. Gumby
Enter command (? for help): quit
```

As you can see, the program reads in the file I created the first time, and Mr. Gumby is still there!

Feel free to experiment with this program, and see if you can extend its functionality and improve its user-friendliness. Perhaps you can think of a version that you have use for yourself? How about a database of your record collection? Or a database to help you keep track of which friends have borrowed which of your books? (I know I could use that last one.)

re

The re module contains support for *regular expressions.* If you've heard about regular expressions before, you probably know how powerful they are; if you haven't, prepare to be amazed.

You should note, however, that mastering regular expressions may be a bit tricky at first. (Okay, very tricky, actually.) The key is to learn about them a little bit at a time—just look up (in the documentation) the parts you need for a specific task. There is no point in memorizing it all up front. This section describes the main features of the re module and regular expressions, and enables you to get started.

TIP *In addition to the standard documentation, Andrew Kuchling's "Regular Expression HOWTO"* (http://py-howto.sourceforge.net/regex) *is a useful source of information on regular expressions in Python.*

What Is a Regular Expression?

A regular expression (also called a *regexp*) is a pattern that can match a piece of text. The simplest form of regular expression is just a plain string, which matches itself. In other words, the regular expression 'python' matches the string 'python'. You can use this matching behavior for such things as searching for patterns in a text, for replacing certain patterns with some computed values, or for splitting a text into pieces.

The Wildcard

A regexp can match more than one string, and we create such a pattern by using some special characters. For instance, the period character ("dot") matches any character (except a newline), so the regular expression '.ython' would match both the string 'python' and the string 'jython'. It would also match strings such as 'qython', '+ython', or ' ython' (in which the first letter is a single space), but not strings such as 'cpython' or 'ython' because the period matches a single letter, and neither two nor zero.

Because it matches "anything" (any single character except a newline), the period is called a *wildcard.*

Escaping Special Characters

When you use special characters such as this, it's important to know that you may run into problems if you try to use them as normal characters. For instance, imagine you want to match the string 'python.org'. Do you simply use the pattern 'python.org'? You could, but that would also match 'pythonzorg', for instance, which you probably wouldn't want. (The dot matches any character except newline, remember?) To make a special character behave like a normal one, you *escape* it, just as we escaped quotes in strings, in Chapter 1. You place a backslash in front of it. Thus, in this example, you would use 'python\\.org', which would match 'python.org', and nothing else.

> **NOTE** *To get a single backslash, which is required here by the* re *module, you need to write two backslashes in the string—to escape it from the interpreter. Thus you have* two levels *of escaping here: (1) from the interpreter, and (2) from the* re *module. (Actually, in some cases you can get away with using a single backslash and have the interpreter escape it for you automatically, but don't rely on it.) If you are tired of doubling up backslashes, use a raw string, such as* r'python\.org'.

Character Sets

Matching any character can be useful, but sometimes you want more control. You can create a so-called *character set* by enclosing a substring in brackets. Such a character set will match any of the characters it contains, so '[pj]ython' would match both 'python' and 'jython', but nothing else. You can also use ranges, such as '[a-z]' to match any character from a to z (alphabetically), and you can combine such ranges by putting one after another, such as '[a-zA-Z0-9]' to match uppercase and lowercase letters and digits. (Note that the character set will match only *one* such character, though.)

To invert the character set, put the character ^ first, as in '[^abc]' to match any character *except* a, b, or c.

Special Characters in Character Sets

In general, special characters such as dots, asterisks, and question marks have to be escaped with a backslash if you want them to appear as literal characters in the pattern, rather than function as regexp operators. Inside character sets, escaping these characters is generally not necessary (although perfectly legal). You should, however, keep in mind the following rules:

You *do* have to escape the caret ("^") if it appears at the beginning of the character set unless you want it to function as a negation operator. (In other words, don't place it at the beginning unless you mean it.)

Similarly, the right bracket ("]") and the dash ("-") must be put either at the beginning of the character set or escaped with a backslash.

Alternatives and Subpatterns

Character sets are nice when you let each letter vary independently, but what if you want to match only the strings 'python' and 'perl'? You can't specify such a specific pattern with character sets or wildcards. Instead, you use the special character for alternatives: the "pipe" character '|'. So, your pattern would be 'python|perl'.

However, sometimes you don't want to use the choice operator on the *entire* pattern—just a part of it. To do that, you enclose the part, or *subpattern*, in parentheses. The previous example could be rewritten as 'p(ython|erl)'. (Note that the term subpattern can also be used about a single character.)

Optional and Repeated Subpatterns

By adding a question mark after a subpattern, you make it optional. It may appear in the matched string, but it isn't strictly required. So, for instance, the (slightly unreadable) pattern

```
r'(http://)?(www\.)?python\.org'
```

would match all of the following strings (and nothing else):

```
'http://www.python.org'
'http://python.org'
'www.python.org'
'python.org'
```

A few things are worth noting here:

- I've escaped the dots, to prevent them from functioning as wildcards.

- I've used a raw string to reduce the number of backslashes needed.

- Each optional subpattern is enclosed in parentheses.

- The optional subpatterns may appear or not, independently of each other.

The question mark means that the subpattern can appear once or not at all. There are a few other operators that allow you to repeat a subpattern more than once:

(*pattern*)*   *pattern* is repeated zero or more times

(*pattern*)+   *pattern* is repeated one or more times

(*pattern*){*m, n*}   *pattern* is repeated from *m* to *n* times

So, for instance r'w*\.python.org' matches 'www.python.org', but also '.python.org', 'ww.python.org', and 'wwwwww.python.org'. Similarly, r'w+\.python.org' matches 'w.python.org' but not '.python.org', and r'w{3,4}\.python.org' matches only 'www.python.org' and 'wwww.python.org'.

NOTE *The term "match" is used loosely here, to mean that the pattern matches the entire string. The* match *function, described in the text that follows, requires only that the pattern matches the beginning of the string.*

The Beginning and End of a String

Until now, you've only been looking at a pattern matching an entire string, but you can also try to find a substring that matches the patterns, such as the substring 'www' of the string 'www.python.org' matching the pattern 'w+'. When you're searching for substrings like this, it can sometimes be useful to anchor this substring either at the beginning or the end of the full string. For instance, you might want to match 'ht+p' at the beginning of a string, but not anywhere else. Then you use a caret ('^') to mark the beginning: '^ht+p' would match 'http://python.org' (and 'httttttp://python.org', for that matter) but not 'www.http.org'. Similarly, the end of a string may be indicated by the dollar sign ('$').

NOTE *For a complete listing of regexp operators, see the standard library reference, in the section "Regular Expression Syntax"* http://www.python.org/doc/lib/re-syntax.html.

Contents of the re Module

Knowing how to write regular expressions isn't much good if you can't use them for anything. The re module contains several useful functions for working with regular expressions. Some of the most important ones are described in Table 10-8.

Table 10-8. Some Important Functions in the re Module

FUNCTION	DESCRIPTION
compile(*pattern[, flags]*)	Creates a pattern object from a string with a regexp
search(*pattern, string[, flags]*)	Searches for *pattern* in *string*
match(*pattern, string[, flags]*)	Matches *pattern* at the beginning of *string*
split(*pattern, string[, maxsplit=0]*)	Splits a *string* by occurrences of *pattern*
findall(*pattern, string*)	Returns a list of all occurrences of *pattern* in *string*
sub(*pat, repl, string[, count=0]*)	Substitutes occurrences of *pat* in *string* with *repl*
escape(*string*)	Escapes all special regexp characters in *string*

The function re.compile transforms a regular expression (written as a string) to a pattern object, which can be used for more efficient matching. If you use regular expressions represented as strings when you call functions such as search or match, they have to be transformed into regular expression objects internally anyway. By doing this once, with the compile function, this step is no longer necessary each time you use the pattern. The pattern objects have the searching/matching functions as methods, so re.search(pat, string) (where pat is a regexp written as a string) is equivalent to pat.search(string) (where pat is a pattern object created with compile). Compiled regexp objects can also be used in the normal re functions.

The function re.search searches a given string to find the first substring, if any, that matches the given regular expression. If one is found, a MatchObject (evaluating to *true*) is returned; otherwise None (evaluating to *false*) is returned.

Due to the nature of the return values, the function can be used in conditional statements, such as

```
if re.search(pat, string):
    print 'Found it!'
```

However, if you need more information about the matched substring, you can examine the returned MatchObject. (More about MatchObjects in the next section.)

The function re.match tries to match a regular expression at the beginning of a given string. So match('p', 'python') returns *true*, while match('p', 'www.python.org') returns *false*. (The return values are the same as those for search.)

NOTE *The* match *function will report a match if the pattern matches the* beginning *of a string; the pattern is* not *required to match the entire string. If you want to do that, you have to add a dollar sign to the end of your pattern; the dollar sign will match the end of the string and thereby "stretch out" the match.*

The function re.split splits a string by the occurrences of a pattern. This is similar to the string method split, except that you allow full regular expressions instead of only a fixed separator string. For instance, with the string method split you could split a string by the occurrences of the string ', ' but with re.split you can split on any sequence of space characters and commas:

```
>>> some_text = 'alpha, beta,,,,gamma    delta'
>>> re.split('[, ]+', some_text)
['alpha', 'beta', 'gamma', 'delta']
```

NOTE *If the pattern contains parentheses, the parenthesized groups are interspersed between the split substrings.*

As you can see from this example, the return value is a list of substrings. The maxsplit argument indicates the maximum number of splits allowed:

```
>>> re.split('[, ]+', some_text, maxsplit=2)
['alpha', 'beta', 'gamma    delta']
>>> re.split('[, ]+', some_text, maxsplit=1)
['alpha', 'beta,,,,gamma    delta']
```

The function re.findall returns a list of all occurrences of the given pattern. For instance, to find all words in a string, you could do the following:

```
>>> pat = '[a-zA-Z]+'
>>> text = '"Hm...Err — are you sure?" he said, sounding insecure.'
>>> re.findall(pat, text)
['Hm', 'Err', 'are', 'you', 'sure', 'he', 'said', 'sounding', 'insecure']
```

Or, you could find the punctuation:

```
>>> pat = r'[.?\-",]+'
>>> re.findall(pat, text)
['"', '...', '—', '?"', ',', '.']
```

Note that the dash ("-") has been escaped so Python won't interpret it as part of a character range (such as a-z).

The function re.sub is used to substitute the leftmost, non-overlapping occurrences of a pattern with a given replacement. Consider the following example:

```
>>> pat = '{name}'
>>> text = 'Dear {name}...'
>>> re.sub(pat, 'Mr. Gumby', text)
'Dear Mr. Gumby...'
```

See the section "Using Group Numbers and Functions in Substitutions" later in this chapter for information on how to use this function more effectively.

The function re.escape is a utility function used to escape all the characters in a string that might be interpreted as a regexp operator. Use this if you have a long string with lots of these special characters and you want to avoid typing a lot of backslashes, or if you get a string from a user (for example, through the raw_input function) and want to use it as a part of a regexp. Here is an example of how it works:

```
>>> re.escape('www.python.org')
'www\\.python\\.org'
>>> re.escape('But where is the ambiguity?')
'But\\ where\\ is\\ the\\ ambiguity\\?'
```

 NOTE *In Table 10-8 you'll notice that some of the functions have an optional parameter called* flags. *This parameter can be used to change how the regular expressions are interpreted. For more information about this, see the standard library reference, in the section about the* re *module at* http://www.python.org/doc/current/lib/module-re.html. *The flags are described in the subsection "Module Contents."*

Match Objects and Groups

The re functions that try to match a pattern against a section of a string all return MatchObjects when a match is found. These objects contain information about the substring that matched the pattern. They also contain information about which parts of the pattern matched which parts of the substring—and these "parts" are called *groups.*

A group is simply a subpattern that has been enclosed in parentheses. The groups are numbered by their left parenthesis. Group zero is the entire pattern. So, in the pattern

```
'There (was a (wee) (cooper)) who (lived in Fyfe)'
```

the groups are as follows:

```
0  There was a wee cooper who lived in Fyfe
1  was a wee cooper
2  wee
3  cooper
4  lived in Fyfe
```

Typically, the groups contain special characters such as wildcards or repetition operators, and thus you may be interested in knowing what a given group has matched. For instance, in the pattern

```
r'www\.(.+)\.com$'
```

group 0 would contain the entire string, and group 1 would contain everything between 'www.' and '.com'. By creating patterns like this, you can extract the parts of a string that interest you.

Some of the more important methods of re match objects are described in Table 10-9.

Table 10-9. Some Important Methods of re Match Objects

METHOD	DESCRIPTION
group([*group1*, …])	Retrieves the occurrences of the given subpatterns ("groups")
start([*group*])	Returns the starting position of the occurrence of a given group
end([*group*])	Returns the ending position (an exclusive limit, as in slices) of the occurrence of a given group
span([*group*])	Returns both the beginning and ending positions of a group

The method group returns the (sub)string that was matched by a given group in the pattern. If no group number is given, group 0 is assumed. If only a single group number is given (or you just use the default, 0) a single string is returned. Otherwise, a tuple of strings corresponding to the given group numbers is returned.

NOTE   *In addition to the entrie match (group 0), you can have only 99 groups, with numbers in the range 1–99.*

The method start returns the starting index of the occurrence of the given group (which defaults to 0, the whole pattern).

The method end is similar to start, but returns the ending index plus one.

The method span returns the tuple (*start, end*) with the starting and ending indices of a given group (which defaults to 0, the whole pattern).

Consider the following example:

```
>>> m = re.match(r'www\.(.*)\..{3}', 'www.python.org')
>>> m.group(1)
```

```
'python'
>>> m.start(1)
4
>>> m.end(1)
10
>>> m.span(1)
(4, 10)
```

Using Group Numbers and Functions in Substitutions

In the first example using re.sub, I simply replaced one substring with another—something I could easily have done with the replace string method (described in the section "String Methods" in Chapter 3). Of course, regular expressions are useful because they allow you to search in a more flexible manner, but they also allow you to perform more powerful substitutions.

The easiest way to harness the power of re.sub is to use group numbers in the substitution string. Any escape sequences of the form '\\\n' in the replacement string are replaced by the string matched by group *n* in the pattern. For instance, let's say you want to replace words of the form '*something*' with 'something', where the former is a normal way of expressing emphasis in plain text documents (such as e-mail), and the latter is the corresponding HTML code (as used in Web pages). Let's first construct the regexp:

```
>>> emphasis_pattern = r'\*([^\*]+)\*'
```

Note that regular expressions can easily become hard to read, so using meaningful variable names (and possibly a comment or two) is important if anyone (including you!) is going to be able to read the code.

TIP *One way to make your regular expressions more readable is to use the* VERBOSE *flag in the* re *functions. This allows you to add whitespace (space characters, tabs, newlines, and so on) to your pattern, which will be ignored by* re—*except when you put it in a character class or escape it with a backslash. You can also put comments in such verbose regexps. The following is a pattern object that is equivalent to the emphasis pattern, but which uses the* VERBOSE *flag:*

```
>>> emphasis_pattern = re.compile(r'''
            \*         # Beginning emphasis tag — an asterisk
            (          # Begin group for capturing phrase
            [^\*]+     # Capture anything except asterisks
            )          # End group
            \*         # Ending emphasis tag
            ''', re.VERBOSE)
```

Now that I have my pattern, I can use `re.sub` to make my substitution:

```
>>> re.sub(emphasis_pattern, r'<em>\1</em>', 'Hello, *world*!')
'Hello, <em>world</em>!'
```

As you can see, I have successfully translated the text from plain text to HTML.

But you can make your substitutions even more powerful by using a *function* as the replacement. This function will be supplied with the MatchObject as its only parameter, and the string it returns will be used as the replacement. In other words, you can do whatever you want to the matched substring, and do elaborate processing to generate its replacement. What possible use could you have for such power, you ask? Once you start experimenting with regular expressions you will surely find countless uses for this mechanism. For one application, see the "Examples" section that follows.

Greedy and Non-Greedy Patterns

The repetition operators are by default *greedy*; that means that they will match as much as possible. For instance, let's say I rewrote the emphasis program to use the following pattern:

```
>>> emphasis_pattern = r'\*(.+)\*'
```

This matches an asterisk, followed by one or more letters, and then another asterisk. Sounds perfect, doesn't it? But it isn't:

```
>>> re.sub(emphasis_pattern, r'<em>\1</em>', '*This* is *it*!')
'<em>This* is *it</em>!'
```

As you can see, the pattern matched everything from the first asterisk to the last—including the two asterisks between! This is what it means to be greedy: Take everything you can.

In this case you clearly don't want this overly greedy behavior. The solution presented in the preceding text (using a character set matching anything *except* an asterisk) is fine when you know that one specific letter is illegal. But let's consider another scenario: What if you used the form '**something**' to signify emphasis? Now it shouldn't be a problem to include single asterisks inside the emphasized phrase. But how do you avoid being too greedy?

Actually, it's quite easy; you just use a non-greedy version of the repetition operator. All the repetition operators can be made non-greedy by putting a question mark after them:

```
>>> emphasis_pattern = r'\*\*(.+?)\*\*'
>>> re.sub(emphasis_pattern, r'<em>\1</em>', '**This** is **it**!')
'<em>This</em> is <em>it</em>!'
```

Here I've used the operator +? instead of +, which means that the pattern will match one or more occurrences of the wildcard. But it will match as few as it can because it is now non-greedy; it will match only the minimum needed to reach the next occurrence of '**', which is the end of the pattern. As you can see, it works nicely.

Finding out who an e-mail is from. Have you ever saved an e-mail as a text file? If you have, you may have seen that it contains a lot of essentially unreadable text at the top, similar to that shown in Listing 10-9.

Listing 10-9. A Set of (Fictitious) E-mail Headers

```
From foo@bar.baz   Thu Dec 20 01:22:50 2001
Return-Path: <foo@bar.baz>
Received: from xyzzy42.bar.com (xyzzy.bar.baz [123.456.789.42])
        by frozz.bozz.floop (8.9.3/8.9.3) with ESMTP id BAA25436
        for <magnus@bozz.floop>; Thu, 20 Dec 2001 01:22:50 +0100 (MET)
Received: from [43.253.124.23] by bar.baz
          (InterMail vM.4.01.03.27 201-229-121-127-20010626) with ESMTP
          id <20011220002242.ADASD123.bar.baz@[43.253.124.23]>;
          Thu, 20 Dec 2001 00:22:42 +0000
User-Agent: Microsoft-Outlook-Express-Macintosh-Edition/5.02.2022
Date: Wed, 19 Dec 2001 17:22:42 -0700
Subject: Re: Spam
From: Foo Fie <foo@bar.baz>
To: Magnus Lie Hetland <magnus@bozz.floop>
CC: <Mr.Gumby@bar.baz>
Message-ID: <B8467D62.84F%foo@baz.com>
In-Reply-To: <20011219013308.A2655@bozz.floop>
Mime-version: 1.0
Content-type: text/plain; charset="US-ASCII"
Content-transfer-encoding: 7bit
Status: RO
Content-Length: 55
Lines: 6

So long, and thanks for all the spam!


Yours,

Foo Fie
```

Let's try to find out who this e-mail is from. If you examine the text, I'm sure you can figure it out in this case (especially if you look at the message itself, at the bottom, of course). But can you see a general pattern? How do you extract the name of the sender, without the e-mail address? Or, how can you list all the e-mail addresses mentioned in the headers? Let's handle the first task first.

The line containing the sender begins with the string 'From: ' and ends with an e-mail address enclosed in angle brackets ('<' and '>'). You want the text found between those. If you use the fileinput module, this ought to be an easy task. A program solving the problem is shown in Listing 10-10.

 NOTE *You could solve this problem without using regular expressions if you wanted.*

Listing 10-10. A Program for Finding the Sender of an E-mail

```
# find_sender.py
import fileinput, re
pat = re.compile('From: (.*?) <.*>$')
for line in fileinput.input():
    m = pat.match(line)
    if m: print m.group(1)
```

You can then run the program like this (assuming that the e-mail message is in the text file message.eml):

```
$ python find_sender.py message.eml
Foo Fie
```

You should note the following about this program:

- I compile the regular expression to make the processing more efficient.

- I enclose the subpattern I want to extract in parentheses, making it a group.

- I use a non-greedy pattern to match the name because I want to stop matching when I reach the first left angle bracket.

- I use a dollar sign to indicate that I want the pattern to match the entire line, all the way to the end.

- I use an `if` statement to make sure that I did in fact match something before I try to extract the match of a specific group.

To list all the e-mail addresses mentioned in the headers, you need to construct a regular expression that matches an e-mail address but nothing else. You can then use the method `findall` to find all the occurrences in each line. To avoid duplicates, you keep the addresses as keys in a dictionary (a standard Python trick), with 1 as the value. (Any value would suffice here because you won't be using it.) Finally, you extract the keys, sort them, and print them out:

```python
import fileinput, re
pat = re.compile(r'[a-z\-\.]+@[a-z\-\.]+', re.IGNORECASE)
addresses = {}
for line in fileinput.input():
    for address in pat.findall(line):
        addresses[address] = 1
addresses = addresses.keys()
addresses.sort()
for address in addresses:
    print address
```

The resulting output when running this program (with the preceding e-mail message as input) is as follows:

```
Mr.Gumby@bar.baz
foo@bar.baz
foo@baz.com
magnus@bozz.floop
```

Note that when sorting, uppercase letters come before lowercase letters.

NOTE *I haven't adhered strictly to the problem specification here. The problem was to find the addresses in the* header, *but in this case the program finds all the addresses in the entire file. To avoid that, you can call* `fileinput.close()` *if you find an empty line because the header can't contain empty lines, and you would be finished. Alternatively you can use* `fileinput.nextfile()` *to start processing the next file, if there is more than one.*

Making a template system. A template is a file you can put specific values into to get a finished text of some kind. For instance, you may have a mail template requiring only the insertion of a recipient name. Python already has an advanced template mechanism: string formatting. However, with regular expressions you can make the system even more advanced. Let's say you want to replace all occurrences of ' [*something*]' (the "fields") with the result of evaluating *something* as an expression in Python. Thus, the string

```
'The sum of 7 and 9 is [7 + 9].'
```

should be translated to

```
'The sum of 7 and 9 is 16.'
```

Also, you want to be able to perform assignments in these fields, so that the string

```
'[name="Mr. Gumby"]Hello, [name]'
```

should be translated to

```
'Hello, Mr. Gumby'
```

This may sound like a complex task, but let's review the available tools:

- You can use a regular expression to match the fields and extract their contents.

- You can evaluate the expression strings with eval, supplying the dictionary containing the scope. You do this in a try/except statement; if a SyntaxError is raised, you probably have a statement (such as an assignment) on your hands and should use exec instead.

- You can execute the assignment strings (and other statements) with exec, storing the template's scope in a dictionary.

- You can use re.sub to substitute the result of the evaluation into the string being processed.

Suddenly it doesn't look so intimidating, does it?

> **TIP** *If a task seems daunting, it almost always helps to break it down into smaller pieces. Also, take stock of the tools at your disposal for ideas on how to solve your problem.*

See Listing 10-11 for a sample implementation.

Listing 10-11. A Template System

```python
# templates.py

import fileinput, re

# Matches fields enclosed in square brackets:
field_pat = re.compile(r'\[(.+?)\]')

# We'll collect variables in this:
scope = {}

# This is used in re.sub:
def replacement(match):
    code = match.group(1)
    try:
        # If the field can be evaluated, return it:
        return str(eval(code, scope))
    except SyntaxError:
        # Otherwise, execute the assignment in the same scope...
        exec code in scope
        # ...and return an empty string:
        return ''

# Get all the text as a single string:
# (There are better ways of doing this; see Chapter 11)
lines = []
for line in fileinput.input():
    lines.append(line)
text = ''.join(lines)

# Substitute all the occurrences of the field pattern:
print field_pat.sub(replacement, text)
```

Simply put, this program does the following:

1. Defines a pattern for matching fields.

2. Creates a dictionary to act as a scope for the template.

3. Defines a replacement function that does the following:

    a. Grabs group 1 from the match and puts it in code.

    b. Tries to evaluate code with the scope dictionary as namespace, converts the result to a string, and returns it. If this succeeds, the field was an expression and everything is fine. Otherwise (i.e., a SyntaxError is raised), go to Step 3c.

    c. Executes the field in the same namespace (the scope dictionary) used for evaluating expressions, and then returns an empty string (because the assignment doesn't evaluate to anything).

4. Uses fileinput to read in all available lines, puts them in a list, and joins them into one big string.

5. Replaces all occurrences of field_pat using the replacement function in re.sub, and prints the result.

 NOTE *It is much more efficient to put the lines into a list and then join them at the end than to do something like this:*

```
# Don't do this:
text = ''
for line in fileinput.input():
    text += line
```

Although this looks elegant, each assignment has to create a new string, which is the old string with the new one appended. This leads to a terrible waste of resources and makes your program slow. Don't do this. If you want a more elegant way to read in all the text of a file, take a peek at Chapter 11, "Files and Stuff."

So, I have just created a really powerful template system in just 15 lines of code (not counting whitespace and comments). I hope you're starting to see how powerful Python becomes when you use the standard libraries. Let's finish this example by testing the template system. Try running it on the simple file shown in Listing 10-12.

Listing 10-12. A Simple Template Example

```
[x = 2]
[y = 3]
The sum of [x] and [y] is [x + y].
```

You should see this:

```
The sum of 2 and 3 is 5.
```

NOTE *It may not be obvious, but there are three empty lines in the preceding output—two above and one below the text. Although the first two fields have been replaced by empty strings, the newlines following them are still there. Also, the* print *statement adds a newline, which accounts for the empty line at the end.*

But wait, it gets better! Because I have used fileinput, I can process several files in turn. That means that I can use one file to define values for some variables, and then another file as a template where these values are inserted. For instance, I might have one file with definitions as in Listing 10-13, named magnus.txt, and a template file as in Listing 10-14, named template.txt.

Listing 10-13. Some Template Definitions

```
[name     = 'Magnus Lie Hetland' ]
[email    = 'magnus@foo.bar'      ]
[language = 'python'              ]
```

Listing 10-14. A Template

```
[import time]
Dear [name],

I would like to learn how to program. I hear you use
the [language] language a lot — is it something I
should consider?

And, by the way, is [email] your correct email address?


Fooville, [time.asctime()]

Oscar Frozzbozz
```

The import time isn't an assignment (which is the statement type I set out to handle), but because I'm not being picky and just use a simple try/except statement, my program supports any statement or expression that works with eval or exec. You can run the program like this (assuming a UNIX command line):

```
$ python templates.py magnus.txt template.txt
```

You should get some output similar to that in Listing 10-15.

Listing 10-15. Sample Output from the Template System

```
Dear Magnus Lie Hetland,

I would like to learn how to program. I hear you use
the python language a lot — is it something I
should consider?

And, by the way, is magnus@foo.bar your correct email address?


Fooville, Wed Apr 24 20:34:29 2002

Oscar Frozzbozz
```

Even though this template system is capable of some quite powerful substitutions, it still has some flaws. For instance, it would be nice if you could write the definition file in a more flexible manner. If it were executed with execfile you could simply use normal Python syntax. That would also fix the problem of getting lots of blank lines at the top of the output.

Can you think of other ways of improving it? Can you think of other uses for the concepts used in this program? The best way (in my opinion) to become really proficient in any programming language is to play with it—test its limitations and discover its strengths. See if you can rewrite this program so it works better and suits your needs.

Other Interesting Standard Modules

Even though this chapter has covered a lot of material, I have barely scratched the surface of the standard libraries. To tempt you to dive in, I'll quickly mention a few more cool libraries:

difflib. This library enables you to compute how similar two sequences are. It also enables you to find the sequences (from a list of possibilities) that are "most similar" to an original sequence you provide. Could be used to create a simple searching program, for instance.

md5 and sha. These modules can compute small "signatures" (numbers) from strings; and if you compute the signatures for two different strings, you can be almost certain that the two signatures will be different. You can use this on large text files. Several uses in cryptography and security.

rexec and Bastion. These modules enable you to execute code while giving the code *restricted rights*—you can decide what the code will be allowed to do. Thus you can execute code from other "untrusted" people without running a great security risk. (You should not trust these modules for applications where security is critical.)

cmd. This module enables you to write a command-line interpreter, somewhat like the Python interactive interpreter. You can define your own commands that the user can execute at the prompt. Perhaps you could use this as the user interface to one of your programs?

A Quick Summary

In this chapter you've learned about modules: how to create them, how to explore them, and how to use some of those included in the standard Python libraries.

Modules. A module is basically a subprogram whose main function is to *define things*, such as functions, classes, and variables. If a module contains any test code, it should be placed in an `if` statement that checks whether `__name__=='__main__'`. Modules can be imported if they are in the PYTHONPATH. You import a module stored in the file `foo.py` with the statement `import foo`.

Packages. A package is just a module that contains other modules. Packages are implemented as directories that contain a file named `__init__.py`.

Exploring modules. After you have imported a module into the interactive interpreter, you can explore it in many ways. Among them are using `dir`, examining the `__all__` variable, and using the `help` function. The documentation and the source code can also be excellent sources of information and insight.

The standard library. Python comes with several modules included, collectively called the standard library. Some of these were reviewed in this chapter:

- `sys`: A module that gives you access to several variables and functions that are tightly linked with the Python interpreter.

- `os`: A module that gives you access to several variables and functions that are tightly linked with the operating system.

- `fileinput`: A module that makes it easy to iterate over the lines of several files or streams.

- `time`: A module for getting the current time, and for manipulating and formatting times and dates.

- `random`: A module with functions for generating random numbers, choosing random elements from a sequence, or shuffling the elements of a list.

- shelve: A module for creating a persistent mapping, which stores its contents in a database with a given file name.

- re: A module with support for regular expressions.

If you are curious to find out more, I again urge you to browse the Python Library Reference (http://python.org/doc/lib). It's really interesting reading.

New Functions in This Chapter

FUNCTION	DESCRIPTION
dir(*obj*)	Returns an alphabetized list of attribute names
help([*obj*])	Interactive help or help about a specific object
reload(*module*)	Returns a reloaded version of a module that has already been imported

What Now?

If you have grasped at least a few of the concepts in this chapter, your Python prowess has probably taken a great leap forward. With the standard libraries at your fingertips, Python changes from powerful to extremely powerful. With what you have learned so far, you can write programs to tackle a wide range of problems. In the next chapter you learn more about using Python to interact with the outside world of files and networks, and thereby tackle problems of greater scope.

CHAPTER 11

Files and Stuff

So far we've mainly been working with data structures that reside in the interpreter itself. What little interaction our programs have had with the outside world has been through input, raw_input, and print. In this chapter, we go one step further and let our programs catch a glimpse of a larger world: the world of files and streams. The functions and objects described in this chapter will enable us to store data between program invocations and to process data from other programs, even data stored remotely on a network (such as the Internet).

Opening Files

You can open files with the open function, which has the following syntax:

open(*filename*[, *mode*[, *buffering*]])

The open function takes a file name as its only mandatory argument, and returns a file object. The mode and buffering arguments are both optional and will be explained in the material that follows.

....

The open Function and the File Type

In earlier versions of Python, open was a separate function, but from version 2.2 onwards, open is the same as file, the file type. So when you call it as a function, you are actually using the file constructor to create a file object.

....

So, assuming that you have a text file (created with your text editor, perhaps) called somefile.txt stored in the directory C:\text (or something like ~/text in UNIX), you can open it like this:

```
>>> f = open(r'C:\text\somefile.txt')
```

If the file doesn't exist, you may see an exception traceback like this:

```
Traceback (most recent call last):
File "<pyshell#0>", line 1, in ?
```

```
f = open(r'C:\text\somefile.txt')
IOError: [Errno 2] No such file or directory: "C:\\text\\somefile.txt"
```

You'll see what you can do with such file objects in a little while, but first, let's take a look at the other two arguments of the open function.

The Mode Argument

If you use open with only a file name as a parameter, you get a file object you can read from. If you want to write to the file, you have to state that explicitly, supplying a *mode*. (Be patient—I get to the actual reading and writing in a little while.) The mode argument to the open function can have several values, as summarized in Table 11-1.

Table 11-1. Possible Values for the Mode Argument of the open *Function*

VALUE	DESCRIPTION
'r'	Read mode
'w'	Write mode
'a'	Append mode
'b'	Binary mode (added to other mode)
'+'	Read/write mode (added to other mode)

Explicitly specifying read mode has the same effect as not supplying a mode string at all. The write mode enables you to write to the file.

The '+' can be added to any of the other modes to indicate that both reading and writing is allowed. So, for instance, 'r+' can be used when opening a text file for reading and writing. (For this to be useful, you will probably want to use seek as well; see the sidebar about random access later in this chapter.)

The 'b' mode changes the way the file is handled. Generally, Python assumes that you are dealing with text files (containing characters). Typically, this is not problem. But if you are processing some other kind of file (called a *binary* file) such as a sound clip or an image, you should add a 'b' to your mode: for example, 'rb' to read a binary file.

Why Use Binary Mode?

If you use binary mode when you read (or write) a file, things won't be much different. You are still able to read a number of bytes (basically the same as characters), and perform other operations associated with text files. The main point is that when you use binary mode, Python gives you exactly the contents found in the file—and in text mode it won't necessarily do that.

If you find it shocking that Python manipulates your text files, don't worry. The only "trick" it employs is to standardize your line endings. Generally, in Python, you end your lines with a newline character ('\n'), as is the norm in UNIX systems. This is not standard in Windows, however. In Windows, a line ending is marked with '\r\n'. To hide this from your program (so it can work seamlessly across different platforms), Python does some automatic conversion here: When you read text from a file in text-mode in Windows, it converts '\r\n' to '\n'. Conversely, when you write text to a file in text-mode in Windows, it converts '\n' to '\r\n'. (The Macintosh version does the same thing, but converts between '\n' and '\r'.)

The problem occurs when you work with a binary file, such as a sound clip. It may contain bytes that can be interpreted as the line-ending characters mentioned in the previous paragraph, and if you are using text mode, Python performs its automatic conversion. However, that will probably destroy your binary data. So, to avoid that, you simply use binary mode, and no conversions are made.

Note that this distinction is not important on platforms (such as UNIX) where the newline character is the standard line terminator because no conversion is performed there anyway.

Buffering

The open function takes a third (optional) parameter, which controls the *buffering* of the file. If the parameter is 0, I/O (input/output) is unbuffered (all reads and writes go directly from/to the disk); if it is 1, I/O is buffered (meaning that Python may use memory instead of disk space to make things go faster, and only update when you use flush or close—see the section "Closing Your Files," later in this chapter). Larger numbers indicate the buffer size (in bytes), while 1 sets the buffer size to the default.

The Basic File Methods

Now you know how to open files; the next step is to do something useful with them. In this section, you learn about some basic methods that file objects (and some other "file-like" objects, sometimes called *streams*) have.

Three Standard Streams

In Chapter 10, in the section about the sys module, I mentioned three standard streams. These are actually files (or "file-like" objects): you can apply most of what you learn about files to them.

A standard source of data input is sys.stdin. When a program reads from standard input, you can either supply text by typing it, or you can link it with the standard output of another program, using a *pipe*. (This is a standard UNIX concept—there is an example later in this section.)

The text you give to print appears in sys.stdout. The prompts for input and raw_input also go there. Data written to sys.stdout typically appears on your screen, but can be linked to the standard input of another program with a pipe, as mentioned.

Error messages (such as stack traces) are written to sys.stderr. In many ways it is similar to sys.stdout.

Reading and Writing

The most important capabilities of files (or streams) are supplying and receiving data. If you have a file-like object named f you can write data (in the form of a string) with the method f.write, and read data (also as a string) with the method f.read.

Each time you call f.write(*string*), the string you supply is written to the file after those you have written previously.

```
>>> f = open('somefile.txt', 'w')
>>> f.write('Hello, ')
>>> f.write('World!')
>>> f.close()
```

Notice that I call the close method when I'm finished with the file. You learn more about it in the section "Closing Your Files" later in this chapter.

Reading is just as simple. Just remember to tell the stream how many characters (bytes) you want to read.

Example (continuing where I left off):

```
>>> f.read(4)
'Hell'
>>> f.read()
'o, World!'
```

First, I specify how many characters to read (4), and then I simply read the rest of the file (by not supplying a number). Note that I could have dropped the mode specification from the call to open because 'r' is the default.

EXAMPLE

In a UNIX shell (such as GNU bash) you can write several commands after one another, linked together with *pipes*, as in this example (assuming GNU bash):

```
$ cat somefile.txt | python somescript.py | sort
```

 NOTE *GNU* bash *is also available in Windows. For more information, take a look at* http://www.cygwin.org.

This pipeline consists of three commands:

- cat somefile.txt simply writes the contents of the file somefile.txt to standard output (sys.stdout).

- python somescript.py executes the Python script somescript.

- sort reads all the text from standard input (sys.stdin), sorts the lines alphabetically, and writes the result to standard output.

But what is the point of these pipe characters ('|'), and what does somescript.py do?

The pipes link up the standard output of one command with the standard input of the next. Clever, eh? So you can safely guess that somescript.py reads data from its sys.stdin (which is what cat somefile.txt writes) and writes some result to its sys.stdout (which is where sort gets its data).

A simple script (`somescript.py`) that uses `sys.stdin` is shown in Listing 11-1. The contents of the file `somefile.txt` is shown in Listing 11-2, and the result that is printed out when running the command

```
$ cat somefile.txt | python somescript.py
```

is shown in Listing 11-3.

Listing 11-1. Simple Script That Counts the Words in `sys.stdin`

```
# somescript.py
import sys
text = sys.stdin.read()
words = text.split()
wordcount = len(words)
print 'Wordcount:', wordcount
```

Listing 11-2. A File Containing Some Nonsensical Text

```
Your mother was a hamster and your
father smelled of elderberries.
```

Listing 11-3. The Result of `cat somefile.txt | python somescript.py`

```
Wordcount: 11
```

Random Access

In this chapter, I treat files only as streams—you can read data only from start to finish, strictly in order. In fact, you can also move around a file, accessing only the parts you are interested in (called "random access") by using the two file-object methods `seek` and `tell`:

`seek(`*offset*`[, `*whence*`])`: Moves the "current position" (where reading or writing is performed) to the position described by *offset* and *whence*. *offset* is a byte (character) count. *whence* defaults to 0, which means that the offset is from the beginning of the file (the offset must be non-negative); *whence* may also be set to 1 (move relative to current position: the offset may be negative), or 2 (move relative to the end of the file).

Consider this example:

```
>>> f = open(r'c:\text\somefile.txt', 'w')
>>> f.write('01234567890123456789')
```

```
>>> f.seek(5)
>>> f.write('Hello, World!')
>>> f.close()
>>> f = open(r'c:\text\somefile.txt')
>>> f.read()
'01234Hello, World!89'
```

tell(): Returns the current file position as in the following example:

```
>>> f = open(r'c:\text\somefile.txt')
>>> f.read(3)
'012'
>>> f.read(2)
'34'
>>> f.tell()
5L
```

Note that the number returned from f.tell in this case was a long integer. That may not always be the case.

Reading and Writing Lines

Actually, what I've been doing until now is a bit impractical. Usually, I could just as well be reading in the lines of a stream as reading letter by letter. You can read a single line (text from where you have come so far, up to and including the first line separator you encounter) with the method file.readline. You can either use it without any arguments (in which case a line is simply read and returned) or with a non-negative integer, which is then the maximum number of characters (or bytes) that readline is allowed to read. So if someFile.readline() returns 'Hello, World!\n', someFile.readline(5) returns 'Hello'. To read all the lines of a file and have them returned as a list, use the readlines method.

 NOTE *An alternative to* readlines *that can be useful when iterating is* xreadlines. *For more information, see the section "Iterating over File Contents," later in this chapter.*

The method writelines is the opposite of readlines: Give it a list (or, in fact, any sequence or iterable object) of strings, and it writes all the strings to the file (or stream). Note that newlines are *not* added: you have to add those yourself. Also, there is no writeline method because you can just use write.

> **NOTE** *On platforms that use other line separators, substitute "carriage return" (Mac) or "carriage return and newline" (Windows) for "newline."*

Closing Your Files

You should remember to close your files by calling their close method. Usually, a file object is closed automatically when you quit your program (and possibly before that), and not closing files you have been *reading* from isn't really that important (although it can't hurt, and might help to avoid keeping the file uselessly "locked" against modification in some operating systems and settings). But you should always close a file you have *written* to because Python may *buffer* (keep stored temporarily somewhere, for efficiency reasons) the data you have written, and if your program crashes for some reason, the data might not be written to the file at all. The safe thing is to close your files after you're finished with them. If you want to be certain that your file is closed, you should use a try/finally statement with the call to close in the finally clause:

```
# Open your file here
try:
    # Write data to your file
finally:
    file.close()
```

TIP *After writing something to a file, you usually want the changes to appear in that file, so other programs reading the same file can see the changes. Well, isn't that what happens, you say. Not necessarily. As mentioned, the data may be buffered (stored temporarily somewhere in memory), and not written until you close the file. If you want to keep working with the file (and not close it) but still want to make sure the file on disk is updated to reflect your changes, call the file object's* flush *method. (Note, however, that* flush *might not allow other programs running at the same time to access the file, due to locking considerations that depend on your operating system and settings. Whenever you can conveniently close the file, that is preferable.)*

EXAMPLES

Assume that somefile.txt contains the text in Listing 11-4. What can you do with it?

Listing 11-4. A Simple Text File

```
Welcome to this file
There is nothing here except
This stupid haiku
```

Let's try the methods you know:
read(*n*):

```
>>> f = open(r'c:\text\somefile.txt')
>>> f.read(7)
'Welcome'
>>> f.read(4)
' to '
>>> f.close()
```

read():

```
>>> f = open(r'c:\text\somefile.txt')
>>> print f.read()
Welcome to this file
There is nothing here except
This stupid haiku
>>> f.close()
```

readline():

```
>>> f = open(r'c:\text\somefile.txt')
>>> for i in range(3):
        print str(i) + ': ' + f.readline(),
0: Welcome to this file
1: There is nothing here except
2: This stupid haiku
>>> f.close()
```

readlines():

```
>>> import pprint
>>> pprint.pprint(open(r'c:\text\somefile.txt').readlines())
['Welcome to this file\n',
 'There is nothing here except\n',
 'This stupid haiku']
```

Note that I relied on the file object being closed automatically in this example.

write(*string*):

```
>>> f = open(r'c:\text\somefile.txt', 'w')
>>> f.write('this\nis no\nhaiku')
>>> f.close()
```

After running this, the file contains the text in Listing 11-5.

Listing 11-5. The Modified Text File

```
this
is no
haiku
```

```
writelines(list):

>>> f = open(r'c:\text\somefile.txt')
>>> lines = f.readlines()
>>> f.close()
>>> lines[1] = "isn't a\n"
>>> f = open(r'c:\text\somefile.txt', 'w')
>>> f.writelines(lines)
>>> f.close()
```

After running this, the file contains the text in Listing 11-6.

Listing 11-6. The Text File, Modified Again

```
this
isn't a
haiku
```

Iterating Over File Contents

Now you've seen some of the methods file objects present to us, and you've learned how to acquire such file objects. One of the common operations on files is to iterate over their contents, repeatedly performing some action as you go. There are many ways of doing this, and although you can find your favorite and stick to that, others may have done it differently, and to understand their programs, you should know all the basic techniques. Some of these techniques are just applications of the methods you've already seen (read, readline, and readlines) while some are new (for example, xreadlines and file iterators).

In all the examples in this section, I use a fictitious function called process to represent the processing of each character or line. Feel free to implement it any way you like. One simple example would be the following:

```
def process(string):
    print 'Processing: ', string
```

More useful implementations could do such things as storing data in a data structure, computing a sum, replacing patterns with the re module, or perhaps adding line numbers.

Also, to try out the examples, you should set the variable filename to the name of some actual file.

Doing It Byte by Byte

One of the most basic (but probably least common) ways of iterating over file contents is to use the read method in a while loop. For instance, you might want to loop over every character (byte) in the file. You could do that as shown in Listing 11-7.

Listing 11-7. Looping Over Characters with read

```
f = open(filename)
char = f.read(1)
while char:
    process(char)
    char = f.read(1)
```

This program works because when you have reached the end of the file, the read method returns an empty string, but until then, the string always contains one character (and thus has the Boolean value *true*). So as long as char is true, you know that you aren't finished yet.

As you can see, I have repeated the assignment char = f.read(1), and code repetition is generally considered a bad thing. (Laziness is a virtue, remember?) To avoid that, I can use the while 1/break technique you first encountered in Chapter 5. The resulting code is shown in Listing 11-8.

Listing 11-8. Writing the Loop Differently

```
f = open(filename)
while 1:
    char = f.read(1)
    if not char: break
    process(char)
```

As mentioned in Chapter 5, you shouldn't use the break statement too often (because it tends to make the code more difficult to follow); even so, the approach shown in Listing 11-8 is usually preferred to that in Listing 11-7, precisely because you avoid duplicated code.

One Line at a Time

When dealing with text files, you are often interested in iterating over the *lines* in the file, not each individual character. You can do this easily in the same way as we did with characters, using the readline method (described earlier, in the section "Reading and Writing Lines"), as shown in Listing 11-9.

Listing 11-9. Using readline *in a* while *Loop*

```
f = open(filename)
while 1:
    line = f.readline()
    if not line: break
    process(line)
```

Reading Everything

If the file isn't too large, you can just read the whole file in one go, using the read method with no parameters (to read the entire file as a string), or the readlines method (to read the file into a list of strings, in which each string is a line). Listings 11-10 and 11-11 show how easy it is to iterate over characters and lines when you read the file like this. Note that reading the contents of a file into a string or a list like this can be useful for other things besides iteration. For instance, you might apply a regular expression to the string, or you might store the list of lines in some data structure for further use.

Listing 11-10. Iterating Over Characters with read

```
f = open(filename)
for char in f.read():
    process(char)
```

Listing 11-11. Iterating Over Lines with readlines

```
f = open(filename)
for line in f.readlines():
    process(line)
```

Lazy Line Iteration with `fileinput` *and* `xreadlines`

Sometimes you have to iterate over the lines in a very large file, and `readlines` would use too much memory. You could use a `while` loop with `readline`, of course, but in Python `for` loops are preferable when they are available. It just so happens that they are in this case. You can use a method called *lazy line iteration:* lazy because it only reads the parts of the file actually needed (more or less).

You have already encountered `fileinput` in Chapter 10; see Listing 11-12 for an example using it. Note that the `fileinput` module takes care of opening the file. You just have to give it a file name.

Listing 11-12. Iterating Over Lines with `fileinput`

```
import fileinput
for line in fileinput.input(filename):
    process(line)
```

You can also perform lazy line iteration by using the `xreadlines` method. It works almost like `readlines` except that it doesn't read all the lines into a list. Instead it creates an `xreadlines` object.

You can use an `xreadlines` object just like a sequence in a `for` loop, but if you try to use it like a normal sequence, you'll find that it behaves a bit strangely. You can access each element only once, and you have to access them in order. (That's exactly what the `for` loop does.) An example using `xreadlines` is shown in Listing 11-13. As you can see, it's almost exactly like using `readlines`.

 NOTE *Using* `xreadlines` *will probably give you a speedup compared to using* `readline` *in a* `while` *loop because* `xreadlines` *"reads ahead," thereby requiring fewer disk accesses.*

Listing 11-13. Iterating Over Lines with `xreadlines`

```
f = open(filename)
for line in f.xreadlines():
    process(line)
```

The New Kids on the Block: File Iterators

It's time for the coolest technique of all. If Python had had this since the beginning, I suspect that several of the other methods (at least xreadlines) would
never have appeared. So what is this cool technique? From Python 2.2, files are
iterable, which means that you can use them directly in for loops to iterate over
their lines. See Listing 11-14 for an example. Pretty elegant, isn't it?

Listing 11-14. Iterating Over a File

```
f = open(filename)
for line in f:
    process(line)
```

In these iteration examples, I've been pretty casual about closing my files.
Although I probably should have closed them, it's not critical, as long as I don't
write to the file. If you are willing to let Python take care of the closing (as I have
done so far), you could simplify the example even further, as shown in
Listing 11-15. Here I don't assign the opened file to a variable (like the variable f
I've used in the other examples), and therefore I have no way of explicitly
closing it.

Listing 11-15. Iterating Over a File Without Storing the File Object in a Variable

```
for line in open(filename):
    process(line)
```

Note that sys.stdin is iterable, just like other files, so if you want to iterate
over all the lines in standard input, you can use

```
import sys
for line in sys.stdin:
    process(line)
```

Also, you can do all the things you can do with iterators in general, such as
converting them into lists of strings (by using list(open(filename))), which
would simply be equivalent to using readlines.
Consider the following example:

```
>>> f = open('somefile.txt', 'w')
>>> print >> f, 'This is the first line'
>>> print >> f, 'This is the second line'
```

```
>>> print >> f, 'This is the third line'
>>> f.close()
>>> first, second, third = open('somefile.txt')
>>> first
'This is the first line\n'
>>> second
'This is the second line\n'
>>> third
'This is the third line\n'
```

In this example, it's important to note the following:

- I've used print to write to the file; this automatically adds newlines after the strings I supply.

- I use sequence unpacking on the opened file, putting each line in a separate variable. (This isn't exactly common practice because you usually won't know the number of lines in your file, but it demonstrates the "iterat-orness" of the file object.)

- I close the file after having written to it, to ensure that the data is flushed to disk. (As you can see, I haven't closed it after reading from it. Sloppy, perhaps, but not critical.)

Accessing Remote Files with urllib

Now that you know how to handle files, let's take a look at a standard module that enables you to access files across a network, just as if they were located on your computer. This simple extension opens up a new world of possibilities: virtually anything you can refer to with a URL (Uniform Resource Locator) can be used as input to your program. Just imagine the possibilities you get if you combine this with the re module: You can download Web pages, extract information, and create automatic reports of your findings.

....

More Network Programming

The capability to access files remotely is only one of many possibilities for using a computer network in your programs. For some other possibilities, check out the following standard library modules:

MODULE	DESCRIPTION
asynchat	Additional functionality for asyncore
asyncore	Asynchronous socket handler
BaseHTTPServer	Basic, extendable Web server
cgi	Basic CGI support
ftplib	FTP client module
gopherlib	gopher client module
httplib	HTTP client module
imaplib	IMAP4 client module
nntplib	NNTP client module
poplib	POP client module
SimpleXMLRPCServer	A simple XML-RPC server
smtplib	SMTP client module
socket	Low-level socket handling
SocketServer	Basic, extendable socket server
telnetlib	telnet client module
urllib2	More advanced version of urllib
xmlrpclib	Support for the XML-RPC remote procedure call protocol

Opening Remote Files

You can open remote files almost exactly as you do local files; the difference is that you can use only read mode, and instead of open (or file), you use urlopen from the urllib module:

```
>>> from urllib import urlopen
>>> webpage = urlopen('http://www.python.org')
```

If you are online, the variable webpage should now contain a file-like object linked to the Python Web page at http://www.python.org.

NOTE   *If you want to experiment with* urllib *but aren't currently online, you can access local files with URLs that start with* file:, *such as* file:c:\text\somefile.txt.

The file-like object that is returned from urlopen supports (among others) the close, read, readline, and readlines methods.

Let's say you want to extract the (relative) URL of the "Tutorial" link on the Python page you just opened. You could do that with regular expressions (see Chapter 10 in the section about the re module; for more info about HTML, see Chapter 13):

```
>>> import re
>>> text = webpage.read()
>>> m = re.search('<a href="([^"]+)">Tutorial</a>', text, re.IGNORECASE)
>>> m.group(1)
'doc/current/tut/tut.html'
```

NOTE   *At the time of writing, this code gave the exact results shown. However, by the time you read this the Python page may have changed, and you may have to modify the regular expression to make the code work.*

File-Like Objects

You will probably run into the term "file-like" repeatedly in your Python career (I've used it a few times already). A file-like object is simply one supporting a few of the same methods as a file, most notably either read or write or both. The objects returned by urllib.urlopen are a good example of this. They support methods such as read, readline, and readlines, but not (at the time of writing) file iteration, for instance.

Retrieving Remote Files

The urlopen function gives you a file-like object you can read from. If you would rather have urllib take care of downloading the file for you, storing a copy in a local file, you can use urlretrieve instead. Rather than returning a file-like object, it returns a tuple (*filename, headers*), where *filename* is the name of the local file (this name is created automatically by urllib), and *headers* contains some information about the remote file. (I'll ignore *headers* here. Look up `urlretrieve` in the standard library documentation of `urllib` if you want to know more about it.) If you want to specify a file name for the downloaded copy, you can supply that as a second parameter. For instance,

```
urlretrieve('http://www.python.org', 'C:\\python_webpage.html')
```

retrieves the Python home page and stores it in the file `C:\python_webpage.html`. If you don't specify a file name, the file is put in some temporary location, available for you to open (with the `open` function), but when you're done with it, you may want to have it removed so that it doesn't take up space on your hard drive. To clean up such temporary files, you can call the function `urlcleanup` without any arguments, and it takes care of things for you.

Some Utilities

In addition to reading and downloading files through URLs, `urllib` also offers some functions for manipulating the URLs themselves. (The following assumes some knowledge of URLs and CGI.) These functions are

quote(*string*[, *safe*]): Returns a string in which all special characters (characters that have special significance in URLs) have been replaced by URL-friendly versions (such as %7E instead of ~). This can be useful if you have a string that might contain such special characters and you want to use it as a URL. The *safe* string includes characters that should not be coded like this: the default is '/'.

quote_plus(*string*[, *safe*]): Works like `quote`, but also replaces spaces with plus signs.

unquote(*string*): The reverse of `quote`.

unquote_plus(*string*): The reverse of `quote_plus`.

urlencode(*query*[, *doseq*]): Converts a mapping (such as a dictionary) or a sequence of two-element tuples—of the form (*key*, *value*)—into a "URL-encoded" string, which can be used in POST queries. (Check the Python documentation for more information.)

A Quick Summary

In this chapter you've seen how to interact with the environment through files and file-like objects, one of the most important techniques for I/O (input/output) in Python. Here are some of the highlights from the chapter:

Opening and closing files. You open a file with the open function (in newer versions of Python, actually just an alias for file), by supplying a file name.

Modes and file types. When opening a file, you can also supply a *mode*, such as 'r' for read-mode or 'w' for write-mode. By appending 'b' to your mode, you can open files as binary files. (This is necessary only on platforms where Python performs line-ending conversion, such as Windows.)

Standard streams. The three standard files (stdin, stdout, and stderr, found in the sys module) are file-like objects that implement the UNIX *standard I/O* mechanism (also available in Windows).

Reading and writing. You read from a file or file-like object using the method read. You write with the method write.

Reading and writing lines. You can read lines from a file using readline, readlines, and (for efficient iteration) xreadlines. You can write files with writelines.

Iterating over file contents. There are many ways of iterating over file contents. It is most common to iterate over the lines of a text file, and you can do this (from version 2.2) by simply iterating over the file itself. There are other methods too, such as readlines and xreadlines, which are compatible with older versions of Python.

Accessing remote files. You can use the urllib module to open (for reading) or retrieve files across a network by using a URL instead of a file name.

File-like objects. A file-like objects is (informally) an object that supports a set of methods such as read and readline (and possibly write and writelines).

New Functions in This Chapter

FUNCTION	DESCRIPTION
file(*name*[, *mode*[, *buffering*]])	Opens a file and returns a file object
open(*name*[, *mode*[, *buffering*]])	Alias for file; use open rather than file when opening files
urllib.urlopen(*url*[, *data*])	Opens a remote file and returns a file-like object
urllib.urlretrieve(*url*, ...)	Retrieves a remote file
urllib.urlcleanup()	Cleans up temporary files from urlretrieve
urllib.quote(*string*[, *safe*])	Quotes (escapes) special URL characters
urllib.quote_plus(*string*[, *safe*])	Same as quote, but also replaces spaces with '+'
urllib.unquote(*string*)	Inverse of quote
urllib.unquote_plus(*string*)	Inverse of quote_plus
urllib.urlencode(*query*[, *doseq*])	Encodes mapping as CGI query data

What Now?

So now you know how to interact with the environment through files; but what about interacting with the user? So far we've used only input, raw_input, and print, and unless the user writes something in a file that your program can read, you don't really have any other tools for creating user interfaces. That changes in the next chapter, when I cover graphical user interfaces, with windows, buttons, and so on.

CHAPTER 12

Graphical User Interfaces

IN THIS CHAPTER YOU LEARN how to make graphical user interfaces (GUIs) for your Python programs: you know, windows with buttons and text fields and stuff like that. Pretty cool, huh?

There are plenty of so-called "GUI toolkits" available for Python, but none of them is recognized as *the* standard GUI toolkit. This has its advantages (greater freedom of choice) and drawbacks (others can't use your programs unless they have the same GUI toolkit installed; fortunately, there is no conflict between the various GUI toolkits available for Python so you can install as many different GUI toolkits as you want). Also, some of the GUI toolkits can be a bit complicated and hard to program. In this chapter you see how the Anygui project tries to solve these problems.

An Example GUI Application

To make things easier to follow, I use a running example throughout this chapter. Your task is to write a basic program that enables you to edit text files. Writing a full-fledged text editor is beyond the scope of this chapter—we'll stick to the essentials. After all, the goal is to demonstrate the basic mechanisms of GUI programming in Python.

The requirements for this minimal text editor are as follows:

- It must allow you to open text files, given their file names.

- It must allow you to edit the text files.

- It must allow you to save the text files.

- It must allow you to quit.

When writing a GUI program, it's often useful to draw a sketch of how you want it to look. Figure 12-1 shows a simple layout that satisfies the requirements.

Figure 12-1. A sketch of the text editor

The elements of the interface can be used as follows:

1. Write a file name in the text field to the left of the buttons and press Open to open a file. The text contained in the file is put in the text area at the bottom.

2. You can edit the text to your heart's content in the large text area.

3. If and when you want to save your changes, press the Save button, which again uses the text field containing the file name—and writes the contents of the text area to the file.

4. There is no Quit button—if the user closes the window, the program quits.

....

What's the Difference Between Text Areas and Text Fields?

In the requirement description, I've used the terms "text area" and "text field." This terminology is quite common: A *text field* is a GUI component that lets the user edit a small piece (a single line) of text; a *text area*, on the other hand, lets the user edit more text (typically several lines) and usually has scroll bars, while a text field usually doesn't. Chances are you have encountered both types of text editing components in Web pages that ask you to enter data into a form.

....

In some languages, writing a program like this is a daunting task, but with Python and the right GUI toolkit it's really a piece of cake. (You may not agree with me right now, but by the end of this chapter I hope you will.)

A Plethora of Platforms

Before writing a GUI program in Python you have to decide what GUI platform you want to use. Simply put, a platform is one specific set of graphical components, accessible through a given Python module, called a *GUI toolkit*. There are many such toolkits available for Python. Some of the most popular ones are listed in Table 12-1. For an even more detailed list, you could search the Vaults of Parnassus (see Appendix C) for the keyword GUI. Cameron Laird also maintains a Web page with an extensive list of GUI toolkits for Python (http://starbase.neosoft.com/~claird/comp.lang.python/python_GUI.html).

Table 12-1. Some Popular GUI Toolkits Available for Python

PACKAGE	DESCRIPTION
Tkinter	Uses the Tk platform. Readily available. Semi-standard.
wxPython	Based on wxWindows. Increasingly popular.
PythonWin	Windows only. Uses native Windows GUI capabilities.
Java Swing	Jython only. Uses native Java GUI capabilities.
PyGTK	Uses the GTK platform. Especially popular on Linux.
PyQt	Uses the Qt platform. Especially popular on Linux.

Information about Tkinter, wxPython, and Jython with Swing can be found in the section "But I'd Rather Use..." later in this chapter. For information about PythonWin, PyGTK, and PyQT, check out the project home pages (see Appendix C).

As you can see, there are plenty of packages to choose from. So which toolkit should you use? It is largely a matter of taste, although each toolkit has its advantages and drawbacks. Tkinter is sort of a de facto standard because it has been used in most "official" Python GUI programs, and it is included as a part of the Windows binary distribution. On UNIX, however, you have to compile and install it yourself. And because not everyone installs it (they may fancy wxPython or PyQt, for instance), your program might not run on those installations. Because this problem exists for all of the packages mentioned so far, so you might think it is irrelevant. Well, that's where Anygui enters the scene.

What Is Anygui?

Anygui is a project I started in the hope of creating a standard Python GUI package without trying to impose a specific platform (such as Tkinter or wxPython) on everyone. The goal is for Anygui to enable you to write programs that can be run with any of the available GUI toolkits, without bothering you with the details.

At the time of this writing, Anygui supports nine platforms, including all those mentioned in Table 12-1, GUI emulation in text-terminals with curses, and even GUI emulation with plain text, using the print statement! The number of platforms supported is increasing, and while the functionality currently available is only a subset of what you might expect from a full GUI toolkit, more is underway.

Anygui is quite simple, which is partly a given because it can support only the intersection of the features available in all its back-end GUI platforms. But it is also by design, to make it useful to beginners (and people like me, who like simple things). Python is becoming increasingly popular as a teaching language, and Anygui is designed to fit that trend. Even if Anygui never becomes as feature-rich as packages such as Tkinter and wxPython, it still covers the basic mechanisms—the basic skills you have to learn before you can write GUI programs. I've chosen to use it in this chapter because even if you ultimately end up using another package, you will have a fundamental understanding to build on.

For more information about Anygui (and the latest version of the software), visit the Web page at http://www.anygui.org.

Downloading and Installing Anygui

To download Anygui, simply visit the download page,
`http://www.anygui.org/download`. From there you will be able to download
a binary installer for Windows (with the file name extension `.exe`), RPM packages, and a `tar.gz` file as described in Chapter 1.

If you are running Python in Windows, simply download the binary installer
and run it. It will take care of all the installation tasks itself. If you are running
a Linux system that uses `rpm`, you can install one of the RPM packages (either the
`noarch.rpm` or the `src.rpm`—it doesn't matter which one).

If you can't use the binary installer or the RPM packages, download the
`tar.gz` file. When you have downloaded it, uncompress it, using either a Windows
compression program such as WinZip or the UNIX `tar` command. In the resulting
directory you will find a file called `INSTALL.txt`, which describes how to install
the software. Basically, what you have to do is execute the enclosed script called
`setup.py` with the command `install`, as follows:

```
$ python setup.py install
```

As an alternative to running this setup script, you can edit your `PYTHONPATH`
environment variable to include the `lib` directory.

After you have installed Anygui, you need to ensure that you have a working
GUI toolkit installed that Anygui can use. Some Python distributions include
such GUI toolkits by default. For instance, the standard Python distribution for
Windows includes Tkinter. You can find more information on installing various
toolkits in their respective documentation. See the section "A Plethora of
Platforms" earlier in this chapter for some pointers on where to find this
documentation.

Getting Started

To get started, import everything from the `anygui` module:

```
from anygui import *
```

Or, if you want to keep your namespace clean, use the following:

```
import anygui as gui
```

You can, of course, drop the `as gui` part. It just saves you some typing later
because you can write `gui.Button` instead of `anygui.Button`, and so forth. In the

examples in this chapter I use the starred import style, but I suggest you give the alternatives good consideration if you're going to develop larger GUI programs.

In addition to importing the anygui module itself, every Anygui program needs an Application object. It manages the windows of the program, and you use it to actually start the *main event loop* (starting the GUI, more or less) with its method run. Not all GUI toolkits have a separate application class like this, but, even among those that don't, most have a function that mirrors the functionality of Application.run.

A skeletal Anygui program looks like this:

```
from anygui import *
app = Application()
# Add code here
app.run()
```

If you run this program, nothing happens. You need some components (buttons and so on) and the windows to put them in.

Creating Windows and Components

Let's return to our example—the text editor. The first thing you need is a window. Creating a window is as easy as instantiating the Window class. To add the window to your application so it appears on your screen, you have to call the add method of your Application object. Listing 12-1 shows this first version of the editor.

Listing 12-1. A GUI Program with Only a Window

```
from anygui import *
app = Application()
win = Window()
app.add(win)
app.run()
```

Not very complicated, is it? Assuming you have installed Anygui, you can run this program and a window appears, as shown in Figure 12-2. The exact appearance depends on which back-end your Anygui installation is using.

Figure 12-2. A GUI program with only a window

From what you have seen so far, you may be able to guess how you create your buttons, text field, and text area, and how you add them to your window. But let me show you anyway.

To create a button, you instantiate the Button class (surprise, surprise) and add it to the window by calling the window's add method:

```
btn = Button()
win.add(btn)
```

If you add these lines to your program (inserting them before app.run()) and run it, you end up with something like Figure 12-3.

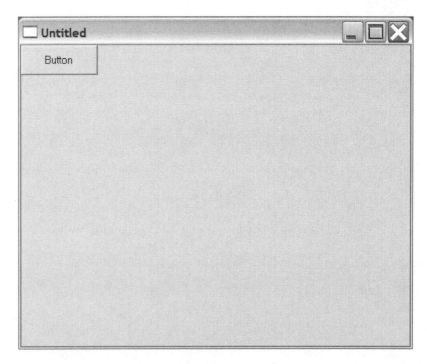

Figure 12-3. The program after adding a button

You use the same process to add other components. For your text field you use the TextField class, and for your text area, you use the TextArea class. (More on those in a little while.)

One thing isn't quite right in Figure 12-3, however. The text on the button says Button, but you want it to say Open or Save. How do you do that?

Attributes

You can customize all the components in Anygui by setting various attributes. For instance, if you want to set the text of a button btn, you simply assign a string to its text attribute:

```
btn.text = 'Open'
```

As a shortcut, you can supply the attributes as keyword arguments to the constructor:

```
btn = Button(text='Open')
```

In your program, you need two buttons—with some more readable names than btn, of course. So, you end up with the program shown in Listing 12-2.

Listing 12-2. Adding Two Buttons with Customized Text

```
from anygui import *
app = Application()
win = Window()
app.add(win)

loadButton = Button(text='Open')
win.add(loadButton)

saveButton = Button(text='Save')
win.add(saveButton)

app.run()
```

The reason I've called the first button loadButton and not openButton will become clear in a little while.

When you run this program, you get the result shown in Figure 12-4. One of the buttons is missing! What happened here?

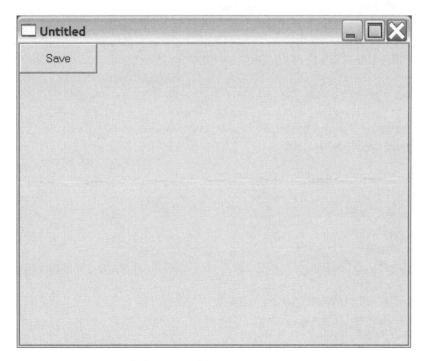

Figure 12-4. A window with layout problems

Layout

Actually, the window in Figure 12-4 does contain both your buttons. The problem is that the Save button is right on top of the Open button, so the latter is obscured. To fix this, you have to position the buttons properly. Such positioning of components is called "layout."

The simplest way to lay out components is to set their size and position directly, through their attributes. To set the position of a component, you can use either its position attribute (setting it to a pair of coordinates, using a tuple) or set its x and y attributes separately. The first line in the following example is equivalent to the last two:

```
loadButton.position = 10, 10  # Set both x and y coordinates
loadButton.x = 10             # Set the x coordinate
loadButton.y = 10             # Set the y coordinate
```

Similarly, the size of the component can be set either through its size attribute, or through its width and height attributes separately. The first line in the following example is equivalent to the last two:

```
loadButton.size = 80, 25  # Set both width and height
loadButton.width = 80     # Set the width
loadButton.height = 25    # Set the height
```

And just to make things really convenient, the geometry attribute allows you to set all of this at once—it's the equivalent of position + size:

```
loadButton.geometry = 10, 10, 80, 25 # Set x, y, width, and height
```

Listing 12-3 shows how to add all the components and lay them out according to the sketch in Figure 12-1.

Listing 12-3. Placing All the Components with Basic Layout

```
from anygui import *
app = Application()
win = Window()
app.add(win)

loadButton = Button(text='Open')
loadButton.geometry = 225, 5, 80, 25
win.add(loadButton)
```

```
saveButton = Button(text='Save')
saveButton.geometry = 315, 5, 80, 25
win.add(saveButton)

filename = TextField()
filename.geometry = 5, 5, 210, 25
win.add(filename)

contents = TextArea()
contents.geometry = 5, 35, 390, 260
win.add(contents)

app.run()
```

If you run this program, you should get something like Figure 12-5.

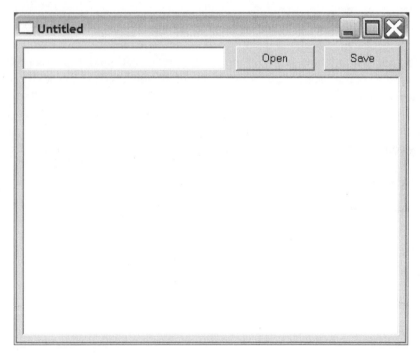

Figure 12-5. The program with correct layout

Advanced Layout

Although specifying the geometry of each component as I did in Listing 12-3 is
easy to understand, it can be a bit tedious. Doodling a bit on graph paper may
help in getting the coordinates right, but there are more serious drawbacks to this
approach than having to play around with numbers. If you run the program and
try to resize the window, you'll notice that the geometries of the components
don't change. This is no disaster, but it does look a bit odd. When you resize
a window, you assume that its contents will be resized and relocated as well.

If you consider how we did the layout, this behavior shouldn't really come as
a surprise. We explicitly set the position and size of each component, but didn't
say anything about how they should behave when the window was resized. There
are many ways of specifying this. The Anygui layout mechanism even enables
you to use your own objects as *layout managers* that arrange the components
every time the window changes its size. (For more information about this topic,
consult the Anygui documentation, available at http://anygui.org/docs.) In our
example we will use the default layout manager.

To get a dynamic layout (as opposed to the static one used so far) you supply
information about how you want the components positioned through keyword
arguments to the add method. Which keyword arguments you can use depend on
which layout scheme you are using. For the default layout manager (called
Placer), the available keywords (in Anygui 0.1.1) are shown in Table 12-2. You
won't be using direction and space here; they are used when adding more than
one component at a time. (For details, see the Anygui documentation.)

Table 12-2. Layout Arguments for the Default Layout Scheme

KEYWORD ARGUMENT	DESCRIPTION
left	The component's left edge
right	The component's right edge
top	The component's top edge
bottom	The component's bottom edge
hmove	Whether to move horizontally on resize
vmove	Whether to move vertically on resize
hstretch	Whether to stretch horizontally on resize
vstretch	Whether to stretch vertically on resize
direction	'left', 'right', 'up', or 'down'
space	Spacing between multiple components

Although the arguments described in Table 12-2 give you quite a few options, things aren't really much more complicated than they were in the examples in the previous section. The left, right, top, and bottom arguments, are a bit like size and position attributes, except that they are a bit more flexible. They may be either set to a number (like the plain geometrical attributes) or a pair (*component, distance*). For instance, if openButton is added to win with the keyword right set to (saveButton, 10), it means that the right edge of openButton should be placed at a distance of 10 pixels from saveButton. That's not too hard, is it? Listing 12-4 shows the layout rewritten to use left, right, top, and bottom.

Listing 12-4. Using the Default Layout Scheme

```
from anygui import *
app = Application()
win = Window()
app.add(win)

saveButton = Button(text='Save', height=25)
# 5 points from the right window edge and 5 points from the top; move button
# horizontally to keep it that way:
win.add(saveButton, right=5, top=5, hmove=1)

loadButton = Button(text='Open', height=25)
# 10 points from saveButton (to the right) and 5 points from the top; move button
# horizontally to keep it that way:
win.add(loadButton, right=(saveButton, 10), top=5, hmove=1)

filename = TextField()
# 10 points from loadButton (to the right), 5 points from the top, and 5 points
# from the left edge of the window; stretch text field horizontally to keep it
# that way:
win.add(filename, right=(loadButton, 10), top=5, left=5, hstretch=1)

contents = TextArea()
# 5 points from filename (above), 5 points from the left edge of the window,
# 5 points from the right edge of the window, and 5 points from the bottom of
# the window; stretch text area both horizontally and vertically to keep it that
# way:
win.add(contents, top=(filename, 5), left=5, right=5, bottom=5,
        hstretch=1, vstretch=1)

app.run()
```

This code gives the same result as that in Listing 12-3, but instead of using lots of absolute coordinates, I am now placing things in relation to one another.

If you look closely at the code you may notice that I've managed to sneak in some arguments relating to stretching and movement as well. These are Boolean variables and are simply used to tell the Placer whether or not you want a given component to stretch/move horizontally/vertically to preserve the geometry you set up with left, right, top, and bottom. In this case, I want the buttons to move horizontally, so I set their hmove to 1. I want the text field to stretch horizontally, so I set its hstretch to 1. Finally, I want the text area to stretch in both directions, so I set both hstretch and vstretch to 1.

And that's it. I've got the layout I wanted. One crucial thing is lacking, however. If you press the buttons, nothing happens.

Event Handling

In GUI lingo, the actions performed by the user (such as clicking a button) are called *events*. You need to make your program notice these events somehow, and then react to them. You accomplish this by linking a function to the component where the event in question might occur. When the event does occur (if ever), that function will then be called. You link the component and its event handler (or handlers—there may be several) with a function called link.

You can use the link function with either two or three arguments. (Actually, there are additional optional arguments, but those are for advanced use only; consult the documentation for details.) If used with three arguments, the first is the component (called the *event source*, or just the *source*), the second is the event type you're interested in (as a string, for example, 'click'), and the third is the function (called the *event handler*, or just the *handler*). If only two arguments are used, a default event type is assumed. (The default event type varies from component to component; see Table 12-3 for some of the most common ones.)

Table 12-3. Default Events for Some Common Components

COMPONENTS	DEFAULT EVENT
Button, CheckBox, RadioButton	click
ListBox, RadioGroup	select
TextField	enterkey

Let's assume that you have written a function responsible for opening a file, and you've called it load. Then you can use that as an event handler for loadButton as follows:

```
link(loadButton, 'click', load)
```

Because you're looking for `'click'` events, and because `'click'` happens to be the default event type for buttons, you can omit the event type, and just use

```
link(loadButton, load)
```

This is pretty intuitive, isn't it? I've linked a function to the button—when the button is pressed, the function is called.

....

What's This load Stuff About?

There is nothing magical about my choice to use `loadButton` and `load` as the button and handler names—even though the button text says "Open." It's just that if I had called the button `openButton`, `open` would have been the natural name for the handler, and that would have made the built-in file-opening function `open` unavailable. While there are ways of dealing with this, I found it easier to use a different name.

....

The Finished Program

Let's fill in the remaining blanks. All you need now are the two event handlers, `load` and `save`. When an event handler is called, it receives a single event object, which holds information about what happened (such as the source, the event type, the time it occurred) but let's ignore that here because you're only interested in the fact that a click occurred.

NOTE *In Anygui releases up to and including 0.1.1, event handlers receive information in the form of keyword arguments, rather than event objects. At the time of writing, 0.1.1 is the current release, but the next version should be out by the time you read this. If you're using 0.1.1, simply change the event handlers from this format:*

```
def someEventHandler(event): ...
```

to this:

```
def someEventHandler(**kwds): ...
```

Even though the event handlers are the meat of the program, they are surprisingly simple. Let's take a look at the load function first. It looks like this:

```
def load(event):
    file = open(filename.text)
    contents.text = file.read()
    file.close()
```

The file opening/reading part ought to be familiar from Chapter 11. As you can see, the file name is found by fetching filename's text attribute (where filename is the text field, remember?). Similarly, to put the text into the text area, you simply assign it to contents.text.

The save function is just as simple: It's the exact reverse of load except that 'w' has been added to open:

```
def save(event):
    file = open(filename.text, 'w')
    file.write(contents.text)
    file.close()
```

And that's it. Now I simply link these to their respective buttons and the program is ready to run. See Listing 12-5 for the final program. Notice that I've set the title attribute of my window as well: It's shown in the window bar on the top.

Listing 12-5. The Final Editor Program

```
from anygui import *

app = Application()
win = Window(title='Simple Editor')
app.add(win)

saveButton = Button(text='Save', height=25)
win.add(saveButton, right=5, top=5, hmove=1)

loadButton = Button(text='Open', height=25)
win.add(loadButton, right=(saveButton, 10), top=5, hmove=1)

filename = TextField(height=25)
win.add(filename, right=(loadButton, 10), top=5, left=5, hstretch=1)

contents = TextArea()
win.add(contents, top=(filename, 5), left=5, right=5, bottom=5,
        hstretch=1, vstretch=1)
```

```
def load(event):
    file = open(filename.text)
    contents.text = file.read()
    file.close()

link(loadButton, load)

def save(event):
    file = open(filename.text, 'w')
    file.write(contents.text)
    file.close()

link(saveButton, save)

app.run()
```

You can try out the editor using the following steps:

1. Run the program. You should get a window like the one in Figure 12-5.

2. Write something in the large text area (for example, "Hello, world!").

3. Write a file name in the small text field (for example, hello.txt). Make sure that this file does not already exist or it will be overwritten.

4. Press the Save button.

5. Close the editor window (just for fun).

6. Restart the program.

7. Type the same file name in the little text field.

8. Press the Open button. The text of the file should reappear in the large text area.

9. Edit the file to your heart's content, and save it again.

Now you can keep opening, editing, and saving until you grow tired of that—then you can start thinking of improvements. (How about allowing your program to download files with urllib, for instance?)

Hey! What About `pyw`?

In Chapter 1, I asked you to give your file the .pyw ending and double-click it (in Windows). Nothing happened, and I promised to explain it later. In Chapter 10, I mentioned it again, and said I'd explain it in this chapter. So I will.

It's no big deal, really. It's just that when you double-click an ordinary Python script in Windows, a DOS window appears with a Python prompt in it. That's fine if you use print and raw_input as the basis of your interface, but now that you know how to make graphical user interfaces, this DOS window will only be in our way. The truth behind the .pyw window is that it will run Python without the DOS window—which is just perfect for GUI programs.

But I'd Rather Use...

Anygui may be nice for writing simple GUI programs, and its simplicity makes it well-suited for beginners. However, it doesn't deal with all the complexities of a full GUI toolkit at least not yet. So once you feel you've grasped the basics of GUI programming, you may want to take a look at the other packages available. There are so many that I can't possibly teach you how to use all of them—but I'll give you some examples from three of the more popular ones (Tkinter, wxPython, and Jython/Swing). I won't discuss which of these (or any of the other available packages) is best. It seems to me that it's largely a matter of taste anyway.

EXAMPLE

To illustrate the various packages, I've created a simple example—simpler, even, than the editor example used earlier in the chapter. It's just a single window containing a single button with the label "Hello" filling the window. When you press the button, it prints out the words "Hello, world!" A simple Anygui version is shown here:

```
from anygui import *
def hello(event): print 'Hello, world!'
btn = Button(text='Hello')
link(btn, hello)

win = Window(title='Hello, Anygui!')
win.add(btn)
```

```
btn.size = win.size = 200, 100
app = Application()
app.add(win)

app.run()
```

 NOTE *If you're using Anygui 0.1.1 or older, remember that the event handler should be defined as* hello(**kwds).

In the interest of simplicity, I'm not using any fancy layout features here. The resulting window is shown in Figure 12-6.

Figure 12-6. A simple GUI example

Using Tkinter

Tkinter is an old timer in the Python GUI business. It is a wrapper around the Tk GUI toolkit (associated with the programming language Tcl). It is included by default in the Windows distribution. The following are some useful URLs:

- http://www.python.org/topics/tkinter/doc.html

- http://www.ibm.com/developerworks/linux/library/l-tkprg

- http://www.nmt.edu/tcc/help/lang/python/tkinter.pdf

Here is the GUI example implemented with Tkinter:

```
from Tkinter import *
def hello(): print 'Hello, world!'
win = Tk() # Tkinter's 'main window'
win.title('Hello, Tkinter!')
win.geometry('200x100') # Size 200, 200

btn = Button(win, text='Hello', command=hello)
btn.pack(expand=YES, fill=BOTH)

mainloop()
```

Using wxPython

The wxPython package is based on the C++ GUI toolkit wxWindows and is rapidly gaining in popularity. Like Tkinter, it is available on most platforms, with a binary installer available for Windows. If you want to explore wxPython, I'd suggest starting at the official Web site at http://www.wxpython.org.

Here is the GUI example implemented with wxPython:

```
from wxPython.wx import *
def hello(event): print 'Hello, world!'
class MyApp(wxApp):
    def OnInit(self):
        win_id = wxNewId()
        win = wxFrame(NULL, win_id, 'Hello, wxPython!',
                        size=wxSize(200, 100))
        btn_id = wxNewId()
        btn = wxButton(win, btn_id, 'Hello')
        EVT_BUTTON(btn, btn_id, hello)
        win.Show(true)
        return true

app = MyApp()
app.MainLoop()
```

Using Jython and Swing

If you're using Jython (the Java implementation of Python), packages such as Tkinter and wxPython aren't available. The only GUI toolkits that are readily available are the Java standard library packages AWT and Swing (Swing is the most recent and considered the standard Java GUI toolkit). The good news is that both of these are automatically available so you don't have to install them separately. For more information, visit the Jython Web site and look into the Swing documentation written for Java:

- http://www.jython.org

- http://java.sun.com/docs/books/tutorial/uiswing

Here is the GUI example implemented with Jython and Swing:

```
from javax.swing import *
import sys

def hello(event): print 'Hello, world!'
btn = JButton('Hello')
btn.actionPerformed = hello

win = JFrame('Hello, Swing!')
win.contentPane.add(btn)

def closeHandler(event): sys.exit()
win.windowClosing = closeHandler

btn.size = win.size = 200, 100
win.show()
```

Note that one additional event handler has been added here (closeHandler) because the Close button doesn't have any useful default behavior in Java Swing. Also note that you don't have to explicitly enter the main event loop because it's running in parallel with the program (in a separate *thread*).

Using Something Else

The basics of most GUI toolkits are the same, which is why I think it makes sense to start with something simple such as Anygui. Unfortunately, however, when learning how to use a new package it takes time to find your way through all the details that enable you to do exactly what you want. So you should take your time before deciding which package you want to work with (the section "A Plethora of Platforms" earlier in this chapter should give you some ideas of where to start), and then immerse yourself in its documentation and start writing code. I hope this chapter has provided the basic concepts you need to make sense of that documentation.

A Quick Summary

Once again, let's review what we've covered in this chapter:

Graphical user interfaces. Graphical user interfaces are useful in making your programs more user-friendly. Not all programs need them, but whenever your program interacts with a user, a GUI is probably helpful.

GUI platforms for Python. Many GUI platforms are available to the Python programmer. Although this richness is definitely a boon, the choice can sometimes be difficult.

Anygui. Anygui is a relatively simple GUI toolkit that can use any of several other packages as its *back-end*. Its goals are to be simple and ubiquitous. Even though you may want to use other packages for more demanding work, Anygui is a good place to start learning the basic concepts of GUI programming.

Components. A GUI program consists of graphical components. In Anygui, you can customize these simply by setting attributes such as text, title, size, or position.

Layout. You can position components quite simply by specifying their geometry directly. However, to make them behave properly when their containing window is resized, you will have to use some sort of layout manager.

Event handling. Actions performed by the user trigger *events* in the GUI toolkit. To be of any use, your program will probably be set up to react to some of these events; otherwise the user won't be able to interact with it. In Anygui, event handlers are added to components with the link function.

New Functions in This Chapter

FUNCTION	DESCRIPTION
anygui.link(*source*[, *event*], *handler*)	Used to link components with event handlers

CONSTRUCTOR/METHOD	DESCRIPTION
Application(...)	Creates an application
Application.add(*win*)	Adds a window to the application (making it appear)
Application.run()	Starts the main event loop
Button(...)	Creates a clickable button
TextArea(...)	Creates a multiline text area
TextField(...)	Creates a single-line text field
Window(...)	Creates a window (without showing it)
Window.add(*comp*)	Adds a component to a window

What Now?

That's it. You're officially finished with the first part of this book. Chapter 13 gives you an introduction to the second part, and starting with Chapter 14 you'll be writing lots of nifty programs—everything from chat servers to arcade games. Prepare to be amazed by the power of Python.

CHAPTER 13

Playful Programming

Welcome to the second part of the book. You have finished the tutorial part and should have a clearer picture of how Python works. Now the rubber hits the road, so to speak, and in the next ten chapters you put your newfound skills to work. Each chapter contains a single do-it-yourself project with lots of room for experimentation, while at the same time giving you the necessary tools to implement a solution.

In this chapter I give you some general guidelines for programming in Python, as well as a short description of how the projects are laid out.

Why Playful?

I think one of the strengths of Python is that it makes programming fun—for me, anyway. It's much easier to be productive when you're having fun; and one of the fun things about Python is that it allows you to be very productive. It's a positive feedback loop, and you get far too few of those in life.

The term *Playful Programming* is one I invented as a less extreme version of *Extreme Programming*, or XP.

 NOTE *Extreme Programming is an approach to software development created by Kent Beck. For more information, see* http://www.extremeprogramming.org.

I like many of the ideas of the XP movement but have been too lazy to commit completely to their principles. Instead, I've picked up a few things, and combined them with what I feel is a natural way of developing programs in Python.

The Ju-Jitsu of Programming

You have perhaps heard of *ju-jitsu?* It's a Japanese martial art, which, like its descendants *judo* and *aikido*, focuses on flexibility of response, or "bending instead of breaking." Instead of trying to impose your preplanned moves on an opponent, you go with the flow, using your opponent's movements against him or her. This way (in theory) you can beat an opponent who is bigger, meaner, and stronger than you.

How does this apply to programming? The key is the syllable "ju" which may be (very roughly) translated as flexibility. When you run into trouble (as you invariably will) while programming, instead of trying to cling stiffly to your initial designs and ideas, be flexible; roll with the punches. Be prepared to change and adapt. Don't treat unforeseen events as frustrating interruptions; treat them as stimulating starting points for creative exploration of new options and possibilities.

The point is that when you sit down and plan how your program should be, you don't have any real experience with that specific program. How could you? After all, it doesn't exist yet. By working on the implementation, you gradually learn new things that could have been useful when you did the original design. Instead of ignoring these lessons you pick up along the way, you should use them to redesign (or *refactor*) your software. I'm not saying that you should just start hacking away with no idea of where you are headed—just that you should prepare for change, and accept that your initial design *will* need to be revised. It's like the old writer's saying: "Writing is rewriting."

This practice of flexibility has many aspects; here I'll touch upon three of them:

- **Prototyping:** One of the nice things about Python is that you can write programs quickly. Writing a prototype program is an excellent way to learn more about your problem.

- **Configuration:** Flexibility comes in many forms. The purpose of configuration is to make it easy to change certain parts of your program, both for you and your users.

- **Testing:** Automated testing is absolutely essential if you want to be able to change your program easily. With tests in place, you can be sure that your program still works after introducing a modification.

These principles are described in greater detail in the material that follows.

Prototyping

In general, if you wonder how something works in Python, just try it. You don't have to do extensive preprocessing, such as compiling or linking, which is necessary in many other languages. You can just run your code directly. And not only that—you can run it piecemeal in the interactive interpreter, prodding at every corner until you thoroughly understand its behavior.

This kind of exploration doesn't only cover language features and built-in functions. Sure, it's useful to be able to find out exactly how, say, the `iter` function works, but even more important is the ability to easily create a prototype of the program you are about to write, just to see how *that* works.

NOTE   *In this context, the word* prototype *means a tentative implementation, a mock-up that implements the main functionality of the final program, but which may have to be completely rewritten at some later stage.*

After you have put some thought into the structure of your program (such as which classes and functions you need), I suggest implementing a simple version of it, possibly with very limited functionality. You'll quickly notice how much easier the process becomes when you have a running program to play with. You can add features, change things you don't like, and so on; you can really see how it works, instead of just thinking about it or drawing diagrams on paper.

You can use prototyping in any programming language, but the strength of Python is that writing a mock-up is a very small investment, so you're not committed to using it. If you find that your design wasn't as clever as it could have been, you can simply toss out your prototype and start from scratch. The process might take a few hours, or a day or two. If you were programming in C++, for instance, much more work would probably be involved in getting something up and running, and discarding it would be a major decision. By committing to one version you lose flexibility; you get locked in by early decisions that may prove wrong in light of the real-world experience you get from actually implementing it.

In the projects that follow, I consistently use prototyping instead of detailed analysis and design up front. Every project is divided into two implementations. The first is a fumbling experiment in which I've thrown together a program that solves the problem (or possibly only a part of the problem) in order to learn about the components needed and what's required of a good solution. The greatest lesson will probably be seeing all the flaws of the program in action.

By building on this newfound knowledge, we take another, hopefully more informed, whack at it. Of course you should feel free to revise the code or even start afresh a third time. Usually, starting from scratch doesn't take as much time as one might think. If you have already thought through the practicalities of the program, the typing shouldn't take too long.

Configuration

In this section, I return to the ever important principle of abstraction. In Chapters 6 and 7, I showed you how to abstract away code by putting it in functions and methods, and hiding larger structures inside classes. Let's take a look at another, much simpler, way of introducing abstraction in your program: extracting *symbolic constants* from your code.

Extracting Constants

By *constants* I mean built-in literal values such as numbers, strings, and lists. Instead of writing these repeatedly in your program, you can gather them in global variables. I know I've been warning you about those, but problems with global variables occur primarily when you start changing them, because it can be difficult to keep track of which part of your code is responsible for which change. I'll leave these variables alone, however, and use them as if they were constant (hence the term *symbolic constants*). To signal that a variable is to be treated as a symbolic constant, you can use a special naming convention, using only capital letters in their variable names, separating words with underscores.

Let's take a look at an example. In a program that calculates the area and circumference of circles, you could keep writing 3.14 every time you needed the value π. But what if you, at some later time, wanted a more exact value, say 3.14159? You would have to search through the code and replace the old value with the new. Not very hard, and in most good text editors it could be done automatically. However, what if you had started out with the value 3? Would you later want to replace every occurrence of the number 3 with 3.14159? Hardly. A much better way of handling this would be to start the program with the line

```
PI = 3.14
```

and then use the name `PI` instead of the number itself. That way you could simply change this single line to get a more exact value at some later time. Just keep this in the back of your mind: Whenever you write a constant (such as the number 42 or the string "Hello, world!") more than once consider placing it in a global variable instead.

> **NOTE** *Actually, the value of π is found in the* math *module, under the name* math.pi:
>
> ```
> >> from math import pi
> >> pi
> 3.1415926535897931
> ```

Configuration Files

Extracting constants for your own benefit is one thing; but some constants can even be exposed to your users. For instance, if they don't like the background color of your GUI program, perhaps you should let them use another color. Or perhaps you could let users decide what greeting message they would like to get when they start your exciting arcade game or the default starting page of the new Web browser you just implemented.

Instead of putting these configuration variables at the top of one of your modules, you can put them in a separate file. The simplest way of doing this is to have a separate module for configuration. For instance, if PI was set in the module file config.py, you could (in your main program) do the following:

```
from config import PI
```

Then, if the user wants a different value for PI, he or she can simply edit config.py without having to wade through your code.

Another possibility is to use the standard library module ConfigParser, which will allow you to use a reasonably standard format for configuration files. It allows both standard Python assignment syntax, such as

```
greeting = 'Hello, world!'
```

and another configuration format used in many programs:

```
greeting: Hello, world!
```

You have to divide the configuration file into *sections*, using headers such as [files] or [colors]. The names can be anything, but you have to enclose them in brackets. A sample configuration file is shown in Listing 13-1, and a program using it is shown in Listing 13-2. For more information on the features of the ConfigParser module, you should consult the library documentation (http://python.org/doc/lib/module-ConfigParser.html).

Listing 13-1. A Simple Configuration File

```
[numbers]

pi: 3.1415926535897931

[messages]
```

```
greeting: Welcome to the area calculation program!
question: Please enter the radius:
result_message: The area is
```

Listing 13-2. A Program Using ConfigParser

```
from ConfigParser import ConfigParser

config = ConfigParser()
# Read the configuration file:
config.read('c:/python/config.txt')

# Print out an initial greeting;
# 'messages' is the section to look in:
print config.get('messages', 'greeting')

# Read in the radius, using a question from the config file:
radius = input(config.get('messages', 'question') + ' ')

# Print a result message from the config file;
# end with a comma to stay on same line:
print config.get('messages', 'result_message'),

# getfloat() converts the config value to a float:
print config.getfloat('numbers', 'pi') * radius**2
```

I won't go into much detail about configuration in the following projects, but I suggest you think about making your programs highly configurable. That way, the user can adapt the program to his or her taste, which can make using it more pleasurable. After all, one of the main frustrations of using software is that you can't make it behave the way you want it to.

Testing

To plan for change and flexibility, it's important to set up tests for the various parts of your program (so-called *unit tests*). It's also a very practical and pragmatic part of designing your application. Let's look at these two issues separately, beginning with the latter.

Precise Requirement Specification

When developing a piece of software, you must first know what problem the software will solve—what objectives it will meet. You can clarify your goals for the program by writing a *requirement specification,* a document (or just some quick notes) describing requirements the program must satisfy. It is then easy to check at some later time whether the requirements are indeed satisfied. But many programmers dislike writing reports and in general prefer to have their computer do as much of their work as possible. Good news: You can specify the requirements in Python, and have the interpreter check whether they are satisfied!

> **NOTE** *There are many types of requirements, including such vague concepts as client satisfaction. In this section I focus on* functional *requirements—that is, what is required of the program's functionality.*

The idea is to start by writing a test program, and *then* write a program that passes the tests. The test program is your requirement specification and helps you stick to those requirements while developing the program.

Let's take a simple example: You want to write a module with a single function that will compute the area of a rectangle with a given height and a given width. Before you start coding, you write a unit test with some examples for which you know the answers. Your test program might look like this:

```
from area import rect_area
height = 3
width = 4
correct_answer = 12
answer = rect_area(height, width)
if answer == correct_answer:
    print 'Test passed '
else:
    print 'Test failed '
```

In this example, I call the function rect_area (which I haven't written yet) on the height 3 and width 4 and compare the answer with the correct one, which is 12. Of course, testing only one case like this won't give you much confidence in the correctness of the code. A real test program would probably be a lot more thorough. Anyway, if you carelessly implement rect_area (in the file area.py) as follows, and try to run the test program, you would get an error message:

```
def rect_area(height, width):
    return height * height # This is wrong...
```

You could then examine the code to see what was wrong, and replace the returned expression with height * width.

Planning for Change

In addition to helping a great deal as you write the program, automated tests help you avoid accumulating errors when you introduce changes. We have already established that you should be prepared to change your code rather than clinging frantically to what you've got; but change has its dangers. When you change some piece of your code, you very often introduce some unforeseen bug. If you have designed your program well (with lots of encapsulation), the effects of a change should be local, and only affect a small piece of the code. That means that debugging is easier *if you spot the bug.*

The point is that if you don't have a thorough set of tests handy, you may not even discover that you have introduced a bug until later, when you no longer know how the error got introduced. And without a good test set, it is much more difficult to pinpoint exactly what is wrong. You can't roll with the punches unless you see them coming.

Support for Testing in the Standard Libraries

You may think that writing lots of tests to make sure that every detail of your program works correctly sounds like a chore. Well, I have good news for you: There is help in the standard libraries (isn't there always?). There are two brilliant modules available to automate the testing process for you: unittest, a generic testing framework, and my favorite, doctest, which is designed for checking documentation, but which is excellent for writing unit tests as well. Let's take a look at doctest, which is a great starting point.

doctest

Throughout this book, I use examples taken directly from the interactive interpreter. I find that this is an effective way to show how things work, and when you have such an example, it's easy to test it for yourself. In fact, interactive interpreter sessions can be a useful form of documentation to put in docstrings. For instance, let's say I write a function for squaring a number, and add an example to its docstring:

```
def square(x):
    '''
    Squares a number and returns the result.

    >>> square(2)
    4
```

```
>>> square(3)
9
'''
    return x*x
```

As you can see, I've included some text in the docstring, too. What does this have to do with testing? Let's say the square function is defined in the module my_math (that is, a file called my_math.py). Then you could add the following code at the bottom:

```
if __name__=='__main__':
    import doctest, my_math
    doctest.testmod(my_math)
```

That's not a lot, is it? You simply import doctest and the my_math module itself, and then run the testmod (for "test module") function from doctest. What does this do? Let's try it:

```
$ python my_math.py
$
```

Nothing seems to have happened, but that's a good thing. The doctest.testmod function reads all the docstrings of a module and seeks out any text that looks like an example from the interactive interpreter; then it checks whether the example represents reality. To get some more input, you can just give the -v switch (for verbose) to your script:

```
$ python my_math.py -v
Running my_math.__doc__
0 of 0 examples failed in my_math.__doc__
Running my_math.square.__doc__
Trying: square(2)
Expecting: 4
ok
Trying: square(3)
Expecting: 9
ok
0 of 2 examples failed in my_math.square.__doc__
1 items had no tests:
    test
1 items passed all tests:
    2 tests in my_math.square
2 tests in 2 items.
```

```
2 passed and 0 failed.
Test passed.
$
```

As you can see, a lot happened behind the scenes. The `testmod` function checks both the module docstring (which, as you can see, contains no tests) and the function docstring (which contains two tests, both of which succeed).

With this in place, you can safely change your code. Let's say that you want to use the Python exponentiation operator instead of plain multiplication, and use x**2 instead of x*x. You edit the code, but accidentally forget to enter the number 2, and end up with x**x. Try it, and then run the script to test the code. What happens? This is the output you get:

```
******************************************************************
Failure in example: square(3)
from line #5 of my_math.square
Expected: 9
Got: 27
******************************************************************
1 items had failures:
    1 of   2 in my_math.square
***Test Failed*** 1 failures.
```

So the bug was caught, and you get a very clear description of what is wrong. Fixing the problem shouldn't be a problem now.

 CAUTION *Don't trust your tests blindly, and be sure to test enough cases. As you can see, the test using* square(2) *does* not *catch the bug because for* x==2, x**2 *and* x**x *are the same thing!*

For more information about the `doctest` module you should again check out the library reference (`http://python.org/doc/lib/module-doctest.html`).

unittest

While `doctest` is very easy to use, `unittest` is more flexible and powerful. It may have a steeper learning curve than `doctest`, but I suggest that you take a look at it because it makes it possible to write very large and thorough test sets in a more

structured manner. The module is described in the library reference
(http://www.python.org/doc/current/lib/module-unittest.html).

Although I won't go into detail about it, let's take a look at a simple example
of how you can use unittest. First, here is a part of a module called my_math:

```
def product(x, y):
    return x * y
```

You then write a separate test program for this module (called
test_my_math.py in this case), using the TestCase class from the unittest module:

```
import unittest, my_math

class ProductTestCase(unittest.TestCase):
    def testIntegers(self):
        for x in xrange(-10, 10):
            for y in xrange(-10, 10):
                p = my_math.product(x, y)
                self.failUnless(p == x*y, 'Integer multiplication failed')

    def testFloats(self):
        for x in xrange(-10, 10):
            for y in xrange(-10, 10):
                x = x/10.0
                y = y/10.0
                p = my_math.product(x, y)
                self.failUnless(p == x*y, 'Float multiplication failed')

if __name__ == '__main__': unittest.main()
```

The function unittest.main takes care of running the tests for us. You can
execute the test program as follows:

```
$ python test_my_math.py
```

The output is simply:

```
..
----------------------------------
Ran 2 tests in 0.015s

OK
```

The dots at the top (there are only two) are the tests.

Just for fun, let's change the product function so that it fails for the specific parameters 7 and 9:

```
def product(x, y):
    if x == 7 and y == 9:
        return 'An insidious bug has surfaced!'
    else:
        return x * y
```

If you run the test script again, you should get an error message:

```
.F
========================================================================
FAIL: testIntegers (__main__.ProductTestCase)
_____

Traceback (most recent call last):
  File "test_my_math.py", line 8, in testIntegers
    self.failUnless(p == x*y, 'Integer multiplication failed')
  File "/home/idi/f/mlh/python/Python-2.2/lib/python2.2/unittest.py", line 262,
in failUnless
    if not expr: raise self.failureException, msg
AssertionError: Integer multiplication failed


_____

Ran 2 tests in 0.045s

FAILED (failures=1)
```

As you can see, one of the tests is now represented as an F (failure) rather than a dot, and you get a full traceback with a description of what went wrong.

Logging

Even though it's not strictly a form of testing, I'll say a few words about logging here because it will help you discover problems and bugs. Logging is basically collecting data about your program as it runs, so you can examine it afterward. A very simple form of logging can be done with the print statement. Just put a statement like this at the beginning of your program:

```
log = open('logfile.txt', 'w')
```

You can then later put any interesting information about the state of your program into this file as follows:

```
print >> log, ('Downloading file from URL %s' % url)
text = urllib.urlopen(url).read()
print >> log, 'File successfully downloaded'
```

This approach won't work well if your program crashes during the download. It would be safer if you opened and closed your file for every log statement. Then, if your program crashed, you could see that the last line in your log file said "Downloading file from..." and you would know that the download wasn't successful. One way of enforcing this opening and closing behavior is to create a log class and instantiate it, as shown in Listing 13-3.

 NOTE *Instead of opening and closing the file like this, you could use the file method* flush *to make sure your changes are stored on disk.*

Listing 13-3. A Simple Logger Class

```
import time

class Logger:
    def __init__(self, filename):
        self.filename = filename
    def __call__(self, string):
        file = open(self.filename, 'a')
        file.write('[' + time.asctime() + '] ')
        file.write(string + '\n')
        file.close()

log = Logger('logfile.txt')
```

Lots of improvements are possible here, of course. The example is only meant to give you an idea of what is possible. Listing 13-4 shows how you can use this logger object.

Listing 13-4. A Program Using the Logger Class

```
log('Starting program')

log('Trying to divide 1 by 0')

print 1 / 0

log('The division succeeded')

log('Ending program')
```

Running that program would result in the following logfile:

```
[Sat Jan 19 12:27:51 2002] Starting program
[Sat Jan 19 12:27:51 2002] Trying to divide 1 by 0
```

As you can see, nothing is logged after trying to divide 1 by 0 because this error effectively kills the program. Because this is such a simple error, you can tell what is wrong by the exception traceback that prints as the program crashes. However, the most difficult type of bug to track down is one that doesn't stop your program but simply makes it behave strangely. Examining a detailed logfile may help you find out what's going on.

If you want to get serious about logging, you shouldn't reinvent the wheel. Do a Web search on "python" and "logging" and you should find some useful classes that can do the job for you.

If You Can't Be Bothered

All this is well and good, you may think, but there's no way I'm going to put that much effort into writing a simple little program. Configuration, testing, logging— it sounds really boring.

Well, that's fine. You may not need it for simple programs. And even if you're working on a larger project, you may not really *need* all of this at the beginning. I would say that the minimum is that you have some way of testing your program, even if it's not based on automatic unit tests. For instance, if you're writing a program that automatically makes you coffee, you should have a coffee pot around, to see if it works.

In the project chapters that follow, I don't write full test suites, intricate logging facilities, and so forth. I present you with some simple test cases to demonstrate that the programs work, and that's it. If you find the core idea of a project interesting, you should take it further—try to enhance and expand it.

And in the process, you should consider the issues you read about in this chapter. Perhaps a configuration mechanism would be a good idea? Or a more extensive test suite? It's up to you.

Project Structure

All the projects follow more or less the same structure, with the following sections:

- **What's the problem?** In this section the main goals of the project are outlined, including some background information.

- **Useful tools.** Here, I describe modules, classes, functions, and so on that might be useful for the project.

- **Preparations.** Here we perform any preparations necessary before starting to program. This may include setting up the necessary framework for testing the implementation.

- **First implementation.** This is the first whack—a tentative implementation to learn more about the problem.

- **Second implementation.** After the first implementation, you will probably have a better understanding of things, which will enable you to create a new and improved version.

- **Further exploration.** Finally, I give pointers for further experimentation and exploration.

A Quick Summary

In this chapter, I described some general principles and techniques for programming in Python, conveniently lumped under the heading "Playful Programming." Here are the highlights:

Flexibility. When designing and programming, you should aim for flexibility. Instead of clinging to your initial ideas, you should be willing to, and even prepared to, revise and change every aspect of your program as you gain insight into the problem at hand.

Prototyping. One important technique for learning about a problem and possible implementations is to write a simple version of your program to see how it works. In Python, this is so easy that you can write several prototypes in the time it takes to write a single version in many other languages.

Configuration. Extracting constants from your program makes it easier to change them at some later point. Putting them in a configuration file makes it possible for your user to configure the program to behave like he or she wants it to.

Testing. Testing is an important technique both for specifying what your program should do, and for ensuring that it still behaves correctly after introducing changes. The `doctest` and `unittest` modules can be of great help in implementing automated tests.

Project structure. All ten projects have a similar structure. First, the problem is outlined along with some useful tools for solving it. Then, after the necessary preparations (such as setting up tests), I present two successive implementations. Finally, I give pointers for further exploration.

What Now?

Indeed, what now? Now is the time to take the plunge and really start programming. It's time for the projects.

CHAPTER 14

Project 1:
Instant Markup

IN THIS PROJECT, you see how to use Python's excellent text processing capabilities, including the capability to use regular expressions to change a plain text file into one marked up in a language such as HTML or XML. You need such skills if you want to use text written by people who don't know these languages in a system that requires the contents to be marked up.

Let's start by implementing a simple prototype that does the basic processing, and then extend that program to make the markup system more flexible.

Alphabet Soup

Never heard of XML? Don't worry about that—if you have only a passing acquaintance with HTML, you'll do fine in this chapter. If you need an introduction to HTML, I suggest you take a look at Dave Raggett's excellent guide "Getting Started with HTML" at the World Wide Web Consortium's Web site (http://www.w3.org/MarkUp/Guide). For more information about XML, see Chapter 16, "Project 3: XML for All Occasions."

What's the Problem?

You want to add some formatting to a plain text file. Let's say you've been handed the file from someone who can't be bothered with writing in HTML, and you need to use the document as a Web page. Instead of adding all the necessary tags manually, you want your program to do it automatically.

Your task is basically to classify various text elements, such as headlines and emphasized text, and then clearly mark them. In the specific problem addressed here, you add HTML markup to the text, so the resulting document can be displayed in a Web browser and used as a Web page. However, once you have built your basic engine, there is no reason why you can't add other kind of markup (such as various forms of XML or perhaps LaTeX codes). After analyzing a text you can even perform other tasks, such as extracting all the headlines to make a table of contents.

What Is L^AT_EX?

You don't have to worry about it while working on this project—but L^AT_EX is another markup system (based on the T_EX typesetting program) for creating various types of technical documents. I mention it here only as an example of what other uses your program may be put to. If you want to know more, you can visit the T_EX Users Group home page at http://www.tug.org.

The text you're given may contain some clues (such as emphasized text being marked *like this*), but you'll probably need some ingenuity in making your program guess how the document is structured.

Specific Goals

Before starting to write your prototype, let's define some goals:

- The input shouldn't be required to contain artificial codes or tags.

- You should be able to deal both with different blocks, such as headings, paragraphs, and list items, as well as inlines, such as emphasized text or URLs.

- While you concentrate on HTML, it should be easy to extend your program to other markup languages.

You may not be able to reach these goals fully in the first version of your program, but that's what it's for. You write the prototype to find flaws in your original ideas and to learn more about how to write a program that solves your problem.

Useful Tools

Consider what tools might be needed in writing this program. You certainly need to read from and write to files (see Chapter 11), or at least read from standard input (sys.stdin) and output with print. You probably need to iterate over the lines of the input (see Chapter 11); you need a few string methods (see Chapter 3); perhaps you'll use a generator or two (see Chapter 9); and you probably need the re module (see Chapter 10). If any of these concepts seem unfamiliar to you, you should perhaps take a moment to refresh your memory.

Preparations

Before you start coding, you need some way of assessing your progress; you need a test suite. In this project a single test may suffice: a test *document* (in plain text). Listing 14-1 contains a sample text that you want to mark up automatically.

*Listing 14-1. A Sample Plain Text Document (*test_input.txt*)*

```
Welcome to World Wide Spam, Inc.


These are the corporate web pages of *World Wide Spam*, Inc. We hope
you find your stay enjoyable, and that you will sample many of our
products.

A short history of the company

World Wide Spam was started in the summer of 2000. The business
concept was to ride the dot-com wave and to make money both through
bulk email and by selling canned meat online.

After receiving several complaints from customers who weren't
satisfied by their bulk email, World Wide Spam altered their profile,
and focused 100% on canned goods. Today, they rank as the world's
13,892nd online supplier of SPAM.

Destinations

From this page you may visit several of our interesting web pages:

  - What is SPAM? (http://wwspam.fu/whatisspam)

  - How do they make it? (http://wwspam.fu/howtomakeit)

  - Why should I eat it? (http://wwspam.fu/whyeatit)
```

```
How to get in touch with us

You can get in touch with us in *many* ways: By phone (555-1234), by
email (wwspam@wwspam.fu) or by visiting our customer feedback page
(http://wwspam.fu/feedback).
```

To test you implementation, you need only to use this document as input and view the results in a Web browser—or perhaps examine the added tags directly.

First Implementation

One of the first things you need to do is split the text into paragraphs. It's obvious from Listing 14-1 that the paragraphs are separated by one or more empty lines. A better word than paragraph might be *block* because this name can apply to headlines and list items as well.

A simple way to find these blocks is to collect all the lines you encounter until you find an empty line, and then return the lines you have collected so far. That would be one block. Then, you could start all over again. You needn't bother collecting empty lines, and you won't return empty blocks (where you have encountered more than one empty line). Also, you should make sure that the last line of the file is empty; otherwise you won't know when the last block is finished. (There are other ways of finding out, of course.)

Listing 14-2 shows an implementation of this approach.

Listing 14-2. A Text Block Generator (util.py)

```python
from __future__ import generators

def lines(file):
    for line in file: yield line
    yield '\n'

def blocks(file):
    block = []
    for line in lines(file):
        if not line.isspace():
            block.append(line)
        elif block:
            yield ''.join(block).strip()
            block = []
```

The `lines` generator is just a little utility that tucks an empty line onto the end of the file. The `blocks` generator implements the approach described. When a block is yielded, its lines are joined, and the resulting string is stripped, giving you a single string representing the block, with excessive whitespace at either end (such as list indentations or newlines) removed.

 NOTE *The* `from __future__ import generators` *statement is necessary in Python version 2.2, but not in 2.3. See also the section "Avoiding Generators" in Chapter 9.*

I've put the code in the file `util.py`, which means that you can import the utility generators in your program later on.

Adding Some Markup

With the basic functionality from Listing 14-2, you can create a simple markup script. The basic steps of this program are as follows:

1. Print some beginning markup.

2. For each block print the block, enclosed in paragraph tags.

3. Print some ending markup.

This isn't very difficult, but it's not extremely useful either. Let's say that instead of enclosing the first block in paragraph tags, you enclose it in top heading tags (h1). Also, you replace any text enclosed in asterisks with emphasized text (using em tags). At least that's a *bit* more useful. Given the `blocks` function, and using `re.sub`, the code is very simple. See Listing 14-3.

Listing 14-3. A Simple Markup Program (`simple_markup.py`*)*

```
from __future__ import generators
import sys, re
from util import *

print '<html><head><title>...</title><body>'

title = 1
for block in blocks(sys.stdin):
```

```
        block = re.sub(r'\*(.+?)\*', r'<em>\1</em>', block)
        if title:
            print '<h1>'
            print block
            print '</h1>'
            title = 0
        else:
            print '<p>'
            print block
            print '</p>'

print '</body></html>'
```

This program can be executed on the sample input as follows:

```
$ python simple_markup.py < test_input.txt > test_output.html
```

The file `test_output.html` will then contain the generated HTML code. Figure 14-1 shows how this HTML code looks in a Web browser.

Figure 14-1. The first attempt at generating a Web page

Although not very impressive, this prototype does perform some important tasks: It divides the text into blocks that can be handled separately, and it applies a filter (consisting of a call to re.sub) to each block in turn. This seems like a good approach to use in your final program.

Now what would happen if you tried to extend this prototype? You would probably add checks inside the for loop to see whether the block was a heading, a list item, or something else. You would add more regular expressions. It could quickly grow into a mess—and, more importantly, it would be very difficult to make it output anything other than HTML; and one of the goals of this project is to make it easy to add other output formats.

Second Implementation

So, what did you learn from this first implementation? To make it more extensible, you need to make your program more *modular* (divide the functionality into independent components). One way of achieving modularity is through object-oriented design (see Chapter 7). You need to find some abstractions to make your program more manageable as its complexity grows. Let's begin by listing some possible components:

- **A parser:** An object that reads the text and manages the other classes.

- **Rules:** You can make one rule for each type of block, which is able to detect the applicable block type and to format it appropriately.

- **Filters:** Use filters to wrap up some regular expressions to deal with inline elements.

- **Handlers:** The parser uses handlers to generate output. Each handler can produce a different kind of markup.

Although this isn't a very detailed design, at least it gives you some ideas about how to divide your code into smaller parts and make each part manageable.

Handlers

Let's begin with the handlers. A handler is responsible for generating the resulting marked up text, but it receives detailed instructions from the parser. Let's say it has a pair of methods for each block type—one for starting the block, and one for ending it. For instance, it might have the methods start_paragraph and end_paragraph to deal with paragraph blocks. For HTML, these could be implemented as follows:

```
class HTMLRenderer:
    def start_paragraph(self):
        print '<p>'
    def end_paragraph(self):
        print '</p>'
```

Of course, you'll need more similar methods for other block types. (For the full code of the HTMLRenderer class, see Listing 14-4 later in this chapter.) This seems flexible enough. If you wanted some other type of markup, you would just make another handler (or renderer) with other implementations of the start and end methods.

NOTE   *The name* Handler *(as opposed to* Renderer, *for instance) was chosen to indicate that it handles the method calls generated by the parser. It doesn't* have *to render the text in some markup language, as* HTMLRenderer *does. A similar handler mechanism is used in the XML parsing scheme called SAX, which is explained in Chapter 16, "Project 3: XML For All Occasions."*

How do you deal with regular expressions? As you may recall, the re.sub function can take a function as its second argument (the replacement). This function is called with the match object, and its return value is inserted into the text. This fits nicely with the handler philosophy discussed previously—you just let the handlers implement the replacement methods. For instance, emphasis can be handled like this:

```
def sub_emphasis(self, match):
    return '<em>%s</em>' % match.group(1)
```

If you don't understand what the group method does, perhaps you should take another look at the re module, described in Chapter 10.

In addition to the start, end, and sub methods, you'll have a method called feed, which you use to feed actual text to the handler. In your simple HTML renderer, you'll just implement it like this:

```
def feed(self, data):
    print data
```

A Handler Superclass

In the interest of flexibility, let's add a Handler class, which will be the superclass of your handlers and which will take care of some administrative details. Instead of having to call the methods by their full name (for example, start_paragraph) it may at times be useful to handle the block types as strings (for example, 'paragraph') and supply the handler with those. You can do this by adding some generic methods called start(*type*), end(*type*), and sub(*type*). In addition, you can make start, end, and sub check whether the corresponding methods (such as start_paragraph for start('paragraph')) are really implemented and do nothing if no such method is found. An implementation of this Handler class follows. (This code is taken from the module handlers shown in Listing 14-4.)

```
class Handler:
    def callback(self, prefix, name, *args):
        method = getattr(self, prefix+name, None)
        if callable(method): return method(*args)
    def start(self, name):
        self.callback('start_', name)
    def end(self, name):
        self.callback('end_', name)
    def sub(self, name):
        def substitution(match):
            result = self.callback('sub_', name, match)
            default = match.group(0)
            return result or default
        return substitution
```

NOTE *This code required nested scopes, which are not available prior to Python 2.1. If you're using Python 2.1, you need to add the line* from __future__ import nested_scopes *at the top of the* handlers *module. (To some degree, nested scopes can be simulated with default arguments. See the sidebar "Nested Scopes" in Chapter 6.)*

Several things in this code warrant some explanation.

The callback method is responsible for finding the correct method (such as start_paragraph), given a prefix (such as 'start_') and a name (such as 'paragraph'), and it performs its task by using getattr with None as the default value. If the object returned from getattr is callable, it is called with any additional arguments supplied. So, for instance, calling handler.callback('start_', 'paragraph') calls the method handler.start_paragraph with no arguments, given that it exists.

The start and end methods are just helper methods that call callback with the respective prefixes start_ and end_.

The sub method is a bit different. It doesn't call callback directly, but returns a new function, which is used as the replacement function in re.sub (which is why it takes a match object as its only argument). Confusing? Let's consider an example (and don't worry about the default part yet—I'll get to that).

Let's say HTMLRenderer is a subclass of Handler and it implements the method sub_emphasis as described in the previous section (see Listing 14-4 for the actual code). Let's say you have an HTMLRenderer instance in the variable handler:

```
>>> from handlers import HTMLRenderer
>>> handler = HTMLRenderer()
```

What then will handler.sub('emphasis') do?

```
>>> handler.sub('emphasis')
<function substitution at 0x168cf8>
```

It returns a function (substitution) that basically calls the handler.sub_emphasis method when you call it. That means that you can use this function in a re.sub statement:

```
>> re.sub(r'\*(.+?)\*', handler.sub('emphasis'), 'This *is* a test')
'This <em>is</em> a test'
```

Magic! (The regular expression matches text bracketed by asterisks, which I'll discuss shortly.) But why go to such lengths? Why not just use r'\1' as I did in the simple version? Because then you'd be committed to using the em tag—and you want the handler to be able to decide what markup to use. If your handler were a (hypothetical) LaTeXRenderer, for instance, you might get another result altogether:

```
>> re.sub(r'\*(.+?)\*', handler.sub('emphasis'), 'This *is* a test')
'This \emph{is} a test'
```

The markup has changed, but the code has not.

Now, what about that or default part of the replacement function? What's that all about? It's a backup, in case no substitution is implemented. The callback method tries to find a suitable sub_something method, but if it doesn't find one, it returns None. Because your function is as a re.sub replacement function, you *don't* want it to return None. Instead, if you find no substitution method, you just return the original match without any modifications. Due to short-circuit logic (see Chapter 5), if the callback returns None, your lambda returns default (which is match.group(0)) instead, which is the original matched text.

Rules

Now that I've made the handlers quite extensible and flexible, it's time to turn to the parsing (interpretation of the original text). Instead of making one big if statement with various conditions and actions such as in my simple markup program I'll make the rules a separate kind of object.

The rules are used by the main program (the parser), which must determine which rules are applicable for a given block, and then make each rule do what is needed to transform the block. In other words, a rule must

- Be able to recognize blocks where it applies (the *condition*)

- Be able to transform blocks (the *action*)

So each rule object must have two methods, condition and action.

The condition method needs only one argument—the block in question. It should return a Boolean value indicating whether the rule is applicable to the given block.

The action method also needs the block as an argument, but to be able to affect the output, it must also have access to the handler object.

In many circumstances, only one rule may be applicable. That is, if you find that a headline rule is used (indicating that the block is a headline), you should *not* attempt to use the paragraph rule. A simple implementation of this would be to have the parser try the rules one by one, and stop the processing of the block once one of the rules is triggered. This would be fine in general, but as you'll see, sometimes a rule may not preclude the execution of other rules. Therefore you add another piece of functionality to your action method: It returns a Boolean value indicating whether the rule processing for the current block should stop or not.

Pseudocode for the headline rule might be:

```
class HeadlineRule:
    def condition(self, block):
        if the block fits the definition of a headline, return 1;
```

```
            otherwise, return 0.
    def action(self, block, handler):
            call methods such as handler.start('headline'), handler.feed(block) and
            handler.end('headline').
            because we don't want to attempt to use any other rules,
            return 1 which will end the rule processing for this block.
```

A Rule Superclass

Although you don't strictly need a common superclass for your rules, several of them may share the same general action—calling the start, feed, and end methods of the handler with the appropriate type string argument, and then returning 1 (to stop the rule processing). Assuming that all the subclasses have an attribute called type containing this type name as a string, you can implement your superclass as shown in the code that follows. (The Rule class is found in the rules module—the full code is shown in Listing 14-5.)

```
class Rule:
    def action(self, block, handler):
        handler.start(self.type)
        handler.feed(block)
        handler.end(self.type)
        return 1
```

The condition method is the responsibility of each subclass. The Rule class and its subclasses are put in the rules module.

Filters

You won't need a separate class for your filters. Given the sub method of your Handler class, each filter can be represented by a regular expression and a name (such as emphasis or url). You see how in the next section, when you deal with the parser.

The Parser

You've come to the heart of your application—the Parser class. It uses a handler and a set of rules and filters to transform a plain text file into a marked-up file—in this specific case, an HTML file. Which methods does it need? It needs a constructor to set things up, a method to add rules, a method to add filters, and a method to parse a given file.

You can see code for the `Parser` class in Listing 14-6. (Let's just worry about the `Parser` class for now—I'll get to the rest soon enough.)

Although there is quite a lot to digest in this class, most of it isn't very complicated. The constructor simply stores the supplied handler as an instance variable (attribute) and then initializes two lists—one of rules, and one of filters. The `addRule` method simply adds a rule to the rule list. The `addFilter` method does a bit more work. Like `addRule`, it adds a filter to the filter list—but before doing so, it creates that filter. The filter is simply a function that applies `re.sub` with the appropriate regular expression (pattern) and uses a replacement from the handler, accessed with `handler.sub(name)`.

NOTE   *Again, you need nested scopes. In Python 2.1, add* `from __future__ import nested_scopes` *to the beginning of the script.*

The `parse` method—although it might look a bit complicated—is perhaps the easiest method to implement because it merely does what you've been planning to do all along. It begins by calling `start('document')` on the handler, and ends by calling `end('document')`. Between these calls it iterates over all the blocks in the text file.

For each block it applies both the filters and the rules. Applying a filter is simply a matter of calling the filter function with the block and handler as arguments, and rebinding the block variable to the result, as follows:

```
block = filter(block, self.handler)
```

This enables each of the filters to do its work, which is replacing parts of the text with marked-up text (such as replacing *this* with this).

There is a bit more logic in the rule loop. For each rule there is an `if` statement, checking whether the rule applies by calling `rule.condition(block)`. If the rule applies, `rule.action` is called with the block and handler as arguments. Remember that the `action` method returns a Boolean value indicating whether to finish the rule application for this block. Finishing the rule application is done by setting the variable `last` to the return value of `action`, and then conditionally breaking out of the `for` loop with

```
if last: break
```

NOTE *You can collapse these two statements into one, eliminating the* last *variable:*

```
if rule.action(block, self.handler): break
```

Whether or not to do so is largely a matter of taste. Removing the temporary variable makes the code simpler, while leaving it in clearly labels the return value.

Constructing the Rules and Filters

Now you have all the tools you need, but you haven't created any specific rules or filters yet. The motivation behind much of the code you've written so far is to make the rules and filters as flexible as the handlers. You can write several independent rules and filters and add them to your parser through the addRule and addFilter methods, making sure to implement the appropriate methods in your handlers.

A complicated ruleset makes it possible to deal with complicated documents. However, let's keep it simple for now: Let's create one rule for the title, one rule for other headings, and one for list items. Because list items should be treated collectively as a list, you'll create a separate list rule, which deals with the entire list. Lastly, you can create a default rule for paragraphs, which covers all blocks not dealt with by the previous rules.

We can specify the rules in informal terms as follows:

- A heading is a block that consists of only one line, which has a length of at most 70 characters. If the block ends with a colon, it is not a heading.

- The title is the first block in the document, provided that it is a heading.

- A list item is a block that begins with a hyphen ("-").

- A list begins between a block that is not a list item and a following list item and ends between a list item and a following block that is not a list item.

These rules follow some of my intuitions about how a text document is structured. Your opinions on this (and your text documents) may differ. Also, the rules have weaknesses (for instance, what happens if the document ends with a list item?)—feel free to improve on them.

The source code for the rules is shown in Listing 14-5 (which also contains the basic Rule class).

Let's begin with the heading rule. The attribute type has been set to the string 'heading', which is used by the action method inherited from Rule. The condition simply checks that the block does not contain a newline (\n) character, that its length is at most 70, and that the last character is not a colon.

The title rule is similar, but only works once—for the first block. After that, it ignores all blocks because its attribute first has been set to a *false* value.

The list item rule condition is a direct implementation of the preceding specification. Its condition is a reimplementation of that found in Rule; the only difference is that it removes the first character from the block (the hyphen) and strips away excessive whitespace from the remaining text. The markup provides its own "list bullet," so you won't need the hyphen anymore.

All the rule actions so far have returned a *true* value (1). The list rule does not, because it is triggered when you encounter a list item after a non-list item or when you encounter a non-list item after a list item. Because it doesn't actually mark up these blocks but merely indicates the beginning and end of a list (a group of list items) you don't want to halt the rule processing—so you return 0.

The list rule requires further explanation. Its condition is always *true* because you want to examine all blocks. In the action method you have two alternatives that may lead to action:

- If the attribute inside (indicating whether the parser is currently inside the list) is *false* (as it is initially), and the condition from the list item rule is *true*, you have just entered a list. Call the appropriate start method of the handler, and set the inside attribute to *true* (1).

- Conversely, if inside is *true*, and the list item rule condition is *false*, you have just left a list. Call the appropriate end method of the handler, and set the inside attribute to *false* (0).

After this processing, the function returns 0 to let the rule handling continue.

The final rule is ParagraphRule. Its condition is always *true* because it is the "default" rule. It is added as the last element of the rule list, and handles all blocks that aren't dealt with by any other rule.

The filters are simply regular expressions. Let's add three filters—one for emphasis, one for URLs, and one for e-mail addresses. Let's use the following three regular expressions:

```
r'\*(.+?)\*'
r'(http://[\.a-zA-Z/]+)'
r'([\.a-zA-Z]+@[\.a-zA-Z]+[a-zA-Z]+)'
```

The first pattern (emphasis) matches an asterisk followed by one or more arbitrary characters (matching as few as possible—hence the question mark), followed by another asterisk. The second pattern (URLs) matches the string 'http://' (here you could add more protocols) followed by one or more characters that are either dots, letters, or slashes. (This pattern will not match all legal URLs—feel free to improve it.) Finally, the e-mail pattern matches a sequence of letters and dots followed by an "at" sign (@) followed by more letters and dots, finally followed by a sequence of letters, ensuring that you don't end with a dot. (Again—feel free to improve this.)

Putting It All Together

You now have only to create a Parser object and add the relevant rules and filters. Let's do that by creating a subclass of Parser that does the initialization in its constructor. Then let's use that to parse sys.stdin. The final program is shown in Listings 14-4 through 14-6. (These listings depend on the utility code in Listing 14-2.) The final program may be run just like the prototype:

```
$ python markup.py < test_input.txt > test_output.html
```

You can see the result of running the program on the sample text in Figure 14-2.

The second implementation is clearly more complicated and extensive than the first version. The added complexity is well worth the effort because the resulting program is much more flexible and extensible. Adapting it to new input and output formats is merely a matter of subclassing and initializing the existing classes, rather than rewriting everything from scratch, as you would have had to do in the first prototype.

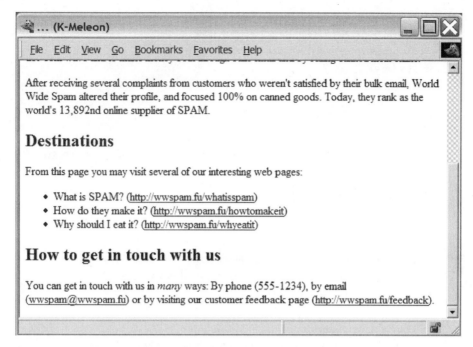

Figure 14-2. The second attempt at generating a Web page

*Listing 14-4. The Handlers (*handlers.py*)*

```python
class Handler:
    """

    An object that handles method calls from the Parser.

    The Parser will call the start() and end() methods at the
    beginning of each block, with the proper block name as
    parameter. The sub() method will be used in regular expression
    substitution. When called with a name such as 'emphasis', it will
    return a proper substitution function.
    """
```

```
        def callback(self, prefix, name, *args):
            method = getattr(self, prefix+name, None)
            if callable(method): return method(*args)
        def start(self, name):
            self.callback('start_', name)
        def end(self, name):
            self.callback('end_', name)
        def sub(self, name):
            return lambda match: self.callback('sub_', name, match) or match.group(0)


class HTMLRenderer(Handler):
    """
    A specific handler used for rendering HTML.

    The methods in HTMLRenderer are accessed from the superclass
    Handler's start(), end(), and sub() methods. They implement basic
    markup as used in HTML documents.
    """
    def start_document(self):
        print '<html><head><title>...</title></head><body>'
    def end_document(self):
        print '</body></html>'
    def start_paragraph(self):
        print '<p>'
    def end_paragraph(self):
        print '</p>'
    def start_heading(self):
        print '<h2>'
    def end_heading(self):
        print '</h2>'
    def start_list(self):
        print '<ul>'
    def end_list(self):
        print '</ul>'
    def start_listitem(self):
        print '<li>'
    def end_listitem(self):
        print '</li>'
    def start_title(self):
        print '<h1>'
    def end_title(self):
        print '</h1>'
```

```python
    def sub_emphasis(self, match):
        return '<em>%s</em>' % match.group(1)
    def sub_url(self, match):
        return '<a href="%s">%s</a>' % (match.group(1), match.group(1))
    def sub_mail(self, match):
        return '<a href="mailto:%s">%s</a>' % (match.group(1), match.group(1))
    def feed(self, data):
        print data
```

*Listing 14-5. The Rules (*rules.py*)*

```python
class Rule:
    """
    Base class for all rules.
    """
    def action(self, block, handler):
        handler.start(self.type)
        handler.feed(block)
        handler.end(self.type)
        return 1

class HeadingRule(Rule):
    """
    A heading is a single line that is at most 70 characters and
    that doesn't end with a colon.
    """
    type = 'heading'
    def condition(self, block):
        return not '\n' in block and len(block) <= 70 and not block[-1] == ':'

class TitleRule(HeadingRule):
    """
    The title is the first block in the document, provided that it is
    a heading.
    """
    type = 'title'
    first = 1
    def condition(self, block):
        if not self.first: return 0
        self.first = 0
        return HeadingRule.condition(self, block)
```

```
class ListItemRule(Rule):
    """
    A list item is a paragraph that begins with a hyphen. As part of
    the formatting, the hyphen is removed.
    """
    type = 'listitem'
    def condition(self, block):
        return block[0] == '-'
    def action(self, block, handler):
        handler.start(self.type)
        handler.feed(block[1:].strip())
        handler.end(self.type)
        return 1

class ListRule(ListItemRule):
    """
    A list begins between a block that is not a list item and a
    subsequent list item. It ends after the last consecutive list
    item.
    """
    type = 'list'
    inside = 0
    def condition(self, block):
        return 1
    def action(self, block, handler):
        if not self.inside and ListItemRule.condition(self, block):
            handler.start(self.type)
            self.inside = 1
        elif self.inside and not ListItemRule.condition(self, block):
            handler.end(self.type)
            self.inside = 0
        return 0

class ParagraphRule(Rule):
    """
    A paragraph is simply a block that isn't covered by any of the
    other rules.
    """
    type = 'paragraph'
    def condition(self, block):
        return 1
```

Listing 14-6. The Main Program (markup.py)

```python
import sys, re
from handlers import *
from util import *
from rules import *

class Parser:
    """
    A Parser reads a text file, applying rules and controlling a
    handler.
    """
    def __init__(self, handler):
        self.handler = handler
        self.rules = []
        self.filters = []
    def addRule(self, rule):
        self.rules.append(rule)
    def addFilter(self, pattern, name):
        def filter(block, handler):
            return re.sub(pattern, handler.sub(name), block)
        self.filters.append(filter)
    def parse(self, file):
        self.handler.start('document')
        for block in blocks(file):
            for filter in self.filters:
                block = filter(block, self.handler)
            for rule in self.rules:
                if rule.condition(block):
                    last = rule.action(block, self.handler)
                    if last: break
        self.handler.end('document')

class BasicTextParser(Parser):
    """
    A specific Parser that adds rules and filters in its
    constructor.
    """
    def __init__(self, handler):
        Parser.__init__(self, handler)
        self.addRule(ListRule())
        self.addRule(ListItemRule())
        self.addRule(TitleRule())
```

```
                    self.addRule(HeadingRule())
                    self.addRule(ParagraphRule())

                    self.addFilter(r'\*(.+?)\*', 'emphasis')
                    self.addFilter(r'(http://[\.a-zA-Z/]+)', 'url')
                    self.addFilter(r'([\.a-zA-Z]+@[\.a-zA-Z]+[a-zA-Z]+)', 'mail')

handler = HTMLRenderer()
parser = BasicTextParser(handler)

parser.parse(sys.stdin)
```

Further Exploration

Several expansions are possible for this program. Here are some possibilities:

- Add support for tables. Find all aligning left word borders and split the block into columns.

- Add support for interpreting all uppercase words as emphasis. (To do this properly, you will need to take into account acronyms, punctuations, names and other capitalized words.)

- Write markup handlers for other markup languages (such as DocBook XML or LaTeX).

- Write a handler that does something other than markup. Perhaps write a handler that analyzes the document in some way.

- Create a script that automatically converts all text files in a directory to HTML files.

What Now?

Phew! After this strenuous (but useful) project, it's time for some lighter material. In the next chapter, you create some graphics based on data that is automatically downloaded from the Internet. Piece of cake.

#### CHAPTER 15

Project 2:
Painting a
Pretty Picture

IN THIS PROJECT YOU LEARN how you can create graphics in Python. More specifically, you create a PDF file with graphics helping you visualize data that you read from a text file. While you could get such functionality from a regular spreadsheet, Python gives you much more power, as you'll see when you get to the second implementation and automatically download your data from the Internet.

Alphabet Soup Revisited

In the previous chapter we looked at HTML and XML—and here is another acronym: PDF, short for Portable Document Format. PDF is a format created by Adobe that can represent any kind of document with graphics and text. The PDF file is not editable (as, say, a Microsoft Word file would be) but there is reader software freely available for most platforms, and the PDF file should look the same no matter which reader you use or which platform you are on (as opposed to HTML where the correct fonts may not be available, you'd have to ship pictures as separate files, and so on).

If you don't already have a PDF reader, Adobe's own Acrobat Reader is freely available from the Adobe Web site
(http://www.adobe.com/products/acrobat/readstep.html).

What's the Problem?

Python is excellent for analyzing data. With its file handling and string processing facilities, it's probably easier to create some form of report from a data file than to create something similar in your average spreadsheet, especially if what you want to do requires some complicated programming logic.

You have seen (in Chapter 3) how you can use string formatting to get pretty output—for instance, if you want to print numbers in columns. However, sometimes plain text just isn't enough. (As they say, a picture is worth a thousand words.) In this project you learn the basics of the ReportLab package, which enables you to create graphics and documents in the PDF format (and a few other formats) almost as easily as you created plain text earlier.

As you play with the concepts in this project, I encourage you to find some application that is interesting to you. I have chosen to use data about sunspots (from the Space Environment Center, a part of the U.S. National Oceanic and Atmospheric Administration) and to create a line diagram from these data.

Specific Goals

The program should be able to do the following:

- Download a data file from the Internet.

- Parse the data file and extract the interesting parts.

- Create PDF graphics based on the data.

As in the previous project, these goals might not be fully met by the first prototype.

Useful Tools

The crucial tool in this project is the graphics-generating package. There are quite a few such packages to choose from. If you visit the Vaults of Parnassus (http://www.vex.net/parnassus) you will find a separate category for graphics. I have chosen to use ReportLab because it is easy to use and has extensive functionality for both graphics and document generation in PDF.

To get the ReportLab package, go to the official Web page at http://www.reportlab.com. There you will find the software, documentation, samples, and even the opportunity to purchase support. (The basic software itself is free.)

Click the download link to find the software. Then simply follow the instructions on the download page, which basically say to do the following:

1. Download the archive file (for example, ReportLab_X.zip, where X is a version number).

2. Uncompress the archive and put the resulting directory in your
    Python path.

When you have done this, you should be able to import the `reportlab` module, as follows:

```
>>> import reportlab
>>>
```

How Does It Work?

Although I show you how some ReportLab features work in this project, much
more functionality is available. To learn more, I suggest you obtain the user guide
and the (separate) graphics guide, made available on the ReportLab Web site (on
the download page). They are quite readable, and are much more comprehensive
than this one chapter could possibly be.

Preparations

Before we start programming, we need some data with which to test our program. I have chosen (quite arbitrarily) to use data about sunspots, available from
the Web site of the Space Environment Center (http://www.sec.noaa.gov). You
can find the data I use in my examples at
http://www.sec.noaa.gov/ftpdir/weekly/Predict.txt.

This data file is updated weekly and contains information about sunspots
and radio flux. (Don't ask me what that means.) Once you've got this file, you're
ready to start playing with the problem.

Here is a part of the file to give you an idea of how the data look:

```
#          Predicted Sunspot Number And Radio Flux Values
#                      With Expected Ranges
#
#          ----Sunspot Number----   ---10.7 cm Radio Flux---
# YR MO   PREDICTED    HIGH     LOW  PREDICTED    HIGH     LOW
#----------------------------------------------------------------



2001 09      114.0    115.0   113.0      189.7    190.7   188.7
2001 10      112.2    115.2   109.2      186.4    189.4   183.4
```

2001 11	111.0	116.0	106.0	184.2	189.2	179.2
2001 12	108.5	115.5	101.5	182.0	189.0	175.0
2002 01	106.4	114.4	98.4	180.3	189.3	171.3
2002 02	105.3	114.3	96.3	178.8	189.8	167.8

First Implementation

In this first implementation, let's just put the data into our source code, as a list of tuples. That way, it's easily accessible. Here is an example of how you can do it:

```
data = [
#    Year  Month  Predicted  High   Low
    (2001,  8,     113.2,     114.2, 112.2),
    (2001,  9,     112.8,     115.8, 109.8),
    # Add more data here
    ]
```

With that out of the way, let's see how you can turn these data into graphics.

Drawing with ReportLab

ReportLab consists of many parts and enables you to create output in several ways. The most basic module for generating PDF is pdfgen. It contains a Canvas class with several low-level methods for drawing. To draw a line on a Canvas called c, you call the c.line method, for instance.

We'll use the more high-level graphics framework (in the package reportlab.graphics and its submodules), which will enable us to create various shape objects and to add them to a Drawing object that we can later output to a file in PDF format.

Listing 15-1 shows a sample program that draws the string "Hello, world!" in the middle of a 100×100-point PDF figure. (You can see the result in Figure 15-1.) As you can see, the structure is reminiscent of the Anygui programs you saw in Chapter 11. You create a drawing of a given size, you create graphical elements (in this case, a String object) with certain properties, and then you add the elements to the drawing. Finally, the drawing is rendered into PDF and is saved to a file.

Listing 15-1. A Simple ReportLab Program

```
from reportlab.graphics.shapes import Drawing, String
from reportlab.graphics import renderPDF

d = Drawing(100, 100)
s = String(50, 50, 'Hello, world!', textAnchor='middle')

d.add(s)

renderPDF.drawToFile(d, 'hello.pdf', 'A simple PDF file')
```

The call to renderPDF.drawToFile saves your PDF file to a file called hello.pdf in the current directory.

The main arguments to the String constructor are its *x* and *y* coordinates and its text. In addition, you can supply various attributes (such as font size, color, and so on). In this case, I've supplied a textAnchor, which is the part of the string that should be placed at the point given by the coordinates.

 NOTE *When you run this program, you may get two warnings: one saying that the Python Imaging Library is not available, and the other that zlib is not available. (If you have installed either of these, that warning will, of course, not appear.) You won't need either of these libraries for the code in this project, so you can simply ignore the warnings.*

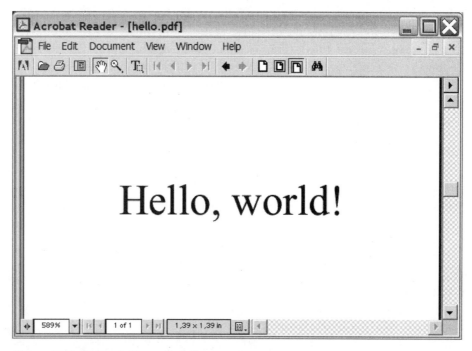

Figure 15-1. A simple ReportLab figure

Constructing Some PolyLines

To create a line diagram (a graph) of the sunspot data, you have to create some lines. In fact, you have to create several lines that are linked. ReportLab has a special class for this: PolyLine.

A PolyLine is created with a list of coordinates as its first argument. This list is of the form [(x0, y0), (x1, y1), ...], with each pair of *x* and *y* coordinate making one point on the PolyLine. See Figure 15-2 for a simple PolyLine.

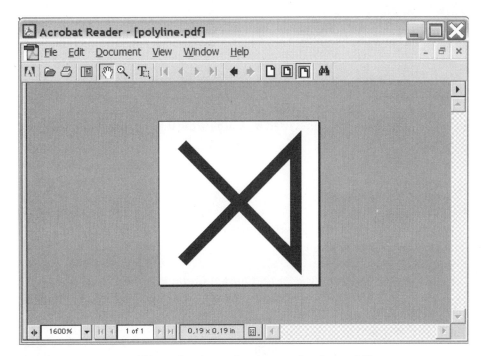

Figure 15-2. PolyLine([(0, 0), (10, 0), (10, 10), (0, 10)])

To make a line diagram, one polyline must be created for each column in the data set. Each point in these polylines will consist of a time (constructed from the year and month) and a value (which is the number of sunspots taken from the relevant column). To get one of the columns (the values) list comprehensions can be useful:

```
pred = [row[2] for row in data]
```

Here pred (for "predicted") will be a list of all the values in the third column of the data. You can use a similar strategy for the other columns. (The time for each row would have to be calculated from both the year and month: for example, *year + month*/12.)

Once you have the values and the time stamps, you can add your polylines to the drawing like this:

```
drawing.add(PolyLine(zip(times, pred), strokeColor=colors.blue))
```

It isn't necessary to set the stroke color, of course, but it makes it easier to tell the lines apart. (Note how zip is used to combine the times and values into a list of tuples.)

The Prototype

You now have what you need to write your first version of the program. The source code is shown in Listing 15-2.

Listing 15-2. The First Prototype for the Sunspot Graph Program

```
from reportlab.lib import colors
from reportlab.graphics.shapes import *
from reportlab.graphics import renderPDF

data = [
#    Year  Month  Predicted  High   Low
    (2001,  8,     113.2,     114.2, 112.2),
    (2001,  9,     112.8,     115.8, 109.8),
    (2001, 10,     111.0,     116.0, 106.0),
    (2001, 11,     109.8,     116.8, 102.8),
    (2001, 12,     107.3,     115.3,  99.3),
    (2002,  1,     105.2,     114.2,  96.2),
    (2002,  2,     104.1,     114.1,  94.1),
    (2002,  3,      99.9,     110.9,  88.9),
    (2002,  4,      94.8,     106.8,  82.8),
    (2002,  5,      91.2,     104.2,  78.2),
    ]

drawing = Drawing(200, 150)

pred = [row[2]-40 for row in data]
high = [row[3]-40 for row in data]
low = [row[4]-40 for row in data]
times = [200*((row[0] + row[1]/12.0) - 2001)-110 for row in data]
```

```
drawing.add(PolyLine(zip(times, pred), strokeColor=colors.blue))
drawing.add(PolyLine(zip(times, high), strokeColor=colors.red))
drawing.add(PolyLine(zip(times, low),  strokeColor=colors.green))

drawing.add(String(65, 115, 'Sunspots', fontSize=18, fillColor=colors.red))

renderPDF.drawToFile(drawing, 'report1.pdf', 'Sunspots')
```

As you can see, I have adjusted the values and time stamps to get the positioning right. The resulting drawing is shown in Figure 15-3.

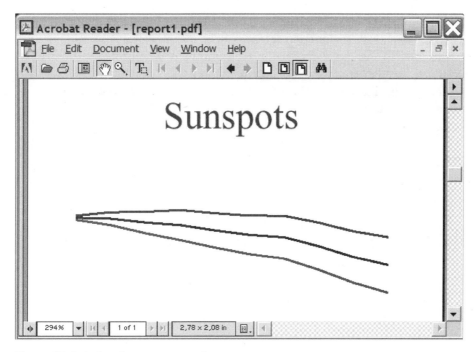

Figure 15-3. A simple sunspot graph

Although it is pleasing to have made a program that works, there is clearly still room for improvement.

Second Implementation

So, what did you learn from your prototype? You've figured out the basics of how to draw stuff with ReportLab. You have also seen how you can extract the data in a way that works well for drawing your graph. However, there are some weaknesses in the program. To position things properly, I had to add some ad hoc modifications to the values and time stamps. And the program doesn't actually get the data from anywhere. (More specifically, it "gets" the data from a list inside the program itself, rather than reading it from an outside source.)

Unlike Project 1, the second implementation won't be much larger or more complicated than the first. It will be an incremental improvement that will use some more appropriate features from ReportLab and actually fetch its data from the Internet.

Getting the Data

As you saw in Chapter 11, you can fetch files across the Internet with the standard module `urllib`. Its function `urlopen` works in a manner quite similar to `open`, but takes a URL instead of a file name as its argument. When you have opened the file and read its contents, you have to filter out what you don't need. The file contains empty lines (consisting of only whitespace) and lines beginning with some special characters ("#" and ":"). The program should ignore these. (See the example file fragment in the section "Preparations" earlier in this chapter.)

Assuming that the URL is stored in a variable called `URL`, and that the variable `COMMENT_CHARS` has been set to the string `'#:'`, you can get a list of rows (as in our original program) like this:

```
data = []
for line in urlopen(URL).readlines():
    if not line.isspace() and not line[0] in COMMENT_CHARS:
        data.append(map(float, line.split()))
```

The preceding code will include all the columns in the data list, although we aren't particularly interested in the ones pertaining to radio flux. However, those columns will be filtered out when we extract the columns we really need (as we did in the original program).

 NOTE *If you are using a data source of your own (or if, by the time you read this, the data format of the sunspot file has changed) you will, of course, have to modify this code accordingly.*

Using the `LinePlot` Class

If you thought getting the data was surprisingly simple, drawing a prettier line plot isn't much of a challenge either. In a situation like this, it's best to thumb through the documentation (in this case, the ReportLab docs) to see if there is a feature already in the system that can do what you need, so you don't have to implement it all yourself. Luckily, there is just such a thing: the `LinePlot` class from the module `reportlab.graphics.charts.lineplots`. Of course we could have looked for this to begin with, but in the spirit of rapid prototyping, we just used what was at hand to see what we could do. Now it's time to go one step further.

The `LinePlot` is instantiated without any arguments, and then you set its attributes before adding it to the `Drawing`. The main attributes you need to set are `x`, `y`, `height`, `width`, and `data`. The first four should be self-explanatory; the latter is simply a list of point-lists, where a point-list is a list of tuples, like the one we used in our `PolyLines`.

To top it off, let's set the stroke color of each line. The final code is shown in Listing 15-3. The resulting figure is shown in Figure 15-4.

Listing 15-3. The Final Sunspot Program

```
from urllib import urlopen
from reportlab.graphics.shapes import *
from reportlab.graphics.charts.lineplots import LinePlot
from reportlab.graphics.charts.textlabels import Label
from reportlab.graphics import renderPDF


URL = 'http://www.sec.noaa.gov/ftpdir/weekly/Predict.txt'
COMMENT_CHARS = '#:'


drawing = Drawing(400, 200)
data = []
for line in urlopen(URL).readlines():
    if not line.isspace() and not line[0] in COMMENT_CHARS:
        data.append(map(float, line.split()))

pred = [row[2] for row in data]
high = [row[3] for row in data]
low = [row[4] for row in data]
times = [row[0] + row[1]/12.0 for row in data]

lp = LinePlot()
lp.x = 50
```

```
lp.y = 50
lp.height = 125
lp.width = 300
lp.data = [zip(times, pred), zip(times, high), zip(times, low)]
lp.lines[0].strokeColor = colors.blue
lp.lines[1].strokeColor = colors.red
lp.lines[2].strokeColor = colors.green


drawing.add(lp)

drawing.add(String(250, 150, 'Sunspots',
            fontSize=14, fillColor=colors.red))


renderPDF.drawToFile(drawing, 'report2.pdf', 'Sunspots')
```

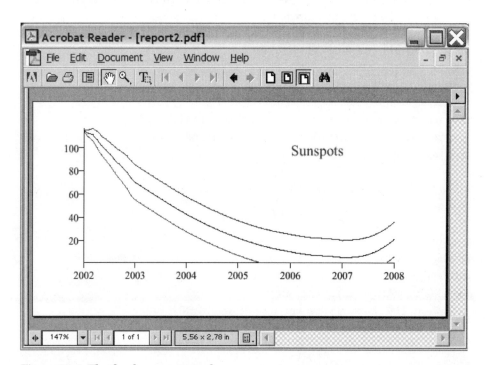

Figure 15-4. The final sunspot graph

Further Exploration

As I mentioned before, many graphics and plotting packages are available for Python. Sping is one such package that is an attempt to make a standard graphics API (based on the older package Piddle, which I helped create). Both Sping and Piddle are available from the Piddle project page (`http://piddle.sf.net`). Sping supports several output formats, including PDF, PostScript, and SVG; various pixmap formats (through the Python Imaging Library); and interactive graphics for Tkinter and wxPython.

Using either ReportLab or Sping you could try to incorporate automatically generated graphics into a document (perhaps generating parts of that as well?). You could use some of the techniques from Chapter 14 to add markup to the text. If you want to create a PDF document, Platypus, a part of ReportLab, is useful for that. (You could also integrate the PDF graphics with some typesetting system such as pdfL^AT_EX.) If you wanted to create a Web page, using Sping to create a picture might be a good choice. (There is experimental support for generating picture formats such as GIF in ReportLab as well, but at the time of this writing, that must be downloaded separately through CVS.)

If your primary goal is to plot data (which is what we did in this project), there are many alternatives to ReportLab. You can find a good list of possibilities at `http://www.python.org/topics/scicomp/plotting.html`. You can also find some at the Vaults of Parnassus.

What Now?

In the first project you learned how to add markup to a plain-text file by creating an extensible parser. In the next project, you learn about analyzing marked-up text (in XML) by using parser mechanisms that already exist in the Python standard library. The goal of the project is to use a single XML file to specify an entire Web site, which will then be generated automatically (with files, directories, added headers and footers) by your program. The techniques you learn in the next project will be applicable to XML parsing in general, and with XML being used in an increasing number of different settings, that can't hurt.

CHAPTER 16

Project 3:
XML for All Occasions

I MENTIONED **XML** BRIEFLY in Project 1—now it's time to examine it in more detail. In this project you see how XML can be used to represent many kinds of data, and how XML files can be processed with the Simple API for XML, or SAX. The goal of this project is to generate a full Web site from a single XML file that describes the various Web pages and directories.

....

Instant XML

In this chapter, I assume that you know what XML is and how to write it. If you know some HTML, you're already familiar with the basics. XML isn't really a specific language (such as HTML); it's more like a set of rules that define a *class* of languages. Basically, you still write tags the same way as in HTML, but in XML you can invent tag names yourself. Such specific sets of tag names and their structural relationships can be described in "document type definitions" or "XML schema"—I won't be discussing those here.

For a concise description of what XML is, see the World Wide Web Consortium's "XML in 10 points" (`http://www.w3.org/XML/1999/XML-in-10-points`). A more thorough tutorial can be found on the W3Schools Web site (`http://www.w3schools.com/xml`). For more information about SAX, see the official SAX Web site (`http://www.saxproject.org`).

....

What's the Problem?

The general problem we'll be attacking in this project is to parse (read and process) XML files. Because you can use XML to represent practically anything, and you can do whatever you want with the data when you parse it, the applications are boundless (as the title of this chapter indicates).

Anything, You Say?

You may be skeptical about what you can really represent with XML. Well, let me give you some examples: XML can be used to mark up text for ordinary document processing—for example, in the form of XHTML (`http://www.w3.org/TR/xhtml1`) or DocBook XML (`http://www.oasis-open.org/docbook/xml`); it can be used to represent music (`http://musicxml.org`), human moods, emotions, and character traits (`http://humanmarkup.org`), or to describe any physical object (`http://xml.coverpages.org/pml-ons.html`). In Project 8, you'll see how it can be used to call Python methods across a network.

A sampling of existing applications of XML may be found on the XML Cover Pages (`http://xml.coverpages.org/xml.html#applications`) or at CBEL (`http://www.cbel.com/xml_markup_languages`).

The specific problem tackled in this chapter is to generate a complete Web site from a single XML file that contains the structure of the site and the basic contents of each page.

Before you proceed with this project, I suggest that you take a few moments to read a bit about XML and to check out the things it's used for. That might give you a better understanding of when it might be a useful file format—and when it would just be overkill. (After all, plain text files can be just fine when they're all you need.)

Specific Goals

Our specific goals are as follows:

- The entire Web site should be described by a single XML file, which should include information about individual Web pages and directories.

- Your program should create the directories and Web pages as needed.

- It should be easy to change the general design of the entire Web site and regenerate all the pages with the new design.

This last point is perhaps enough to make it all worthwhile. But there are other benefits. By placing all your contents in a single XML file you could easily write other programs that use the same XML processing techniques to extract various kinds of information, such as tables of contents, indices for custom search engines, and so on. And even if you don't use this for your Web site, you could use it to create HTML-based slide shows (or, by using something like ReportLab, you could even create PDF slide shows).

Useful Tools

Python has some built-in XML support, but you may have to install some extras yourself. In this project you'll need a functioning SAX parser. To see if you have a usable SAX parser, try to execute the following:

```
>>> from xml.sax import make_parser
>>> parser = make_parser()
```

If this does not raise an exception, you're all set. If it does, you have to install PyXML. First, download the PyXML package from `http://sf.net/projects/pyxml`. There you can find RPM packages for Linux, binary installers for Windows, and source distributions for other platforms. The RPMs are installed with `rpm --install` and the binary Windows distribution is installed simply by executing it. The source distribution is installed through the standard Python installation mechanism, the Distribution Utilities ("distutils"). Simply unpack the `tar.gz` file, change to the unpacked directory and execute the following:

```
$ python setup.py install
```

You should now be able to use the XML tools.

Preparations

Before you can write the program that processes your XML files, you need to design your XML format. What tags do you need, what attributes should they have, and which tags should go where? To find out, let's first consider what it is you want your XML to describe.

The main concepts are Web site, directory, page, name, title, and contents:

Web site. You won't be storing any information about the Web site itself, so this is just the top-level element enclosing all the files and directories.

Directory. A directory is mainly a container for files and other directories.

Page. This is a single Web page.

Name. Both directories and Web pages need names—these will be used as directory names and file names as they will appear in the file system and the corresponding URLs.

Title. Each Web page should have a title (not the same as its file name).

Contents. Each Web page will also have some contents. You'll just use plain XHTML to represent the contents here—that way, you can just pass it through to the final Web pages and let the browsers interpret it.

In short: your document will consist of a single website element, containing several directory and page elements, each of the directory elements optionally containing more pages and directories. The directory and page elements will have an attribute called name, which will contain their name. In addition, the page tag has a title attribute. The page element contains XHTML code (of the type found inside the XHTML body tag). An example file is shown in Listing 16-1.

*Listing 16-1. A Simple Web Site Represented as an XML File (*website.xml*)*

```
<website>
  <page name="index" title="Home Page">
    <h1>Welcome to My Home Page</h1>

    <p>Hi, there. My name is Mr. Gumby, and this is my home page. Here
    are some of my interests:</p>

    <ul>
      <li><a href="interests/shouting.html">Shouting</a></li>
      <li><a href="interests/sleeping.html">Sleeping</a></li>
      <li><a href="interests/eating.html">Eating</a></li>
    </ul>
  </page>
  <directory name="interests">
    <page name="shouting" title="Shouting">
      <h1>Mr. Gumby's Shouting Page</h1>

      <p>...</p>
    </page>
    <page name="sleeping" title="Sleeping">
      <h1>Mr. Gumby's Sleeping Page</h1>

      <p>...</p>
    </page>
```

```
    <page name="eating" title="Eating">
      <h1>Mr. Gumby's Eating Page</h1>

      <p>...</p>
    </page>
  </directory>
</website>
```

First Implementation

At this point we haven't yet looked at how XML parsing works. The approach we are using here (called SAX) consists of writing a set of event handlers (just like in GUI programming) and then letting an existing XML parser call these handlers as it reads the XML document.

....

What About DOM?

There are two common ways of dealing with XML in Python (and other programming languages, for that matter): SAX and DOM (the Document Object Model). A SAX parser reads through the XML file and tells you what it sees (text, tags, attributes), storing only small parts of the document at a time; this makes SAX simple, fast, and memory-efficient, which is why I have chosen to use it in this chapter. DOM takes another approach: It constructs a data structure (the *document tree*), which represents the entire document. This is slower and requires more memory, but can be useful if you want to manipulate the structure of your document, for instance.

For information about using DOM in Python, check out the Python Library Reference (http://www.python.org/doc/lib/module-xml.dom.html). In addition to the standard DOM handling, the standard library contains two other modules, xml.dom.minidom (a simplified DOM) and xml.dom.pulldom (a cross between SAX and DOM, which reduces memory requirements).

A very fast and simple XML parser (which doesn't really use DOM, but which creates a complete document tree from your XML document) is PyRXP (http://www.reportlab.com/xml/pyrxp.html).

....

Creating a Simple Content Handler

There are several event types available when parsing with SAX, but let's restrict ourselves to three: the beginning of an element (the occurrence of an opening tag), the end of an element (the occurrence of a closing tag), and plain text (characters). To parse the XML file, let's use the parse function from the xml.sax module. This function takes care of reading the file and generating the events—but as it generates these events it needs some event handlers to call. These event handlers will be implemented as methods of a *content handler* object. You'll subclass the ContentHandler class from xml.sax.handler because it implements all the necessary event handlers (as dummy operations that have no effect), and you can override only the ones you need.

Let's begin with a minimal XML parser (assuming that your XML file is called website.xml):

```
from xml.sax.handler import ContentHandler
from xml.sax import parse

class TestHandler(ContentHandler): pass
parse('website.xml', TestHandler())
```

If you execute this program, seemingly nothing happens, but you shouldn't get any error messages either. Behind the scenes, the XML file is parsed, and the default event handlers are called—but because they don't do anything, you won't see any output.

Let's try a simple extension. Add the following method to the TestHandler class:

```
def startElement(self, name, attrs):
    print name, attrs.keys()
```

This overrides the default startElement event handler. The parameters are the relevant tag name and its attributes (stored in a dictionary-like object). If you run the program again (using website.xml from Listing 16-1), you see the following output:

```
website []
page [u'name', u'title']
h1 []
p []
ul []
li []
a [u'href']
li []
a [u'href']
li []
a [u'href']
directory [u'name']
page [u'name', u'title']
```

```
h1 []
p []
page [u'name', u'title']
h1 []
p []
page [u'name', u'title']
h1 []
p []
```

How this works should be pretty clear. In addition to startElement, you'll use endElement (which takes only a tag name as its argument), and characters (which takes a string as its argument).

The following is an example that uses all these three methods to build a list of the headlines (the h1 elements) of the Web site file:

```
from xml.sax.handler import ContentHandler
from xml.sax import parse

class HeadlineHandler(ContentHandler):

    in_headline = 0

    def __init__(self, headlines):
        ContentHandler.__init__(self)
        self.headlines = headlines
        self.data = []

    def startElement(self, name, attrs):
        if name == 'h1':
            self.in_headline = 1

    def endElement(self, name):
        if name == 'h1':
            text = ''.join(self.data)
            self.data = []
            self.headlines.append(text)
            self.in_headline = 0

    def characters(self, string):
        if self.in_headline:
            self.data.append(string)
```

```
headlines = []
parse('website.xml', HeadlineHandler(headlines))

print 'The following <h1> elements were found:'
for h in headlines:
    print h
```

Note that the HeadlineHandler keeps track of whether it's currently parsing text that is inside a pair of h1 tags. This is done by setting self.in_headline to *true* when startElement finds an h1 tag, and setting self.in_headline to *false* when endElement finds an h1 tag. The characters method is automatically called when the parser finds some text. As long as the parser is between two h1 tags (self.in_headline is *true*), characters will append the string (which may be just a part of the text between the tags) to self.data, which is a list of strings. The task of joining these text fragments, appending them to self.headlines (as a single string), and resetting self.data to an empty list also befalls endElement. This general approach (of using Boolean variables to indicate whether you are currently "inside" a given tag type) is quite common in SAX programming.

Running this program (again, with the website.xml file from Listing 16-1) you get the following output:

```
The following <h1> elements were found:
Welcome to My Home Page
Mr. Gumby's Shouting Page
Mr. Gumby's Sleeping Page
Mr. Gumby's Eating Page
```

Creating HTML Pages

Now you're ready to make the prototype. For now, let's ignore the directories and concentrate on creating HTML pages. You have to create a slightly embellished event handler that does the following:

- At the start of each page element, opens a new file with the given name, and writes a suitable HTML header to it, including the given title.

- At the end of each page element, writes a suitable HTML footer to the file, and closes it.

- While inside the page element, passes through all tags and characters without modifying them (writes them to the file as they are).

- While not inside a page element, ignores all tags (such as `website` and `directory`).

Most of this is pretty straightforward (at least if you know a bit about how HTML documents are constructed). There are two problems, however, which may not be completely obvious.

First, you can't simply "pass through" tags (write them directly to the HTML file you're building) because you are given their names only (and possibly some attributes). You have to reconstruct the tags (with angle brackets and so forth) yourself.

Second, SAX itself gives you no way of knowing whether you are currently "inside" a page element. You have to keep track of that sort of thing yourself (as we did in the `HeadlineHandler` example). For this project, we're only interested in whether or not to pass through tags and characters, so we'll use a Boolean variable called `passthrough`, which we'll update as we enter and leave the pages.

See Listing 16-2 for the code for the simple program.

Listing 16-2. A Simple Page Maker Script (pagemaker.py)

```python
from xml.sax.handler import ContentHandler
from xml.sax import parse

class PageMaker(ContentHandler):
    passthrough = 0
    def startElement(self, name, attrs):
        if name == 'page':
            self.passthrough = 1
            self.out = open(attrs['name'] + '.html', 'w')
            self.out.write('<html><head>\n')
            self.out.write('<title>%s</title>\n' % attrs['title'])
            self.out.write('</head><body>\n')
        elif self.passthrough:
            self.out.write('<' + name)
            for key, val in attrs.items():
                self.out.write(' %s="%s"' % (key, val))
            self.out.write('>')

    def endElement(self, name):
        if name == 'page':
            self.passthrough = 0
            self.out.write('\n</body></html>\n')
            self.out.close()
        elif self.passthrough:
```

```
            self.out.write('</%s>' % name)
    def characters(self, chars):
        if self.passthrough: self.out.write(chars)


parse('website.xml', PageMaker ())
```

You should execute this in the directory in which you want your files to appear. Note that even if two pages are in two different `directory` elements, they will end up in the same real directory. (That will be fixed in our second implementation.)

Again, using the file `website.xml` from Listing 16-1, you get three HTML files. The file called `index.html` contains the following:

```
<html><head>
<title>Home Page</title>
</head><body>

    <h1>Welcome to My Home Page</h1>

    <p>Hi, there. My name is Mr. Gumby, and this is my home page. Here
    are some of my interests:</p>

    <ul>
      <li><a href="interests/shouting.html">Shouting</a></li>
      <li><a href="interests/sleeping.html">Sleeping</a></li>
      <li><a href="interests/eating.html">Eating</a></li>
    </ul>

</body></html>
```

Figure 16-1 shows how this page looks when viewed in a browser.

Figure 16-1. A generated Web page

Looking at the code you can see two main weaknesses:

- I use `if` statements to handle the various event types. If I need to handle many such event types, my `if` statements will get large and unreadable.

- The HTML code is hard-wired. It should be easy to replace.

Both of these weaknesses will be addressed in the second implementation.

Second Implementation

Because the SAX mechanism is so low-level and basic, you may often find it useful to write a mixin class that handles some administrative details such as gathering character data, managing Boolean state variables (such as passthrough), or dispatching the events to your own custom event handlers. The state and data handling is pretty simple in this project, so let's focus on the handler dispatch.

A Dispatcher Mixin Class

Rather than having to write large if statements in the standard generic event handlers (such as startElement), it would be nice to just write your own specific ones (such as startPage) and have them called automatically. You can implement that functionality in a mixin class, and then subclass the mixin along with ContentHandler.

> **NOTE** *A "mixin" is a class with limited functionality that is meant to be subclassed along with some other more substantial class.*

You want the following functionality in your program: When startElement is called with a name such as 'foo', it should attempt to find an event handler called startFoo and call it with the given attributes. Similarly, if endElement is called with 'foo', it should try to call endFoo. If, in any of these methods, the given handler is not found, a method called defaultStart (or defaultEnd, respectively) will be called, if present. If the default handler isn't present either, nothing should be done.

In addition, some care should be taken with the parameters. The custom handlers (for example, startFoo) do not need the tag name as a parameter, while the custom default handlers (for example, defaultStart) do. Also, only the start handlers need the attributes.

Confused? Let's begin by writing the simplest parts of the class:

```
class Dispatcher:

    # ...

    def startElement(self, name, attrs):
        self.dispatch('start', name, attrs)
```

```
def endElement(self, name):
    self.dispatch('end', name)
```

Here, the basic event handlers are implemented, and they simply call a method called dispatch, which takes care of finding the appropriate handler, constructing the argument tuple, and then calling the handler with those arguments. Here is the code for the dispatch method:

```
def dispatch(self, prefix, name, attrs=None):
    mname = prefix + name.capitalize()
    dname = 'default' + prefix.capitalize()
    method = getattr(self, mname, None)
    if callable(method): args = ()
    else:
        method = getattr(self, dname, None)
        args = name,
    if prefix == 'start': args += attrs,
    if callable(method): method(*args)
```

What happens is this:

1. From a prefix (either 'start' or 'end') and a tag name (for example, 'page') construct the method name of the handler (for example, 'startPage').

2. Using the same prefix, construct the name of the default handler (for example, 'defaultStart').

3. Try to get the handler with getattr, using None as the default value.

4. If the result is callable, assign an empty tuple to args.

5. Otherwise, try to get the default handler with getattr, again using None as the default value. Also, set args to a tuple containing only the tag name (because the default handler needs that).

6. If you are dealing with a start-handler, add the attributes to the argument tuple (args).

7. If your handler is callable (that is, it is either a viable specific handler, or a viable default handler), call it with the correct arguments.

Got that? This basically means that you can now write content handlers like this:

```
class TestHandler(Dispatcher, ContentHandler):
    def startPage(self, attrs):
        print 'Beginning page', attrs['name']
    def endPage(self):
        print 'Ending page'
```

Because the dispatcher mixin takes care of most of the plumbing, the content handler is fairly simple and readable. (Of course we'll add more functionality in a little while.)

Factoring Out the Header, Footer, and Default Handling

This section is much easier than the previous one. Instead of doing the calls to self.out.write directly in the event handler, we'll create separate methods for writing the header and footer. That way you can easily override these methods by subclassing the event handler. Let's make the default header and footer really simple:

```
def writeHeader(self, title):
    self.out.write("<html>\n  <head>\n    <title>")
    self.out.write(title)
    self.out.write("</title>\n  </head>\n  <body>\n")

def writeFooter(self):
    self.out.write("\n  </body>\n</html>\n")
```

Handling of the XHTML contents was also linked a bit too intimately with our original handlers. The XHTML will now be handled by defaultStart and defaultEnd:

```
def defaultStart(self, name, attrs):
    if self.passthrough:
        self.out.write('<' + name)
        for key, val in attrs.items():
            self.out.write(' %s="%s"' % (key, val))
        self.out.write('>')
```

```
def defaultEnd(self, name):
    if self.passthrough:
        self.out.write('</%s>' % name)
```

This works just like before, except that I've moved the code to separate methods (which is usually a good thing). Now, on to the last piece of the puzzle.

Support for Directories

To create the necessary directories, you need a couple of useful functions from the os and os.path modules. One of these functions is os.makedirs, which makes all the necessary directories in a given path. For instance, os.makedirs('foo/bar/baz') creates the directory foo in the current directory, then creates bar in foo, and finally, baz in bar. If foo already exists, only bar and baz are created, and similarly, if bar also exists, only baz is created. However, if baz exists as well, an exception is raised.

To avoid this exception, you need the function os.path.isdir, which checks whether a given path is a directory (that is, whether it exists already). Another useful function is os.path.join, which joins several paths with the correct separator (for example, / in UNIX and so forth).

At all times during the processing, keep the current directory path stored as a list of directory names, referenced by the variable directory. When you enter a directory, append its name; when you leave it, pop the name off. Assuming that directory is set up properly, you can define a function for ensuring that the current directory exists:

```
def ensureDirectory(self):
    path = os.path.join(*self.directory)
    if not os.path.isdir(path): os.makedirs(path)
```

Notice how I've used argument splicing (with the star operator) on the directory list when supplying it to os.path.join.

The base directory of our Web site (for example, public_html) can be given as an argument to the constructor, which then looks like this:

```
def __init__(self, directory):
    self.directory = [directory]
    self.ensureDirectory()
```

The Event Handlers

Finally we've come to the event handlers. We need four of them—two for dealing with directories, and two for pages. The directory handlers simply use the directory list and the ensureDirectory method:

```
def startDirectory(self, attrs):
    self.directory.append(attrs['name'])
    self.ensureDirectory()

def endDirectory(self):
    self.directory.pop()
```

The page handlers use the writeHeader and writeFooter methods. In addition, they set the passthrough variable (to pass through the XHTML), and—perhaps most importantly—they open and close the file associated with the page:

```
def startPage(self, attrs):
    filename = os.path.join(*self.directory+[attrs['name']+'.html'])
    self.out = open(filename, 'w')
    self.writeHeader(attrs['title'])
    self.passthrough = 1

def endPage(self):
    self.passthrough = 0
    self.writeFooter()
    self.out.close()
```

The first line of startPage may look a little intimidating, but it is more or less the same as the first line of ensureDirectory, except that you add the file name (and give it a .html suffix).

The full source code of the program is shown in Listing 16-3. You can find a list of the generated files and directories in Listing 16-4.

*Listing 16-3. The Web Site Constructor (*website.py*)*

```
from xml.sax.handler import ContentHandler
from xml.sax import parse
import os
```

```python
class Dispatcher:

    def dispatch(self, prefix, name, attrs=None):
        mname = prefix + name.capitalize()
        dname = 'default' + prefix.capitalize()
        method = getattr(self, mname, None)
        if callable(method): args = ()
        else:
            method = getattr(self, dname, None)
            args = name,
        if prefix == 'start': args += attrs,
        if callable(method): method(*args)

    def startElement(self, name, attrs):
        self.dispatch('start', name, attrs)

    def endElement(self, name):
        self.dispatch('end', name)

class WebsiteConstructor(Dispatcher, ContentHandler):

    passthrough = 0

    def __init__(self, directory):
        self.directory = [directory]
        self.ensureDirectory()

    def ensureDirectory(self):
        path = os.path.join(*self.directory)
        if not os.path.isdir(path): os.makedirs(path)

    def characters(self, chars):
        if self.passthrough: self.out.write(chars)

    def defaultStart(self, name, attrs):
        if self.passthrough:
            self.out.write('<' + name)
            for key, val in attrs.items():
                self.out.write(' %s="%s"' % (key, val))
            self.out.write('>')

    def defaultEnd(self, name):
        if self.passthrough:
            self.out.write('</%s>' % name)
```

```
    def startDirectory(self, attrs):
        self.directory.append(attrs['name'])
        self.ensureDirectory()

    def endDirectory(self):
        self.directory.pop()

    def startPage(self, attrs):
        filename = os.path.join(*self.directory+[attrs['name']+'.html'])
        self.out = open(filename, 'w')
        self.writeHeader(attrs['title'])
        self.passthrough = 1

    def endPage(self):
        self.passthrough = 0
        self.writeFooter()
        self.out.close()

    def writeHeader(self, title):
        self.out.write('<html>\n  <head>\n    <title>')
        self.out.write(title)
        self.out.write('</title>\n  </head>\n  <body>\n')

    def writeFooter(self):
        self.out.write('\n  </body>\n</html>\n')

parse('website.xml', WebsiteConstructor('public_html'))
```

Listing 16-4. The Files and Directories Created

```
public_html/
public_html/index.html
public_html/interests
public_html/interests/shouting.html
public_html/interests/sleeping.html
public_html/interests/eating.html
```

Encoding Blues

If your XML file contains special characters (those with ordinal numbers above 127) you may be in trouble. The XML parser uses Unicode strings during its processing, and returns those to you (for example, in the characters event handler). Unicode handles the special characters just fine. However, if you want to convert this Unicode string to an ordinary string (which is what happens when you print it, for instance) an exception is raised:

```
>>> some_string = u'Mőőőse'
>>> some_string
u'M\xf6\xf6\xf6se'
>>> print some_string

Traceback (most recent call last):
File "<stdin>", line 1, in ?
UnicodeError: ASCII encoding error: ordinal not in range(128)
```

As you can see, the error message is "ASCII encoding error," which actually means that Python has tried to *encode* the Unicode string with the ASCII encoding, which isn't possible when it contains special characters like this. Encoding is done with the encode method:

```
>>> some_string.encode('ascii')
Traceback (most recent call last):
   File "<stdin>", line 1, in ?
UnicodeError: ASCII encoding error: ordinal not in range(128)
```

To solve this problem, you have to use another encoding—for example, ISO8859-1 (which is fine for most European languages):

```
>>> print some_string.encode('iso8859-1')
Mőőőse
```

You can find more information about such encodings at the World Wide Web Consortium's Web site (http://www.w3.org/International/O-charset.html).

Further Exploration

Now you've got the basic program. What can you do with it? Here are some suggestions:

- Create a new ContentHandler for creating a table of contents or a menu (with links) for the Web site.

- Add navigational aids to the Web pages that tell the user where (in which directory) he or she is.

- Create a subclass of WebsiteConstructor that overrides writeHeader and writeFooter to provide customized design.

- Create another ContentHandler, which constructs a single Web page from the XML file.

- Create a ContentHandler that summarizes your Web site somehow, for instance in RSS (another XML format—see http://www.purl.org/rss/1.0).

- Check out other tools for transforming XML, especially XSLT (see http://www.w3.org/TR/xslt and http://www.4suite.org).

- Create one or more PDF documents based on the XML file, using a tool such as ReportLab's Platypus (http://www.reportlab.com).

- Make it possible to edit the XML file through a Web interface (see Chapter 19).

What Now?

After this foray into the world of XML parsing, let's do some more network programming. In the next chapter, you create a program that can gather news items from various network sources (such as Web pages and Usenet groups) and generate custom news reports for you.

CHAPTER 17

Project 4: In the News

IN THIS PROJECT YOU SEE how you go from a simple prototype without any form of abstraction (no functions, no classes) to a generic system in which some important abstractions have been added. Also, you get a brief introduction to the nntplib library.

What Is NNTP?

NNTP (Network News Transfer Protocol) is a standard network protocol for managing messages posted on Usenet discussion groups. NNTP servers form a global network that collectively manage these newsgroups, and through an NNTP client (also called a "newsreader") you can post and read messages. Most recent Web browsers include NNTP clients, and separate clients exist as well.

For more information about Usenet, you may check out the informational Web site at http://www.usenet.org.

What's the Problem?

The program you write in this project will be an information-gathering agent, a program that will be able to gather information (more specifically, news) and compile a report for you. Given the network functionality you have already encountered, that might not seem very difficult—and it isn't, really. But in this project you go a bit beyond the simple "download a file with urllib" approach. You use another network library that is a bit more difficult to use than urllib, namely nntplib. In addition, you refactor the program to allow many types of news sources and various types of destinations, making a clear separation between the front-end and the back-end, with the main engine in the middle.

 NOTE *"Refactoring" means improving the design of an existing program, usually by adding abstraction and structure.*

Specific Goals

The main goals for the final program are as follows:

- The program should be able to gather news from many different sources.

- It should be easy to add new news sources (and even new kinds of sources).

- The program should be able to dispatch its compiled news report to many different destinations, in many different formats.

- It should be easy to add new destinations (and even new kinds of destinations).

Useful Tools

In this project there is no need to install separate software. What you need, however, are some standard library modules, including one that you haven't seen before, nntplib, which deals with NNTP servers. Instead of explaining all the details of that module, let's examine it through some prototyping.

You will also be using the time module. See Chapter 10 for more information.

Preparations

To be able to use nntplib you need to have access to an NNTP server. If you're not sure whether you do, you could ask your ISP or system administrator for details. In the code examples in this chapter, I use the newsgroup comp.lang.python.announce, so you should make sure that your news (NNTP) server has that group, or you should find some other group you'd like to use. It is important that the NNTP server support the NEWNEWS command—if it doesn't, the programs in this chapter won't work. (If you don't know whether your server supports this command or not, simply try to execute the programs and see what happens.)

If you don't have access to an NNTP server, or your server's NEWNEWS command is disabled, several open servers are available for anyone to use. A quick Web search for "free nntp server" ought to give you a number of servers to choose from. The Web site http://newzbot.com also contains many useful resources.

Assuming that your news server is `news.foo.bar` (this is not a real server name, and won't work), you can test your NNTP server like this:

```
>>> from nntplib import NNTP
>>> server = NNTP('news.foo.bar')
>>> server.group('comp.lang.python.announce')[0]
```

The result of the last line should be a string beginning with `'211'` (basically meaning that the server has the group you asked for), or `'411'` (which means that the server doesn't have the group). It might look something like this:

```
'211 51 1876 1926 comp.lang.python.announce'
```

If the returned string starts with `'411'`, you should use a newsreader to look for another group you might want to use. If an exception is raised, perhaps you got the server name wrong. Another possibility is that you were "timed out" between the time you created the server object and the time you called the group method—the server may only allow you to stay connected for a short period of time (such as 10 seconds). If you're having trouble typing that fast, simply put the code in a script and execute it (with an added `print`) or put the server object creation and method call on the same line (separated by a semicolon).

First Implementation

In the spirit of prototyping, just tackle the problem head on. The first thing you want to do is to download the most recent messages from a newsgroup on an NNTP server. To keep things simple, just print out the result to standard output (with `print`).

Before looking at the details of the implementation, you might want to browse the source code in Listing 17-1, and perhaps even execute the program to see how it works.

The program logic isn't very complicated, but you need to figure out how to use `nntplib`. You'll be using one single object of the `NNTP` class. As you saw in the previous section, this class is instantiated with a single constructor argument—the name of an NNTP server. You need to call three methods on this instance: `newnews`, which returns a list of articles posted after a certain date and time; `head`, which gives you various information about the articles (most notably their subjects); and `body`, which gives you the main text of the articles.

The `newnews` method requires a date string (in the form *yymmdd*) and an hour string (in the form *hhmmss*) in addition to the group name. To construct these, you need some functions from the `time` module, namely `time`, `localtime`, and `strftime`. (See Chapter 10 for more information on the `time` module.).

Let's say you want to download all new messages since yesterday—then you have to construct a date and time 24 hours before the current time. The current time (in seconds) is found with the `time` function; to find the time yesterday, all you have to do is subtract 24 hours (in seconds). To be able to use this time with `strftime`, it must be converted to a time tuple (see Chapter 10) with the `localtime` function. The code for finding "yesterday" then becomes:

```
from time import time, localtime
day = 24 * 60 * 60 # Number of seconds in one day
yesterday = localtime(time() - day)
```

The next step is to format the time correctly, as two strings. For that you use `strftime`, as in the following example:

```
>>> from time import strftime
>>> strftime('%y%m%d')
'020409'
>>> strftime('%H%M%S')
'141625'
```

The string argument to `strftime` is a *format string*, which specifies the format you want the time to be in. Most characters are used directly in the resulting time string, but those preceded by a percent sign are replaced with various time-related values. For instance, %y is replaced with the last two digits of the year, %m with the month (as a two-digit number), and so on. For a full list of these codes, consult the Python Library Reference (http://www.python.org/doc/lib/module-time.html). When supplied only with a format string, `strftime` uses the current time. Optionally, one may supply a time tuple as a second argument:

```
from time import strftime
date = strftime('%y%m%d', yesterday)
hour = strftime('%H%M%S', yesterday)
```

Now that you've got the date and time in correct format for the `newnews` method, you only have to instantiate a server and call the method. Using the same fictitious server name as earlier, the code becomes:

```
servername = 'news.foo.bar'
group = 'comp.lang.python.announce'
server = NNTP(servername)

ids = server.newnews(group, date, hour)[1]
```

Note that I've extracted the second argument of the tuple that is returned from `newnews`. It's sufficient for our purposes: a list of *article IDs* of the articles that were posted after the given date and hour. (The newnews method sends a NEWNEWS command to the NNTP server. As described in the "Preparations" section, this command may be disabled, in which case you should find another server.)

You need the article IDs when you call the head and body methods later, to tell the server which article you're talking about.

So, you're all set to start using head and body (for each of the IDs) and printing out the results. Just like newnews, head and body return tuples with various information (such as whether or not the command succeeded), but you care only about the returned data itself, which is the fourth element—a list of strings. The body of the article with a given ID can be fetched like this:

```
body = server.body(id)[3]
```

From the head (a list of lines containing various information about the article, such as the subject, the date it was posted, and so on) you want only the subject. The subject line is in the form "Subject: Hello, world!", so you need to find the line that starts with "Subject:" and extract the rest of the line. Because (according to the NNTP standard) "subject" can also be spelled as all lowercase, all uppercase, or any kind of combination of upper- and lowercase letters, you simply call the lower method on the line and compare it to "subject". Here is the loop that finds the subject within the data returned by the call to head:

```
head = server.head(id)[3]
for line in head:
    if line.lower().startswith('subject'):
        subject = line[9:]
        break
```

The break isn't strictly necessary, but when you've found the subject, there's no need to iterate over the rest of the lines.

After having extracted the subject and body of an article, you have only to print it, for instance, like this:

```
print subject
print '-'*len(subject)
print '\n'.join(body)
```

After printing all the articles, you call server.quit(), and that's it. In a UNIX shell such as bash you could run this program like this:

```
$ python newsagent1.py | less
```

The use of less is useful for reading the articles one at a time. (If you have no such pager program available, you could rewrite the print part of the program to store the resulting text in a file, which you'll also be doing in the second implementation. See Chapter 11 for more information on file handling.) The source code for the simple news gathering agent is shown in Listing 17-1.

Listing 17-1. A Simple News Gathering Agent (newsagent1.py)

```
from nntplib import NNTP
from time import strftime, time, localtime

day = 24 * 60 * 60 # Number of seconds in one day

yesterday = localtime(time() - day)
date = strftime('%y%m%d', yesterday)
hour = strftime('%H%M%S', yesterday)

servername = 'news.foo.bar'
group = 'comp.lang.python.announce'
server = NNTP(servername)

ids = server.newnews(group, date, hour)[1]

for id in ids:
    head = server.head(id)[3]
    for line in head:
        if line.lower().startswith('subject'):
            subject = line[9:]
            break

    body = server.body(id)[3]

    print subject
    print '-'*len(subject)
    print '\n'.join(body)

server.quit()
```

Second Implementation

The first implementation worked, but was quite inflexible in that it only let you retrieve news from Usenet discussion groups. In the second implementation, you fix that by refactoring the code a bit. You add structure and abstraction by creating some classes and methods to represent the various parts of the code. Once you've done that, some of the parts may be replaced by other classes much more easily than you could replace parts of the code in the original program.

Again, before immersing yourself in the details of the second implementation, you might want to skim (and perhaps execute) the code in Listing 17-2.

So, what classes do you need? Let's just do a quick review of the nouns in the problem description, as suggested in Chapter 7 (I've already filtered out some of the ones I don't think you'll need): information, agent, news, report, network, news source, destination, front-end, back-end, main engine. Just glancing at this list of nouns, I'd suggest the following main classes (or kinds of classes): NewsAgent, NewsItem, Source, and Destination. The various sources will constitute the front-end and the destinations will constitute the back-end, with the news agent sitting in the middle.

The easiest of these is NewsItem—it represents only a piece of data, consisting of a title and a body (a short text). That can be implemented as follows:

```
class NewsItem:

    def __init__(self, title, body):
        self.title = title
        self.body = body
```

To find out exactly what is needed from the news sources and the news destinations, it could be a good idea to start by writing the agent itself. The agent must maintain two lists: one of sources and one of destinations. Adding sources and destinations can be done through the methods addSource and addDestination:

```
class NewsAgent:

    def __init__(self):
        self.sources = []
        self.destinations = []

    def addSource(self, source):
        self.sources.append(source)

    def addDestination(self, dest):
        self.destinations.append(dest)

    # The rest of the code is developed later in the chapter
```

The only thing missing now is a method to distribute the news items from the sources to the destinations. During distribution, each destination must have a method that returns all its news items, and each source needs a method for receiving all the news items that are being distributed. Let's call these methods getItems and receiveItems. In the interest of flexibility, let's just require getItems to return an arbitrary iterator of NewsItems. To make the destinations easier to implement, however, let's assume that receiveItems is callable with a sequence argument (which can be iterated over more than once, to make a table of contents before listing the news items, for example). After this has been decided, the distribute method simply becomes:

```
def distribute(self):
    items = []
    for source in self.sources:
        items.extend(source.getItems())
    for dest in self.destinations:
        dest.receiveItems(items)
```

This iterates through all the sources, building a list of news items. Then it iterates through all the destinations and supplies each of them with the full list of news items.

Now, all you need is a couple of sources and destinations. To begin testing, you can simply create a destination that works like the printing in the first prototype:

```
class PlainDestination:

    def receiveItems(self, items):
        for item in items:
            print item.title
            print '-'*len(item.title)
            print item.body
```

The formatting is the same—the difference is that you have *encapsulated* the formatting. It is now one of several alternative destinations, rather than a hard-coded part of the program. A slightly more complicated destination (HTMLDestination, which produces HTML) can be seen in Listing 17-2. It builds on the approach of PlainDestination with a couple of extra features:

- The text it produces is HTML.

- It writes the text to a specific file, rather than standard output.

- It creates a table of contents in addition to the main list of items.

And that's it, really. The table of contents is created using hyperlinks that link to parts of the page. You accomplish this by using links of the form `<a href="#42">...</a>` (where 42 might be some other number), which leads to the headline with the enclosing anchor tag `<a name="42">...</a>` (where, again, 42 could be another number, but should be the same as in the table of contents). The table of contents and the main listing of news items are built in two different `for` loops. You can see a sample result (using the upcoming `NNTPSource`) in Figure 17-1.

Figure 17-1. An automatically generated news page

It's important to notice the following here: When thinking about the design, I considered using a generic superclass to represent news sources and one to represent news destinations. As it turns out, the sources and destinations don't really share any behavior, so there is no point in using a common superclass. As long as they implement the necessary methods (`getItems` and `receiveItems`) correctly, the `NewsAgent` will be happy. (This is an example of using a protocol, as described in Chapter 9, rather than a specific class.)

When creating an NNTPSource, much of the code can be snipped from the original prototype. As you can see in Listing 17-2, the main differences from the original are the following:

- The code has been encapsulated in the getItems method. The servername and group variables are now arguments to the constructor. Also a window (a time window) is added, instead of assuming that you want the news since yesterday (which is equivalent to setting window to 1).

- To extract the subject, a Message object from the email module is used (constructed with the message_from_string function). This is the sort of thing you might add to later versions of your program as you thumb through the docs (as mentioned in Chapter 15, in the section "Using the LinePlot Class").

- Instead of printing each news item directly, a NewsItem object is yielded (making getItems a generator).

To use this code in Python 2.2 you must include the from __future__ import generators at the top of the program file. (See the section "Avoiding Generators" in Chapter 9 for an alternative.)

To show the flexibility of the design, let's add another news source—one that can extract news items from Web pages (using regular expressions; see Chapter 10 for more information). SimpleWebSource (see Listing 17-2) takes a URL and two regular expressions (one representing titles, and one representing bodies) as its constructor arguments. In getItems, it uses the regexp methods findall to find all the occurrences (titles and bodies) and zip to combine these. It then iterates over the list of (*title, body*) pairs, yielding a NewsItem for each. As you can see, adding new kinds of sources (or destinations, for that matter) isn't very difficult.

To put the code to work, let's instantiate an agent, some sources, and some destinations. In the function runDefaultSetup (which is called if the module is run as a program) several such objects are instantiated:

- A SimpleWebSource is constructed for the BBC News Web site. It uses two simple regular expressions to extract the information it needs. (Note that the layout of the HTML on these pages might change, in which case you need to rewrite the regexps. This also applies if you are using some other page—just view the HTML source and try to find a pattern that applies.)

- An NNTPSource for comp.lang.python. The time window is set to 1, so it works just like the first prototype.

- A PlainDestination, which prints all the news gathered.

- An HTMLDestination, which generates a news page called news.html.

When all of these objects have been created and added to the NewsAgent, the distribute method is called.

You can run the program like this:

```
$ python newsagent2.py
```

The resulting news.html page is shown in Figure 17-2.

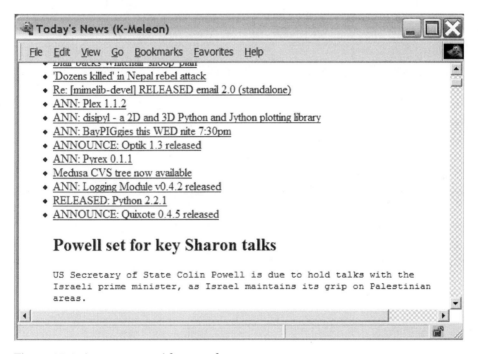

Figure 17-2. A news page with more than one source

What's This wrap Function?

The wrap function takes a string and splits it into lines with lengths less
than a given maximum (default 70). This is used by SimpleWebSource when
displaying text retrieved from Web pages (which may not contain many new-
lines). Because the text is wrapped in <pre> tags (for preformatted text) such
line breaks are necessary. The algorithm it uses is quite simple: it keeps
adding words (and blanks) until adding another word would exceed the line
width. Then it pops off the last blank (if there is one), adds a newline, and
starts working on the next line.

The full source code of the second implementation is found in Listing 17-2.

Listing 17-2. A More Flexible News Gathering Agent (newsagent2.py)

```python
from __future__ import generators
from nntplib import NNTP
from time import strftime, time, localtime
from email import message_from_string
from urllib import urlopen
import re

day = 24 * 60 * 60 # Number of seconds in one day

def wrap(string, max=70):
    """
    Wraps a string to a maximum line width.
    """
    words = string.split()
    parts = []
    length = 0
    for word in words:
        if length+len(word) > max:
            try: parts.pop() # Remove last space character
            except IndexError: pass
            parts.append('\n')
            length = 0
        parts.append(word)
        parts.append(' ')
        length += len(word) + 1
    return ''.join(parts)
```

```
class NewsAgent:
    """
    An object that can distribute news items from news
    sources to news destinations.
    """

    def __init__(self):
        self.sources = []
        self.destinations = []

    def addSource(self, source):
        self.sources.append(source)

    def addDestination(self, dest):
        self.destinations.append(dest)

    def distribute(self):
        """
        Retrieve all news items from all sources, and
        Distribute them to all destinations.
        """
        items = []
        for source in self.sources:
            items.extend(source.getItems())
        for dest in self.destinations:
            dest.receiveItems(items)

class NewsItem:
    """
    A simple news item consisting of a title and a body text.
    """

    def __init__(self, title, body):
        self.title = title
        self.body = body

class NNTPSource:
    """
    A news source that retrieves news items from an NNTP group.
    """

    def __init__(self, servername, group, window):
        self.servername = servername
        self.group = group
        self.window = window
```

```python
    def getItems(self):

        start = localtime(time() - self.window*day)
        date = strftime('%y%m%d', start)
        hour = strftime('%H%M%S', start)

        server = NNTP(self.servername)

        ids = server.newnews(self.group, date, hour)[1]

        for id in ids:
            lines = server.article(id)[3]
            message = message_from_string('\n'.join(lines))

            title = message['subject']
            body = message.get_payload()

            yield NewsItem(title, body)

        server.quit()

class SimpleWebSource:
    """
    A news source that extracts news items from a Web page using
    regular expressions.
    """
    def __init__(self, url, titlePattern, bodyPattern):
        self.url = url
        self.titlePattern = re.compile(titlePattern)
        self.bodyPattern = re.compile(bodyPattern)

    def getItems(self):
        text = urlopen(self.url).read()
        titles = self.titlePattern.findall(text)
        bodies = self.bodyPattern.findall(text)
        for title, body in zip(titles, bodies):
            yield NewsItem(title, wrap(body))

class PlainDestination:
    """
    A news destination that formats all its news items as
    plain text.
    """
```

```
    def receiveItems(self, items):
        for item in items:
            print item.title
            print '-'*len(item.title)
            print item.body

class HTMLDestination:
    """
    A news destination that formats all its news items
    as HTML.
    """
    def __init__(self, filename):
        self.filename = filename

    def receiveItems(self, items):

        out = open(self.filename, 'w')
        print >>> out, """
        <html>
          <head>
            <title>Today's News</title>
          </head>
          <body>
          <h1>Today's News</h1>
        """

        print >>> out, '<ul>'
        id = 0
        for item in items:
            id += 1
            print >>> out, '  <li><a href="#%i">%s</a></li>' % (id, item.title)
        print >>> out, '</ul>'

        id = 0
        for item in items:
            id += 1
            print >>> out, '<h2><a name="%i">%s</a></h2>' % (id, item.title)
            print >>> out, '<pre>%s</pre>' % item.body

        print >>> out, """
          </body>
        </html>
        """
```

```
def runDefaultSetup():
    """
    A default setup of sources and destination. Modify to taste.
    """
    agent = NewsAgent()

    # A SimpleWebSource that retrieves news from the
    # BBC news site:
    bbc_url = 'http://news.bbc.co.uk'
    bbc_title = 'class="h.">([^<]+)'
    bbc_body = '>([^<]+)<BR CLEAR=ALL>'
    bbc = SimpleWebSource(bbc_url, bbc_title, bbc_body)

    agent.addSource(bbc)

    # An NNTPSource that retrieves news from comp.lang.python.announce:
    clpa_server = 'news.foo.bar' # Insert real server name
    clpa_group = 'comp.lang.python.announce'
    clpa_window = 1
    clpa = NNTPSource(clpa_server, clpa_group, clpa_window)

    agent.addSource(clpa)

    # Add plain text destination and an HTML destination:
    agent.addDestination(PlainDestination())
    agent.addDestination(HTMLDestination('news.html'))

    # Distribute the news items:
    agent.distribute()

if __name__ == '__main__': runDefaultSetup()
```

Further Exploration

Because of its extensible nature, this project invites much further exploration.
Here are some ideas:

- Create a more ambitious WebSource, using either htmllib or HTMLParser
  (see the Python Library Reference).

- Create an RSSSource, which parses RSS (an XML format). For more about
  RSS, see http://backend.userland.com/rss092. (See the section "Further
  Exploration" in Chapter 16 for another reference.)

- Improve the layout for the HTMLDestination.

- Create a page monitor that gives you a news item if a given Web page has changed since the last time you examined it. (Just download a copy when it has changed and compare that later. Take a look at the standard library module filecmp for comparing files.)

- Create a CGI version of the news script (see Chapter 19).

- Create an EmailDestination, which sends you an e-mail with news items. (See the standard library module smtplib module for sending e-mail.)

- Add command-line switches to decide what news formats you want. (See the standard library module getopt for some techniques. Also, take a look at Optik, which may end up in the standard library in Python 2.3: http://optik.sf.net.)

- Add a configuration file (see Chapter 13) for setting up sources and destinations.

- Give the destinations information about where the news comes from, to allow a fancier layout.

- Try to categorize your news items (by searching for keywords, perhaps?).

- Create an XMLDestination, which produces XML files suitable for the site builder in Chapter 16. Voilà—you have a news Web site.

What Now?

You've done a lot of file creation and file handling (including downloading the required files), and although that is very useful for a lot of things, it isn't very interactive. In the next project you create a chat server, where you can chat with your friends online. You can even extend it to create your own virtual (textual) environment.

Project 5:
A Virtual Tea Party

IN THIS PROJECT YOU do some serious network programming. You write a chat server—a program that lets several people connect via the Internet and chat with each other in real-time. There are many ways to create such a beast in Python. The approach used here is based on the standard library modules asyncore and asynchat. Another approach is to use *threads*. Although you won't be using those here, I discuss that alternative briefly, too.

What's the Problem?

Online chatting is becoming quite commonplace. There are many chat services of various kinds (IRC, ICQ, and so forth) available all over the Internet; some of these are even full-fledged text-based virtual worlds (see http://www.mudconnect.com for a long list). If you want to set up a chat server, there are many free server programs you can download and install—but writing one yourself is useful for two reasons:

- You learn about network programming.

- You can customize it as much as you want.

The second point suggests that you can start with a simple chat server and develop it into basically any kind of server (including a virtual world), with all the power of Python at your fingertips. Pretty awesome, isn't it?

What Are Sockets?

A basic component in network programming is the *socket*. A socket is basically an "information channel" with a program on both ends. The programs may be on different computers (connected through a network) and may send information to each other through the socket. The modules used in this project hide the basic workings of the Python socket module, so you won't be interacting with the sockets directly. However, if you want to know more about them, a good place to start is Gordon McMillan's Socket Programming HOWTO (http://www.python.org/doc/howto/sockets).

Specific Goals

Specifically, the program we create must be able to do the following:

- Receive multiple connections from different users

- Let the users act *in parallel*

- Interpret commands such as say or logout

- Enable each individual session to behave according to the state the user is in (connected, logged in, logging out, and so on)

- Be easily extensible

The two things that will require special tools are the network connections and the parallel nature of the program.

Useful Tools

The only new tool you need in this project is the asyncore module from the standard library and its undocumented relative asynchat. I'll describe the basics of how these work; you can find more details about asyncore in the Python Library Reference (http://www.python.org/doc/lib/module-asyncore.html). At the time of writing, the asynchat module is not described in the standard documentation, but it may be in a future release. If you want details about how asynchat works beyond what I've described here, you might want to take a peek at the source code. The asyncore framework (including asynchat) is also thoroughly discussed in Chapter 7 of Steve Holden's book *Python Web Programming* (New Riders, 2002).

What's It For?

As mentioned earlier, the basic component in a network program is the *socket*. Sockets can be created directly by importing the socket module and using the functions there. So what do you need asyncore for?

The asyncore framework enables you to juggle several users who are connected simultaneously. Imagine a scenario in which you have no special tools for handling this. When you start up the server, it awaits connecting users. When one user is connected, it starts reading data from that user and supplying results through a socket. But what happens if another user is connected? The second user must wait until the first one has finished. In some cases that will work just fine, but when you're writing a chat server, the whole point is that more than one user can be connected—how else could users chat with one another?

The asyncore framework is based on an underlying mechanism (the select function from the select module) that allows the server to serve all the connected users in a piecemeal fashion. Instead of reading *all* the available data from one user before going on to the next, only *some* data is read. Also, the server reads only from the sockets where there *is* data to be read. This is done again and again, in a loop. Writing is handled similarly. You could implement this yourself using just the modules socket and select but asyncore and asynchat provide a very useful framework that takes care of the details for you.

Pointers for a Multithreaded Chat Server

The asyn part of the asyncore and asynchat names stands for "asynchronous." A synchronous server would handle one user at a time, reading everything available (as well as writing everything available). Normally, this is not a useful approach to something like a chat server. However, you could write a server that had one synchronous handler for each user, and then run these handlers *in parallel*. There are several ways of handling parallel execution in Python (for example, the fork function from the os module), but the one most appropriate for a chat server would probably be *threading*.

A thread is a light-weight process that can run in parallel with several other threads, all accessing the same data. That means that each handler could run in a separate thread and only concentrate on its own user.

Although basic threading is pretty straightforward (simply instantiate a Thread object from the threading module and call its start method) getting a multi-threaded application right can be a pain. Therefore I have chosen not to use this approach here. If you would like to try it out, I suggest the following sources of information:

- The standard documentation of the threading module (http://python.org/doc/lib/module-threading.html).

- The standard documentation of the SocketServer module (http://python.org/doc/lib/module-SocketServer.html). You would probably be using a ThreadingTCPServer.

- The standard documentation of the Queue module (http://python.org/doc/lib/module-Queue.html). If you can implement your application with Queue (and without Locks) you probably should.

In general, I recommend that you try to avoid using threads if possible. They certainly have their uses, but in many cases you can solve your problem in a different manner, and the result will probably be easier to debug and maintain. (If you are experienced in the field of thread programming, feel free to use all the threads you want to.)

Preparations

The first thing you need is a computer that's connected to a network (such as the Internet)—otherwise others won't be able to connect to your chat server. (It is possible to connect to the chat server from your own machine, but that's not much fun in the long run, is it?) To be able to connect, the user has to know the address of your machine (a machine name such as foo.bar.baz.com or an IP number). In addition, the user must know the *port number* used by your server. You can set this in your program; in the code in this chapter I use the (rather arbitrary) number 5005.

> **NOTE** *Certain port numbers are restricted and require administrator privileges. In general, numbers greater than 1,023 are okay.*

To test your server you need a *client*—the program on the user side of the interaction. A simple program for this sort of thing is telnet (which basically lets you connect to any socket server). In UNIX, you probably have this program available on the command line:

```
$ telnet some.host.name 5005
```

The command above connects to the machine some.host.name on port 5005. To connect to the same machine on which you're running the telnet command, simply use the machine name localhost. (You might want to supply an escape character through the -e switch to make sure you can quit telnet easily. See the man page for more details.)

In Windows, you can use either the standard telnet command (in a DOS window) or a terminal emulator with telnet functionality, such as PuTTY (software and more information available at http://www.chiark.greenend.org.uk/~sgtatham/putty). However, if you are installing new software, you might as well get a client program tailored to chatting. MUD (or MUSH or MOO or some other related acronym) clients are quite suitable for this sort of thing. My client of

choice is TinyFugue (software and more information available at
`http://www.muq.org/~hawkeye/tf`). It is mainly designed for use in UNIX. (There
are several clients available for Windows as well; just do a Web search for "mud
client" or something similar.)

First Implementation

Let's break things down a bit. We need to create two main classes: one representing
the chat server and one representing each of the chat sessions (the connected users).

The ChatServer *Class*

To create the basic `ChatServer` we subclass the `dispatcher` class from `asyncore`.
The `dispatcher` is basically just a socket object, but with some extra event handling features, which we'll be using in a minute.

See Listing 18-1 for a basic chat server program (that does very little).

Listing 18-1. A Minimal Server Program

```
from asyncore import dispatcher
import asyncore

class ChatServer(dispatcher): pass

s = ChatServer()
asyncore.loop()
```

If you run this program, nothing happens. To make the server do anything
interesting, we should call its `create_socket` method to create a socket, and its
`bind` and `listen` methods to bind the socket to a specific port number and to
tell it to listen for incoming connections. (That is what servers do, basically.) In
addition, we'll override the `handle_accept` event handling method to actually do
something when the server accepts a client connection. The resulting program is
shown in Listing 18-2.

Listing 18-2. A Server That Accepts Connections

```
from asyncore import dispatcher
import socket, asyncore

class ChatServer(dispatcher):
```

```
    def handle_accept(self):
        conn, addr = self.accept()
        print 'Connection attempt from', addr[0]

s = ChatServer()
s.create_socket(socket.AF_INET, socket.SOCK_STREAM)
s.bind(('', 5005))
s.listen(5)
asyncore.loop()
```

The handle_accept method calls self.accept, which lets the client connect. This returns a connection (a socket that is specific for this client) and an address (information about which machine is connecting). Instead of doing anything useful with this connection, the handle_accept method simply prints that a connection attempt was made. addr[0] is the IP address of the client.

The server initialization calls create_socket with two arguments that specify the type of socket we want. We could use different types, but those shown here are what you usually want. The call to the bind method simply binds the server to a specific address (host name and port). The host name is empty (an empty string, meaning "localhost") and the port number is 5005. The call to listen tells the server to listen for connections; it also specifies a backlog of five connections. The final call to asyncore.loop starts the server's listening loop as before.

This server actually works. Try to run it and then connect to it with your client. The client should immediately be disconnected, and the server should print out the following:

```
Connection attempt from 127.0.0.1
```

The IP address will be different if you don't connect from the same machine as your server.

To stop the server, simply use a keyboard interrupt: Ctrl+C in UNIX, Ctrl+Break in DOS.

Ending the server with a keyboard interrupt results in a stack trace; to avoid that, we can wrap the loop in a try/except statement (with a print statement to move to the next line). With some other cleanups, our basic server ends up as shown in Listing 18-3.

Listing 18-3. The Basic Server with Some Cleanups

```
from asyncore import dispatcher
import socket, asyncore

PORT = 5005
```

```
class ChatServer(dispatcher):

    def __init__(self, port):
        dispatcher.__init__(self)
        self.create_socket(socket.AF_INET, socket.SOCK_STREAM)
        self.set_reuse_addr()
        self.bind(('', port))
        self.listen(5)

    def handle_accept(self):
        conn, addr = self.accept()
        print 'Connection attempt from', addr[0]

if __name__ == '__main__':
    s = ChatServer(PORT)
    try: asyncore.loop()
    except KeyboardInterrupt: pass
```

The added call to set_reuse_addr lets us reuse the same address (specifically, the port number) even if the server isn't shut down properly. (Without this call, you may have to wait for a while before the server can be started again—or change the port number each time the server crashes—because your program may not be able to properly notify your operating system that it's finished with the port.)

The ChatSession Class

The basic ChatServer doesn't do much good. Instead of ignoring the connection attempts, a new dispatcher object should be created for each connection. However, these objects will behave differently from the one used as the main server. They won't be listening on a port for incoming connections; they already *are* connected to a client. Their main task is collecting data (text) coming from the client, and responding to it. We could implement this functionality ourselves by subclassing dispatcher and overriding various methods, but, luckily, there is a module that already does most of the work: asynchat.

Despite the name, it isn't designed for the type of streaming (continuous) chat application that we're working on. (The word "chat" in the name refers to "chat-style" or command-response protocols.) The good thing about the async_chat class (found in the asynchat module) is that it hides the most basic socket reading and writing operations: They can be a bit difficult to get right. All that's needed to make it work is to override two methods: collect_incoming_data and found_terminator. The former is called each time a bit of text has been read from the socket, and the latter is called when a *terminator* is read. The terminator (in our case) is just a line break. (We'll have to tell the async_chat object about that by calling set_terminator as part of the initialization.)

An updated program, now with a ChatSession class, is shown in Listing 18-4.

Listing 18-4. Server Program with ChatSession *Class*

```python
from asyncore import dispatcher
from asynchat import async_chat
import socket, asyncore

PORT = 5005

class ChatSession(async_chat):

    def __init__(self, sock):
        async_chat.__init__(self, sock)
        self.set_terminator("\r\n")
        self.data = []

    def collect_incoming_data(self, data):
        self.data.append(data)

    def found_terminator(self):
        line = ''.join(self.data)
        self.data = []
        # Do something with the line...
        print line

class ChatServer(dispatcher):

    def __init__(self, port):
        dispatcher.__init__(self)
        self.create_socket(socket.AF_INET, socket.SOCK_STREAM)
        self.set_reuse_addr()
        self.bind(('', port))
        self.listen(5)
        self.sessions = []

    def handle_accept(self):
        conn, addr = self.accept()
        self.sessions.append(ChatSession(conn))
```

```
if __name__ == '__main__':
    s = ChatServer(PORT)
    try: asyncore.loop()
    except KeyboardInterrupt: print
```

Several things are worth noting in this new version:

- The set_terminator method is used to set the line terminator to "\r\n",
  which is the commonly used line terminator in network protocols.

- The ChatSession object keeps the data it has read so far as a list of strings
  called data. When more data is read, collect_incoming_data is called automatically, and it simply appends the data to the list. Using a list of strings
  and later joining them (with the join string method) is much more efficient than incrementally adding strings because each addition would
  require a new string object.

- The found_terminator method is called when a terminator is found. The
  current implementation creates a line by joining the current data items,
  and resets self.data to an empty list. However, because we don't have anything useful to do with the line yet, it is simply printed.

- The ChatServer keeps a list of sessions.

- The handle_accept method of the ChatServer now creates a new
  ChatSession object and appends it to the list of sessions.

Try running the server and connect with two (or more) clients simultaneously. Every line you type in a client should be printed in the terminal where your
server is running. That means that the server is now capable of handling several
simultaneous connections. Now all that's missing is the capability for the clients
to see what the others are saying!

Putting It Together

Before the prototype can be considered a fully functional (albeit simple) chat
server, one main piece of functionality is lacking: What the users say (each line
they type) should be broadcast to the others. That functionality can be implemented by a simple for loop in the server, which loops over the list of sessions
and writes the line to each of them. To write data to a async_chat object, you use
the push method.

This broadcasting behavior also adds another problem: We must make sure that connections are removed from the list when the clients disconnect. We can do that by overriding the event handling method handle_close. The final version of the first prototype can be seen in Listing 18-5.

Listing 18-5. A Simple Chat Server (simple_chat.py)

```python
from asyncore import dispatcher
from asynchat import async_chat
import socket, asyncore

PORT = 5005
NAME = 'TestChat'

class ChatSession(async_chat):
    """
    A class that takes care of a connection between the server
    and a single user.
    """
    def __init__(self, server, sock):
        # Standard setup tasks:
        async_chat.__init__(self, sock)
        self.server = server
        self.set_terminator("\r\n")
        self.data = []
        # Greet the user:
        self.push('Welcome to %s\r\n' % self.server.name)

    def collect_incoming_data(self, data):
        self.data.append(data)

    def found_terminator(self):
        """
        If a terminator is found, that means that a full
        line has been read. Broadcast it to everyone.
        """
        line = ''.join(self.data)
        self.data = []
        self.server.broadcast(line)

    def handle_close(self):
        async_chat.handle_close(self)
        self.server.disconnect(self)
```

```
class ChatServer(dispatcher):
    """
    A class that receives connections and spawns individual
    sessions. It also handles broadcasts to these sessions.
    """
    def __init__(self, port, name):
        # Standard setup tasks
        dispatcher.__init__(self)
        self.create_socket(socket.AF_INET, socket.SOCK_STREAM)
        self.set_reuse_addr()
        self.bind(('', port))
        self.listen(5)
        self.name = name
        self.sessions = []

    def disconnect(self, session):
        self.sessions.remove(session)

    def broadcast(self, line):
        for session in self.sessions:
            session.push(line + '\r\n')

    def handle_accept(self):
        conn, addr = self.accept()
        self.sessions.append(ChatSession(self, conn))

if __name__ == '__main__':
    s = ChatServer(PORT, NAME)
    try: asyncore.loop()
    except KeyboardInterrupt: print
```

Second Implementation

The first prototype may be a fully functioning chat server, but its functionality is quite limited. The most obvious limitation is that you can't discern who is saying what. Also, it does not interpret commands (such as say or logout), which our original specification requires. So, we need to add support for identity (one unique name per user) and command interpretation, and we must make the behavior of each session depend on the state it's in (just connected, logged in, and so on)—all of this in a manner that lends itself easily to extension.

Basic Command Interpretation

I'll model the command interpretation on the Cmd class of the cmd module in the standard library. (Unfortunately we can't use this class directly because it can only be used with sys.stdin and sys.stdout and we're working with several streams.)

What we need is a function or method that can handle a single line of text (as typed by the user). It should split off the first word (the command) and call an appropriate method based on it. For instance, the line

```
say Hello, world!
```

might result in the call

```
do_say('Hello, world!')
```

possibly with the session itself as an added argument (so do_say would know who did the talking). Here is a simple implementation, with an added method to express that a command is unknown:

```
class CommandHandler:
    """
    Simple command handler similar to cmd.Cmd from the standard
    library.
    """

    def unknown(self, session, cmd):
        session.push('Unknown command: %s\r\n' % cmd)

    def handle(self, session, line):
        if not line.strip(): return
        parts = line.split(' ', 1)
        cmd = parts[0]
        try: line = parts[1].strip()
        except IndexError: line = ''
        meth = getattr(self, 'do_'+cmd, None)
        if callable(meth):
            meth(session, line)
        else:
            self.unknown(session, cmd)
```

The use of getattr in this class is similar to that in Chapter 14.

With the basic command handling out of the way, we need to define some actual commands—and which commands are available (and what they do) should depend on the current state of the session. How do you represent that state?

Rooms

Each state can be represented by a custom command handler. This is easily combined with the standard notion of chat rooms (or locations in a MUD). Each room is a CommandHandler with its own, specialized commands. In addition, it should keep track of which users (sessions) are currently inside it. Here is a generic superclass for all our rooms:

```
class EndSession(Exception): pass

class Room(CommandHandler):
    """
    A generic environment which may contain one or more users
    (sessions). It takes care of basic command handling and
    broadcasting.
    """

    def __init__(self, server):
        self.server = server
        self.sessions = []

    def add(self, session):
        self.sessions.append(session)

    def remove(self, session):
        self.sessions.remove(session)

    def broadcast(self, line):
        for session in self.sessions:
            session.push(line)

    def do_logout(self, session, line):
        raise EndSession
```

In addition to the basic add and remove methods, a broadcast method simply calls push on all of the users (sessions) in the room. There is also a single command defined—logout (in the form of the do_logout method). It raises an exception (EndSession), which will have to be dealt with elsewhere. (I'll get to that in a little while.)

Login and Logout Rooms

In addition to representing normal chat rooms (this project includes only one such chat room), the Room subclasses can represent other states, which was indeed the intention. For instance, when a user connects to the server, he or she is put in a dedicated LoginRoom (with no other users in it). The LoginRoom prints a welcome message when the user enters (in the add method). It also overrides the unknown method to tell the user to log in; the only command it responds to is the login command, which checks whether the name is acceptable (not the empty string, and not used by another user already).

The LogoutRoom is much simpler. Its only job is to delete the user's name from the server (which has a dictionary called users where the sessions are stored). If the name isn't there (because the user never logged in), the resulting KeyError is ignored.

For the source code of these two classes, see Listing 18-2.

 NOTE *Even though the server's* users *dictionary keeps references to all the sessions, no session is ever retrieved from it. The* users *dictionary is used only to keep track of which names are in use. However, instead of using some arbitrary value (such as 1), I decided to let each user name refer to the corresponding session. Even though there is no immediate use for it, it may be useful in some later version of the program.*

The Main Chat Room

The main chat room also overrides the add and remove methods. In add, it broadcasts a message about the user who is entering, and it adds the user's name to the users dictionary in the server. The remove method broadcasts a message about the user who is leaving.

In addition to these methods, the ChatRoom class implements three commands:

- The say command (implemented by do_say) broadcasts a single line, prefixed with the name of the user who spoke.

- The look command (implemented by do_look) tells the user which users are currently in the room.

- The who command (implemented by do_who) tells the user which users are currently logged in. In this simple server, look and who are equivalent, but if you extend it to contain more than one room, their functionality will differ.

For the source code, see Listing 18-6.

The New Server

I've now described most of the functionality. The main additions to ChatSession and ChatServer are as follows:

- ChatSession has a method called enter, which is used to enter a new room.

- The ChatSession constructor uses LoginRoom.

- The handle_close method uses LogoutRoom.

- The ChatServer constructor adds the dictionary users and the ChatRoom called main_room to its attributes.

Notice also how handle_accept no longer adds the new ChatSession to a list of sessions because the sessions are now managed by the rooms.

> **NOTE** *In general, if you simply instantiate an object, like the* ChatSession *in* handle_accept, *without binding a name to it or adding it to a container, it will be lost, and may be garbage collected (which means that it will disappear completely). Because all* dispatchers *are handled (referenced) by* asyncore *(and* async_chat *is a subclass of* dispatcher*) this is not a problem here.*

The final version of the chat server is shown in Listing 18-6. For your convenience, I've listed the available commands in Table 18-1. An example chat session is shown in Figure 18-1—the server in that example was started with the command

```
python chatserver.py
```

and the user dilbert connected to the server using the command

```
telnet localhost 5005
```

Listing 18-6. A Slightly More Complicated Chat Server (chatserver.py)

```
from asyncore import dispatcher
from asynchat import async_chat
import socket, asyncore

PORT = 5005
NAME = 'TestChat'

class EndSession(Exception): pass

class CommandHandler:
    """
    Simple command handler similar to cmd.Cmd from the standard
    library.
    """

    def unknown(self, session, cmd):
        'Respond to an unknown command'
        session.push('Unknown command: %s\r\n' % cmd)

    def handle(self, session, line):
        'Handle a received line from a given session'
        if not line.strip(): return
        # Split off the command:
        parts = line.split(' ', 1)
        cmd = parts[0]
        try: line = parts[1].strip()
        except IndexError: line = ''
        # Try to find a handler:
        meth = getattr(self, 'do_'+cmd, None)
        # If it is callable...
        if callable(meth):
            # ...call it:
            meth(session, line)
        else:
            # Otherwise, respond to the unknown command:
            self.unknown(session, cmd)

class Room(CommandHandler):
    """
    A generic environment that may contain one or more users
    (sessions). It takes care of basic command handling and
```

```
    broadcasting.
    """

    def __init__(self, server):
        self.server = server
        self.sessions = []

    def add(self, session):
        'A session (user) has entered the room'
        self.sessions.append(session)

    def remove(self, session):
        'A session (user) has left the room'
        self.sessions.remove(session)

    def broadcast(self, line):
        'Send a line to all sessions in the room'
        for session in self.sessions:
            session.push(line)

    def do_logout(self, session, line):
        'Respond to the logout command'
        raise EndSession

class LoginRoom(Room):
    """
    A room meant for a single person who has just connected.
    """

    def add(self, session):
        Room.add(self, session)
        # When a user enters, greet him/her:
        self.broadcast('Welcome to %s\r\n' % self.server.name)

    def unknown(self, session, cmd):
        # All unknown commands (anything except login or logout)
        # results in a prodding:
        session.push('Please log in\nUse "login <nick>"\r\n')

    def do_login(self, session, line):
        name = line.strip()
        # Make sure the user has entered a name:
        if not name:
```

```python
            session.push('Please enter a name\r\n')
        # Make sure that the name isn't in use:
        elif name in self.server.users:
            session.push('The name "%s" is taken.\r\n' % name)
            session.push('Please try again.\r\n')
        else:
            # The name is OK, so it is stored in the session, and
            # the user is moved into the main room.
            session.name = name
            session.enter(self.server.main_room)

class ChatRoom(Room):
    """
    A room meant for multiple users who can chat with the others in
    the room.
    """

    def add(self, session):
        # Notify everyone that a new user has entered:
        self.broadcast(session.name + ' has entered the room.\r\n')
        self.server.users[session.name] = session
        Room.add(self, session)

    def remove(self, session):
        Room.remove(self, session)
        # Notify everyone that a user has left:
        self.broadcast(session.name + ' has left the room.\r\n')

    def do_say(self, session, line):
        self.broadcast(session.name+': '+line+'\r\n')

    def do_look(self, session, line):
        'Handles the look command, used to see who is in a room'
        session.push('The following are in this room:\r\n')
        for other in self.sessions:
            session.push(other.name + '\r\n')

    def do_who(self, session, line):
        'Handles the who command, used to see who is logged in'
        session.push('The following are logged in:\r\n')
        for name in self.server.users:
            session.push(name + '\r\n')
```

```
class LogoutRoom(Room):
    """
    A simple room for a single user. Its sole purpose it is to remove
    the user's name from the server.
    """

    def add(self, session):
        # When a session (user) enters the LogoutRoom it is deleted
        try: del self.server.users[session.name]
        except KeyError: pass

class ChatSession(async_chat):
    """
    A single session, which takes care of the communication with a
    single user.
    """

    def __init__(self, server, sock):
        async_chat.__init__(self, sock)
        self.server = server
        self.set_terminator("\r\n")
        self.data = []
        self.name = None
        # All sessions begin in a separate LoginRoom:
        self.enter(LoginRoom(server))

    def enter(self, room):
        # Remove self from current room and add self to
        # next room...
        try: cur = self.room
        except AttributeError: pass
        else: cur.remove(self)
        self.room = room
        room.add(self)

    def collect_incoming_data(self, data):
        self.data.append(data)

    def found_terminator(self):
        line = ''.join(self.data)
        self.data = []
        try: self.room.handle(self, line)
        except EndSession:
            self.handle_close()
```

```
        def handle_close(self):
            async_chat.handle_close(self)
            self.enter(LogoutRoom(self.server))

class ChatServer(dispatcher):
    """
    A chat server with a single room.
    """

    def __init__(self, port, name):
        dispatcher.__init__(self)
        self.create_socket(socket.AF_INET, socket.SOCK_STREAM)
        self.set_reuse_addr()
        self.bind(('', port))
        self.listen(5)
        self.name = name
        self.users = {}
        self.main_room = ChatRoom(self)

    def handle_accept(self):
        conn, addr = self.accept()
        ChatSession(self, conn)

if __name__ == '__main__':
    s = ChatServer(PORT, NAME)
    try: asyncore.loop()
    except KeyboardInterrupt: print
```

Table 18-1. The Commands Available in the Chat Server

COMMAND	AVAILABLE IN...	DESCRIPTION
login *name*	Login room	Used to log into the server
logout	All rooms	Used to log out of the server
say *statement*	Chat room(s)	Used to say something
look	Chat room(s)	Used to find out who is in the same room
who	Chat room(s)	Used to find out who is logged on to the server

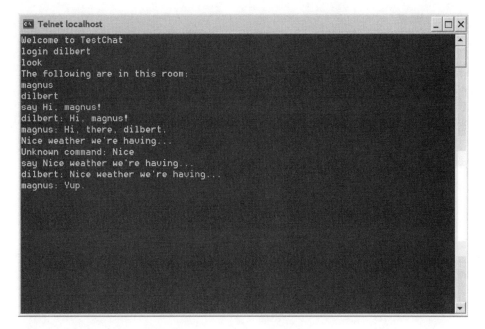

Figure 18-1. A sample chat session

Further Exploration

You can do a lot to extend and enhance the basic server presented in this chapter:

- You could make a version with multiple chat rooms and you could extend the command set to make it behave in any way you want.

- You might want to make the program recognize only certain commands (such as `login` or `logout`) and treat all other text entered as general chatting, thereby avoiding the need for a `say` command.

- You could prefix all commands with a special character (for example, a slash, giving commands like `/login` and `/logout`) and treat everything that doesn't start with the specified character as general chatting.

- You might want to create your own GUI client—but that's a bit trickier than it might seem. The server has one event loop, and the GUI toolkit will have another. To make them cooperate, you will need to use threading. (For an example of how this can be done in simple cases where the various threads don't directly access each other's data, see Chapter 22.)

What Now?

Now you've got your very own chat server. In the next project you tackle a different type of network programming: CGI, the mechanism underlying most Web applications (you know, Web pages with forms that you fill out). The specific application of this technology in the next project is "remote editing," which enables several users to collaborate on developing the same document. You may even use it to edit your own Web pages remotely.

#### CHAPTER 19

Project 6: Remote Editing with CGI

THIS PROJECT DEALS WITH A BASIC Web programming technology: the Common Gateway Interface, or CGI. The specific application is "remote editing"—editing a document on another machine via the Web. This can be useful in collaboration systems (groupware), for instance, where several people may be working on the same document. It can also be useful for updating your Web pages.

....

What Is CGI?

CGI is a standard mechanism by which a Web server can pass your queries (typically supplied through a Web form) to a dedicated program (for example, your Python program) and display the result as a Web page. It is a simple way of creating Web applications without writing your own special-purpose application server. For more information about CGI programming in Python, see the Web Programming Topic Guide on the Python Web site (http://www.python.org/topics/web).

....

What's the Problem?

The problem is quite simple: You have a document stored on one machine and want to be able to edit it from another machine via the Web. This enables you to have a shared document edited by several collaborating authors—you won't need to use FTP or similar file transfer technologies, and you won't need to worry about synchronizing multiple copies. To edit the file, all you need is a browser.

Specific Goals

The system should be able to do the following:

- Display the document as a normal Web page

- Display the document in a text area in a Web form

- Let you save the text from the form

- Protect the document with a password

- Be easily extensible to more than one document

As you'll see, all of this is quite easy to do with the standard Python library module cgi and some plain Python coding. However, the techniques used in this application can be used for creating Web interfaces to all of your Python programs—pretty useful. (For instance, you use the same CGI techniques in Chapter 20.)

Useful Tools

The key tool in Python CGI programming is the cgi module. You can find a thorough description of it in the Python Library Reference (http://www.python.org/doc/lib/module-cgi.html). Another module that can be very useful during the development of CGI scripts is cgitb—more about that later.

Preparations

Before you can make your CGI scripts accessible (and runable) through the Web, you need to put them where a Web server can access them, add a "pound bang" line, and set the proper file permissions. These three steps are explained in the following sections.

Step 1. The Web Server

I'm assuming that you have access to a Web server—in other words, that you can put stuff on the Web. Usually, that is a matter of putting your Web pages, images, and so on in a particular directory (in UNIX, typically called `public_html`). If you don't know how to do this, you should ask your ISP or system administrator.

Your CGI programs must also be put in a directory where they can be accessed via the Web. In addition, they must somehow be identified as CGI scripts, so the Web server doesn't just serve the plain source code as a Web page. There are two typical ways of doing this:

- Put the script in a directory called `cgi-bin`.

- Give your script the file name extension `.cgi`.

Exactly how this works varies from server to server—again, check with your ISP or system administrator.

Step 2. Adding the "Pound Bang" Line

When you've put the script in the right place (and possibly given it a specific file name extension), you must add a "pound bang" line to the beginning of the script. I mentioned this in Chapter 1 as a way of executing your scripts without having to explicitly execute the Python interpreter. Usually, this is just convenient, but for CGI scripts it's crucial; without it, the Web server won't know how to execute your script. (For all it knows, the script could be written in some other programming language such as Perl or Ruby.) In general, simply adding the following line to the beginning of your script will do:

```
#!/usr/bin/env python
```

Note that it has to be the very first line. (No empty lines before it.) If that doesn't work, you have to find out exactly where the Python executable is and use the full path in the pound bang line, as in the following:

```
#!/usr/bin/python
```

In Windows, you would use the full path to your Python binary, such as

```
#!C:\Python22\python.exe
```

Step 3. Setting the File Permissions

The last thing you have to do (at least if your Web server is running on a UNIX or Linux machine) is to set the proper file permissions. You must make sure that everyone is allowed to *read* and *execute* your script file (otherwise the Web server wouldn't be able to run it), but also make sure that only you are allowed to *write* to it (so nobody can change your script).

TIP *Sometimes, if you edit a script in Windows and it's stored on a UNIX disk server (you may be accessing it through Samba or FTP) the file permissions may be fouled up after you've made a change to your script. So if your script won't run, make sure that the permissions are still correct.*

The UNIX command for changing file permissions (or file *mode*) is chmod. Simply run the following command (if your script is called somescript.cgi):

```
chmod 755 somescript.cgi
```

After having performed all these preparations, you should be able to open the script as if it were a Web page and have it execute.

NOTE *You shouldn't open it in your browser as a local file— you must open it with a full URL so that you actually fetch it via the Web (through your Web server).*

Your CGI script won't normally be allowed to modify any files on your computer. Because you want it to store the edited file, you have to explicitly give it permission to do so. You have two options. If you have root (system administrator) privileges, you may create a specific user account for your script and change ownership of the files that need to be modified. If you don't have root access, you can set the file permissions for the file so all users on the system (including that used by the Web server to run your CGI scripts) are allowed to write to the file. You can set the file permissions with this command:

```
chmod 666 edit.dat
```

CAUTION *This also means that everyone that has a user account on the machine can edit your file. You should be extremely cautious about this, especially if the file you are modifying is accessible through your Web server. If you are in doubt, ask your ISP or system administrator for advice. See also the following section "CGI Security Risks."*

CGI Security Risks

Note that there are security issues involved in using CGI programs. If you allow your CGI script to write to files on your server, that may be used to destroy data unless you code your program carefully. Similarly, if you evaluate data supplied by a user as if it were Python code (for example, with exec or eval) or as a shell command (for example, with os.system) you risk performing arbitrary commands, which is a *huge* risk. For a relatively comprehensive source of information about Web security, see the World Wide Web Consortium's security FAQ (http://www.w3.org/Security/Faq). See also the security note on the subject in the Python Library Reference (http://python.org/doc/lib/cgi-security.html).

First Implementation

The simplest possible CGI script is something like this:

```
#!/usr/bin/env python

print 'Content-type: text/plain'
print # Prints an empty line, to end the headers

print 'Hello, world!'
```

If you save this in a file called simple1.cgi and open it through your Web server (as described in the "Preparations" section) you should see a Web page containing only the words "Hello, world!" in plain text. To be able to open this file through a Web server you must put it where the Web server can access it. In a typical UNIX environment, putting it in a directory called public_html in your home directory would enable you to open it with the URL http://localhost/~username/ simple1.cgi (substitute your user name for username). Ask your ISP or system administrator for details.

As you can see, everything the program writes to standard output (for example, with `print`) ends up in the resulting Web page—at least almost. The fact is that the first things you print are HTTP headers—lines of information *about* the page. The only header we'll use in our program is `Content-type`. As you can see, the phrase "`Content-type`" is followed by a colon, a space, and the type `text/plain`. This indicates that the page is plain text; to indicate HTML, this line should instead be:

```
print 'Content-type: text/html'
```

> **NOTE** *The strings* `'text/plain'` *and* `'text/html'` *are MIME (Multipurpose Internet Mail Extensions) types. For a list of official MIME types, see* `http://www.iana.org/assignments/media-types`.

After all the headers have been printed, a single empty line is printed to signal that the document itself is about to begin. And, as you can see, in this case the document is simply the string `'Hello, world!'`.

Sometimes a programming error makes your program terminate with a stacktrace due to an uncaught exception. When running the program through CGI, this will most likely result in an unhelpful error message from the Web server. In Python 2.2, a new module called `cgitb` (for CGI traceback) was added to the standard library. By importing it and calling its `enable` function, you can get a quite helpful Web page with information about what went wrong. Listing 19-1 gives an example of how you might use the `cgitb` module.

Listing 19-1. A CGI Script That Invokes a Traceback (`faulty.cgi`*)*

```
#!/usr/bin/env python

import cgitb; cgitb.enable()

print 'Content-type: text/html'

print

print 1/0

print 'Hello, world!'
```

The result of accessing this script in a browser (through a Web server) is shown in Figure 19-1.

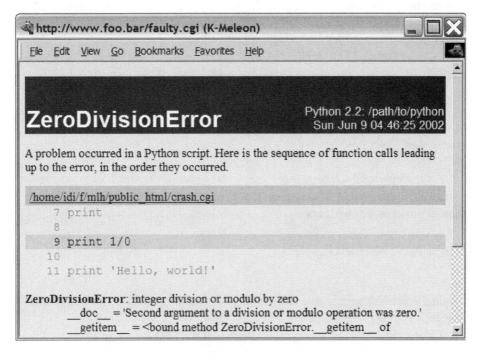

Figure 19-1. A CGI traceback from the cgitb *module*

Note that you might want to turn off the cgitb functionality after developing the program; the traceback page isn't meant for the casual user of your program. (An alternative is to turn off the display and log the errors to files instead. See the Python Library Reference for more information.)

Using the cgi Module

So far the programs have only produced output; they haven't used any form of input. Input is supplied to the CGI script from an HTML form (described in the next section) as key-value pairs, or *fields*. You can retrieve these fields in your CGI script using the FieldStorage class from the cgi module. When you create your FieldStorage instance (you should create only one) it fetches the input variables (or fields) from the request and presents them to your program through a dictionary-like interface. The values of the FieldStorage can be accessed through ordinary key lookup, but due to some technicalities (related to file uploads, which we won't be dealing with here) the elements of the FieldStorage aren't really the values you're after. For instance, if you know the request contained a value named name, you couldn't simply do this:

```
form = cgi.FieldStorage()
name = form['name']
```

You'd have to do this:

```
form = cgi.FieldStorage()
name = form['name'].value
```

A simpler way of fetching the values is the getvalue method, which is similar to the dictionary method get, except that it returns the value of the value attribute of the item. For instance:

```
form = cgi.FieldStorage()
name = form.getvalue('name', 'Unknown')
```

In the preceding example I have supplied a default value. If you don't supply one, None will be the default.

Listing 19-2 contains a simple example that uses cgi.FieldStorage.

Listing 19-2. A CGI Script That Retrieves a Single Value from a FieldStorage *(simple2.cgi)*

```
#!/usr/bin/env python

import cgi
form = cgi.FieldStorage()

name = form.getvalue('name', 'world')

print 'Content-type: text/plain'
print

print 'Hello, %s!' % name
```

Invoking CGI Scripts Without Forms

Input to CGI scripts generally comes from Web forms that have been submitted, but it is also possible to call the CGI program with parameters directly. You do this by adding a question mark after the URL to your script, and then adding *key=value* pairs separated by ampersands (&). For instance, if the URL to the script in Listing 19-2 were `http://www.someserver.com/simple2.cgi` you could call it with `name=Gumby` and `age=42` as with the URL `http://www.someserver.com/simple2.cgi?name=Gumby&age=42`. If you try that, you should get the message "Hello, Gumby!" instead of "Hello, world!" from your CGI script. (Note that the age parameter isn't used.)

A Simple Form

Now you have the tools for handling a user request. It's time to create a form that the user can submit. That form can be a separate page, but in this application I just put it all in the same script.

To find out more about writing HTML forms (or HTML in general) you should perhaps get a good book on HTML (your local bookstore probably has several). You can also find plenty of information on the subject online. Here are some resources:

- `http://www.webreference.com/htmlform`

- `http://www.htmlhelp.com/faq/html/forms.html`

- `http://www.cs.tut.fi/~jkorpela/forms`

- `http://www.htmlgoodies.com/tutors/fm.html`

Let's return to our script. In the beginning, the CGI parameter `name` is retrieved, with the default `'world'`. If you just opened the script in your browser without submitting anything, the default is used.

Then, a simple HTML page is printed, containing `name` as a part of the headline. In addition, this page contains an HTML form whose `action` attribute is set to the name of the script itself (`simple3.py`). That means that if the form is submitted, you are taken back to the same script. The only input element in the form is a text field called `name`. Thus, if you submit the field with a new name, the headline should change because the `name` parameter now has a value. Listing 19-3 contains the source code for this script.

Listing 19-3. A Greeting Script with an HTML Form (simple3.cgi)

```python
#!/usr/bin/env python

import cgi
form = cgi.FieldStorage()

name = form.getvalue('name', 'world')

print """Content-type: text/html

<html>
  <head>
    <title>Greeting Page</title>
  </head>
  <body>
    <h1>Hello, %s!</h1>

    <form action='simple3.cgi'>
    Change name <input type='text' name='name' />
    <input type='submit' />
    </form>
  </body>
</html>
""" % name
```

Figure 19-2 shows the result of accessing the script in Listing 19-3 through a Web server.

Figure 19-2. The result of executing the CGI script in Listing 19-3

Adding Some File Handling

Now we're almost ready to produce the first prototype. All that is lacking is the file handling. We need to store the edited text between invocations of the script. Also, the form should be made a bit bigger (and changed into a text area, rather than a one-line text field) and we should use the POST CGI method instead of the default GET. (Using POST is normally the thing to do if you are submitting large amounts of data.)

The general logic of the program is as follows:

1. Get the CGI parameter text with the current value of the data file as the default.

2. Save the text to the data file.

3. Print out the form, with the text in the textarea.

In order for the script to be allowed to write to your data file, you must first create such a file (for example, called simple_edit.dat). It can be empty or perhaps contain the initial document (a plain text file, possibly containing some form of markup such as XML or HTML). Then you must set the permissions as described in the "Preparations" section earlier in this chapter. The resulting code is shown in Listing 19-4.

Listing 19-4. A Simple Web Editor (simple_edit.cgi)

```
#!/usr/bin/env python

import cgi
form = cgi.FieldStorage()

text = form.getvalue('text', open('simple_edit.dat').read())
f = open('simple_edit.dat', 'w')
f.write(text)
f.close()

print """Content-type: text/html

<html>
  <head>
    <title>A Simple Editor</title>
  </head>
  <body>
    <form action='simple_edit.cgi' method='POST'>
    <textarea rows='10' cols='20' name='text'>%s</textarea><br />
    <input type='submit' />
    </form>
  </body>
</html>
""" % text
```

When accessed through a Web server, the CGI script checks for an input value called text. If such a value is submitted, the text is written to the file simple_edit.dat. The default value is the file's current contents. Finally, a Web page (containing the field for editing and submitting the text) is shown. A screenshot of this page is shown in Figure 19-3.

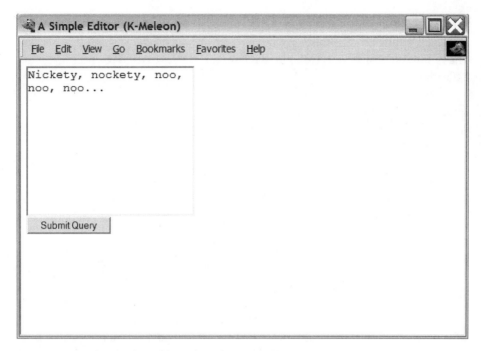

Figure 19-3. The `simple_edit.cgi` *script in action*

Second Implementation

Now that we've gotten the first prototype on the road, what's missing? The system should be able to edit more than one file, and it should use password protection. (Because the document can be viewed by opening it directly in a browser, I won't be paying much attention to the viewing part of the system.)

The main difference from the first prototype is that we'll split the functionality into several scripts—one for each "action" our system should be able to perform:

> `index.html`: This isn't a script. It's just a plain Web page with a form where we can enter a file name. It also has an Open button, which triggers `edit.cgi`.

> `edit.cgi`: Displays a given file in a text area; has a text field for password entry and a Save button, which triggers `save.cgi`.

> `save.cgi`: Saves the text it receives to a given file and displays a simple message (for example, "The file has been saved"). This script should also take care of the password checking.

index.html

The file index.html is an HTML file that contains the form used to enter a file name:

```html
<html>
  <head>
    <title>File Editor</title>
  </head>
  <body>
    <form action='edit.cgi' method='POST'>
      <b>File name:</b><br />
      <input type='text' name='filename' />
      <input type='submit' value='Open' />
  </body>
</html>
```

Note how the text field is named "filename"—that ensures that its contents will be supplied as the CGI parameter filename to the edit.cgi script (which is the action attribute of the form tag.) If you open this file in a browser, enter a file name in the text field and press Open; the edit.cgi script will be run.

edit.cgi

The page displayed by edit.cgi should contain a text area containing the current text of the file you're editing, and a text field for entering a password. The only input needed is the file name, which the script receives from the form in index.html. Note, however, that it is fully possible to open the edit.cgi script directly, without submitting the form in index.html. In that case, you have no guarantee that the filename field of cgi.FieldStorage is set. So you have to add a check to ensure that there *is* a file name. If there is, the file will be opened from a directory that contains the files that may be edited. Let's call the directory data.

 CAUTION *Note that by supplying a file name that contains path elements such as .. ("dot-dot") it may be possible to access files outside this directory. To make sure that the files accessed are within the given directory, you should perform some extra checking, such as listing all the files in the directory (using the glob module, for instance) and checking that the supplied file name is one of the candidate files. See the section "Validating File Names" in Chapter 21 for another approach.*

The code, then, becomes something like Listing 19-5.

Listing 19-5. The Editor Script (`edit.cgi`*)*

```python
#!/usr/bin/env python

print 'Content-type: text/html\n'

from os.path import join, abspath
import cgi, sys

BASE_DIR = abspath('data')

form = cgi.FieldStorage()
filename = form.getvalue('filename')
if not filename:
    print 'Please enter a file name'
    sys.exit()
text = open(join(BASE_DIR, filename)).read()

print """
<html>
  <head>
    <title>Editing...</title>
  </head>
  <body>
    <form action='save.cgi' method='POST'>
      <b>File:</b> %s<br />
      <input type='hidden' value='%s' name='filename' />
      <b>Password:</b><br />
      <input name='password' type='password' /><br />
      <b>Text:</b><br />
      <textarea name='text' cols='40' rows='20'>%s</textarea><br />
      <input type='submit' value='Save' />
    </form>
  </body>
</html>
""" % (filename, filename, text)
```

Note that the abspath function has been used to get the absolute path of the data directory. Also note that the file name has been stored in a hidden form element so that it will be relayed to the next script (save.cgi) without giving the user an opportunity to change it. (We have no guarantees of that, of course, because the user may write his/her own forms, put them on another machine, and have them call our CGI scripts with custom values.)

For password handling I've used an input element of type password rather than text, which means that the characters entered will all be displayed as asterisks.

save.cgi

The script that performs the saving is the last component of our simple system. It receives a file name, a password, and some text. It checks that the password is correct, and if it is, the program stores the text in the file with the given file name. (The file should have its permissions set properly. See the description earlier in this chapter.)

Just for fun, I've used the sha module in the password handling. SHA (Secure Hash Algorithm) is a way of extracting an essentially meaningless string of seemingly random data (a "digest") from an input string. The idea behind the algorithm is that it is almost impossible to construct a string that has a given digest, so if I know the digest of a password (for instance) there is no way I can reconstruct the password or invent one that will reproduce the digest. This means that I can safely compare the digest of a supplied password with a stored digest (of the correct password) instead of comparing the passwords themselves. By using this approach I don't have to store the password itself in the source code, and someone reading the code would be none the wiser about what the password actually *was*.

CAUTION *As I said, this "security" feature is mainly for fun. Unless you are using a secure connection with SSL or some similar technology (which is beyond the scope of this project) it is still possible to pick up the password being submitted over the network.*

Here is an example of how you can use sha:

```
>> from sha import sha
>> sha('foobar').hexdigest()
'8843d7f92416211de9ebb963ff4ce28125932878'
>> sha('foobaz').hexdigest()
'21eb6533733a5e4763acacd1d45a60c2e0e404e1'
```

As you can see, a small change in the password gives you a completely different digest. You can see the code for save.cgi in Listing 19-6.

Listing 19-6. The Saving Script (save.cgi)

```python
#!/usr/bin/env python

print 'Content-type: text/html\n'

from os.path import join, abspath
import cgi, sha, sys

BASE_DIR = abspath('data')

form = cgi.FieldStorage()

text = form.getvalue('text')
filename = form.getvalue('filename')
password = form.getvalue('password')

if not (filename and text and password):
    print 'Invalid parameters.'
    sys.exit()

if sha.sha(password).hexdigest() != '8843d7f92416211de9ebb963ff4ce28125932878':
    print 'Invalid password'
    sys.exit()
```

```
f = open(join(BASE_DIR,filename), 'w')
f.write(text)
f.close()

print 'The file has been saved.'
```

Running the Editor

Follow these steps to use the editor:

1. Open the page index.html in a Web browser. Be sure to open it through a Web server (by using a URL of the form http://www.someserver.com/index.html) and not as a local file. The result is shown in Figure 19-4.

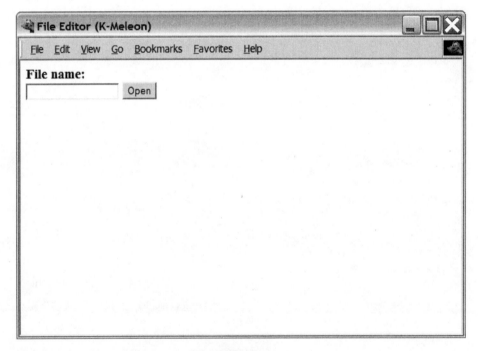

Figure 19-4. The opening page of the CGI editor

2. Enter a file name of a file that your CGI editor is permitted to modify, and press Open. Your browser should then contain the output of the edit.cgi script, as shown in Figure 19-5.

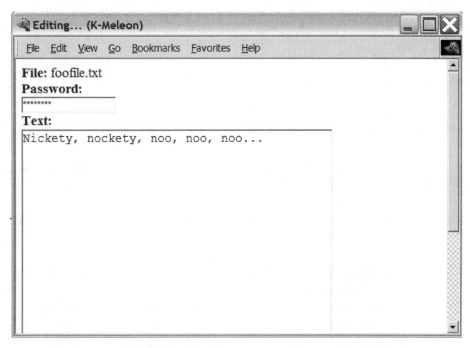

Figure 19-5. The editing page of the CGI editor

3. Edit the file to taste, enter the password, and press Save. Your browser should then contain the output of the save.cgi script, which is simply the message "The file has been saved."

4. If you want to verify that the file has been modified, you may repeat the process of opening the file (Steps 1 and 2).

Further Exploration

With the techniques shown in this project, you can develop all kinds of Web systems. Some possible additions to the existing system are as follows:

- Version control: save old copies of the edited file so you can "undo" your changes.

- Add support for user names so you know who changed what.

- Add file locking (for instance with the `fcntl` module) so two users can't edit the file at the same time.

- Add a `view.cgi` script that automatically adds markup to the files (like the one in Chapter 14).

- Make the scripts more robust by checking their input more thoroughly and adding more user friendly error messages.

- Avoid printing a confirmation message like "The file has been saved." You can either add some more useful output, or redirect the user to another page/script. Redirection can be done with the `Location` header, which works like `Content-type`. Just add `Location:` followed by a space and a URL to the header section of the output (*before* the first empty line).

In addition to expanding the capabilities of this CGI system you might want to check out some more complex Web environments for Python, such as Webware (`http://webware.sf.net`) or Zope (`http://www.zope.org`).

What Now?

Now you've seen how to write CGI scripts. In the next project, we expand on that by using an SQL database for storage. With that powerful combination we'll implement a fully functional Web-based bulletin board.

#### CHAPTER 20

Project 7: Your Own Bulletin Board

MANY KINDS OF SOFTWARE enable you to communicate with other people over the Internet. You've seen a few already (for example, the Usenet groups in Chapter 17 and the chat server in Chapter 18), and in this chapter you will implement another such system: a Web-based discussion forum.

What's the Problem?

In this project we create a simple system for posting and responding to messages via the Web. This has utility in itself, as a discussion forum. One famous example of such a forum is Slashdot (`http://www.slashdot.org`). The system developed in this chapter is quite simple, but the basic functionality is there, and it should be capable of handling quite a large number of postings.

However, the material covered in this chapter has uses beyond developing stand-alone discussion forums. It could be used to implement a more general system for collaboration, for instance, or an issue tracking system, or something completely different. The combination of CGI (or similar technologies) and a solid database (in this case, an SQL database) is quite powerful and versatile.

TIP *Even though it's fun and educational to write your own software, in many cases it's more cost-effective to search for existing software. In the case of discussion forums and the like, chances are that you can find quite a few well-developed systems freely available already.*

Specific Goals

The final system should support the following:

- Displaying the subjects of all current messages

- Message threading (displaying replies indented under the message they reply to)

- Viewing existing messages

- Posting new messages

- Replying to existing messages

In addition to these functional requirements, it would be nice if the system was reasonably stable, could handle a large number of messages, and avoided such problems as two users writing to the same file at the same time. The desired robustness can be achieved by using a database server of some sort, instead of writing the file-handling code ourselves.

Useful Tools

In addition to the CGI stuff from Chapter 19, you'll need an SQL database. Two excellent, freely available databases are

- PostgreSQL (http://www.postgresql.org)

- MySQL (http://www.mysql.org)

In this chapter I use PostgreSQL, but the code should work with most SQL databases (including MySQL) with few edits.

Before moving on, you should make sure that you have access to an SQL database server and check its documentation for instructions on how to manage it.

In addition to the database server itself, you'll need a Python module that can interface with the server (and hide the details from you). Most such modules support the Python DB-API. For more information about this API and a list of quite a few available database modules, see the Python Database Topic Guide (http://www.python.org/topics/database). In this chapter I use psycopg (http://initd.org/Software/psycopg), a robust front-end for PostgreSQL. If you're using MySQL, the MySQLdb module (http://sourceforge.net/projects/mysql-python) is a good choice.

After you have installed your database module, you should be able to import it without raising any exceptions. For psycopg:

```
>>> import psycopg
>>>
```

For MySQLdb:

```
>>> import MySQLdb
>>>
```

You get the idea.

Preparations

Before writing the code that uses your database, you should *create* that database. To do that, you need to use the SQL language. I won't give you a tutorial of that here—the documentation for your SQL database probably has lots of material on this. To get some practice, you might want to check out http://www.sqlcourse.com or Michael Kofler's book *MySQL* (Apress, 2001).

The database structure is intimately linked with the problem and can be a bit tricky to change once you've created it and populated it with data (messages). Let's keep it simple: We'll have only one table, which will contain one row for each message. Each message will have a unique ID (an integer), a subject, a sender (or poster), and some text (the body).

In addition, because we want to be able to display the messages hierarchically (threading), each message should store a reference to the message it is a reply to. The resulting create SQL command becomes

```
create table messages (

    id          serial primary key,
    subject     text not null,
    sender      text not null,
    reply_to    integer references messages,
    text        text not null
);
```

Note that this command uses some PostgreSQL-specific features (serial, which ensures that each message automatically receives a unique id, the text datatype, and references, which makes sure that reply_to contains a valid message id). A more MySQL-friendly version would be as follows:

```
create table messages (
    id          int not null auto_increment,
    subject     varchar(100) not null,
    sender      varchar(15) not null,
    reply_to    int,
    text        mediumtext not null,
    primary key(id)
);
```

I've kept these code snippets simple (an SQL guru would certainly find ways to improve them) because the focus of this chapter is, after all, the Python code. The SQL statements create a new table with the following five fields (columns):

id: Used to identify the individual messages. Each message automatically receives a unique id by the database manager, so you don't have to worry about assigning those from your Python code.

subject: A string that contains the subject of the message.

sender: A string that contains the sender's name or e-mail address or something like that.

reply_to: If the message is a reply to another message, this field contains the id of the other message. (Otherwise, the field won't contain anything.)

text: A string that contains the body of the message.

When you've created this database and set the permissions on it so that your Web server is allowed to read its contents and insert new rows, you're ready to start coding the CGI.

 NOTE *Setting permissions in an SQL database is done with the SQL command* GRANT. *Consult your database documentation for details.*

First Implementation

In this project the first prototype will be very limited. It will be a single script that uses the database functionality so that you can get a feel for how it works. Once you've got that pegged, writing the other necessary scripts won't be very hard.

The CGI part of the code is very similar to that in Chapter 19. If you haven't read that chapter yet, you might want to take a look at it. You should also be sure to review the section "CGI Security Risks" in that chapter.

NOTE   *In the CGI scripts in this chapter, I've imported and enabled the* cgitb *module. This is very useful to uncover flaws in your code, but you should probably remove the call to* cgitb.enable *before deploying the software—you probably wouldn't want an ordinary user to face a full* cgitb *traceback.*

The first thing you need to know is how the DB API works. A full reference is available from the Database Topic Guide (mentioned earlier in this chapter), but the core functionality you'll need is the following (replace db with the name of your database module—for example, psycopg or MySQLdb):

conn = db.connect('user=foo dbname=bar'): Connects to the database named foo as user bar and stores the returned connection object in conn. (Note that the parameter to connect is a string.)

CAUTION   *In this project I assume that you have a dedicated machine on which the database and Web server run. The given user (*foo*) should only be allowed to connect from that machine to avoid unwanted access. If you have other users on your machine, you should probably protect your database with a password, which may also be supplied in the parameter string to* connect. *To find out more about this, you should consult the documentation for your database (and your Python database module).*

curs = conn.cursor(): Gets a *cursor* object from the connection object. The cursor is used to actually execute SQL statements and fetch the results.

conn.commit(): Commits the changes caused by the SQL statements since the last commit.

conn.close(): Closes the connection.

curs.execute(*sql string*): Executes an SQL statement.

curs.fetchone(): Fetches one result row as a sequence—for example, a tuple.

curs.dictfetchone(): Fetches one result row as a dictionary. (Not part of the standard, and therefore not available in all modules.)

curs.fetchall(): Fetches all result rows as a sequence of sequences—for example, a list of tuples.

curs.dictfetchall(): Fetches all result rows as a sequence (for example, a list) of dictionaries. (Not part of the standard, and therefore not available in all modules.)

Here is a simple test (assuming psycopg)—retrieving all the messages in the database (which is currently empty, so we won't get any):

```
>>> import psycopg
>>> conn = psycopg.connect('user=foo dbname=bar')
>>> curs = conn.cursor()
>>> curs.execute('select * from messages')
>>> curs.fetchall()
[]
```

Because we haven't implemented the Web interface yet, we have to enter messages manually if we want to test the database. We can do that either through an administrative tool (such as mysql for MySQL or psql for PostgreSQL) or we can use the Python interpreter with our database module.

Here is a useful piece of code you can use for testing purposes:

```
# addmessage.py


import psycopg
conn = psycopg.connect('user=foo dbname=bar')
curs = conn.cursor()

reply_to = raw_input('Reply to: ')
subject = raw_input('Subject: ')
sender = raw_input('Sender: ')
text = raw_input('Text: ')
```

```
if reply_to:
    query = """
    insert into messages(reply_to, sender, subject, text)
    values(%s, '%s', '%s', '%s')""" % (reply_to, sender, subject, text)
else:
    query = """
    insert into messages(sender, subject, text)
    values('%s', '%s', '%s')""" % (sender, subject, text)

curs.execute(query)
conn.commit()
```

Note that this code is a bit crude—it doesn't keep track of IDs for you (you'll have to make sure that what you enter as reply_to, if anything, is a valid ID), and it doesn't deal properly with text containing single quotes (this can be problematic because single quotes are used as string delimiters in SQL). These issues will be dealt with in the final system, of course.

Try to add a few messages and examine the database at the interactive Python prompt—if everything seems okay, it's time to write a CGI script that accesses the database.

Now that we've got the database handling code figured out, and some ready-made CGI code we can pinch from Chapter 19, writing a script for viewing the message subjects (a simple version of the "main page" of the forum) shouldn't be too hard. We must do the standard CGI setup (in this case, mainly printing the Content-type string), do the standard database setup (get a connection and a cursor), execute a simple SQL select command to get all the messages, and then retrieve the resulting rows with curs.fetchall or curs.dictfetchall.

Listing 20-1 shows a script that does these things. The only really new stuff in the listing is the formatting code, which is used to get the threaded look where replies are displayed below and to the right of the messages they are replies to.

It basically works like this:

1. For each message, get the reply_to field. If it is None (not a reply), add the message to the list of top-level messages. Otherwise, append the message to the list of children stored in children[parent_id].

2. For each top-level message, call format.

The format function prints the subject of the message. Also, if the message has any children, it opens a blockquote element (HTML), then calls format (recursively) for each child, and ends the blockquote element.

If you open the script in your Web browser (see Chapter 19 for information on how to run CGI scripts) you should see a threaded view of all the messages you've added (or their subjects, anyway).

For an idea of what the bulletin board looks like, see Figure 20-1 later in this chapter.

Listing 20-1. The Main Bulletin Board (`simple_main.cgi`)

```python
#!/usr/bin/python


print 'Content-type: text/html\n'

import cgitb; cgitb.enable()

import psycopg
conn = psycopg.connect('dbname=foo user=bar')
curs = conn.cursor()

print """
<html>
  <head>
    <title>The FooBar Bulletin Board</title>
  </head>
  <body>
    <h1>The FooBar Bulletin Board</h1>
    """

curs.execute('select * from messages')
rows = curs.dictfetchall()

toplevel = []
children = {}

for row in rows:
    parent_id = row['reply_to']
    if parent_id is None:
        toplevel.append(row)
    else:
        children.setdefault(parent_id,[]).append(row)

def format(row):
    print row['subject']
```

```
    try: kids = children[row['id']]
    except KeyError: pass
    else:
        print '<blockquote>'
        for kid in kids:
            format(kid)
        print '</blockquote>'

print '<p>'

for row in toplevel:
    format(row)

print """
    </p>
  </body>
</html>
"""
```

Second Implementation

The first implementation was quite limited in that it didn't even allow users to post messages. In this section we expand on the simple system in the first proto-type, which contains the basic structure for the final version. Some measures will be added to check the supplied parameters (such as checking whether reply_to is really a number, and whether the required parameters are really supplied), but you should note that making a system like this robust and user-friendly is a tough task. If you intend to use the system (or, I hope, an improved version of your own) you should be prepared to work quite a bit on these issues.

But before you can even think of improving stability, you need something that works, right? So—where do you begin? How do you structure the system?

A simple way of structuring Web programs (using technologies such as CGI) is to have one script per action performed by the user. In the case of our system, that would mean the following scripts:

main.cgi: Displays the subjects of all messages (threaded) with links to the articles themselves.

view.cgi: Displays a single article, and contains a link that will let you reply to it.

edit.cgi: Displays a single article in editable form (with text fields and text areas, just like in Chapter 19). Its "Submit" button is linked to the save script.

save.cgi: Receives information about an article (from edit.cgi) and saves it by inserting a new row into the database table.

Let's deal with these separately.

main.cgi

This script is very similar to the simple_main.cgi script from the first prototype. The main difference is the addition of links. Each subject will be a link to a given message (to view.cgi) and at the bottom of the page we'll add a link that allows the user to post a new message (a link to edit.cgi).

Take a look at the code in Listing 20-2. The line containing the link to each article (part of the format function) looks like this:

```
print '<p><a href="view.cgi?id=%(id)i">%(subject)s</a></p>' % row
```

Basically, it creates a link to view.cgi?id=*someid* where *someid* is the id of the given row. This syntax (the question mark and key=val) is simply a way of passing parameters to a CGI script—that means that if someone clicks this link, they are taken to view.cgi with the id parameter properly set.

The "Post message" link is just a link to edit.cgi.

So, let's see how view.cgi handles the id parameter.

Listing 20-2. The Main Bulletin Board (main.cgi)

```
#!/usr/bin/python

print 'Content-type: text/html\n'

import cgitb; cgitb.enable()

import psycopg
conn = psycopg.connect('dbname=foo user=bar')
curs = conn.cursor()

print """
<html>
  <head>
```

```
        <title>The FooBar Bulletin Board</title>
      </head>
      <body>
        <h1>The FooBar Bulletin Board</h1>
        """

curs.execute('select * from messages')
rows = curs.dictfetchall()

toplevel = []
children = {}

for row in rows:
    parent_id = row['reply_to']
    if parent_id is None:
        toplevel.append(row)
    else:
        children.setdefault(parent_id,[]).append(row)

def format(row):
    print '<p><a href="view.cgi?id=%(id)i">%(subject)s</a></p>' % row
    try: kids = children[row['id']]]
    except KeyError: pass
    else:
        print '<blockquote>'
        for kid in kids:
            format(kid)
        print '</blockquote>'

print '<p>'

for row in toplevel:
    format(row)

print """
    </p>
    <hr />
    <p><a href="edit.cgi">Post message</a></p>
  </body>
</html>
"""
```

view.cgi

The view script uses the supplied CGI parameter id to retrieve a single message from the database. It then formats a simple HTML page with the resulting values. This page also contains a link back to the main page (main.cgi) and, perhaps more interestingly, to edit.cgi, but this time with the reply_to parameter set to id, to ensure that the new message will be a reply to the current one. (See Listing 20-3 for the code of view.cgi.)

*Listing 20-3. The Message Viewer (*view.cgi*)*

```
#!/usr/bin/python

print 'Content-type: text/html\n'

import cgitb; cgitb.enable()

import psycopg
conn = psycopg.connect('dbname=foo user=bar')
curs = conn.cursor()

import cgi, sys
form = cgi.FieldStorage()
id = form.getvalue('id')

print """
<html>
  <head>
    <title>View Message</title>
  </head>
  <body>
    <h1>View Message</h1>
    """

try: id = int(id)
except:
    print 'Invalid message ID'
    sys.exit()
```

```
curs.execute('select * from messages where id = %i' % id)
rows = curs.dictfetchall()

if not rows:
    print 'Unknown message ID'
    sys.exit()

row = rows[0]
print """
    <p><b>Subject:</b> %(subject)s<br />
    <b>Sender:</b> %(sender)s<br />
    <pre>%(text)s</pre>
    </p>
    <hr />
    <a href='main.cgi'>Back to the main page</a>
    | <a href="edit.cgi?reply_to=%(id)s">Reply</a>
  </body>
</html>
""" % row
```

edit.cgi

The edit script actually performs a dual function—it is used to edit new messages, but also to edit replies. The difference isn't all that great: If a reply_to is supplied in the CGI request, it is stored in a *hidden input* in the edit form. Also, the subject is set to "Re: *parentsubject*" by default (unless the subject already begins with "Re:"—you don't want to keep adding those). Here is the code snippet that takes care of these details:

```
subject = ''

if reply_to is not None:
    print '<input type="hidden" name="reply_to" value="%s"/>' % reply_to
    curs.execute('select subject from messages where id = %s' % reply_to)
    subject = curs.fetchone()[0]
    if not subject.startswith('Re: '):
        subject = 'Re: ' + subject
```

TIP *Hidden inputs are used to temporarily store infor-mation in a Web form. They don't show up to the user as text areas and the like do, but their value is still passed to the CGI script that is the* action *of the form. That way the script that generates the form can pass information to the script that will eventually process the same form.*

Listing 20-4 shows the source code for the edit script.

*Listing 20-4. The Message Editor (*edit.cgi*)*

```python
#!/usr/bin/python

print 'Content-type: text/html\n'

import cgitb; cgitb.enable()

import psycopg
conn = psycopg.connect('dbname=foo user=bar')
curs = conn.cursor()

import cgi, sys
form = cgi.FieldStorage()
reply_to = form.getvalue('reply_to')

print """
<html>
  <head>
    <title>Compose Message</title>
  </head>
  <body>
    <h1>Compose Message</h1>

    <form action='save.cgi' method='POST'>
    """

subject = ''
if reply_to is not None:
    print '<input type="hidden" name="reply_to" value="%s"/>' % reply_to
    curs.execute('select subject from messages where id = %s' % reply_to)
```

```python
    subject = curs.fetchone()[0]
    if not subject.startswith('Re: '):
        subject = 'Re: ' + subject

print """
    <b>Subject:</b><br />
    <input type='text' size='40' name='subject' value='%s' /><br />
    <b>Sender:</b><br />
    <input type='text' size='40' name='sender' /><br />
    <b>Message:</b><br />
    <textarea name='text' cols='40' rows='20'></textarea><br />
    <input type='submit' value='Save'/>
    </form>
    <hr />
    <a href='main.cgi'>Back to the main page</a>'
  </body>
</html>
""" % subject
```

save.cgi

Now on to our final script. The save script will receive information about a message (from edit.cgi) and will store it in the database. That means using an SQL insert command, and because the database has been modified, conn.commit must be called so the changes aren't lost when the script terminates.

Listing 20-5 shows the source code for the save script.

Listing 20-5. The Saving Script (save.cgi)

```python
#!/usr/bin/python


print 'Content-type: text/html\n'

import cgitb; cgitb.enable()

def quote(string):
    if string:
        return string.replace("'", "\\'")
    else:
        return string
```

```
import psycopg
conn = psycopg.connect('dbname=foo user=bar')
curs = conn.cursor()

import cgi, sys
form = cgi.FieldStorage()

sender = quote(form.getvalue('sender'))
subject = quote(form.getvalue('subject'))
text = quote(form.getvalue('text'))
reply_to = form.getvalue('reply_to')

if not (sender and subject and text):
    print 'Please supply sender, subject, and text'
    sys.exit()

if reply_to is not None:
    query = """
    insert into messages(reply_to, sender, subject, text)
    values(%i, '%s', '%s', '%s')""" % (int(reply_to), sender, subject, text)
else:
    query = """
    insert into messages(sender, subject, text)
    values('%s', '%s', '%s')""" % (sender, subject, text)

curs.execute(query)
conn.commit()

print """
<html>
  <head>
    <title>Message Saved</title>
  </head>
  <body>
    <h1>Message Saved</h1>
    <hr />
    <a href='main.cgi'>Back to the main page</a>
  </body>
</html>
"""
```

Trying It Out

To test this system, start by opening main.cgi. From there, press the "Post message" link. That should take you to edit.cgi. Enter some values in all the fields and press "Save." That should take you to save.cgi, which will display the message "Message Saved." Press the "Back to the main page" link to get back to main.cgi. The listing should now include your new message.

To view your message, simply click its subject—that should take you to view.cgi with the correct ID. From there, try to click "Reply," which should take you to edit.cgi once again, but this time with reply_to set (in a hidden input tag) and with a default subject. Once again, enter some text, press "Save," and go back to the main page. It should now show your reply, displayed under the original subject. (If it's not showing, try to reload the page.)

The main page is shown in Figure 20-1, the message viewer in Figure 20-2, and the message composer in Figure 20-3.

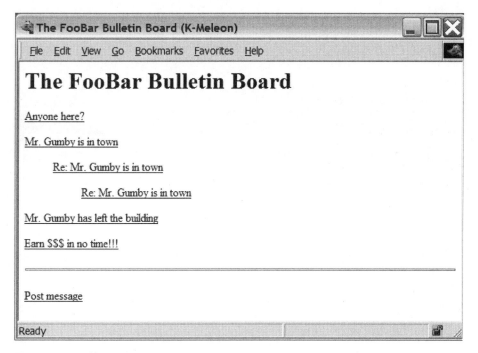

Figure 20-1. The main page

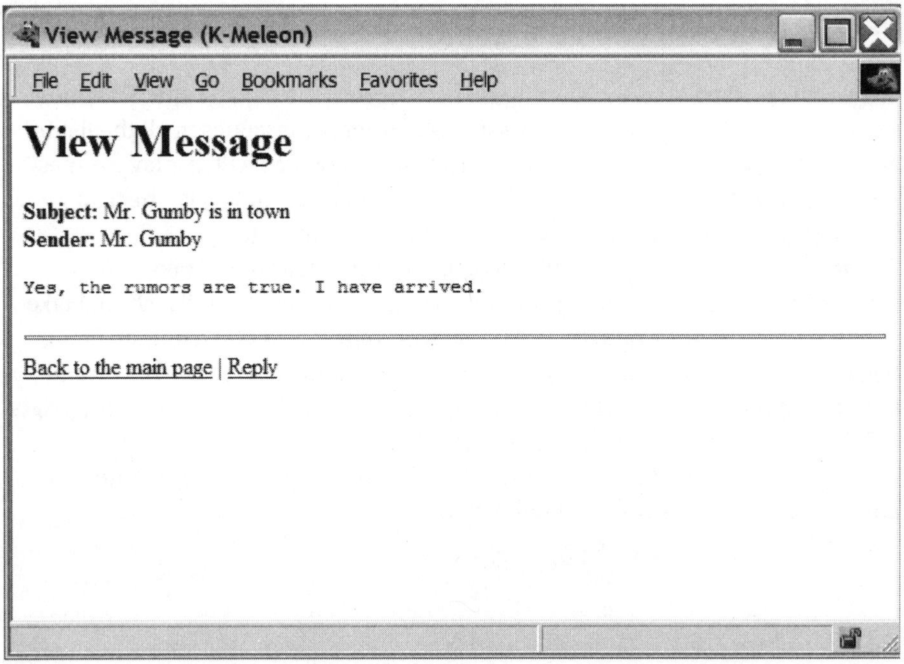

Figure 20-2. The message viewer

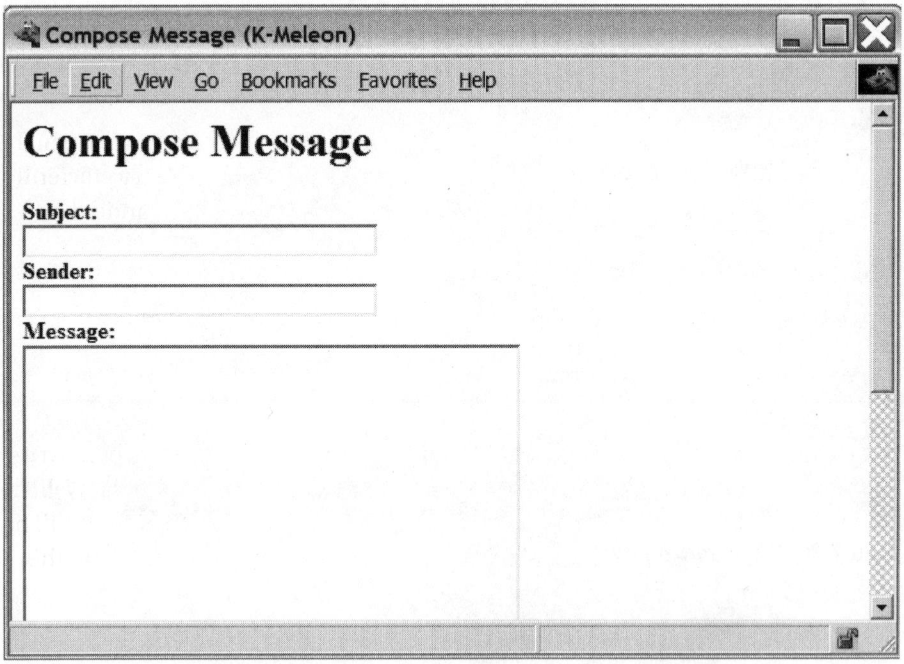

Figure 20-3. The message composer

Further Exploration

Now that you have the power to develop huge and powerful Web applications with reliable and efficient storage, there are lots of things you can sink your teeth into:

- How about making a Web front-end to a database of your favorite Monty Python sketches?

- If you're interested in improving the system in this chapter, you should think about abstraction. How about creating a utility module with a function to print a standard header and another to print a standard footer? That way you wouldn't have to write the same HTML stuff in each script. Also, it might be useful to add a user database with some password handling.

- If you'd like a storage solution that doesn't require a dedicated server, you might want to check out Metakit, a really neat little database package that lets you store an entire database in a single file (http://www.equi4.com/metakit/python.html). It doesn't use SQL directly, but an add-on called MkSQL is available (http://www.mcmillan-inc.com/mksqlintro.html), which makes Metakit behave like most other SQL databases.

- Another database you might want to consider is Gadfly (http://gadfly.sf.net), an SQL database implemented completely in Python.

- Another alternative is the Berkeley DB (http://www.sleepycat.com), which is quite simple but can handle astonishing amounts of data very efficiently. (The Berkeley DB is accessible, when installed, through the standard library modules bsddb, dbhash, or anydbm.)

What Now?

If you think writing your own discussion forum software is cool, how about writing your own peer-to-peer file sharing program, like Napster or Gnutella? Well, in the next project, that's exactly what you'll do—and the good news is that it will be easier than most of the network programming you've done so far, thanks to the wonder of remote procedure calls.

CHAPTER 21

Project 8:
File Sharing
with XML-RPC

IN THIS CHAPTER YOU WRITE a simple file sharing application. You may be familiar with the concept of file sharing from such applications as Napster (no longer downloadable in its original form), Gnutella (available from http://www.gnutella.com), KaZaA (available from http://www.kazaa.com), and many others—what you'll be writing is in many ways similar to these, although quite a bit simpler.

The main technology you'll use is XML-RPC, a protocol for calling procedures (functions) remotely, possibly across a network.

 NOTE *RPC stands for Remote Procedure Call, and XML is the language you've already encountered several times, in Project 1, for example. You can find information about XML-RPC at* http://www.xmlrpc.com.

If you want, you can quite easily use plain socket programming (possibly using the asyncore module, as described in Project 3) to implement the functionality of this project. That might even give you better performance because the XML-RPC protocol does come with a certain overhead. However, XML-RPC is very easy to use, and will most likely simplify your code considerably.

What's the Problem?

What we want to create is a peer-to-peer file sharing program. *File sharing* basically means exchanging files (everything from text files to sound clips) between programs running on different machines. *Peer-to-peer* is a buzzword that describes a type of interaction between computer programs, as opposed to the common *client–server* interaction, where a client may connect to a server but not vice versa. In a peer-to-peer interaction, any peer may connect to any other. In such a (virtual) network of peers there is no central authority (as represented by the server in a client–server architecture), which makes the network more robust. It won't collapse unless you shut down most of the peers.

 TIP *If you're interested in learning more about peer-to-peer systems, you should do a Web search on the phrase "peer-to-peer," which ought to give you several interesting hits.*

Many issues are involved in constructing a peer-to-peer system—in this project we take a very simple approach to things. In a system such as Gnutella, a peer may disseminate a query to all of its neighbors (the other peers it knows about), and they may subsequently disseminate the query further. Any peer that responds to the query can then send a reply through the chain of peers back to the initial one. The peers work individually and in parallel. To simplify things, our system will contact each neighbor in turn, waiting for its response before moving on. Not quite as efficient, but good enough for our purposes.

Also, most peer-to-peer systems have clever ways of organizing their structure—that is, which peers are "next to" which—and how this structure evolves over time, as peers connect and disconnect. We'll keep that very simple in this project, but leave things open for improvements.

Specific Goals

Here are some requirements that our program must satisfy:

- Each node must keep track of a set of known nodes, from which it can ask for help. It must be possible for a node to introduce itself to another node (and thereby be included in this set).

- It must be possible to ask a node for a file (by supplying a file name). If the node has the file in question, it should return it; otherwise it should ask each of its neighbors in turn for the same file (and they, in turn, may ask *their* neighbors). If any of these have the file, it is returned.

- To avoid loops (A asking B, which in turn asks A) and to avoid overly long chains of neighbors asking neighbors (A asking B asking...asking Z) it must be possible to supply a *history* when querying a node. This history is just a list of which nodes have participated in the query up until this point. By not asking nodes already in the history we avoid loops, and by limiting the length of the history we avoid overly long query chains.

- There must be some way of connecting to a node and identifying yourself as a trusted party. By doing so you should be given access to functionality that is not available to untrusted parties (such as other nodes in the peer-to-peer network). This functionality may include asking the node to download and store a file from the other peers in the network (through a query).

- We must have some user interface that lets us connect to a node (as a trusted party) and make it download files. It should be easy to extend and, for that matter, replace this interface.

All of this may seem a bit steep, but as you'll see, implementing isn't all that hard. And you'll probably find that once we've got this in place, adding functionality of your own won't be all that difficult either.

Useful Tools

In this project you'll use quite a few standard library modules. I won't describe them all in detail; refer to Chapter 10 and the Python Library Reference for additional details.

The main new modules we'll be using are `xmlrpclib` and its close friend `SimpleXMLRPCServer`. The `xmlrpclib` module is used to connect to XML-RPC servers, and `SimpleXMLRPCServer` is a class you can use to write such servers. Both of these are new in Python 2.2 but may be downloaded and installed separately, and can thus be used with Python 2.1.

CAUTION *The version of* `SimpleXMLRPCServer` *that ships with Python 2.2 contains a serious flaw in its handling of exceptions. If you use this version, the programs in this chapter (and the next) may appear to work, but in fact they won't be working correctly. Either use a newer version of Python (for example, version 2.3) or download a new version of* `SimpleXMLRPCServer.py` *from* http://www.sweetapp.com/ xmlrpc, *and replace your current version with the downloaded one.*

To show you how easy xmlrpclib is to use, here is an example that connects to the XML-RPC server at The Covers Project (http://covers.wiw.org), a database of cover songs:

```
>>> from xmlrpclib import ServerProxy
>>> server = ServerProxy('http://covers.wiw.org/RPC.php')
>>> covers = server.covers.Covered('Monty Python')
>>> for cover in covers:
...     if cover['song'] == 'Brave Sir Robin':
...         print cover['artist']
...
Happy Rhodes
```

The ServerProxy object looks like a normal object with various methods we can call, but in fact whenever we call one of its methods, it sends a request to the server, which responds to the requests and returns an answer. So, in a way, we're calling the method covers.Covered on the server itself. Network programming could hardly be any easier than this. (For more information about the XML-RPC methods supplied by The Covers Project, see http://covers.wiw.org/xmlrpc.php.)

NOTE *XML-RPC procedure (function/method) names may contain dots, as in the preceding example. The name* covers.Covered *does not imply the existence of an object named* covers *on the server—the dots are only used to structure the names.*

Here is a slightly more complicated example, which uses the news service Meerkat to find some articles about Python:

```
>>> from xmlrpclib import ServerProxy
>>> query = {'search': 'Python', 'num_items': 5}
>>> s = ServerProxy('http://www.oreillynet.com/meerkat/xml-rpc/server.php')
>>> items = s.meerkat.getItems(query)
>>> [i['title'] for i in items]
['MacHack: Meet Dylan the Yoot', 'Hap Debugger', 'Project and proposal for
integrating validation with processing pipelines', 'Spam Check', 'ZCoMIX 1.0
Final Released']
>>> items[0].keys()
```

```
['link', 'description', 'title']
>>> items[3]['link']
'http://aspn.activestate.com/ASPN/Cookbook/Python/Recipe/134945'
```

As you can see, the method `meerkat.getItems` is called with a mapping parameter that contains various arguments (in this case a search query and the number of items to be returned) and returns a list of mappings, each of which has a title, a description, and a link. Actually, there is a lot more to Meerkat than this—if you want to experiment, take a look at the Meerkat Web site (`http://www.oreillynet.com/meerkat`) or one of the many online tutorials about the Meerkat XML-RPC API (for example, `http://www.oreillynet.com/pub/a/rss/2000/11/14/meerkat_xmlrpc.html`).

For the interface to the file sharing program, we'll be using a module from the standard library, called `cmd`; to get some (very limited) parallelism, we'll use the `threading` module, and to extract the components of a URL, we'll use the `urlparse` module. All of these modules are explained later in the chapter.

Other modules you might want to brush up on are `random`, `string`, `time`, and `os.path`.

Preparations

First of all, you must make sure you have the proper libraries, (that you can import `xmlrpclib` and `SimpleXMLRPCServer`). Make sure you've got the right version of `SimpleXMLRPCServer`, as explained in the previous section.

You don't strictly have to be connected to a network to use the software in this project, but it will make things more interesting. If you have access to two (or more) separate machines that are connected, you can run the software on each of these machines and have them communicate with each other. For testing purposes it is also possible to run multiple file sharing nodes on the same machine.

First Implementation

Before you can write a first prototype of the `Node` class (a single node or peer in the system) you have to learn a bit about how the `SimpleXMLRPCServer` class works. It is instantiated with a tuple of the form (*servername, port*). The server name is the name of the machine on which the server will run (you can use an empty string here to indicate `localhost`, the machine where you're actually executing the program). The port number can be any port you have access to, typically 1024 and above.

After you have instantiated the server, you may register an instance that implements its "remote methods," with the `register_instance` method.

Alternatively, you can register individual functions with the `register_function` method. When you're ready to run the server (so that it can respond to requests from outside) you call its method `serve_forever`. You can easily try this out. Start two interactive Python interpreters. In the first one, enter the following:

> **CAUTION** *You may not be able to stop the server easily when you run it in an interpreter like this. You should be prepared to terminate the interpreter itself. An alternative is to enter the following code in a script and run that from the command line. Then you should be able to terminate the server with Ctrl+C (UNIX) or Ctrl+Break (Windows).*

```
>>> from SimpleXMLRPCServer import SimpleXMLRPCServer
>>> s = SimpleXMLRPCServer(("", 4242)) # Localhost at port 4242
>>> def twice(x): # Example function
...     return x*2
...
>>> s.register_function(twice) # Add functionality to the server
>>> s.serve_forever() # Start the server
```

After executing the last statement, the interpreter should seem to "hang." Actually, it's waiting for RPC requests.

To make such a request, switch to the other interpreter and execute the following:

```
>>> from xmlrpclib import ServerProxy # ...or simply Server, if you prefer
>>> s = ServerProxy('http://localhost:4242') # Localhost again...
>>> s.twice(2)
4
```

Pretty impressive, eh? Especially considering that the client part (using `xmlrpclib`) could be run on a different machine. (In that case you would have to use the actual name of the server machine instead of simply `localhost`.)

Now that we've got the XML-RPC technicalities covered, let's get started with the coding. (The full source code of the first prototype is found in Listing 21-1, at the end of this section.)

To find out where to begin, it might be a good idea to review our requirements from earlier in this chapter. We're mainly interested in two things: what information must our `Node` hold (attributes) and what actions must it be able to perform (methods)?

The Node must have at least the following attributes:

- A directory name, so it knows where to find/store its files.

- A "secret" (or password) that can be used by others to identify themselves (as trusted parties).

- A set of known peers (URLs) represented by a dictionary where the URLs are stored as keys, for fast lookup. (You could also use a list—the performance loss would be minimal.)

- A URL, which may be added to the query history, or possibly supplied to other Nodes. (This project won't implement the latter.)

The Node constructor will simply set these four attributes. In addition we'll need a method for querying the Node, a method for making it fetch and store a file, and a method to introduce another Node to it. Let's call these methods query, fetch, and hello. The following is a sketch of the class, written as pseudocode:

```
class Node:

    def __init__(self, url, dirname, secret):
        self.url = url
        self.dirname = dirname
        self.secret = secret
        self.known = {}

    def query(self, query):
        Look for a file (possibly asking neighbors), and return it as
        a string

    def fetch(self, query, secret):
        If the secret is correct, perform a regular query and store
        the file

    def hello(self, other):
        Add the other Node to the known peers
```

Assuming that the set (dictionary) of known URLs is called known, the hello method is very simple—it simply assigns a value to self.known[other], where other is the only parameter (a URL). However, XML-RPC requires all methods to return a value; None is not accepted. So, let's define two result "codes" that indicate success or failure:

```
OK = 1
FAIL = 2
```

Then the hello method can be implemented as follows:

```
def hello(self, other):
    self.known[other] = 1
    return OK
```

When the Node is registered with a SimpleXMLRPCServer, it will be possible to call this method from the "outside."

The query and fetch methods are a bit more tricky. Let's begin with fetch because it's the simpler of the two. It must take two parameters—the query and the "secret," which is required so that our Node can't be arbitrarily manipulated by anybody. (Note that calling fetch causes the Node to download a file. Access to this method should therefore be more restricted than, for example, query, which simply passes the file through.)

If the supplied secret is not equal to self.secret (the one supplied at startup) fetch simply returns FAIL. Otherwise, it calls query to get the file corresponding to the given query (a file name). But what does query return? When we call query, we would like to know whether or not the query succeeded, and we would like to have the contents of the relevant file returned if it did. So, let's define the return value of query as the pair (tuple) code, data where code is either OK or FAIL, and data is the sought-after file (if code equals OK) stored in a string, or an arbitrary value (for example, an empty string) otherwise.

In fetch, the code and the data are retrieved. If the code is FAIL, then fetch simply returns FAIL as well. Otherwise, it opens a new file (in write-mode) whose name is the same as the query, and which is found in self.dirname (we use os.path.join to join the two). The data are written to the file, the file is closed, and OK is returned. See Listing 21-1 for the relatively straightforward implementation.

Now, let's turn our attention to query. It receives a query as a parameter, but it should also accept a history (which contains URLs that should not be queried because they are already waiting for a response to the same query). Because this history is empty in the first call to query, we can use an empty list as a default value.

If you take a look at the code in Listing 21-1 you'll see that I've abstracted away part of the behavior of query by creating two utility methods called _handle and _broadcast. Note that their names begin with underscores—that means that they won't be accessible through XML-RPC. (This is part of the behavior of SimpleXMLRPCServer, not a part of XML-RPC itself.) That is useful because these methods aren't meant to provide separate functionality to an outside party, but are there to structure the code.

For now, let's just assume that _handle takes care of the internal handling of a query (checks whether the file exists at this specific Node, fetches the data, and so forth) and that it returns a code and some data, just like query itself is supposed to. As you can see from the listing, if code == OK then code, data is returned straight away—the file was found. However, what should query do if the code returned from _handle is FAIL? Then it has to ask all other known Nodes for help. The first step in this process is to add self.url to history.

> **NOTE** *Neither the* += *operator nor the* append *list method has not been used when updating the history because we don't want to modify the default value itself.*

If the new history is too long, query returns FAIL (along with an empty string). The max length is arbitrarily set to 6 and kept in the global "constant" MAX_HISTORY_LENGTH.

....

Why Is MAX_HISTORY_LENGTH Set to Six?

The idea is that any peer in the network should be able to reach another in, at most, six steps. This, of course, depends on the structure of the network (which peers know which), but is supported by the hypothesis of "six degrees of separation," which applies to people and who they know. For a description of this hypothesis, see the Small World Research Project (http://smallworld.sociology.columbia.edu).

Using this number in our program may not be very scientific, but at least it seems like a good guess. On the other hand, in a large network with many nodes, the sequential nature of our program may lead to bad performance for large values of MAX_HISTORY_LENGTH so you might want to reduce it if things get slow.

....

If history isn't too long, the next step is to broadcast the query to all known peers—which is done with the _broadcast method. The _broadcast method isn't very complicated. (See the listing for full source.) It iterates over self.known.keys().

If a peer is found in history, the loop continues to the next peer (using the continue statement). Otherwise, a ServerProxy is constructed, and the query method is called on it. Its return value is used as the return value from _broadcast, provided that no exceptions occur. Such exceptions may be due to network problems, a faulty URL, or the fact that the peer doesn't support the query method. If such an exception occurs, the peer's URL is deleted from self.known (in the except clause of the try statement enclosing the query). Finally, if control reaches the end of the function (nothing has been returned yet), FAIL is returned, along with an empty string.

NOTE *You shouldn't simply iterate over the dictionary* self.known *or* self.known.iterkeys() *because the dictionary will be modified during the iteration. Using the* keys *method is safe because it extracts the keys as a list, which is, in effect, a copy that is not affected by the modification.*

The _start method creates a SimpleXMLRPCServer (using the little utility function getPort, which extracts the port number from a URL), with logRequests set to *false* (we don't want to keep a log). It then registers self with register_instance and calls the server's serve_forever method.

Finally, the main method of the module extracts a URL, a directory, and a secret (password) from the command line; creates a Node; and calls its _start method.

For the full code of the prototype, see Listing 21-1.

*Listing 21-1. A Simple Node Implementation (*simple_node.py*)*

```python
from xmlrpclib import ServerProxy
from os.path import join, isfile
from SimpleXMLRPCServer import SimpleXMLRPCServer
from urlparse import urlparse
import sys

MAX_HISTORY_LENGTH = 6

OK = 1
FAIL = 2
EMPTY = ''

def getPort(url):
    'Extracts the port from a URL'
    name = urlparse(url)[1]
```

```
        parts = name.split(':')
        return int(parts[-1])


class Node:
    """
    A node in a peer-to-peer network.
    """
    def __init__(self, url, dirname, secret):
        self.url = url
        self.dirname = dirname
        self.secret = secret
        self.known = {}

    def query(self, query, history=[]):
        """
        Performs a query for a file, possibly asking other known Nodes for
        help. Returns the file as a string.
        """
        code, data = self._handle(query)
        if code == OK:
            return code, data
        else:
            history = history + [self.url]
            if len(history) >= MAX_HISTORY_LENGTH:
                return FAIL, EMPTY
            return self._broadcast(query, history)

    def hello(self, other):
        """
        Used to introduce the Node to other Nodes.
        """
        self.known[other] = 1
        return OK

    def fetch(self, query, secret):
        """
        Used to make the Node find a file and download it.
        """
        if secret != self.secret: return FAIL
        code, data = self.query(query)
        if code == OK:
            f = open(join(self.dirname, query), 'w')
            f.write(data)
```

```
                f.close()
                return OK
            else:
                return FAIL

    def _start(self):
        """
        Used internally to start the XML-RPC server.
        """
        s = SimpleXMLRPCServer(("", getPort(self.url)), logRequests=0)
        s.register_instance(self)
        s.serve_forever()

    def _handle(self, query):
        """
        Used internally to handle queries.
        """
        dir = self.dirname
        name = join(dir, query)
        if not isfile(name): return FAIL, EMPTY
        return OK, open(name).read()

    def _broadcast(self, query, history):
        """
        Used internally to broadcast a query to all known Nodes.
        """
        for other in self.known.keys():
            if other in history: continue
            try:
                s = ServerProxy(other)
                return s.query(query, history)
            except:
                del self.known[other]
        return FAIL, EMPTY

def main():
    url, directory, secret = sys.argv[1:]
    n = Node(url, directory, secret)
    n._start()

if __name__ == '__main__': main()
```

Let's take a look at a simple example of how this program may be used. Make sure you have several terminals (xterms, DOS windows or equivalent) open. Let's say you want to run two peers (both on the same machine): create a directory for each of them, for instance files1 and files2. Put some file (for example, test.txt) into files2. Then, in one terminal, run the following command:

```
python simple_node.py http://localhost:4242 files1 secret1
```

In a real application you would use the full machine name instead of localhost and you would probably use something a bit more cryptic instead of secret1.

This is our first peer. Let's create another one. In a different terminal, run the following command:

```
python simple_node.py http://localhost:4243 files2 secret2
```

As you can see, this peer serves files from a different directory, uses another port number (4243), and has another secret. If you have followed these instructions, you should have two peers running (each in a separate terminal window). Let's start up an interactive Python interpreter and try to connect to one of them:

```
>>> from xmlrpclib import *
>>> mypeer = ServerProxy('http://localhost:4242') # The first peer
>>> code, data = mypeer.query('test.txt')
>>> code
2
```

As you can see, the first peer fails when asked for the file test.txt. (2 is the code for failure, remember?) Let's try the same thing with the second peer:

```
>>> otherpeer = ServerProxy('http://localhost:4243') # The second peer
>>> code, data = otherpeer.query('test.txt')
>>> code
1
```

This time the query succeeds because the file test.txt is found in the second peer's file directory. If your test file doesn't contain too much text, you can display the contents of the data variable to make sure that the contents of the file have been transferred properly:

```
>>> data
'This is a test\n'
```

So far so good. How about introducing the first peer to the second one?

```
>>> mypeer.hello('http://localhost:4243') # Introducing mypeer to otherpeer
```

Now the first peer knows the URL of the second, and thus may ask it for help. Let's try querying the first peer again—this time the query should succeed:

```
>>> s1.query('test.txt')
[1, 'This is a test\n']
```

Bingo!

Now there is only one thing left to test: can we make the first node actually download and store the file from the second one?

```
>>> s1.fetch('test.txt', 'secret1')
1
```

Well, the return value indicates success. And if you look in the files1 directory, you should see that the file test.txt has miraculously appeared. Cool, eh? Feel free to start several peers (on different machines, if you want to), and introduce them to each other. When you grow tired of playing, proceed to the next implementation.

Second Implementation

The first implementation has plenty of flaws and shortcomings. I won't address all of them (some possible improvements are discussed in the section "Further Exploration," at the end of this chapter) but here are some of the more important ones:

- If you try to stop a Node and then restart it, you will probably get some error message about the port being in use already.

- We should have a more user friendly interface than using xmlrpclib in an interactive Python interpreter.

- The return codes are inconvenient—a more natural and Pythonic solution would be to use a custom exception if the file can't be found.

- The Node doesn't check whether the file it returns is actually inside the file directory. By using paths such as '../somesecretfile.txt' a sneaky cracker may get unlawful access to any of your other files.

The first problem is easy to solve. We simply set the `allow_reuse_address` attribute of the `SimpleXMLRPCServer` to *true:*

```
SimpleXMLRPCServer.allow_reuse_address = 1
```

If you don't want to modify this class directly, you can create your own subclass. The other changes are a bit more involved, and are discussed in the following sections. The source code is shown in Listings 21-2 and 21-3. (You might want to take a quick look at these listings before reading on.)

The Client Interface

The client interface uses the `Cmd` class from the `cmd` module. For details about how this works, see the Python Library Reference. Simply put, you subclass `Cmd` to create a command-line interface, and implement a method called do_foo for each command `foo` you want it to be able to handle. This method will receive the rest of the command line as its only argument (as a string). For instance, if you type

```
say hello
```

in the command-line interface, the method do_say is called with the string `'hello'` as its only argument. The prompt of the `Cmd` subclass is determined by the `prompt` attribute.

The only commands implemented in our interface will be `fetch` (to download a file) and `exit` (to exit the program). The `fetch` command simply calls the `fetch` method of the server (I'll get to that in a minute), printing an error message if the file could not be found. (The `UNHANDLED` stuff will be explained in the next section, "The Exceptions.") The `exit` commands prints an empty line (for aesthetic reasons only) and calls `sys.exit`. (The `EOF` command corresponds to "end of file," which occurs when the user presses Ctrl+D in UNIX.)

But what is all the stuff going on in the constructor? Well—we want each client to be associated with a peer of its own. We *could* simply create a `Node` object and call its _start method, but then our `Client` couldn't do anything until the _start method returned—which makes the `Client` completely useless. To fix this, the `Node` is started in a separate *thread*. Normally, using threads involves a lot of safeguarding and synchronization with locks and the like, all of which is beyond the scope of this book. However, because a `Client` only interacts with its `Node` through XML-RPC, we don't need any of this. (You should be careful if you rewrite this code, however. The minute your `Client` starts interacting directly with the `Node` object or vice versa you may easily run into trouble. Make sure you fully understand threading before you do this.) To run the _start method in a separate thread we only have to put the following code into our program at some suitable place:

```
from threading import Thread
n = Node(url, dirname, self.secret)
t = Thread(target=n._start)
t.start()
```

To make sure that the server is fully started before we start connecting to it with XML-RPC, we'll give it a head start, and wait for a moment with time.sleep.

Afterward, we'll go through all the lines in a file of URLs and introduce our server to them with the hello method.

You don't really want to be bothered with coming up with a clever secret password. Instead, you can use the utility function randomString in Listing 21-3, which generates a random secret string that is shared between the Client and the Node.

The Exceptions

Instead of returning a code indicating success or failure, we'll just assume success and raise an exception in the case of failure. In XML-RPC, exceptions (or "faults") are identified by numbers. In Listing 21-2 you can see that I have (arbitrarily) chosen the numbers 100 and 200 for ordinary failure (an unhandled request) and a request refusal (access denied), respectively. The exceptions are subclasses of xmlrpclib.Fault—when they are raised in the server, they are passed on to the client with the same faultCode. If an ordinary exception (such as IOException) is raised in the server, an instance of the Fault class is still created, so we can't simply use arbitrary exceptions here. (Make sure you have a version of SimpleXMLRPCServer that handles exceptions properly. See the caution in the section "Useful Tools" earlier in this chapter for more information.)

As you can see from the source code, the logic is still basically the same, but instead of using if statements for checking returned codes, the program now uses exceptions. (Because we can only use Fault objects, we need to check the faultCodes. If we weren't using XML-RPC we would have used different exception classes instead, of course.)

Validating File Names

The last issue to deal with is to check whether a given file name is found within a given directory. There are several ways to do this, but to keep things platform-independent (so it works in Windows, in UNIX, and in Mac OS, for instance) you should use the module os.path.

The simple approach taken here is to create an absolute path from the directory name and the file name (so that, for example, '/foo/bar/../baz' is converted to '/foo/baz'), the directory name is joined with an empty file name (using os.path.join) to ensure that it ends with a file separator (such as '/'), and then we check that the absolute file name begins with the absolute directory name. If it does, the file is actually inside the directory.

Trying Out the Second Implementation

The full source code for the second implementation is found in Listings 21-2 and 21-3. Let's see how the program is used. It is started like this:

```
python client.py urls.txt directory http://servername.com:4242
```

The file urls.txt should contain one URL per line—the URLs of all the other peers you know of. The directory given as the second argument should contain the files you want to share (and will be the location where new files are downloaded). The last argument is the URL to the peer. When you run this command, you should get a prompt like this:

```
>
```

Try fetching a non-existent file:

```
> fetch fooo
Couldn't find the file fooo
```

By starting several nodes (either on the same machine, using different ports, or on different machines) that know about each other (just put all the URLs in the URL files) you can try these out as we did with the first prototype. When you get bored with this, move on to the next section, "Further Exploration."

Listing 21-2. A New Node Implementation (server.py)

```
from xmlrpclib import ServerProxy, Fault
from os.path import join, abspath, isfile
from SimpleXMLRPCServer import SimpleXMLRPCServer
from urlparse import urlparse
import sys
```

```
SimpleXMLRPCServer.allow_reuse_address = 1

MAX_HISTORY_LENGTH = 6

UNHANDLED      = 100
ACCESS_DENIED = 200

class UnhandledQuery(Fault):
    """

    An exception that represents an unhandled query.
    """
    def __init__(self, message="Couldn't handle the query"):
        Fault.__init__(self, UNHANDLED, message)

class AccessDenied(Fault):
    """

    An exception that is raised if a user tries to access a
    resource for which he or she is not authorized.
    """
    def __init__(self, message="Access denied"):
        Fault.__init__(self, ACCESS_DENIED, message)

def inside(dir, name):
    """

    Checks whether a given file name lies within a given directory.
    """

    dir = abspath(dir)
    name = abspath(name)
    return name.startswith(join(dir, ''))

def getPort(url):
    """

    Extracts the port number from a URL.
    """

    name = urlparse(url)[1]
    parts = name.split(':')
    return int(parts[-1])

class Node:
    """

    A node in a peer-to-peer network.
    """

    def __init__(self, url, dirname, secret):
```

```python
        self.url = url
        self.dirname = dirname
        self.secret = secret
        self.known = {}

    def query(self, query, history=[]):
        """
        Performs a query for a file, possibly asking other known Nodes for
        help. Returns the file as a string.
        """
        try:
            return self._handle(query)
        except UnhandledQuery:
            history = history + [self.url]
            if len(history) >= MAX_HISTORY_LENGTH: raise
            return self._broadcast(query, history)

    def hello(self, other):
        """
        Used to introduce the Node to other Nodes.
        """
        self.known[other] = 1
        return 0

    def fetch(self, query, secret):
        """
        Used to make the Node find a file and download it.
        """
        if secret != self.secret: raise AccessDenied
        result = self.query(query)
        f = open(join(self.dirname, query), 'w')
        f.write(result)
        f.close()
        return 0

    def _start(self):
        """
        Used internally to start the XML-RPC server.
        """
        s = SimpleXMLRPCServer(("", getPort(self.url)), logRequests=0)
        s.register_instance(self)
        s.serve_forever()
```

```
    def _handle(self, query):
        """
        Used internally to handle queries.
        """          dir = self.dirname
        name = join(dir, query)
        if not isfile(name): raise UnhandledQuery
        if not inside(dir, name): raise AccessDenied
        return open(name).read()


    def _broadcast(self, query, history):
        """
        Used internally to broadcast a query to all known Nodes.
        """
        for other in self.known.keys():
            if other in history: continue
            try:
                s = ServerProxy(other)
                return s.query(query, history)
            except Fault, f:
                if f.faultCode == UNHANDLED: pass
                else: del self.known[other]
            except:
                del self.known[other]
        raise UnhandledQuery

def main():
    url, directory, secret = sys.argv[1:]
    n = Node(url, directory, secret)
    n._start()


if __name__ == '__main__': main()
```

*Listing 21-3. A Node Controller Interface (*client.py*)*

```
from xmlrpclib import ServerProxy, Fault
from cmd import Cmd
from random import choice
from string import lowercase
from server import Node, UNHANDLED
from threading import Thread
from time import sleep
import sys
```

```
HEAD_START = 0.1 # Seconds
SECRET_LENGTH = 100

def randomString(length):
    """
    Returns a random string of letters with the given length.
    """
    chars = []
    letters = lowercase[:26]
    while length > 0:
        length -= 1
        chars.append(choice(letters))
    return ''.join(chars)

class Client(Cmd):
    """
    A simple text based interface to the Node class.
    """

    prompt = '> '

    def __init__(self, url, dirname, urlfile):
        """
        Sets the url, dirname, and urlfile, and starts the Node
        Server in a separate thread.
        """
        Cmd.__init__(self)
        self.secret = randomString(SECRET_LENGTH)
        n = Node(url, dirname, self.secret)
        t = Thread(target=n._start)
        t.setDaemon(1)
        t.start()
        # Give the server a head start:
        sleep(HEAD_START)
        self.server = ServerProxy(url)
        for line in open(urlfile):
            line = line.strip()
            self.server.hello(line)

    def do_fetch(self, arg):             """
        Handler for the 'fetch' command. Calls the fetch method of the
        Server. If an exception is raised with faultCode == UNHANDLED,
```

```
                    an error message is printed.
                    """
                    try:
                        self.server.fetch(arg, self.secret)
                    except Fault, f:
                        if f.faultCode != UNHANDLED: raise
                        print "Couldn't find the file", arg

            def do_exit(self, arg):
                """
                Handler for the 'exit' command.
                """
                print
                sys.exit()

            do_EOF = do_exit # End-Of-File is synonymous with 'exit'

    def main():
        urlfile, directory, url = sys.argv[1:]
        client = Client(url, directory, urlfile)
        client.cmdloop()

    if __name__ == '__main__': main()
```

Further Exploration

You can probably think of several ways to improve and extend the system described in this chapter, but here are some ideas:

- Add caching: If you node relays a file through a call to query, why not store the file at the same time? That way you can respond more quickly the next time someone asks for the same file. You could perhaps set a maximum size for the cache, remove old files, and so on.

- Use a threaded or asynchronous server (a bit difficult). That way you can ask several other nodes for help without waiting for their replies, and they can later give you the reply by calling a reply method.

- Allow more advanced queries, such as querying on the contents of text files.

- Use the `hello` method more extensively. When you discover a new peer (through a call to `hello`), why not introduce it to all the peers you know? Perhaps you can think of more clever ways of discovering new peers?

- Read the `SimpleXMLRPCServer` code.

What Now?

Now that we have a peer-to-peer file sharing system working, how about making it more user-friendly? In the next chapter, we add a GUI as an alternative to the current `cmd`-based interface.

Project 9: File Sharing II—Now with GUI!

THIS IS A RELATIVELY SHORT project because much of the functionality we need has already been written—in Project 8. In this chapter, you see how easy it can be to add a graphical user interface (GUI) to an existing Python program.

What's the Problem?

In this project you expand the file sharing system developed in Project 8 with a GUI client. This will make the program much easier to use, which means that more people might choose to use it—and if there is to be any point in a file sharing program, there should be more than one user. A secondary goal of this project is to show that a program that has a sufficiently modular design can be quite easy to extend (one of the arguments for using object-oriented programming).

Specific Goals

The GUI client should satisfy the following requirements:

- It should allow you to enter a file name and submit it to the server's fetch method.

- It should list the files currently available in the server's file directory.

That's it. Because you already have much of the system working, the GUI part is a relatively simple extension.

Useful Tools

In addition to the tools used in Project 8, you will need the anygui module. For more information about (and installation instructions for) Anygui, see Chapter 12.

If you want to use another GUI toolkit, feel free to do so. The implementation in this chapter will give you the general idea of how you can build your own, with your favorite tools. (Chapter 12 describes several GUI toolkits.)

Preparations

Before you begin this project, you should have Project 8 in place, and a usable GUI toolkit installed, as mentioned in the previous section. Beyond that, no significant preparations are necessary for this project.

First Implementation

If you want to take a peek at the full source code for the first implementation, it can be found in Listing 22-1. Much of the functionality is quite similar to that of Project 8. The client presents an interface (the fetch method) through which the user may access the functionality of the server. Let's review the GUI-specific parts of the code.

The client in Project 8 was a subclass of cmd.Cmd; the Client described in this chapter subclasses anygui.Application. While you're not required to subclass Application (you could create a completely separate Client class) it can be a natural way of organizing your code. The GUI-related set-up is placed in a separate method, called setUp. It performs the following steps:

1. It creates a Window with the title 'File Sharing Client' and adds it to self (the Application instance).

2. It creates a TextField and assigns it to the attribute self.input (and, for convenience, to the local variable input). It also creates a button with the text 'Fetch' and the same height as the TextField.

3. It adds the Button to the Window, with a distance of 10 pixels to the top and right edges, and lets the Window move the button horizontally if needed (hmove=1). Note that the default layout manager (Placer) is used here. Feel free to use another layout manager if you want to.

4. It adds the TextField to the Window, with a distance of 10 pixels from the top and left edges, and a distance of 10 pixels from the Button (to the

right). It also lets the Window stretch the TextField horizontally if needed
(hstretch=1).

5.   Finally, it links the button with an event handler, called fetchHandler.

The event handler is quite similar to the similar handler do_fetch from
Project 8. It retrieves the query from self.input (the TextField); if the query is
empty, it simply returns. Otherwise, it calls self.server.fetch inside
a try/except statement. Note that the event handler receives an event object as
its only argument.

 NOTE   *If you are using version 0.1 of Anygui, you should
change the method signature to* fetchHandler(self, **kwds).
See Chapter 12 for details.

Except for the relatively simple code explained previously, the GUI client
works just like the text-based client in Project 8. You can run it in the same manner, too. This implementation only performs part of the job it's supposed to,
though. It should also list the files available in the server's file directory. To do
that, the server (Node) itself must be extended.

The source code for the first implementation is shown in Listing 22-1.

*Listing 22-1. A Simple GUI Client (*simple_guiclient.py*)*

```
from xmlrpclib import ServerProxy, Fault
from server import Node, UNHANDLED
from client import randomString
from threading import Thread
from time import sleep
from os import listdir
import sys
from anygui import *

HEAD_START = 0.1 # Seconds
SECRET_LENGTH = 100

class Client(Application):
    """
    The main client class, which takes care of setting up the GUI and
    starts a Node for serving files.
    """
```

```
def __init__(self, url, dirname, urlfile):
    """

    Creates a random secret, instantiates a Node with that secret,
    starts a Thread with the Node's _start method (making sure the
    Thread is a daemon so it will quit when the application quits),
    reads all the URLs from the URL file and introduces the Node to
    them. Finally, sets up the GUI.
    """
    Application.__init__(self)
    self.secret = randomString(SECRET_LENGTH)
    n = Node(url, dirname, self.secret)
    t = Thread(target=n._start)
    t.setDaemon(1)
    t.start()
    # Give the server a head start:
    sleep(HEAD_START)
    self.server = ServerProxy(url)
    for line in open(urlfile):
        line = line.strip()
        self.server.hello(line)
    self.setUp()

def setUp(self):
    """

    Sets up the GUI. Creates a Window, a TextField, and a Button, and
    lays them out. Binds the submit Button to self.fetchHandler.
    """
    win = Window(title='File Sharing Client')
    self.add(win)

    self.input = input = TextField()
    submit = Button(text='Fetch', height=input.height)

    win.height = input.height + 20

    win.add(submit,
            top=10,
            right=10,
            hmove=1)
```

```
        win.add(input,
                top=10,
                left=10,
                right=(submit, 10),
                hstretch=1)

        link(submit, self.fetchHandler)

    def fetchHandler(self, event):
        """
        Called when the user clicks the 'Fetch' button. Reads the
        query from the TextField, and calls the fetch method of the
        server Node. If the query is not handled, an error message
        is printed.
        """
        query = self.input.text
        try:
            self.server.fetch(query, self.secret)
        except Fault, f:
            if f.faultCode != UNHANDLED: raise
            print "Couldn't find the file", query

def main():
    urlfile, directory, url = sys.argv[1:]
    client = Client(url, directory, urlfile)
    client.run()

if __name__ == '__main__': main()
```

To run this program you need a URL file, a directory of files to share, and a URL for your Node. Here is a sample run:

```
$ python simple_guiclient.py urlfile.txt files/ http://localhost:8080
```

Note that the file urlfile.txt must contain the URLs of some other Nodes for the program to be of any use. You can either start several programs on the same machine (with different port numbers) for testing purposes, or run them on different machines.

See Figure 22-1 for a screenshot of the client.

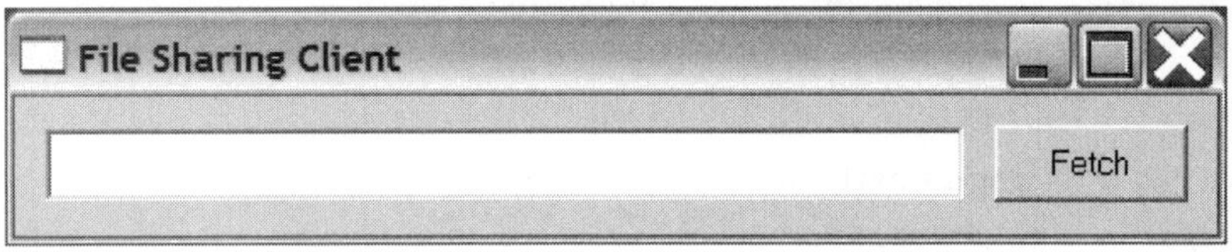

Figure 22-1. The simple GUI client

Second Implementation

The first prototype was very simple. It did its job as a file sharing system, but wasn't very user-friendly. It would help a lot if the user could see which files he or she had available (either located in the file directory when the program starts, or subsequently downloaded from another Node). The second implementation will address this file listing issue. The full source code can be found in Listing 22-2.

To get a listing from a Node, you must add a method. You could protect it with a password like you have done with `fetch`, but making it publicly available may be useful, and it doesn't represent any real security risk. Extending an object is really easy: you can do it through subclassing. You simply construct a subclass of Node called `ListableNode`, with a single additional method, `list`, which uses the method `os.listdir`, which returns a list of all the files in a directory:

```
class ListableNode(Node):

    def list(self):
        return listdir(self.dirname)
```

To access this server method, the method `updateList` is added to the client:

```
def updateList(self):
    self.files.items = self.server.list()
```

The attribute `self.files` refers to a `ListBox`, which has been added in the `setUp` method. The `updateList` method is called in `setUp` at the point where the `ListBox` is created, and again each time `fetchHandler` is called (because calling `fetchHandler` may potentially alter the list of files).

And that's it. You now have a GUI-enabled peer-to-peer file sharing program, which can be run with the command

```
$ python guiclient.py urlfile.txt files/ http://localhost:8080
```

To see what it looks like, see Figure 22-2. The full source code is found in Listing 22-2.

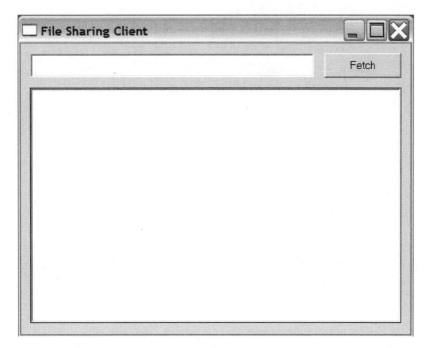

Figure 22-2. The finished GUI client

Of course there are plenty of ways to expand the program. For some ideas, see the next section, "Further Exploration," as well as the section with the same title in Chapter 21. Beyond that, just let your imagination go wild.

Listing 22-2. The Finished GUI Client (guiclient.py)

```python
from xmlrpclib import ServerProxy, Fault
from server import Node, UNHANDLED
from client import randomString
from threading import Thread
from time import sleep
from os import listdir
import sys
from anygui import *

HEAD_START = 0.1 # Seconds
SECRET_LENGTH = 100


class ListableNode(Node):
    """
    An extended version of Node, which can list the files
```

```
        in its file directory.
        """

    def list(self):
        return listdir(self.dirname)

class Client(Application):                    .
    """
    The main client class, which takes care of setting up the GUI and
    starts a Node for serving files.
    """

    def __init__(self, url, dirname, urlfile):
        """
        Creates a random secret, instantiates a ListableNode with that secret,
        starts a Thread with the ListableNode's _start method (making sure the
        Thread is a daemon so it will quit when the application quits),
        reads all the URLs from the URL file and introduces the Node to
        them. Finally, sets up the GUI.
        """

        Application.__init__(self)
        self.secret = randomString(SECRET_LENGTH)
        n = ListableNode(url, dirname, self.secret)
        t = Thread(target=n._start)
        t.setDaemon(1)
        t.start()
        # Give the server a head start:
        sleep(HEAD_START)
        self.server = ServerProxy(url)
        for line in open(urlfile):
            line = line.strip()
            self.server.hello(line)
        self.setUp()

    def updateList(self):
        """
        Updates the ListBox with the names of the files available
        from the server Node.
        """

        self.files.items = self.server.list()

    def setUp(self):
        """
        Sets up the GUI. Creates a Window, a TextField, and a Button, and
        a ListBox, and lays them out. Binds the submit Button to
```

```
        self.fetchHandler.
        """

        win = Window(title='File Sharing Client')
        self.add(win)

        self.input = input = TextField()
        submit = Button(text='Fetch', height=input.height)

        self.files = files = ListBox()
        self.updateList()

        win.add(submit,
                top=10,
                right=10,
                hmove=1)

        win.add(input,
                top=10,
                left=10,
                right=(submit, 10),
                hstretch=1)

        win.add(files,
                top=(input,10),
                left=10,
                right=10,
                bottom=10,
                hstretch=1,
                vstretch=1)

        link(submit, self.fetchHandler)

    def fetchHandler(self, event):
        """
        Called when the user clicks the 'Fetch' button. Reads the
        query from the TextField, and calls the fetch method of the
        server Node. After handling the query, updateList is called.
        If the query is not handled, an error message is printed.
        """
        query = self.input.text
        try:
            self.server.fetch(query, self.secret)
            self.updateList()
```

```
            except Fault, f:
                if f.faultCode != UNHANDLED: raise
                print "Couldn't find the file", query

def main():
    urlfile, directory, url = sys.argv[1:]
    client = Client(url, directory, urlfile)
    client.run()

if __name__ == '__main__': main()
```

Further Exploration

Some ideas for extending the file sharing system are given in Chapter 21. Here are some more:

- Add a status bar that displays such messages as "Downloading" or "Couldn't find file foo.txt."

- Figure out ways for Nodes to share their "friends." For example, when one Node is introduced to another, each of them could introduce the other to the Nodes it already knows. Also, before a Node shuts down, it might tell all its current neighbors of all the Nodes it knows.

- Add a list of known Nodes (URLs) to the GUI. Make it possible to add new URLs and save them in a URL file.

What Now?

Now you've written a full-fledged GUI-enabled peer-to-peer file sharing system. Although that sounds pretty challenging, it wasn't all that hard, was it? Now it's time to face the last and greatest challenge: writing your own arcade game.

#### CHAPTER 23

Project 10:
Do-It-Yourself
Arcade Game

WELCOME TO THE FINAL PROJECT. Now that you've sampled several of Python's many capabilities, it's time to go out with a bang. In this chapter you learn how to use Pygame, an extension that enables you to write full-fledged, full-screen arcade games in Python. Although easy to use, Pygame is quite powerful and consists of several components that are thoroughly documented in the Pygame documentation (available on the Pygame Web site, `http://pygame.org`). This project introduces you to some of the main Pygame concepts, but because this chapter is only meant as a starting point, I've skipped several interesting features such as sound and video handling. I would recommend that you look into these yourself, once you've familiarized yourself with the basics.

What's the Problem?

So, how do you write a computer game? The basic design process is similar to the one you use when writing any other program (as described in Chapter 7), but before you can develop an object model, you need to design the game itself. What are its characters, its setting, its objectives?

I'll keep things reasonably simple here, so as not to clutter the presentation of the basic Pygame concepts. Feel free to create a much more elaborate game if you like. I'll base my game on the well-known Monty Python sketch "Self-Defense Against Fresh Fruit." In this sketch, a Sergeant Major (John Cleese) is instructing his soldiers in self-defense techniques against attackers wielding fresh fruit such as pomegranates, mangoes in syrup, greengages, and bananas. The defense techniques include using a gun, unleashing a tiger, and dropping a 16-ton weight on top of the attacker. In this game, I turn things around—the player controls a banana that desperately tries to survive a course in self-defense, avoiding a barrage of 16-ton weights dropping from above. I guess a fitting name for the game might be Squish.

TIP *If you'd like to try your hand at a game of your own as you follow this chapter, feel free to do so. If you just want to change the look and feel of the game, simply replace the graphics (a couple of GIF or PNG images) and some of the descriptive text.*

Specific Goals

The specific goals of this project revolve around the game design. The game should behave as it was designed (the banana should be movable, and the 16-ton weight should drop from above). In addition, the code should be modular and easily extensible (as always). A useful requirement might be that game states (such as the game introduction, the various game levels, the "game over" state) should be part of the design, and that new states should be easy to add.

Useful Tools

The only new tool you need in this project is Pygame, which you can download from the Pygame Web site (http://pygame.org). To get Pygame to work in UNIX, you may need to install some extra software, but it's all documented in the Pygame installation instructions (also available from the Pygame Web site). The Windows binary installer is very easy to use—simply execute the installer and follow the instructions.

NOTE *The Pygame distribution does not include Numerical Python, which may be useful for manipulating sounds and images. Although it's not needed for this project, you might want to check it out (http://www.pfdubois.com/numpy). The Pygame documentation thoroughly describes how to use Numerical Python with Pygame.*

The Pygame distribution consists of several modules, most of which you won't need in this project. The following sections describe the modules you do need. (Only the specific functions or classes needed are discussed here.) In addition to the functions described in the following sections, the various objects used (such as surfaces, groups, or sprites) have several useful methods that I discuss as they are used in the implementation sections.

TIP *You can find a nice introduction to Pygame in the "Line-by-Line Chimp Tutorial," on the Pygame Web site* (http://pygame.org/docs/tut/ChimpLineByLine.html). *It addresses a few issues not discussed here, such as playing sound clips.*

pygame

This module automatically imports all the other Pygame modules, so if you place "import pygame" at the top of your program, you can automatically access the other modules, such as pygame.display or pygame.font.

The pygame module contains (among other things), the Surface function, which returns a new surface object. Surface objects are simply blank images of a given size that you can use for drawing and *blitting*. To blit (calling a surface object's blit method) simply means to transfer the contents of one surface to another. (The word "blit" is derived from the technical term "block transfer," which is abbreviated BLT.)

The init function is central to any Pygame game. It must be called before your game enters its main event loop. This function automatically initializes all the other modules (such as font and image).

You need the error class when you want to catch Pygame-specific errors.

pygame.locals

This module contains names (variables) you might want in your own module's scope. It contains names for event types, keys, video modes, and more. It is designed to be safe to use with starred import (from pygame.locals import *), although if you know what you need, you may want to be more specific (for example, from pygame.locals import FULLSCREEN).

pygame.display

This module contains functions for dealing with the Pygame display, which either may be contained in a normal window, or occupy the entire screen. In this project you need the following functions:

- flip: In general, when you modify the current screen, you do that in two steps. First, you perform all the necessary modifications to the surface object returned from the get_surface function, and then you call pygame.display.flip to update the display to reflect your changes.

- update: Used instead of flip when you only want to update a part of the screen. It can be used with the list of rectangles returned from the draw method of the RenderUpdates class (described in the section "pygame.sprite," which follows) as its only parameter.

- set_mode: Used to set the display size and the type of display. There are several variations possible, but here we'll restrict ourselves to the FULLSCREEN version, and the default "display in a window" version.

- set_caption: Used to set a caption for the Pygame program. The set_caption function is primarily useful when you run your game in a window (as opposed to full-screen) because the caption is used as the window title.

- get_surface: Returns a surface object you can draw your graphics on before calling pygame.display.flip or pygame.display.blit. The only surface method used for drawing in this project is blit, which transfers the graphics found in one surface object onto another one, at a given location. (In addition, the draw method of a Group object will be used to draw Sprite objects onto the display surface.)

pygame.font

This module contains the Font function. Font objects are used to represent different typefaces. They can be used to render text as images that may then be used as normal graphics in Pygame.

pygame.sprite

This module contains two very important classes: Sprite and Group.

The Sprite class is the base class for all visible game objects—in the case of this project, the banana and the 16-ton weight. To implement your own game objects, you subclass Sprite, override its constructor to set its image and rect properties (which determine how the Sprite looks, and where it is placed), and override its update method, which is called whenever the sprite might need updating.

Instances of the Group class (and its subclasses) are used as containers for Sprites. In general, using groups is a Good Thing. In simple games (such as in this project) simply create a group called sprites or allsprites or something similar, and add all your Sprites to it. When you call the Group object's update method, the update methods of all your Sprite objects will then be called automatically. Also, the Group object's draw method can be used to draw all the Sprite objects it contains.

In this project I use the RenderUpdates subclass of Group, whose draw method returns a list of rectangles that have been affected. These may then be passed to pygame.display.update to update only the parts of the display that need to be updated. This can greatly improve the performance of the game.

pygame.mouse

In Squish, I use this module for just two things: hiding the mouse cursor, and getting the mouse position. You hide the mouse with pygame.mouse.set_visible(0), and you get the position with pygame.mouse.get_pos().

pygame.event

This module keeps track of various events such as mouse clicks, mouse motion, keys that are pressed or released, and so on. To get a list of the most recent events, use the function pygame.event.get.

> **NOTE** *If you rely only on state information such as the mouse position returned by* pygame.mouse.get_pos, *you don't have to use* pygame.event.get. *However, you need to keep the Pygame updated ("in sync"), which you can do by calling the function* pygame.event.pump *regularly.*

pygame.image

This module is used to deal with images, such as those stored in GIF, PNG, or JPEG files (or indeed several other formats). In this project you only need the load function, which reads an image file and creates a surface object containing the image.

Preparations

Now that you know a bit about what some of the different Pygame modules do, it's almost time to start hacking away at the first prototype game. There are, however, a couple of preparations you need to make before you can get the prototype up and running. First of all, you should make sure that you have Pygame installed, including the image and font modules. (You might want to import both of these in an interactive Python interpreter to make sure they are available.)

You also need a couple of images. If you want to stick to the theme of the game as presented in this chapter, you need one image depicting a 16-ton weight, and one depicting a banana. Their exact sizes aren't all that important, but you might want to keep them in the range 100×100 through 200×200 pixels. (You might also want a separate image for the *splash screen,* the first screen that greets the user of your game. In this project I simply use the weight symbol for that as well.) You should have these two images available in a common image file format such as GIF, PNG, or JPEG.

Figure 23-1 shows the weight and banana graphics used in my version of the game.

Figure 23-1. A 16-ton weight and a banana, ready for action

First Implementation

When you use a new tool such as Pygame, it often pays off to keep the first prototype as simple as possible and to focus on learning the basics of the new tool, rather than the intricacies of the program itself. Let's restrict the first version of Squish to an animation of 16-ton weights falling from above. The steps needed for this are as follows:

1. Initialize Pygame, using pygame.init, pygame.display.set_mode, and pygame.mouse.set_visible. Get the screen surface with pygame.display.get_surface. Fill the screen surface with a solid white color (with the fill method) and call pygame.display.flip to display this change.

2. Load the weight image.

3. Create an instance of a custom Weight class (a subclass of Sprite) using the image. Add this object to a RenderUpdates group called (for example) sprites. (This will be particularly useful when dealing with multiple sprites.)

4. Get all recent events with pygame.event.get. Check all the events in turn—if an event of type QUIT is found, or if an event of type KEYDOWN representing the escape key (K_ESCAPE) is found, exit the program. (The event types and keys are stored in the attributes type and key in the event object. Constants such as QUIT, KEYDOWN, and K_ESCAPE can be imported from the module pygame.locals.)

5. Call the update method of the sprites group. This in turn calls the update method of the Weight instance. (You have to implement the latter method yourself.)

6. Call sprites.draw with the screen surface as the argument to draw the Weight sprite at its current position. (This position changes each time update is called.)

7. Call pygame.display.update with the rectangle list returned from sprites.draw to update the display only in the right places. (If you don't need the performance, you can use pygame.display.flip here to update the entire display.)

8. Go to Step 4.

See Listing 23-1 for code that implements these steps. The QUIT event would occur if the user quit the game—for example, by closing the window.

Listing 23-1. A Simple "Falling Weights" Animation (weights.py)

```python
import sys, pygame
from pygame.locals import *
from random import randrange


class Weight(pygame.sprite.Sprite):

    def __init__(self):
        pygame.sprite.Sprite.__init__(self)
        # image and rect used when drawing sprite:
        self.image = weight_image
        self.rect = self.image.get_rect()
        self.reset()

    def reset(self):
        """
        Move the weight to a random position at the top of the screen.
        """
        self.rect.top = -self.rect.height
        self.rect.centerx = randrange(screen_size[0])

    def update(self):
        """
        Update the weight for display in the next frame.
        """
        self.rect.top += 1
        if self.rect.top > screen_size[1]:
            self.reset()

# Initialize things
pygame.init()
screen_size = 800, 600
pygame.display.set_mode(screen_size, FULLSCREEN)
pygame.mouse.set_visible(0)

# Load the weight image
weight_image = pygame.image.load('weight.png')
weight_image = weight_image.convert() # ...to match the display

# Create a sprite group and add a Weight
sprites = pygame.sprite.RenderUpdates()
sprites.add(Weight())
```

```
# Get the screen surface and fill it
screen = pygame.display.get_surface()
white = (255, 255, 255)
screen.fill(white)
pygame.display.flip()

while 1:
    # Check for quit events:
    for event in pygame.event.get():
        if event.type == QUIT:
            sys.exit()
        if event.type == KEYDOWN and event.key == K_ESCAPE:
            sys.exit()
    # Update all sprites:
    sprites.update()
    # Draw all sprites:
    updates = sprites.draw(screen)
    # Update the necessary parts of the display:
    pygame.display.update(updates)
```

You can run this program with the following command:

```
$ python weights.py
```

You should make sure that both weights.py and weight.png (the weight image) are in the current directory when you execute this.

 NOTE   *I have used a PNG image with transparency here, but a GIF image might work just as well. JPEG images aren't really well-suited for transparency.*

Figure 23-2 shows a screenshot of the program created in Listing 23-1.

Figure 23-2. A simple animation of falling weights

Most of the code should speak for itself. There are, however, a few points that need explaining:

- All sprite objects should have two attributes called image and rect. The former should contain a surface object (an image) and the latter should contain a rectangle object (just use self.image.get_rect() to initialize it). These two attributes will be used when drawing the sprites. By modifying self.rect you can move the sprite around.

- Surface objects have a method called convert, which can be used to create a copy with a different color model. You don't have to worry about the details, but using convert without any arguments creates a surface that is tailored for the current display, and displaying it will be as fast as possible.

- Colors are specified through RGB triples (red-green-blue, with each value being 0–255), so the tuple (255, 255, 255) represents white.

You modify a rectangle (such as self.rect in this case) by assigning to its attributes (top, bottom, left, right, topleft, topright, bottomleft, bottomright, size, width, height, center, centerx, centery, midleft, midright, midtop, midbottom) or calling methods such as inflate or move. (These are all described in the Pygame documentation at http://pygame.org/docs/ref/Rect.html).

Now that the Pygame technicalities are in place, it's time to extend and refactor our game logic a bit.

Second Implementation

In this section, instead of walking you through the design and implementation step by step, I have added copious comments and docstrings to the source code (shown in Listings 23-2 through 23-4). You can examine the source ("use the source," remember?) to see how it works, but here is a short rundown of the essentials (and some not-quite-intuitive particulars):

- The game consists of five files: config.py, which contains various configuration variables; objects.py, which contains the implementations of the game objects; squish.py, which contains the main Game class and the various game state classes; and weight.png and banana.png, the two images used in the game.

- The rectangle method clamp ensures that a rectangle is placed within another rectangle, moving it if necessary. This is used to ensure that the banana doesn't move off-screen.

- The rectangle method inflate resizes (inflates) a rectangle by a given number of pixels in the horizontal and vertical direction. This is used to shrink the banana boundary, to allow some overlap between the banana and the weight before a hit (or "squish") is registered.

- The game itself consists of a game object and various game states. The game object only has one state at a time, and the state is responsible for handling events and displaying itself on the screen. The states may also tell the game to switch to another state. (A Level state may, for instance, tell the game to switch to a GameOver state.)

That's it. You may run the game by executing the squish.py file, as follows:

```
$ python squish.py
```

You should make sure that the other files are in the same directory. In Windows, you can simply double-click the squish.py file.

TIP *If you rename* squish.py *to* squish.pyw, *double-clicking it in Windows won't pop up a gratuitous terminal window. If you want to put the game on your desktop (or somewhere else) without moving all the modules and image files along with it, simply create a shortcut to the* squish.pyw *file.*

Some screenshots of the game are shown in Figures 23-3 through 23-6.

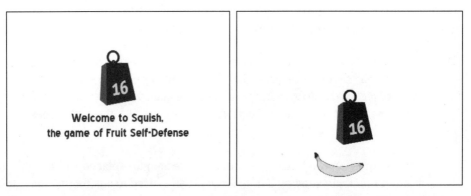

Figure 23-3. The Squish opening screen

Figure 23-4. A banana about to be squished

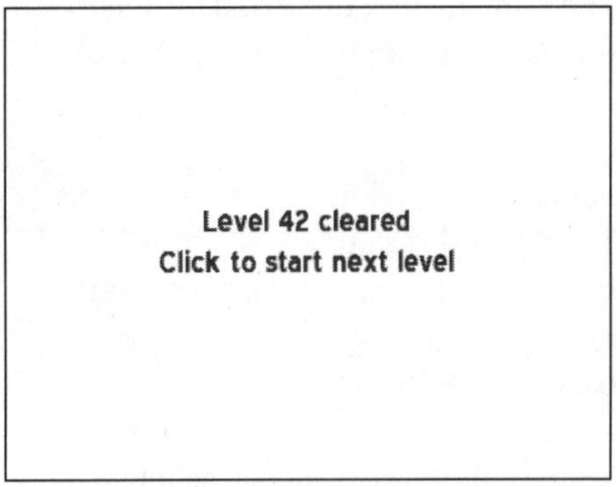

Figure 23-5. The "level cleared" screen

Figure 23-6. The "game over" screen

*Listing 23-2. The Squish Configuration File (*config.py*)*

```
# Configuration file for Squish
# -----------------------------

# Feel free to modify the configuration variables below to taste.

# Change these to use other images in the game:
banana_image = 'banana.png'
weight_image = 'weight.png'
splash_image = 'weight.png'

# Change these to affect the general appearance:
screen_size = 800, 600
background_color = 255, 255, 255
margin = 30
full_screen = 1
font_size = 48

# These affect the behavior of the game:
drop_speed = 5
banana_speed = 10
speed_increase = 1
weights_per_level = 10
banana_pad_top = 40
banana_pad_side = 20
```

*Listing 23-3. The Squish Game Objects (*objects.py*)*

```
import pygame, config, os
from random import randrange

"This module contains the game objects of the Squish game."

class SquishSprite(pygame.sprite.Sprite):

    """
    Generic superclass for all sprites in Squish.  The constructor
    takes care of loading an image, setting up the sprite rect, and
    the area within which it is allowed to move. That area is governed
    by the screen size and the margin.
    """
```

```
        def __init__(self, image):
            pygame.sprite.Sprite.__init__(self)
            self.image = pygame.image.load(image).convert()
            self.rect = self.image.get_rect()
            screen = pygame.display.get_surface()
            shrink = -config.margin * 2
            self.area = screen.get_rect().inflate(shrink, shrink)


class Weight(SquishSprite):

    """
    A falling weight. It uses the SquishSprite constructor to set up
    its weight image, and will fall with a speed given as a parameter
    to its constructor.
    """

    def __init__(self, speed):
        SquishSprite.__init__(self, config.weight_image)
        self.speed = speed
        self.reset()

    def reset(self):
        """
        Move the weight to the top of the screen (just out of sight)
        and place it at a random horizontal position.
        """
        x = randrange(self.area.left, self.area.right)
        self.rect.midbottom = x, 0

    def update(self):
        """
        Move the weight vertically (downwards) a distance
        corresponding to its speed. Also set the landed attribute
        according to whether it has reached the bottom of the screen.
        """
        self.rect.top += self.speed
        self.landed = self.rect.top >= self.area.bottom
```

```
class Banana(SquishSprite):

    """
    A desperate banana. It uses the SquishSprite constructor to set up
    its banana image, and will stay near the bottom of the screen,
    with its horizontal position governed by the current mouse
    position (within certain limits).
    """

    def __init__(self):
        SquishSprite.__init__(self, config.banana_image)
        self.rect.bottom = self.area.bottom

        # These paddings represent parts of the image where there is
        # no banana. If a weight moves into these areas, it doesn't
        # constitute a hit (or, rather, a squish):
        self.pad_top = config.banana_pad_top
        self.pad_side = config.banana_pad_side

    def update(self):
        """
        Set the Banana's center x-coordinate to the current mouse
        x-coordinate, and then use the rect method clamp to ensure
        that the Banana stays within its allowed range of motion.
        """
        self.rect.centerx = pygame.mouse.get_pos()[0]
        self.rect = self.rect.clamp(self.area)

    def touches(self, other):
        """
        Determines whether the banana touches another sprite (e.g. a
        Weight). Instead of just using the rect method colliderect, a
        new rectangle is first calculated (using the rect method
        inflate with the side and top paddings) which does not include
        the 'empty' areas on the top and sides of the banana.
        """
        # Deflate the bounds with the proper padding:
        bounds = self.rect.inflate(-self.pad_side, -self.pad_top)
        # Move the bounds so they are placed at the bottom of the Banana:
        bounds.bottom = self.rect.bottom
        # Check whether the bounds intersect with the other object's rect:
        return bounds.colliderect(other.rect)
```

Listing 23-4. The Main Game Module (squish.py)

```python
import os, sys, pygame
from pygame.locals import *
import objects, config

"This module contains the main game logic of the Squish game."

class State:

    """
    A generic game state class that can handle events and display
    itself on a given surface.
    """

    def handle(self, event):
        """
        Default event handling only deals with quitting.
        """
        if event.type == QUIT:
            sys.exit()
        if event.type == KEYDOWN and event.key == K_ESCAPE:
            sys.exit()

    def firstDisplay(self, screen):
        """
        Used to display the State for the first time. Fills the screen
        with the background color.
        """
        screen.fill(config.background_color)
        # Remember to call flip, to make the changes visible:
        pygame.display.flip()

    def display(self, screen):
        """
        Used to display the State after it has already been displayed
        once. The default behavior is to do nothing.
        """
        pass
```

```
class Level(State):

    """

    A game level. Takes care of counting how many weights have been
    dropped, moving the sprites around, and other tasks relating to
    game logic.
    """

    def __init__(self, number=1):
        self.number = number
        # How many weights remain to dodge in this level?
        self.remaining = config.weights_per_level

        speed = config.drop_speed
        # One speed_increase added for each level above 1:
        speed += (self.number-1) * config.speed_increase

        # Create the weight and banana:
        self.weight = weight = objects.Weight(speed)
        self.banana = banana = objects.Banana()
        both = self.weight, self.banana # This could contain more sprites...
        self.sprites = pygame.sprite.RenderUpdates(both)

    def update(self, game):
        "Updates the game state from the previous frame."
        # Update all sprites:
        self.sprites.update()
        # If the banana touches the weight, tell the game to switch to
        # a GameOver state:
        if self.banana.touches(self.weight):
            game.nextState = GameOver()
        # Otherwise, if the weight has landed, reset it. If all the
        # weights of this level have been dodged, tell the game to
        # switch to a LevelCleared state:
        elif self.weight.landed:
            self.weight.reset()
            self.remaining -= 1
            if self.remaining == 0:
                game.nextState = LevelCleared(self.number)

    def display(self, screen):
        """

        Displays the state after the first display (which simply wipes
```

the screen). As opposed to firstDisplay, this method uses
pygame.display.update with a list of rectangles that need to
be updated, supplied from self.sprites.draw.
"""

```
screen.fill(config.background_color)
updates = self.sprites.draw(screen)
pygame.display.update(updates)
```

```
class Paused(State):
```

```
    """
    A simple, paused game state, which may be broken out of by pressing
    either a keyboard key or the mouse button.
    """
```

```
    finished = 0  # Has the user ended the pause?
    image = None  # Set this to a file name if you want an image
    text = ''     # Set this to some informative text
```

```
    def handle(self, event):
        """
        Handles events by delegating to State (which handles quitting
        in general) and by reacting to key presses and mouse
        clicks. If a key is pressed or the mouse is clicked,
        self.finished is set to true.
        """
        State.handle(self, event)
        if event.type in [MOUSEBUTTONDOWN, KEYDOWN]:
            self.finished = 1
```

```
    def update(self, game):
        """
        Update the level. If a key has been pressed or the mouse has
        been clicked (i.e. self.finished is true), tell the game to
        move to the state represented by self.nextState() (should be
        implemented by subclasses).
        """
        if self.finished:
            game.nextState = self.nextState()
```

```
    def firstDisplay(self, screen):
        """
        The first time the Paused state is displayed, draw the image
```

```
(if any) and render the text.
"""
# First, clear the screen by filling it with the background color:
screen.fill(config.background_color)

# Create a Font object with the default appearance, and specified size:
font = pygame.font.Font(None, config.font_size)

# Get the lines of text in self.text, ignoring empty lines at
# the top or bottom:
lines = self.text.strip().splitlines()

# Calculate the height of the text (using font.get_linesize()
# to get the height of each line of text):
height = len(lines) * font.get_linesize()

# Calculate the placement of the text (centered on the screen):
center, top = screen.get_rect().center
top -= height // 2

# If there is an image to display...
if self.image:
    # load it:
    image = pygame.image.load(self.image).convert()
    # get its rect:
    r = image.get_rect()
    # move the text down by half the image height:
    top += r.height // 2
    # place the image 20 pixels above the text:
    r.midbottom = center, top - 20
    # blit the image to the screen:
    screen.blit(image, r)

antialias = 1      # Smooth the text
black = 0, 0, 0  # Render it as black

# Render all the lines, starting at the calculated top, and
# move down font.get_linesize() pixels for each line:
for line in lines:
    text = font.render(line.strip(), antialias, black)
    r = text.get_rect()
    r.midtop = center, top
    screen.blit(text, r)
    top += font.get_linesize()
```

```
            # Display all the changes:
            pygame.display.flip()


class Info(Paused):

    """
    A simple paused state that displays some information about the
    game. It is followed by a Level state (the first level).
    """

    nextState = Level
    text = '''
In this game you are a banana,
trying to survive a course in
self-defense against fruit, where the
participants will "defend" themselves
against you with a 16 ton weight.'''


class StartUp(Paused):

    """
    A paused state that displays a splash image and a welcome
    message. It is followed by an Info state.
    """

    nextState = Info
    image = config.splash_image
    text = '''
Welcome to Squish,
the game of Fruit Self-Defense'''


class LevelCleared(Paused):

    """
    A paused state that informs the user that he or she has cleared a
    given level.  It is followed by the next level state.
    """

    def __init__(self, number):
        self.number = number
```

```
            self.text = '''Level %i cleared
            Click to start next level''' % self.number

        def nextState(self):
            return Level(self.number+1)


class GameOver(Paused):

    """
    A state that informs the user that he or she has lost the
    game. It is followed by the first level.
    """

    nextState = Level
    text = '''
Game Over
Click to Restart, Esc to Quit'''


class Game:

    """
    A game object that takes care of the main event loop, including
    changing between the different game states.
    """

    def __init__(self, *args):
        # Get the directory where the game and the images are located:
        path = os.path.abspath(args[0])
        dir = os.path.split(path)[0]
        # Move to that directory (so that the images files may be
        # opened later on):
        os.chdir(dir)
        # Start with no state:
        self.state = None
        # Move to StartUp in the first event loop iteration:
        self.nextState = StartUp()

    def run(self):
        """
        This method sets things in motion. It performs some vital
        initialization tasks, and enters the main event loop.
```

```
                """
                pygame.init() # This is needed to initialize all the pygame modules

                # Decide whether to display the game in a window or to use the
                # full screen:
                flag = 0                      # Default (window) mode
                if config.full_screen:
                    flag = FULLSCREEN         # Full screen mode
                screen_size = config.screen_size
                screen = pygame.display.set_mode(screen_size, flag)

                pygame.display.set_caption('Fruit Self Defense')
                pygame.mouse.set_visible(0)

                # The main loop:
                while 1:
                    # (1) If nextState has been changed, move to the new state, and
                    #      display it (for the first time):
                    if self.state != self.nextState:
                        self.state = self.nextState
                        self.state.firstDisplay(screen)
                    # (2) Delegate the event handling to the current state:
                    for event in pygame.event.get():
                        self.state.handle(event)
                    # (3) Update the current state:
                    self.state.update(self)
                    # (4) Display the current state:
                    self.state.display(screen)


        if __name__ == '__main__':
            game = Game(*sys.argv)
            game.run()
```

Further Exploration

Here are some ideas for how you can improve the game:

- Add sounds to it.

- Keep track of the score. Each weight dodged could be worth 16 points, for instance. How about keeping a high-score file? Or even an online high-score server (using `asyncore` or XML-RPC)?

- Make more objects fall simultaneously.

- Give the player more than one "life."

For a much more elaborate (and extremely entertaining) example of Pygame programming, check out the SolarWolf game by Pete Shinners, the Pygame maintainer (`http://www.pygame.org/shredwheat/solarwolf`). You can find plenty of information and several other games at the Pygame Web site. If playing with Pygame gets you hooked on game development, you might want to check out these Web sites:

- `http://www.gdse.com`

- `http://www.gamedev.net`

- `http://www.flipcode.com`

What Now?

Well, this is it. You have finished the last project. If you take stock of what you have accomplished (assuming that you have followed all the projects) you should be rightfully impressed with yourself. The breadth of the topics presented has given you a taste of the possibilities that await you in the world of Python programming. I hope you have enjoyed the trip this far, and I wish you good luck on your continued journey as a Python programmer.

APPENDIX A

The Short Version

THIS IS A MINIMAL introduction to Python, based on my popular Web tutorial, "Instant Python" (http://hetland.org/python/instant-python). It targets programmers who already know a language or two, but who want to get up to speed with Python. For information on downloading and executing the Python interpreter, see Chapter 1.

The Basics

To get a basic feel for the Python language, think of it as pseudocode—it's pretty close to the truth. Variables don't have types, so you don't have to declare them. They appear when you assign to them, and disappear when you don't use them anymore. Assignment is done with the = operator, like this:

```
x = 42
```

Note that equality is tested by the == operator.
You can assign several variables at once, like this:

```
x,y,z = 1,2,3
first, second = second, first
a = b = 123
```

Blocks are indicated through indentation, and *only* through indentation. (No begin/end or braces.) The following are some common control structures:

```
if x < 5 or (x > 10 and x < 20):
    print "The value is OK."

if x < 5 or 10 < x < 20:
    print "The value is OK."
```

```
for i in [1,2,3,4,5]:
    print "This is iteration number", i


x = 10
while x >= 0:
    print "x is still not negative."
    x = x-1
```

The first two examples are equivalent.

The index variable given in the for loop iterates through the elements of a *list* (written as in the example). To make an "ordinary" for loop (that is, a counting loop), use the built-in function range:

```
# Print out the values from 0 to 99 inclusive
for value in range(100):
    print value
```

The line beginning with # is a comment and is ignored by the interpreter.

Now you know enough (in theory) to implement any algorithm in Python. Let's add some basic user interaction. To get input from the user (from a text prompt), use the built-in function input:

```
x = input("Please enter a number: ")
print "The square of that number is", x*x
```

The input function displays the (optional) prompt given and lets the user enter any valid Python value. In this case we were expecting a number. If something else (such as a string) is entered, the program would halt with an error message. To avoid that you would have to add some error checking. I won't go into that here; suffice it to say that if you want the user input stored *verbatim* as a string (so that *anything* can be entered), use the function raw_input instead. If you wanted to convert an input string s to an integer, you could then use int(s).

 NOTE *If you want to input a string with* input, *the user has to write the quotes explicitly. In Python, strings can be enclosed in either single or double quotes.*

So, we have control structures, input, and output covered—now we need some snazzy data structures. The most important ones are *lists* and *dictionaries*. Lists are written with brackets, and can (naturally) be nested:

```
name = ["Cleese", "John"]
x = [[1,2,3],[y,z],[[[]]]]
```

One of the nice things about lists is that you can access their elements separately or in groups, through *indexing* and *slicing*. Indexing is done (as in many other languages) by writing the index in brackets after the list. (Note that the first element has index 0.)

```
print name[1], name[0] # Prints "John Cleese"
name[0] = "Smith"
```

Slicing is almost like indexing, except that you indicate both the start and stop index of the result, with a colon (:) separating them:

```
x = ["SPAM","SPAM","SPAM","SPAM","SPAM","eggs","and","SPAM"]
print x[5:7] # Prints the list ["eggs","and"]
```

Notice that the end is non-inclusive. If one of the indices is dropped, it is assumed that you want everything in that direction. In other words, the slice x[:3] means "every element from the beginning of x up to element 3, non-inclusive." (It could be argued that it would actually mean element 4 because the counting starts at 0. Oh, well.) The slice x[3:] would, on the other hand, mean "every element from x, starting at element 3 (inclusive) up to, and including, the last one." For really interesting results, you can use negative numbers, too: x[-3] is the third element from the end of the list.

> **TIP** *While on the subject of indexing, you might be interested to know that the built-in function* len *gives you the length of a list.*

Now, then—what about dictionaries? To put it simply, they are like lists, except that their contents aren't ordered. How do you index them then? Well, every element has a *key*, or a "name," which is used to look up the element just as in a real dictionary. The following example demonstrates the syntax used to create dictionaries:

```
phone = { "Alice" : 23452532, "Boris" : 252336,
          "Clarice" : 2352525, "Doris" : 23624643}

person = { 'first name': "Robin", 'last name': "Hood",
           'occupation': "Scoundrel" }
```

Now, to get person's occupation, you use the expression person["occupation"]. If you wanted to change his last name, you could write:

```
person['last name'] = "of Locksley"
```

Simple, isn't it? Like lists, dictionaries can hold other dictionaries. Or lists, for that matter. And naturally lists can hold dictionaries, too. That way, you can easily make some quite advanced data structures.

Functions

Next step: abstraction. You want to give a name to a piece of code, and call it with a couple of parameters. In other words, you want to define a function (also called a procedure). That's easy. Use the keyword def as follows:

```
def square(x):
    return x*x

print square(2) # Prints out 4
```

The return statement is used to return a value from the function.

When you pass a parameter to a function, you bind the parameter to the value, thus creating a new reference. This means that you can modify the original value directly inside the function, but if you make the parameter name refer to something else (rebind it), that change won't affect the original. This works just like in Java, for instance. Let's take a look at an example:

```
def change(x):
    x[1] = 4

y = [1,2,3]
change(y)
print y # Prints out [1,4,3]
```

As you can see, it is the original list that is passed in, and if the function modifies it, these modifications carry over to the place where the function was called. Note the behavior in the following example, however, where the function body *rebinds* the parameter:

```
def nochange(x):
    x = 0

y = 1
nochange(y)
print y # Prints out 1
```

Why doesn't y change now? Because you *don't change the value!* The value that is passed in is the number 1—you can't change a number in the same way that you change a list. The number 1 is (and will always be) the number 1. What I *did* do is change what the parameter x *refers to*, and this does *not* carry over to the environment.

Python has all kinds of nifty things such as *named arguments* and *default arguments* and can handle a variable number of arguments to a single function. For more info on this, see Chapter 6.

If you know how to use functions in general, what I've told you so far is basically what you need to know about them in Python.

It might be useful to know, however, that functions are *values* in Python. So if you have a function such as square, you could do something like the following:

```
queeble = square
print queeble(2) # Prints out 4
```

To call a function without arguments you must remember to write doit()
and not doit. The latter, as shown, only returns the function itself, as a value. This
goes for methods in objects, too. Methods are described in the next section.

Objects and Stuff...

I assume you know how object-oriented programming works. (Otherwise, this
section might not make much sense. No problem. Start playing without the
objects; or check out Chapter 7.) In Python you define classes with the (surprise!)
class keyword, as follows:

```
class Basket:

    # Always remember the *self* argument
    def __init__(self, contents=None):
        self.contents = contents or []

    def add(self, element):
        self.contents.append(element)

    def print_me(self):
        result = ""
        for element in self.contents:
            result = result + " " + `element`
        print "Contains:" + result
```

Several things are worth noting in the previous example:

- All methods (functions in an object) receive an additional argument at the
  start of the argument list, containing the object itself. (Called self in this
  example, which is customary.)

- Methods are called like this: object.method(arg1, arg2).

- Some method names, such as __init__ (and __str__, which is
  discussed later), are predefined, and mean special things. __init__ is the
  name of the *constructor* of the class (it is the method that is called when
  you create an instance).

- Some arguments can be *optional* and given a default value (as mentioned before, under the section on functions). This is done by writing the definition like

```
def spam(age=32): ...
```

Here, spam can be called with one or zero parameters. If none is used, then the parameter age will have the value 32.

- There is a rather mysterious use of the logical operator or. This use, based on so-called *short-circuit logic*, will be explained a bit later in this section.

- Backticks convert an object to its string representation. (So if element contains the number 1, then `element` is the same as "1" whereas 'element' is a literal string.)

- The plus sign + is used also for concatenating sequences, and strings are really just sequences of characters (which means that you can use indexing and slicing and the len function on them. Cool, huh?)

> **NOTE** *The strategy of building a string piecemeal with the plus operator is simple but not particularly efficient. If possible, it's better to gather the component strings in a list, and join them with the* join *string method. See Chapter 3 for more details.*

No methods or member variables (attributes) are protected (or private or the like) in Python. Encapsulation is pretty much a matter of programming style. (If you *really* need it, there are naming conventions that will allow some privacy, such as prefixing a name with a single or double underscore).

Now, about that short-circuit logic...

All values in Python can be used as logic values. Some of the more empty ones, such as [], 0, "", and None (and, from Python 2.3, False) represent logical falsity, while most other values (such as [0], 1, or "Hello, world") represent logical truth.

Logical expressions such as a and b are evaluated like this: First, check if a is true. If it is *not*, then simply return it. If it *is*, then simply return b (which will represent the truth value of the expression). The corresponding logic for a or b is: If a is true, then return it. If it isn't, then return b.

This short-circuit mechanism enables you to use and and or like the Boolean operators they are supposed to implement, but it also enables you to write short and sweet little conditional expressions. For instance, the statement

```
if a:
    print a
else:
    print b
```

could instead be written

```
print a or b
```

Actually, this is somewhat of a Python idiom, so you might as well get used to it. The Basket constructor (Basket.__init__) uses this strategy in handling default parameters. The argument contents has a default value of None (which is, among other things, false); therefore, to check if it had a value, you could write:

```
if contents:
    self.contents = contents
else:
    self.contents = []
```

Instead, the constructor uses the simple statement

```
self.contents = contents or []
```

Why don't you give it the default value of [ ] in the first place? Because of the way Python works, this would give all the Baskets the same empty list as default contents. As soon as one of them started to fill up, they all would contain the same elements, and the default would not be empty anymore. To learn more about this, see the discussion about the difference between *identity* and *equality* in Chapter 5.

NOTE   *When using* None *as a placeholder as done in the* Basket.__init__ *method, using* contents is None *as the condition is safer than simply checking the argument's Boolean value, since this will allow you to pass in a false value such as an empty list of your own (to which you could keep a reference outside the object).*

If you would like to use an empty list as default value, you can avoid the problem of sharing this among instances by doing the following:

```
def __init__(self, contents=[]):
    self.contents = contents[:]
```

Can you guess how this works? Instead of using the same empty list everywhere, you use the expression contents[:] to make a copy. (You simply slice the entire thing.)

So, to actually make a Basket and to use it (to call some methods on it) you would do something like this:

```
b = Basket(['apple','orange'])
b.add("lemon")
b.print_me()
```

This would print out the contents of the Basket—an apple, an orange, and a lemon.

There are other magic methods than __init__. One such method is __str__, which defines how the object wants to look if it is treated like a string. You could use this in the basket instead of print_me:

```
def __str__(self):
    result = ""
    for element in self.contents:
        result = result + " " + `element`
    return "Contains:" + result
```

Now, if you wanted to print the basket b, you could just use

```
print b
```

Cool, huh?

Subclassing is done like this:

```
class SpamBasket(Basket):
    # ...
```

Python allows multiple inheritance so you can have several superclasses in the parentheses, separated by commas. Classes are instantiated like this: x = Basket(). Constructors are, as I said, made by defining the special member function __init__. Let's say that SpamBasket had a constructor __init__(self, type). Then you could make a spam basket like this: y = SpamBasket("apples").

> **NOTE** *You can use the special method __del__ to implement destructor behavior, but because you don't know exactly when an object is deleted (the deallocation is done automatically by garbage collection), you should not rely too much on this method.*

If you, in the constructor of SpamBasket, needed to call the constructor of one or more superclasses, you could call it like this: Basket.__init__(self). Note that in addition to supplying the ordinary parameters, you have to explicitly supply self because the superclass __init__ doesn't know which instance it is dealing with.

For more about the wonders of object-oriented programming in Python, see Chapter 7.

Some Loose Ends

Let me just quickly go review a few other useful things before ending this appendix. Most useful functions and classes are put in *modules*, which are really text files with the file name extension .py that contain Python code. You can import these and use them in your own programs. For instance, to use the function sqrt from the standard module math, you can do either...

```
import math
x = math.sqrt(y)
```

or...

```
from math import sqrt
x = sqrt(y)
```

For more information on the standard library modules, see Chapter 10.

All the code in the module/script is run when it is imported. If you want your program to be both an importable module and a runnable program, you might want to add something like this at the end of it:

```
if __name__ == "__main__": main()
```

This is a magic way of saying that if this module is run as an executable script (that is, it is not being imported into another script), then the function main should be called. Of course, you could do anything after the colon there.

And for those of you who want to make an executable script in UNIX, use the following first line to make it run by itself:

```
#!/usr/bin/env python
```

Finally, a brief mention of an important concept: *exceptions*. Some operations (such as dividing something by zero or reading from a non-existent file) produce an error condition or *exception*. You can even make your own and raise them at the appropriate times.

If nothing is done about the exception, your program ends and prints out an error message. You can avoid this with a try/except-statement. For instance:

```
def safe_division(a, b):
    try:
        return a/b
    except ZeroDivisionError: pass
```

ZeroDivisionError is a standard exception. In this case, you *could* have checked if b was zero, but in many cases, that strategy is not feasible. And besides, if you removed the try/except statement in safe_division, thereby making it a risky function to call (called something like unsafe_division), you could still do the following:

```
try:
    unsafe_division(a, b)
except ZeroDivisionError:
    print "Something was divided by zero in unsafe_division"
```

In cases in which you *typically* would not have a specific problem, but it *might* occur, using exceptions enables you to avoid costly testing and so forth.

Well, that's it. Hope you learned something. Now go and play. And remember the Python motto of learning: "Use the source" (which basically means, read all the code you can get your hands on).

Python Reference

THIS IS NOT A FULL PYTHON reference by far—you can find that in the standard Python documentation (`http://python.org/doc/ref`). Rather, this is a handy "cheat sheet" that can be useful for refreshing your memory as you start out programming in Python.

Expressions

This section summarizes Python expressions. Table B-1 lists the most important basic (literal) values in Python; Table B-2 lists the Python operators, along with their precedence (those with high precedence are evaluated before those with low precedence); Table B-3 describes some of the most important built-in functions; Tables B-4 through B-6 describe the list methods, dictionary methods, and string methods, respectively.

Table B-1. Basic (Literal) Values

TYPE	DESCRIPTION	SYNTAX SAMPLES
Integer	Numbers without a fractional part	`42`
Long integer	Large integer numbers	`42L`
Float	Numbers with a fractional part	`42.5, 42.5e-2`
Complex	Sum of a real (integer or float) and imaginary number	`38 + 4j, 42j`
String	An immutable sequence of characters	`'foo', "bar", """baz""", r'\n'`
Unicode	An immutable sequence of Unicode characters	`u'foo', u"bar", u"""baz"""`

Table B-2. Operators

OPERATOR	DESCRIPTION	PRECEDENCE
lambda	Lambda expression	1
or	Logical or	2
and	Logical and	3
not	Logical negation	4
in	Membership test	5
not in	Negative membership test	5
is	Identity test	6
is not	Negative identity test	6
<	Less than	7
>	Greater than	7
<=	Less or equal	7
>=	Greater or equal	7
==	Equal to	7
!=	Not equal to	7
|	Bitwise or	8
^	Bitwise exclusive or	9
&	Bitwise and	10
<<	Left shift	11
>>	Right shift	11
+	Addition	12
-	Subtraction	12
*	Multiplication	13
/	Division	13
%	Remainder	13
+	Unary identity	14
-	Unary negation	14

continued

Table B-2. Operators (continued)

OPERATOR	DESCRIPTION	PRECEDENCE
~	Bitwise complement	15
**	Exponentiation	16
x.attribute	Attribute reference	17
x[*index*]	Subscription	17
x[*index1*:*index2*]	Slicing	17
f(*args...*)	Function call	17
(...)	Parenthesized expression or tuple display	17
[...]	List display	17
{*key*:*value*, ...}	Dictionary display	17
`` `expressions...` ``	String conversion	17

Table B-3. Some Important Built-in Functions

FUNCTION	DESCRIPTION
abs(*number*)	Returns the absolute value of a number
apply(*function*[, *args*[, *kwds*]])	Calls a given function, optionally with parameters
callable(*object*)	Checks whether an object is callable
chr(*number*)	Returns a character whose ASCII code is the given number
cmp(*x*, *y*)	Compares x and y—if $x<y$ it returns a negative number, if $x>y$ it returns a positive number, and if $x==y$ it returns zero
complex(*real*[, *imag*])	Returns a complex number with the given real (and, optionally, imaginary) component
delattr(*object*, *name*)	Deletes the given attribute from the given object
dict([*mapping-or-sequence*])	Constructs a dictionary, optionally from another mapping or a list of (*key*, *value*) pairs
dir([*object*])	Lists (most of) the names in the currently visible scopes, or optionally (most of) the attributes of the given object

continued

Table B-3. Some Important Built-in Functions (continued)

FUNCTION	DESCRIPTION
divmod(*a*, *b*)	Returns (*a*//*b*, *a*%*b*) (with some special rules for floats)
eval(*string*[, *globals*[, *locals*]])	Evaluates a string containing an expression, optionally in a given global and local scope
execfile(*file*[, *globals*[, *locals*]])	Executes a Python file, optionally in a given global and local scope
file(*filename*[, *mode*[, *bufsize*]])	Creates a file object with a given file name, optionally with a given mode and buffer size
filter(*function, sequence*)	Returns a list of the elements from the given sequence for which *function* returns *true*
float(*object*)	Converts a string or number to a float
getattr(*object, name*[, *default*])	Returns the value of the named attribute of the given object, optionally with a given default value
globals()	Returns a dictionary representing the current global scope
hasattr(*object, name*)	Checks whether the given object has the named attribute
help([*object*])	Invokes the built-in help system, or prints a help message about the given object
hex(*number*)	Converts a number to a hexadecimal string
id(*object*)	Returns the unique ID for the given object
input([*prompt*])	Equivalent to eval(raw_input(*prompt*))
int(*object*[, *radix*])	Converts a string (optionally with a given radix) or number to an integer
isinstance(*object, classinfo*)	Checks whether the given object is an instance of the given *classinfo* value, which may be either a class object, a type object, or a tuple of class and type objects
issubclass(*class1, class2*)	Checks whether *class1* is a subclass of *class2* (every class is a subclass of itself)
iter(*object*[, *sentinel*])	Returns an iterator object, which is either *object*.__iter__(), an iterator constructed for iterating a sequence (if object supports __getitem__), or, if *sentinel* is supplied, an iterator that keeps calling *object* in each iteration until *sentinel* is returned

continued

Table B-3. Some Important Built-in Functions (continued)

FUNCTION	DESCRIPTION
len(*object*)	Returns the length (number of items) of the given object
list([*sequence*])	Constructs a list, optionally with the same items as the supplied sequence
locals()	Returns a dictionary representing the current local scope (do *not* modify this dictionary)
long(*object*[, *radix*])	Converts a string (optionally with a given radix) or number to a long integer
map(*function, sequence, ...*)	Creates a list consisting of the values returned by the given function when applying it to the items of the supplied sequence(s)
max(*object1*, [*object2*, ...])	If *object1* is a non-empty sequence, the largest element is returned; otherwise, the largest of the supplied arguments (*object1*, *object2*, ...) is returned
min(*object1*, [*object2*, ...])	If *object1* is a non-empty sequence, the smallest element is returned; otherwise, the smallest of the supplied arguments (*object1*, *object2*, ...) is returned
oct(*number*)	Converts an integer number to an octal string
open(*filename*[, *mode*[, *bufsize*]])	An alias for file (use open, not file, when opening files)
ord(*char*)	Returns the ASCII value of a single character (a string or Unicode string of length 1)
pow(*x*, *y*[, *z*])	Returns *x* to the power of *y*, optionally modulo *z*
range([*start*,]*stop*[, *step*])	Returns a numeric range (as a list) with the given *start* (inclusive, default 0), *stop* (exclusive), and *step* (default 1)
raw_input([*prompt*])	Returns data input by the user as a string, optionally using a given prompt
reduce(*function, sequence*[, *initializer*])	Applies the given function cumulatively to the items of the sequence, using the cumulative result as the first argument and the items as the second argument, optionally with a start value (*initializer*)
reload(*module*)	Reloads an already loaded module and returns it
repr(*object*)	Returns a string representation of the object, often usable as an argument to eval

continued

Table B-3. Some Important Built-in Functions (continued)

FUNCTION	DESCRIPTION
round(*float*[, *n*])	Rounds off the given float to *n* digits after the decimal point (default zero)
setattr(*object, name, value*)	Sets the named attribute of the given object to the given value
str(*object*)	Returns a nicely formatted string representation of the given object
tuple([*sequence*])	Constructs a tuple, optionally with the same items as the supplied sequence
type(*object*)	Returns the type of the given object
unichr(*number*)	The Unicode version of chr
unicode(*object*[, *encoding*[, *errors*]])	Returns a Unicode encoding of the given object, possibly with a given encoding, and a given mode for handling errors (either 'strict' or 'ignore', 'strict' being default)
vars([*object*])	Returns a dictionary representing the local scope, or a dictionary corresponding to the attributes of the given object (do *not* modify the returned dictionary)
xrange([*start*,]*stop*[, *step*])	Similar to range, but the returned object uses less memory, and should only be used for iteration
zip(*sequence1*, ...)	Returns a list of tuples, where each tuple contains an item from each of the supplied sequences. The returned list has the same length as the shortest of the supplied sequences

Table B-4. List Methods

METHOD	DESCRIPTION
list.append(*object*)	Equivalent to *list*[len(*list*):len(*list*)] = [*object*]
list.count(*object*)	Returns the number of *i*'s for which *list*[*i*] == *object*
list.extend(*sequence*)	Equivalent to *list*[len(*list*):len(*list*)] = *sequence*
list.index(*object*)	Returns the smallest *i* for which *list*[*i*] == *object* (or raises a ValueError if no such *i* exists)
list.insert(*index, object*)	Equivalent to *list*[*index*:*index*] = [*object*] if *index* >= 0; if *index* < 0, object is prepended to the list
list.pop([*index*])	Removes and returns the item with the given index (default –1)
list.remove(*object*)	Equivalent to del *list*[*list*.index(*object*)]
list.reverse()	Reverses the items of list in place
list.sort()	Sorts the items of list in place

Table B-5. Dictionary Methods

METHOD	DESCRIPTION
dict.clear()	Removes all the items of *dict*
dict.copy()	Returns a copy of *dict*
dict.get(*key*[, *default*])	Returns *dict*[*key*] if it exists, otherwise it returns the given default value (default None)
dict.has_key(*key*)	Checks whether *dict* has the given key
dict.items()	Returns a list of (*key, value*) pairs representing the items of *dict*
dict.iteritems()	Returns an iterable object over the same (*key, value*) pairs as returned by *dict*.items
dict.iterkeys()	Returns an iterable object over the keys of *dict*
dict.itervalues()	Returns an iterable object over the values of *dict*
dict.keys()	Returns a list of the keys of *dict*
dict.pop(*key*)	Removes and returns the value corresponding to the given key (new in Python 2.3)
dict.popitem()	Removes an arbitrary item from *dict* and returns it as a (*key, value*) pair

continued

Table B-5. Dictionary Methods (continued)

METHOD	DESCRIPTION
dict.setdefault(*key*[, *default*])	Returns *dict*[*key*] if it exists, otherwise it returns the given default value (default None) and binds *dict*[*key*] to it
dict.update(*other*)	For each item in *other*, adds the item to *dict* (possibly overwriting existing items)
dict.values()	Returns a list of the values in *dict* (possibly containing duplicates)

Table B-6. String Methods

METHOD	DESCRIPTION
string.capitalize()	Returns a copy of the string in which the first character is capitalized
string.center(*width*)	Returns a string of length max(len(*string*), *width*) in which a copy of *string* is centered, padded with spaces
string.count(*sub*[, *start*[, *end*]])	Counts the occurrences of the substring *sub*, optionally restricting the search to *string*[*start*: *end*]
string.decode([*encoding*[, *errors*]])	Returns decoded version of the string using the given encoding, handling errors as specified by *errors* ('strict', 'ignore', or 'replace')
string.encode([*encoding*[, *errors*]])	Returns encoded version of the string using the given encoding, handling errors as specified by *errors* ('strict', 'ignore', or 'replace')
string.endswith(*suffix*[, *start*[, *end*]])	Checks whether *string* ends with *suffix*, optionally restricting the matching with the given indices *start* and *end*
string.expandtabs([*tabsize*])	Returns a copy of the string in which tab characters have been expanded using spaces, optionally using the given *tabsize* (default 8)
string.find(*sub*[, *start*[, *end*]])	Returns the first index where the substring *sub* is found, or −1 if no such index exists, optionally restricting the search to *string*[*start*: *end*]
string.index(*sub*[, *start*[, *end*]])	Returns the first index where the substring *sub* is found, or raises a ValueError if no such index exists, optionally restricting the search to *string*[*start*: *end*]

continued

Table B-6. String Methods (continued)

METHOD	DESCRIPTION
string.isalnum()	Checks whether the string consists of alphanumeric characters
string.isalpha()	Checks whether the string consists of alphabetic characters
string.isdigit()	Checks whether the string consists of digits
string.islower()	Checks whether all the case-based characters (letters) of the string are lowercase
string.isspace()	Checks whether the string consists of whitespace
string.istitle()	Checks whether all the case-based characters in the string following non case-based letters are uppercase and all other case-based characters are lowercase
string.isupper()	Checks whether all the case-based characters of the string are uppercase
string.join(*sequence*)	Returns a string in which the string elements of *sequence* have been joined by *string*
string.ljust(*width*)	Returns a string of length max(len(*string*), *width*) in which a copy of *string* is left justified, padded with spaces
string.lower()	Returns a copy of the string in which all case-based characters have been lowercased
string.lstrip()	Returns a copy of the string in which all whitespace has been stripped from the beginning of the string
string.replace(*old, new*[, *max*])	Returns a copy of the string in which the occurrences of *old* have been replaced with *new*, optionally restricting the number of replacements to *max*
string.rfind(*sub*[, *start*[, *end*]])	Returns the last index where the substring *sub* is found, or −1 if no such index exists, optionally restricting the search to *string*[*start*: *end*]
string.rindex(*sub*[, *start*[, *end*]])	Returns the last index where the substring *sub* is found, or raises a ValueError if no such index exists, optionally restricting the search to *string*[*start*: *end*]
string.rjust(*width*)	Returns a string of length max(len(*string*), *width*) in which a copy of *string* is right justified, padded with spaces
string.rstrip()	Returns a copy of the string in which all whitespace has been stripped from the end of the string

continued

Table B-6. String Methods (continued)

METHOD	DESCRIPTION
string.split([*sep*[, *maxsplit*]])	Returns a list of all the words in the string, using *sep* as the separator (splits on all whitespace if left unspecified), optionally limiting the number of splits to *maxsplit*
string.splitlines([*keepends*])	Returns a list with all the lines in *string*, optionally including the line breaks (if *keepends* is supplied and is *true*)
string.startswith (*prefix*[, *start*[, *end*]])	Checks whether *string* starts with *suffix*, optionally restricting the matching with the given indices *start* and *end*
string.strip()	Returns a copy of the string in which all whitespace has been stripped from the beginning and the end of the string
string.swapcase()	Returns a copy of the string in which all the case-based characters have had their case swapped
string.title()	Returns a copy of the string in which all the words are capitalized
string.translate(*table*[, *deletechars*])	Returns a copy of the string in which all characters have been translated using *table* (constructed with the maketrans function in the string module), optionally deleting all characters found in the string *deletechars*
string.upper()	Returns a copy of the string in which all the case-based characters have been uppercased

Statements

This section gives you a quick summary of each of the statement types in Python.

Simple Statements

Simple statements consist of a single (logical) line.

Expression Statements

Expressions can be statements on their own. This is especially useful if the expression is a function call or a documentation string.
Example:

```
raw_input('Press <Enter> when ready')
```

Assert Statements

Assert statements check whether a condition is true and raises an `AssertionError` (optionally with a supplied error message) if it isn't.
Example:

```
assert age >= 12, 'Children under the age of 12 are not allowed'
```

Assignment Statements

Assignment statements bind variables to values. Multiple variables may be assigned to simultaneously (through sequence unpacking) and assignments may be chained.
Examples:

```
x = 42                   # Simple assignment
name, age = 'Gumby', 60  # Sequence unpacking
x = y = z = 10           # Chained assignments
```

Augmented Assignment Statements

Assignments may be augmented by operators. The operator will then be applied to the existing value of the variable and the new value, and the variable will be rebound to the result. If the original value is mutable, it may be modified instead (with the variable staying bound to the original).
Examples:

```
x *= 2                     # Doubles x
x += 5                     # Adds 5 to x
```

The pass Statement

The pass statement is a "no-op," which does nothing. It is useful as a placeholder, or as the only statement in syntactically required blocks where you want no action to be performed.
Example:

```
try: x.name
except AttributeError: pass
else: print 'Hello', x.name
```

The del Statement

The del statement unbinds variables and attributes, and removes parts (positions, slices, or slots) from data structures (mappings or sequences). It cannot be used to delete values directly because values are only deleted through garbage collection.
Examples:

```
del x                 # Unbinds a variable
del seq[42]           # Deletes a sequence element
del seq[42:]          # Deletes a sequence slice
del map['foo']        # Deletes a mapping item
```

The print *Statement*

The print statement writes one or more values (automatically formatted with str, separated by single spaces) to a given stream, with sys.stdout being the default. It adds a line break to the end of the written string unless the print statement ends with a comma.

Examples:

```
print 'Hello, world!'      # Writes 'Hello, world\n' to sys.stdout
print 1, 2, 3              # Writes '1 2 3\n' to sys.stdout
print >> somefile, 'xyz'   # Writes 'xyz' to somefile
print 42,                  # Writes '42 ' to sys.stdout
```

The return *Statement*

The return statement halts the execution of a function and returns a value. If no value is supplied, None is returned.

Examples:

```
return              # Returns None from the current function
return 42           # Returns 42 from the current function
return 1, 2, 3      # Returns (1, 2, 3) from the current function
```

The yield *Statement*

The yield statement temporarily halts the execution of a generator and yields a value. A generator is a form of iterator and can be used in for loops, among other things.

Example:

```
yield 42            # Returns 42 from the current function
```

The raise *Statement*

The raise statement raises an exception. It may be used without any arguments (inside an except clause, to re-raise the currently caught exception), with a subclass of Exception and an optional argument (in which case an instance is constructed), or with an instance of a subclass of Exception.
Examples:

```
raise                      # May only be used inside except clauses
raise IndexError
raise IndexError, 'index out of bounds'
raise IndexError('index out of bounds')
```

The break *Statement*

The break statement ends the immediately enclosing loop statement (for or while) and continues execution immediately after that loop statement.
Example:

```
while 1:
    line = file.readline()
    if not line: break
    print line
```

The continue *Statement*

The continue statement is similar to the break statement in that it halts the current iteration of the immediately enclosing loop, but instead of ending the loop completely, it continues execution at the beginning of the next iteration.
Example:

```
while 1:
    line = file.readline()
    if not line: break
    if line.isspace(): continue
    print line
```

The import *Statement*

The import statement is used to import names (variables bound to functions, classes, or other values) from an external module.
Examples:

```
import math
from math import sqrt
from math import sqrt as squareroot
from math import *
```

The global *Statement*

The global statement is used to mark a variable as global. It is used in functions to allow statements in the function body to rebind global variables. Using the global statement is generally considered poor style and should be avoided whenever possible.
Example:

```
count = 1
def inc():
    global count
    count += 1
```

The exec *Statement*

The exec statement is used to execute strings containing Python statements, optionally with a given global and local namespace (dictionaries).
Examples:

```
exec 'print "Hello, world!"'
exec 'x = 2' in globals, locals
```

Compound Statements

Compound statements contain groups (blocks) of other statements.

The if Statement

The if statement is used for conditional execution, and it may include elif and else clauses.
Example:

```
if x < 10:
    print 'Less than ten'
elif 10 <= x < 20:
    print 'Less than twenty'
else:
    print 'Twenty or more'
```

The while Statement

The while statement is used for repeated execution (looping) while a given condition is true. It may include an else clause (which is executed if the loop finishes normally, without any break or return statements, for instance).
Example:

```
x = 1
while < 100:
    x *= 2
print x
```

The for Statement

The for statement is used for repeated execution (looping) over the elements of sequences or other iterable objects (objects having an __iter__ method that returns an iterator). It may include an else clause (which is executed if the loop finishes normally, without any break or return statements, for instance).
Example:

```
for i in range(10, 0, -1):
    print i
print 'Ignition!'
```

The try *Statement*

The try statement is used to enclose pieces of code where one or more known exceptions may occur, and enables your program to trap these exceptions and perform exception handling code if an exception is trapped.
Example:

```
try:
    1/0
except ZeroDivisionError:
    print "Can't divide anything by zero."
```

Function Definitions

Function definitions are used to create function objects and to bind global or local variables to these function objects.
Example:

```
def double(x):
    return x*2
```

Class Definitions

Class definitions are used to create class objects and to bind global or local variables to these class objects.
Example:

```
class Doubler:
    def __init__(self, value):
        self.value = value
    def double(self):
        self.value *= 2
```

APPENDIX C

Online Resources

As you learn Python, the Internet is an invaluable resource. This appendix describes some of the Web sites that may be of interest to you as you are starting out. If you are looking for something Python-related that isn't described here, I suggest that you first look at the official Python Web site (http://python.org), and then use your favorite Web search engine, or the other way around. There is a lot of information about Python online; chances are you'll find something. If you don't, you can always try comp.lang.python (described later in this chapter).

Python Distributions

Several Python distributions are available. Here are some of the more prominent ones:

> **Official Python Distribution** (http://python.org/download). This comes with a default IDE (integrated development environment) called IDLE (for more information, see http://python.org/idle).

> **ActivePython** (http://activestate.com). This is ActiveState's Python distribution, which includes several non-standard packages in addition to the official distribution. This is also the home of Visual Python, a Python plug-in for Visual Studio .NET.

> **PythonWare** (http://www.pythonware.com/products/python). The PythonWare Python distribution is small but complete and very easy to install. It can coexist with other Python installations.

> **Jython** (http://jython.org). Jython is the Java implementation of Python.

> **MacPython** (http://www.cwi.nl/~jack/macpython.html). MacPython is the Macintosh port of Python.

> **win32all** (http://starship.python.net/crew/mhammond). The Python for Windows extensions. If you have ActivePython installed, you already have all these extensions.

Python Documentation

Answers to most of your Python questions are most likely somewhere on the `python.org` Web site. The documentation can be found at `http://python.org/doc`, with the following subdivisions:

> **The Official Python Tutorial** (`http://python.org/doc/tut`). A relatively simple introduction to the language.

> **The Python Language Reference** (`http://python.org/doc/ref`). This document contains a precise definition of the Python language. It may not be the place to start when learning Python, but it contains precise answers to most questions you might have about the language.

> **The Python Library Reference** (`http://python.org/doc/lib`). This is probably the most useful piece of Python documentation you'll ever find. It describes all (or most) of the modules in the standard Python library. If you are wondering how to solve a problem in Python, this should be the first place you look—perhaps the solution already exists in the libraries.

> **Extending and Embedding the Python Interpreter**
> (`http://python.org/doc/ext`). This is a document that describes how to write Python extension modules in the C language, and how to use the Python interpreter as a part of larger C programs. (Python itself is implemented in C.)

> **Macintosh Library Modules** (`http://python.org/doc/mac`). This document describes functionality specific to the Macintosh port of Python.

> **The Python/C API Reference Manual** (`http://python.org/doc/api`). This is a rather technical document describing the details of the Python/C API (application programming interface), which enables C programs to interface with the Python interpreter.

Two other useful documentation resources are Pydoc Online (`http://pydoc.org`) and pyhelp.cgi (`http://starship.python.net/crew/theller/pyhelp.cgi`), which allow you to search the standard Python documentation.

The future of Python is decided by the language's Benevolent Dictator For Life (BDFL), Guido van Rossum, but his decisions are guided and informed by

so-called Python Enhancement Proposals, which may be accessed at
`http://python.org/peps`. Various HOWTO documents (relatively specific tutorials) can be found at `http://python.org/doc/howto`.

Useful Toolkits and Modules

The main source for finding software implemented in Python (including useful toolkits and modules you can use in your own programs) is the Vaults of Parnassus (`http://www.vex.net/parnassus`). If you can't find what you're looking for there, try a standard Web search.

Table C-1 lists the URLs of some of the most well-known GUI toolkits available for Python (all of them usable with Anygui). For a more thorough description, see Chapter 12. Table C-2 lists the URLs of the third-party packages used in the ten projects.

Table C-1. Some Well-Known GUI Toolkits for Python

PACKAGE	URL
Tkinter	`http://python.org/topics/tkinter/doc.html`
wxPython	`http://www.wxpython.org`
PythonWin	`http://starship.python.net/crew/mhammond`
Java Swing	`http://java.sun.com/docs/books/tutorial/uiswing`
PyGTK	`http://www.daa.com.au/~james/pygtk`
PyQt	`http://www.thekompany.com/projects/pykde`

Table C-2. The Third-Party Modules Used in the Ten Projects

PACKAGE	URL
Anygui	`http://www.anygui.org`
Psycopg	`http://initd.org/Software/psycopg`
MySQLdb	`http://sourceforge.net/projects/mysql-python`
Pygame	`http://www.pygame.org`
PyXML	`http://sourceforge.net/projects/pyxml`
ReportLab	`http://www.reportlab.com`
SimpleXMLRPCServer	`http://www.sweetapp.com/xmlrpc`

Newsgroups and Mailing Lists

An important forum for Python discussion is the Usenet group `comp.lang.python`. If you're serious about Python, I recommend that you at least skim this group regularly. Its companion group `comp.lang.python.announce` contains announcements about new Python software (both new Python distributions, Python extensions, and software written using Python).

Several official mailing lists are available. For instance, the `comp.lang.python` group is mirrored in the `python-list@python.org` mailing list. If you have a Python problem and need help, simply send an e-mail to `help@python.org` (assuming that you've exhausted all other options, of course). For learning about programming in Python, the tutor list (`tutor@python.org`) may be useful. For information about how to join these (and other) mailing lists, see `http://python.org/psa/MailingLists.html`.

Index

XML-RPC
  defining result codes for, 508
  file sharing with, 501–523
  Web site address for information
    about, 501
XML-RPC file sharing program
  calling the fetch method in, 508
  calling the query method in, 508
  client interface, 515–516
  exceptions handling in, 516
  first implementation, 505–514
  implementing the hello method, 508
  second implementation, 514–522
  some flaws in the first implement-
    ation, 514–515
  starting the program, 517
  testing first implementation, 506
  testing the second implementation,
    517–522

validating file names in, 516–517
xmlrpclib module, connecting to XML-
    RPC servers with, 503–505
xrange function, 127
  using, 112
xreadlines object, lazy line iteration
    with, 316

Y
yield statement, 230–231

Z
zero (0), conversion specifier, 65
zero padding, of numbers in strings,
    67
ZeroDivisionError class, built-in
    exception, 196
zip function, for zipping sequences
    together, 114

Apress Titles

ISBN	PRICE	AUTHOR	TITLE
1-893115-73-9	$34.95	Abbott	Voice Enabling Web Applications: VoiceXML and Beyond
1-893115-01-1	$39.95	Appleman	Dan Appleman's Win32 API Puzzle Book and Tutorial for Visual Basic Programmers
1-893115-23-2	$29.95	Appleman	How Computer Programming Works
1-893115-97-6	$39.95	Appleman	Moving to VB .NET: Strategies, Concepts, and Code
1-59059-023-6	$39.95	Baker	Adobe Acrobat 5: The Professional User's Guide
1-59059-039-2	$49.95	Barnaby	Distributed .NET Programming
1-893115-09-7	$29.95	Baum	Dave Baum's Definitive Guide to LEGO MINDSTORMS
1-893115-84-4	$29.95	Baum, Gasperi, Hempel, and Villa	Extreme MINDSTORMS: An Advanced Guide to LEGO MINDSTORMS
1-893115-82-8	$59.95	Ben-Gan/Moreau	Advanced Transact-SQL for SQL Server 2000
1-893115-91-7	$39.95	Birmingham/Perry	Software Development on a Leash
1-893115-48-8	$29.95	Bischof	The .NET Languages: A Quick Translation Guide
1-59059-053-8	$44.95	Bock/Stromquist/Fischer/Smith	.NET Security
1-893115-67-4	$49.95	Borge	Managing Enterprise Systems with the Windows Script Host
1-59059-019-8	$49.95	Cagle	SVG Programming: The Graphical Web
1-893115-28-3	$44.95	Challa/Laksberg	Essential Guide to Managed Extensions for C++
1-893115-39-9	$44.95	Chand	A Programmer's Guide to ADO.NET in C#
1-59059-015-5	$39.95	Clark	An Introduction to Object Oriented Programming with Visual Basic .NET
1-893115-44-5	$29.95	Cook	Robot Building for Beginners
1-893115-99-2	$39.95	Cornell/Morrison	Programming VB .NET: A Guide for Experienced Programmers
1-893115-72-0	$39.95	Curtin	Developing Trust: Online Privacy and Security
1-59059-014-7	$44.95	Drol	Object-Oriented Macromedia Flash MX
1-59059-008-2	$29.95	Duncan	The Career Programmer: Guerilla Tactics for an Imperfect World
1-893115-71-2	$39.95	Ferguson	Mobile .NET
1-893115-90-9	$49.95	Finsel	The Handbook for Reluctant Database Administrators
1-59059-024-4	$49.95	Fraser	Real World ASP.NET: Building a Content Management System
1-893115-42-9	$44.95	Foo/Lee	XML Programming Using the Microsoft XML Parser
1-893115-55-0	$34.95	Frenz	Visual Basic and Visual Basic .NET for Scientists and Engineers
1-893115-85-2	$34.95	Gilmore	A Programmer's Introduction to PHP 4.0
1-893115-36-4	$34.95	Goodwill	Apache Jakarta-Tomcat
1-893115-17-8	$59.95	Gross	A Programmer's Introduction to Windows DNA
1-893115-62-3	$39.95	Gunnerson	A Programmer's Introduction to C#, Second Edition
1-59059-030-9	$49.95	Habibi/Patterson/Camerlengo	The Sun Certified Java Developer Exam with J2SE 1.4
1-59059-009-0	$49.95	Harris/Macdonald	Moving to ASP.NET: Web Development with VB .NET

ISBN	PRICE	AUTHOR	TITLE
1-893115-30-5	$49.95	Harkins/Reid	SQL: Access to SQL Server
1-59059-006-6	$39.95	Hetland	Practical Python
1-893115-10-0	$34.95	Holub	Taming Java Threads
1-893115-04-6	$34.95	Hyman/Vaddadi	Mike and Phani's Essential C++ Techniques
1-893115-96-8	$59.95	Jorelid	J2EE FrontEnd Technologies: A Programmer's Guide to Servlets, JavaServer Pages, and Enterprise JavaBeans
1-893115-49-6	$39.95	Kilburn	Palm Programming in Basic
1-893115-50-X	$34.95	Knudsen	Wireless Java: Developing with Java 2, Micro Edition
1-893115-79-8	$49.95	Kofler	Definitive Guide to Excel VBA
1-893115-57-7	$39.95	Kofler	MySQL
1-893115-87-9	$39.95	Kurata	Doing Web Development: Client-Side Techniques
1-893115-75-5	$44.95	Kurniawan	Internet Programming with VB
1-893115-38-0	$24.95	Lafler	Power AOL: A Survival Guide
1-893115-46-1	$36.95	Lathrop	Linux in Small Business: A Practical User's Guide
1-893115-19-4	$49.95	Macdonald	Serious ADO: Universal Data Access with Visual Basic
1-893115-06-2	$39.95	Marquis/Smith	A Visual Basic 6.0 Programmer's Toolkit
1-893115-22-4	$27.95	McCarter	David McCarter's VB Tips and Techniques
1-59059-021-X	$34.95	Moore	Karl Moore's Visual Basic .NET: The Tutorials
1-893115-76-3	$49.95	Morrison	C++ For VB Programmers
1-59059-003-1	$39.95	Nakhimovsky/Meyers	XML Programming: Web Applications and Web Services with JSP and ASP
1-893115-80-1	$39.95	Newmarch	A Programmer's Guide to Jini Technology
1-893115-58-5	$49.95	Oellermann	Architecting Web Services
1-59059-020-1	$44.95	Patzer	JSP Examples and Best Practices
1-893115-81-X	$39.95	Pike	SQL Server: Common Problems, Tested Solutions
1-59059-017-1	$34.95	Rainwater	Herding Cats: A Primer for Programmers Who Lead Programmers
1-59059-025-2	$49.95	Rammer	Advanced .NET Remoting (C# Edition)
1-59059-062-7	$49.95	Rammer	Advanced .NET Remoting in VB .NET
1-893115-20-8	$34.95	Rischpater	Wireless Web Development
1-893115-93-3	$34.95	Rischpater	Wireless Web Development with PHP and WAP
1-893115-89-5	$59.95	Shemitz	Kylix: The Professional Developer's Guide and Reference
1-893115-40-2	$39.95	Sill	The qmail Handbook
1-893115-24-0	$49.95	Sinclair	From Access to SQL Server
1-59059-026-0	$49.95	Smith	Writing Add-ins for Visual Studio .NET
1-893115-94-1	$29.95	Spolsky	User Interface Design for Programmers
1-893115-53-4	$44.95	Sweeney	Visual Basic for Testers
1-59059-002-3	$44.95	Symmonds	Internationalization and Localization Using Microsoft .NET
1-59059-010-4	$54.95	Thomsen	Database Programming with C#
1-893115-29-1	$44.95	Thomsen	Database Programming with Visual Basic .NET
1-893115-65-8	$39.95	Tiffany	Pocket PC Database Development with eMbedded Visual Basic

ISBN	PRICE	AUTHOR	TITLE
1-59059-027-9	$59.95	Torkelson/Petersen/Torkelson	Programming the Web with Visual Basic .NET
1-893115-59-3	$59.95	Troelsen	C# and the .NET Platform
1-59059-011-2	$59.95	Troelsen	COM and .NET Interoperability
1-893115-26-7	$59.95	Troelsen	Visual Basic .NET and the .NET Platform
1-893115-54-2	$49.95	Trueblood/Lovett	Data Mining and Statistical Analysis Using SQL
1-893115-68-2	$54.95	Vaughn	ADO.NET and ADO Examples and Best Practices for VB Programmers, Second Edition
1-59059-012-0	$49.95	Vaughn/Blackburn	ADO.NET Examples and Best Practices for C# Programmers
1-893115-83-6	$44.95	Wells	Code Centric: T-SQL Programming with Stored Procedures and Triggers
1-893115-95-X	$49.95	Welschenbach	Cryptography in C and C++
1-893115-05-4	$39.95	Williamson	Writing Cross-Browser Dynamic HTML
1-893115-78-X	$49.95	Zukowski	Definitive Guide to Swing for Java 2, Second Edition
1-893115-92-5	$49.95	Zukowski	Java Collections
1-893115-98-4	$54.95	Zukowski	Learn Java with JBuilder 6

Available at bookstores nationwide or from Springer Verlag New York, Inc. at 1-800-777-4643;
fax 1-212-533-3503. Contact us for more information at sales@apress.com.

Apress Titles Publishing *SOON!*

ISBN	AUTHOR	TITLE
1-59059-022-8	Alapati	Expert Oracle 9i Database Administration
1-59059-041-4	Bock	CIL Programming: Under the Hood of .NET
1-59059-000-7	Cornell	Programming C#
1-59059-033-3	Fraser	Managed C++ and .NET Development
1-59059-038-4	Gibbons	Java Development to .NET Development
1-59059-044-9	MacDonald	.NET User Interfaces with VB .NET: Windows Forms and Custom Controls
1-59059-001-5	McMahon	A Programmer's Introduction to ASP.NET WebForms in Visual Basic .NET
1-893115-74-7	Millar	Enterprise Development: A Programmer's Handbook
1-893115-27-5	Morrill	Tuning and Customizing a Linux System
1-59059-028-7	Rischpater	Wireless Web Development, Second Edition
1-893115-43-7	Stephenson	Standard VB: An Enterprise Developer's Reference for VB 6 and VB .NET
1-59059-035-X	Symmonds	GDI+ Programming in C# and VB .NET
1-59059-032-5	Thomsen	Database Programming with Visual Basic .NET, Second Edition
1-59059-007-4	Thomsen	Building Web Services with VB .NET
1-59059-018-X	Tregar	Writing Perl Modules for CPAN
1-59059-004-X	Valiaveedu	SQL Server 2000 and Business Intelligence in an XML/.NET World

Available at bookstores nationwide or from Springer Verlag New York, Inc. at 1-800-777-4643;
fax 1-212-533-3503. Contact us for more information at sales@apress.com.

books for professionals by professionals™

About Apress

Apress, located in Berkeley, CA, is a fast-growing, innovative publishing company devoted to meeting the needs of existing and potential programming professionals. Simply put, the "A" in Apress stands for *"The Author's Press™"* and its books have *"The Expert's Voice™"*. Apress' unique approach to publishing grew out of conversations between its founders Gary Cornell and Dan Appleman, authors of numerous best-selling, highly regarded books for programming professionals. In 1998 they set out to create a publishing company that emphasized quality above all else. Gary and Dan's vision has resulted in the publication of over 50 titles by leading software professionals, all of which have *The Expert's Voice™*.

Do You Have What It Takes to Write for Apress?

Apress is rapidly expanding its publishing program. If you can write and refuse to compromise on the quality of your work, if you believe in doing more than rehashing existing documentation, and if you're looking for opportunities and rewards that go far beyond those offered by traditional publishing houses, we want to hear from you!

Consider these innovations that we offer all of our authors:

- **Top royalties with *no* hidden switch statements**
  Authors typically only receive half of their normal royalty rate on foreign sales. In contrast, Apress' royalty rate remains the same for both foreign and domestic sales.

- **A mechanism for authors to obtain equity in Apress**
  Unlike the software industry, where stock options are essential to motivate and retain software professionals, the publishing industry has adhered to an outdated compensation model based on royalties alone. In the spirit of most software companies, Apress reserves a significant portion of its equity for authors.

- **Serious treatment of the technical review process**
  Each Apress book has a technical reviewing team whose remuneration depends in part on the success of the book since they too receive royalties.

Moreover, through a partnership with Springer-Verlag, New York, Inc., one of the world's major publishing houses, Apress has significant venture capital behind it. Thus, we have the resources to produce the highest quality books *and* market them aggressively.

If you fit the model of the Apress author who can write a book that gives the "professional what he or she needs to know™," then please contact one of our Editorial Directors, Dan Appleman (dan_appleman@apress.com), Gary Cornell (gary_cornell@apress.com), Jason Gilmore (jason_gilmore@apress.com), Simon Hayes (simon_hayes@apress.com), Karen Watterson (karen_watterson@apress.com), or John Zukowski (john_zukowski@apress.com) for more information.